Culinary Careers
FOR
DUMMIES®

by Michele Thomas, Annette Tomei, and Tracey Vasil Biscontini

WILEY

John Wiley & Sons, Inc.

Culinary Careers For Dummies®

Published by
John Wiley & Sons, Inc.
111 River St.
Hoboken, NJ 07030-5774
www.wiley.com

Copyright © 2011 by John Wiley & Sons, Inc.

Published by John Wiley & Sons, Inc., Hoboken, New Jersey

Published simultaneously in Canada

For general information on our other products and services, please contact our Customer Care Department within the U.S. at 877-762-2974, outside the U.S. at 317-572-3993, or fax 317-572-4002.

For technical support, please visit www.wiley.com/techsupport.

Wiley also publishes its books in a variety of electronic formats and by print-on-demand. Some content that appears in standard print versions of this book may not be available in other formats. For more information about Wiley products, visit us at www.wiley.com.

Library of Congress Control Number: 2011936933

ISBN 978-1-118-07774-0 (pbk); ISBN 978-1-118-16835-6 (ebk); ISBN 978-1-118-16836-3 (ebk); ISBN 978-1-118-16837-0 (ebk)

Manufactured in the United States of America

10 9 8 7 6 5 4 3 2

WILEY

About the Authors

As managing editor at International Culinary Center of New York, **Michele Thomas** oversees editorial production and distribution of the school's proprietary curricula for its professional and amateur French and Italian cooking, pastry, and bread-baking classes. She was introduced to the thrills of cooking and candy-making as a child through her mother's work with holiday gingerbread displays. After studying communication and media at Fordham University, she started a career developing K-12 picture books, textbooks, and teaching materials in science, mathematics, and reading for several major publishers, including Macmillan/McGraw-Hill, Harcourt School Publishers, Pearson Education, Houghton Mifflin, Rosen Publishing Group, and Newbridge Educational Publishing, as well as the Department of Education for the US Virgin Islands. She has also covered food, fitness, nutrition, fashion, education, home, and lifestyle for Metro Newspaper Service, where she also wrote marketing materials for diverse clients, such as Disaronno Amaretto, OXO, the Platinum Guild, the Accessories Council, The Scotts Miracle-Gro Company, and Armstrong Floors. A Brooklyn, New York, native, Michele teaches high school academic-essay writing for Legal Outreach, a New York-based nonprofit mentoring organization. She also teaches creative writing as a volunteer with Girls Write Now, one of the top 10 after-school programs in the United States.

Chef Annette Tomei is a food and beverage educator based in New York City. She is a 1994 graduate of The French Culinary Institute (FCI) and holds a master's degree in gastronomy from the University of Adelaide with Le Cordon Bleu Australia. She has been a chef, an educator, and a speaker covering an array of subjects from basic knife skills to aphrodisiacs in the kitchen to beverage pairing. Her work takes her from New York and California to Italy and beyond.

Annette is the co-author of *Chile Aphrodisia* (Rio Nuevo) and a contributor to *Fork Me, Spoon Me: the Sensual Cookbook* (Life of Reiley). She has also written curriculum and designed and managed educational programs for both The French Culinary Institute and The Culinary Institute of America at Greystone.

Tracey Vasil Biscontini is the founder, president, and CEO of Northeast Editing, Inc., a company specializing in the creation of educational content for publishers. She holds bachelor's degrees in mass communications and education from King's College and a master's degree in English from the University of Scranton. Recently named one of the "Top 25 Women in Business in Northeast Pennsylvania," she is a former educator, journalist, and newspaper columnist whose award-winning writing has appeared in national magazines. Since founding Northeast Editing, Inc., in 1992, she has managed educational projects and authored test-preparation and library-reference content for some of the largest publishers in the United States.

Northeast Editing, Inc., is located in a former rectory in Jenkins Township, a small community nestled between Wilkes-Barre and Scranton in northeastern Pennsylvania. Tracey's company boasts a relaxed working environment that serves as her staff's home away from home. When they're not hard at work, the editors and writers at Northeast Editing, Inc., enjoy breaks in a large backyard and welcome hugs from Prince, a former stray that is now a resident office cat. Tracey lives in Avoca, Pennsylvania, with her husband Nick, son Tyler, and daughter Morgan.

Authors' Acknowledgments

Special thanks to Angela Harmon and Nicole Frail, editors at Northeast Editing, Inc., who devoted countless hours of research and writing to help create this book. We also thank Tracy Boggier, our acquisitions editor, who got the ball rolling; Linda Brandon, our incredible project editor, who offered advice and guidance every step of the way; our wonderful copy editor Caitie Copple; and our knowledgeable technical editor, Russ Zito.

Publisher's Acknowledgments

We're proud of this book; please send us your comments at http://dummies.custhelp.com. For other comments, please contact our Customer Care Department within the U.S. at 877-762-2974, outside the U.S. at 317-572-3993, or fax 317-572-4002.

Some of the people who helped bring this book to market include the following:

Acquisitions, Editorial, and Vertical Websites

Project Editor: Linda Brandon

Acquisitions Editor: Tracy Boggier

Copy Editor: Caitie Copple

Assistant Editor: David Lutton

Editorial Program Coordinator: Joe Niesen

Technical Editor: Russ Zito

Editorial Managers: Jennifer Ehrlich, Carmen Krikorian

Editorial Assistant: Alexa Koschier

Art Coordinator: Alicia B. South

Cover Photos: © iStockphoto.com / Kelly Cline

Cartoons: Rich Tennant (www.the5thwave.com)

Composition Services

Project Coordinator: Katherine Crocker

Layout and Graphics: Lavonne Roberts, Corrie Socolovitch

Proofreader: BIM Indexing & Proofreading Services

Indexer: Claudia Bourbeau

Publishing and Editorial for Consumer Dummies

Kathleen Nebenhaus, Vice President and Executive Publisher

Kristin Ferguson-Wagstaffe, Product Development Director

Ensley Eikenburg, Associate Publisher, Travel

Kelly Regan, Editorial Director, Travel

Publishing for Technology Dummies

Andy Cummings, Vice President and Publisher

Composition Services

Debbie Stailey, Director of Composition Services

Contents at a Glance

Table of Contents

Introduction

So you're considering a career in culinary arts. Good for you! Culinary careers are both rewarding and challenging, and some even allow you to utilize an artistic flair. The job outlook for culinary careers is good, in part because culinary professionals work in so many different places. For starters, they work in all types of restaurants — upscale restaurants, hotel restaurants, chain restaurants, diners, and more. Some work in pastry shops and bakeries. Others work for caterers and in institutions such as schools, universities, hospitals, and nursing homes. Some lucky culinary professionals cook food for guests in resorts and spas and on cruise ships. Those with an independent streak seek employment as personal and private chefs. Wherever you find a commercial kitchen, you find culinary professionals hard at work.

Some culinary careers require you to know about food but don't require you to cook it. Food writers earn a living writing reviews of restaurants and articles about food for magazines and websites. Food photographers snap shots of food for advertisements, product labels, cookbooks, and menus. A food stylist arranges food to be photographed or filmed — a task that's much harder than you may think. They have to think creatively and use tools such as staples, tweezers, and glue to make the "food" look delicious (Although it certainly doesn't have to taste that way and in some cases it isn't even food at all!). Other non-cooking culinary careers include brewing beer, selling culinary equipment, handling public relations for restaurants, and marketing culinary services and products.

To land a job as a culinary professional today, most people must attend culinary school. Working your way up the culinary ladder is still possible without education, but you have a better chance of getting your foot in the door with a culinary diploma or degree. You have many options when it comes to choosing a culinary school. You can attend a local community college or technical school or attend a large, prestigious culinary school such as The Culinary Institute of America.

When it comes to finding your first culinary job, be humble. You won't walk in a restaurant and be offered the position of executive chef. You won't walk into a *pâtisserie* (pastry shop) and be made a pastry chef. The same goes for a culinary school, you can't expect to teach culinary school without culinary training and experience. Do you see what we're trying to say here? You need experience and a culinary education to land many jobs within the culinary field, so you most likely won't land the job of your dreams right away — that is, until you acquire needed knowledge and skills. You must be willing to start at the bottom and work your way up the ladder.

About This Book

The culinary arts field is an ever-growing and ever-changing industry. Think about all of the restaurants located in the area where you live. Now think about how many people these establishments employ. Many culinary opportunities also exist outside of restaurants and hotels such as in schools, catering companies, newspapers, grocery stores, and even private homes. If you decide you want to pursue a culinary career, you have a lot of decisions to make, and *Culinary Careers For Dummies* is designed to help you with these decisions, as well as educate you about the various careers within the field and the steps you need to take to land a job.

This book begins with a general overview of the culinary industry, exploring the places where culinary professionals seek employment, whether you should attend culinary school, and which culinary education is right for you. It then explains the different culinary jobs that exist in traditional establishments, such as restaurants, hotels, bakeries, and catering companies, and nontraditional settings, such as publications, labs, commissary kitchens, wineries, retail shops, and more. We also provide information about how to land your first culinary job, switch careers within the culinary field, and open your own business.

Culinary Careers For Dummies will give you all the information you need to prepare for, find, and land a culinary job that's right for you.

Conventions Used in This Book

The following conventions are used throughout the text to make things consistent and easy to understand:

- ✔ We use the phrase *culinary arts* to refer to the art of cooking and preparing foods and the phrase *pastry arts* to refer to the art of preparing pastries and baked goods. Degrees are offered in culinary arts and pastry arts, and cooks, chefs, and bakers all participate in the art of cooking or the art of preparing pastries.

- ✔ We use the phrase *culinary professional* to refer to any job in the culinary world. Chefs, cooks, servers, and dishwashers are all culinary professionals. Food writers and photographers are also culinary professionals.

- ✔ We use the phrase *culinary school* to refer to any type of school giving classes about cooking or the culinary profession. A technical school offering a culinary certificate is a culinary school, as are schools such as the prestigious French Culinary Institute.

✔ We carefully distinguish between a chef and a cook. A *chef* typically holds a higher degree than a cook or has received more formal culinary education. A chef may also earn a high salary and oversee staff. A *cook,* on the other hand, prepares items on a menu that a chef creates. A cook typically does not earn as much money as a chef, nor manages other staff.

✔ We use *italics* to introduce new terms that are defined.

✔ Websites are printed `monofont` so they stand out from regular text.

What You're Not to Read

Of course, we'd love it if you read every word of advice in this book — we wrote it, after all. We also understand, however, that life is hectic and time is limited, so we've outlined a few areas of the book that you may want to skip and return to when you have more time:

✔ **Text in sidebars:** Sidebars are shaded boxes that provide extra information or detailed examples. Although you'll likely enjoy the gems of knowledge in the sidebars, they won't necessarily give you an edge in landing a job, so feel free to read them later.

✔ **Specific chapters:** You can skip certain chapters if you think they don't pertain to your needs. For example, if you're just starting out and trying to determine what you have to do to land an entry-level job in culinary arts, you can skip Chapters 17 and Chapter 18, which deal with changing jobs and becoming a culinary entrepreneur. Or if you know that would never want to be a caterer or cook for an institution, you can skip Chapter 7 on volume cooking.

✔ **Our bios:** Yes, it's true. Although we think our lives are intriguing, you're not going to be asked about them on a job interview. Sigh.

Foolish Assumptions

We all know what happens when we assume, but while writing this book, we decided to live dangerously and make the following assumptions about you:

✔ You enjoy cooking and probably have for most of your life.

✔ You're interested in a career in culinary arts, pastry arts, or hotel/restaurant management and want to know more about jobs in these fields and where to find them.

✔ You're not familiar with the title and job duties of each person who works in different culinary settings such as restaurants, bakeries, and wineries.

    ✔ You don't know what it takes to specialize in a particular culinary field, such as cake decorating or beer brewing.

    ✔ You're not sure if culinary school is a good idea for you.

How This Book Is Organized

This book is divided into six parts and 20 chapters. The table of contents outlines the specifics, but following is an overview of what you can expect to see.

Part I: An Introduction to the World of Culinary Arts

In Part I of this book, you explore the basics: you learn the meaning of the words *culinary arts* and what a culinary professional does on the job. Culinary professionals come in all shapes and sizes — they are high school graduates, graduates of prestigious culinary schools, and career changers who decided to switch gears to pursue their dream. To become a chef, you can attend school or get an entry-level kitchen job and try to work your way up. Chapter 3 gives you the pros and cons of culinary school, and Chapter 4 describes various culinary schools, both in the United States and abroad.

Part II: Exploring Popular Career Paths

When you think of culinary professionals, you probably think of cooks in a chaotic restaurant kitchen, working hard to get tasty meals to hungry customers. Restaurant work is indeed one of the most popular career paths for people who love food. In this part of the book, we tell you what it's like to work in a restaurant, including those in hotels and spas. You find out about the kitchen brigade, or the chain of command in a restaurant kitchen, so you can see where you'd like to fit in some day. In this part, we also explore some other common places culinary professional work: hotels and resorts, catering companies, and cafeterias in schools, hospitals, retirement homes, and even prisons.

Part III: Taking a Specialized Approach

Some individuals choose to take the road less traveled and specialize in a unique area of the culinary field. Part III teaches you about some of these careers, which include pastry chef, baker, personal or private chef, food artisan, food scientist, and culinarians who specialize in beverages such as wine.

If you love food in general but a particular kind of food (or drink) in particular, this part can help you decide if a focus is right for you.

Part IV: Checking Out Non-Cooking Careers

Plenty of workers in the culinary industry never spend a day working in a kitchen or dining room. Perhaps your dream is to be a food critic (wouldn't that be fun?). Chapter 12 discusses this possible career and other off-the-beaten-track culinary jobs, such as test-kitchen staff and food stylist. Some culinary professionals even work as public relations and marketing professionals for food-service companies or restaurants, as Chapter 13 details. You can also check out Chapters 14 and 15 for information on more non-cooking jobs, from culinary instructor to grocery store manager.

Part V: Landing the Job, Moving Up the Ladder, and More

Part V gets to the crux of the matter — landing a job in the culinary industry. Think of yourself as a product that you have to sell to an employer. Creating a top-notch résumé and cover letter is the first step in the process. Then you need to stop, breathe, and look around you for places to apply for work. Today's job market requires that you be proactive and go out and visit establishments rather than just looking at help-wanted ads in newspapers and online. Visit restaurants, talk to the staff, and network with instructors, friends, and family. This part of the book also gives you tips for climbing the culinary job ladder when you're ready to do so.

If your dream is to one day open your own restaurant or catering company, this part can also guide you on that path. Chapter 18 tells you what you need to know to go it on your own.

Part VI: The Part of Tens

The Part of Tens is a standard element of *For Dummies* books. Chapter 19 gives you ten reasons to work in the culinary industry, and Chapter 20 gives you ten tips to thrive in the culinary industry.

Icons Used in This Book

To make this book easier to read and simpler to use, we include some icons that can help you find key ideas and information. Keep an eye out for them.

This icon appears next to interesting information about the culinary industry. The information marked by this icon is not essential but can help you better understand the world of culinary arts.

Text next to this icon details little tricks you can use in any arena of the culinary field. We use this icon to draw attention to skills that are important for certain positions and approaches that work better for some jobs.

When you see this icon, you know the information that follows is especially important in landing a culinary job or succeeding on the job.

This icon highlights information that may pose a threat to you while on the job. It gives you the not-so-good news about the culinary industry.

Where to Go from Here

The great thing about *For Dummies* books is that you can start wherever you want and still find complete information. You don't have to read this book from cover to cover; you can start wherever you think you need the most help. Want to know what you need to do to become a pastry chef? Turn ahead to Chapter 8. Are you certain that you will one day open your own catering company? Read about caterers in Chapter 7 and running your business in Chapter 18.

If you're not sure where to start, we suggest Part I, which gives you basic information about the culinary industry such as the typical duties of culinary jobs and the job outlook over the next decade.

Wherever you decide to start, we wish you well on your culinary search. As Julia Child once said, "Find something you're passionate about and keep tremendously interested in it."

Part I

An Introduction to the World of Culinary Arts

"I'd get up, but I'm trying to soften a stick of butter to move dinner along."

In this part . . .

Culinary arts is the art of preparing and cooking food. If you have a love of food and want to learn everything you can about preparing it, then working toward a certificate or degree in culinary arts may be just right for you. When it comes to a culinary education, you have many avenues to choose from. You can obtain a bachelor's degree in the culinary arts, an associate's degree in baking or pastry, or even a certification in molecular gastronomy. Taking business, design, photography, marketing, and various other courses will also help you succeed in this industry. With the proper education and experience, you can easily attain many culinary positions.

In this part, we give an overview of the culinary arts profession, explaining what culinary professionals do, examining where they work, comparing on-the-job training with culinary school, and, finally, choosing a school. We also weigh the pros and cons of obtaining a culinary degree versus jumping right into the culinary industry.

Chapter 1

A Snapshot of the Culinary Arts Profession

In This Chapter

▶ Understanding what culinary professionals do

▶ Considering whether school or work is better preparation for a culinary career

▶ Finding work in a culinary field

▶ Exploring the outlook for cooking jobs

*I*f you're reading this book, you must be considering a career in culinary arts. Entering a new career field can be exciting and a little scary, so congratulations on taking the first step! Culinary arts is a challenging, rewarding, and creative field, and the future job outlook is favorable. That's the good news. The bad news? Succeeding in the culinary world takes skill, knowledge, determination, and experience. Depending on the position you hope to land, you may have to go to culinary school. And even if you go to school, restaurant experience may be a requirement. (Think server, dishwasher, or fast-food cook.)

More good news: Culinary professionals enjoy their work. Most can't imagine earning a living any other way. Why? It's all about the food! Culinary professionals eat, sleep, and dream about food. They enjoy preparing it, cooking it, plating it, serving it, and, of course, eating it. If you're reading this, chances are that you're among the food obsessed, and a career in culinary arts may be a good choice for you.

What Does It Mean to Work in the Culinary Arts?

Think about the words *culinary* and *arts*. What do these words mean? Anything related to food is referred to as being *culinary*. Anyone associated with food, from chefs to dishwashers, work in the culinary field. *Arts* is a whole different matter. Everyone who works in a creative field is an artist. Painter Leonardo da Vinci and poet Emily Dickinson were artists. An executive chef, a pastry chef, and baker are also artists, but of a different kind. Their canvas is a plate and their medium is food.

Culinary arts, then, is the art of food, and culinary artists are people who do creative things with food. Their work goes beyond cooking a tuna casserole for dinner. They create dishes that are a feast for the eyes as well as the palate. And they do this in many different places in many different capacities.

Working in culinary arts is not easy or glamorous, and only the strong survive. Culinary professionals work long hours, often when the rest of us are at home relaxing or asleep. They work weekends and holidays and spend the majority of their time on their feet. They work under pressure in crowded, hot kitchens where tempers fly. The noise in a commercial kitchen may be nerve-wracking. Chefs and cooks shout out orders, shout at the staff, and may even cuss. Working in a culinary kitchen is no day at the beach. The thin-skinned need not apply.

Where cooking professionals work

Many culinary professionals work in restaurants, but you find them in other places as well. We give you the lowdown on the variety of establishments that employ culinary pros in Chapter 2, but for now, here's a brief list. You're certain to find culinary professionals that cook in these places:

- ✔ Restaurants, large and small (see Chapter 5)
- ✔ Hotel restaurants and kitchens, which may include banquet halls (see Chapter 6)
- ✔ Resorts and spas (see Chapter 6)
- ✔ Pastry shops and bakeries (see Chapter 8)
- ✔ Catering companies (see Chapter 7)
- ✔ Institutions such as hospitals, airlines, cruise ships, schools, and correctional centers (see Chapter 7)
- ✔ Kitchens in homes as personal and private chefs (see Chapter 9); as artisans (see Chapter 10); or as culinary entrepreneurs (see Chapter 18)
- ✔ Culinary schools (see Chapter 14)
- ✔ Test kitchens (see Chapters 10 and 12)
- ✔ Commissary kitchens (see Chapters 3, 5, 6, and 8)

What non-cooking culinary professionals do

Lots of culinary jobs are available even if you're not interested in actually cooking for a living. Check out these non-cooking culinary professional roles:

- Food writers, cookbook editors, and television and radio hosts (see Chapter 12)
- Food photographers and stylists (see Chapters 12 and 14)
- Food scientists (see Chapter 10)
- Retail salespeople and purchasers (see Chapter 15)
- Beverage and wine experts (see Chapter 11)
- Food-related public relations and marketing professionals (see Chapter 13)

Looking Beyond Food Prep: What Culinary Professionals Do

If you enter a culinary profession that involves cooking, you'll perform other tasks in addition to cooking food for customers. Your specific job duties depend on the place where you work and the position you hold. For example, the executive chef is typically the top dog in a kitchen, and a line cook is much lower in the chain of command, so the duties of those two jobs are different. (To learn more about the kitchen brigade, turn ahead to Chapter 5.)

Most culinary professionals involved in cooking have some or all of these job duties:

- Prepping food (washing, cutting, chopping, peeling, and pounding)
- Preparing ingredients (mixing, weighing, and measuring)
- Lifting heavy items (such as pots and sacks of flour and potatoes)
- Purchasing supplies and ingredients
- Baking, roasting, broiling, and steaming meats and fish
- Baking, steaming, roasting, and sautéing vegetables
- Frying potatoes and other foods
- Baking breads, cakes, and pastries
- Arranging, plating, and garnishing food
- Estimating costs and maintaining budgets

- ✔ Cleaning and organizing the kitchen
- ✔ Developing recipes and menus
- ✔ Hiring and training new staff
- ✔ Determining production schedules
- ✔ Communicating with other members of the kitchen brigade and front-of-the-house staff

But not all culinary professionals cook. These professionals may have duties similar to those in other non-culinary professions. For example, the duties of a food writer are similar to those of other writers, except that the subject matter and publication they write for are likely different. The same goes for food photographers, restaurant supply salespeople, food scientists, and others. People in these professions are tied together by their love of food and the fact that they work with food — even if they don't cook or work directly with food. For more information on non-cooking professions, as well as their duties, check out the chapters in Part IV.

Asking the Age-Old Question: School or Work?

You may have heard of chefs who began their career as a dishwasher or server and climbed the culinary ladder to earn fame and fortune as an executive chef or the owner of a three-star restaurant. Is this possible? Sure. Is it likely? Nope. Many chefs who have never attended culinary school will not hire you unless you've done so. Deciding whether to go to culinary school or to earn your stripes working is a tough one. A culinary degree or diploma is often a must these days and may give you the edge that you need to land a job. On the other hand, the experience you garner from working in real-life situations is invaluable. Often, the decision depends on what your career goals are and what your circumstances are. Check out Chapter 3 for more on choosing the right path for you.

Even famous chefs must start at the bottom and work their way up the culinary ladder. Emeril Lagasse once worked as a part-time bread baker in a Portuguese bakery and was paid only $50 for each episode of *Essence of Emeril,* his first television show. Chef and restaurateur Mario Batali worked as a dishwasher in a New Jersey restaurant called Stuff Yer Face. Batali was quickly promoted to pizza maker. TV personality Rachael Ray never attended culinary school and instead honed her skills in her Italian family's kitchen.

Choosing to go to culinary school

Culinary school gives you a broad foundation on which to build your skills. Culinary students work in actual kitchens under the supervision of a chef. Different chefs teach different classes, so students learn many skills. Expect to learn about the following subjects and skills in culinary school:

- ✔ Applying cooking techniques (roasting, baking, grilling, frying, sautéing)
- ✔ Learning knife skills (chopping, slicing, dicing, cutting, julienning —yes, there is a difference!)
- ✔ Operating kitchen equipment (stoves, fryers, mixers, grills, scales)
- ✔ Measuring and weighing ingredients
- ✔ Using kitchen tools (spatulas, whisks, tongs, thermometer)
- ✔ Following food safety procedures (keeping conditions sanitary, avoiding cross contamination, dealing with waste, controlling temperature)
- ✔ Managing (accounting, budgeting, hiring, purchasing)
- ✔ Preparing and planning menus
- ✔ Following nutrition guidelines

Do you think you're too old to carry a book bag and head back to class? Many culinary schools report that the average age of their students is now 30 or older. And culinary students are as diverse as the meals they prepare. They range in age from 18 to more than 60, and more than half are career-changers.

You have many options when choosing a culinary school, from earning a certificate from a community college or technical school to earning a four-year degree from a top-notch establishment such as the Culinary Institute of America or the International Culinary Schools at the Art Institutes. Of course, in a perfect world, everyone could attend the school of his or her choosing, even to study abroad, but our world is far from perfect. Reality demands that you consider these factors when choosing a culinary school:

- ✔ **Your location:** Think about how far you can travel and whether moving is a feasible option.
- ✔ **The time you can devote:** If you're like most people, you're planning to work while attending school, so a part-time program at a community college may be the most flexible option for you.
- ✔ **The amount of money you can spend:** Smaller, local programs cost only a fraction of the tuition charged at major culinary institutes.

You have the following options in terms of the degree you earn at a culinary school:

- **Diploma or a certificate:** These programs run from several months to a year.
- **Associate's degree:** Earning an associate's degree takes two years as a full-time student.
- **Bachelor's degree:** You'll need to be a full-time student for four years to earn a bachelor's degree.

To learn more about culinary schools, flip ahead to Chapter 4.

Landing an apprenticeship

An apprenticeship is a great way to gain practical, hands-on experience. What is an apprenticeship, you ask? It's an arrangement in which you volunteer your services without pay, usually, in exchange for instruction. An apprenticeship is a great go-between school and actually working. In the past, many culinary professionals completed an apprenticeship instead of going to culinary school, but it's no longer the norm. Most culinary professionals go to school and may serve an apprenticeship as part of their schooling. In this case, they work for school credit. However, if the culinary school you attend does not include an apprenticeship as part of its curriculum, or if you're opting out of culinary school, you may be able to land one on your own.

Some culinary students or graduates choose to do a *stagiaire,* or stage, to gain employment. A *stagiaire* is nothing more than volunteering your time to prove to a restaurant that you have what it takes to work there. You typically set up a time with an establishment to come in and work. You can also use a stagiaire as an opportunity to learn more culinary skills from people already in the profession.

Convincing professionals in any field to give you an apprenticeship is not easy. They may not have the time or the energy to teach you how to do their job. However, if you can devote a significant amount of time, they may find the idea of free labor appealing. Be persistent and humble.

When a chef does agree to give you an apprenticeship, realize that you're at the bottom in terms of experience in the kitchen. Expect to perform bottom-of-the-barrel duties, such as slicing vegetables or even washing dishes. Be grateful for any instruction you're given. Say please and thank you and work hard. Keep in mind that if you prove yourself, your apprenticeship may lead to a job in that same kitchen.

Sizzling hot cooking shows

Today's cooking television shows are a far cry from those of the past, such as Julia Child's *The French Chef,* which attracted millions of viewers in the 1960s. Modern viewers care more about being entertained than being instructed, and reality-cooking shows such as *Hell's Kitchen* and *Top Chef* do not disappoint. *Hell's Kitchen* is a cooking competition hosted by celebrity chef Gordon Ramsay in which the final two contestants must design and run their own restaurants. With a goal of winning money to open their own restaurant, the culinary pros on *Top Chef* must make gourmet creations on a shoestring budget while living in the same house. The personality clashes are as much fun as the competition. *Top Chef Masters* is a

spin-off of the *Top Chef* series. In this reality competition, 24 chefs compete in various challenges, with the top chef winning $100,000 for his or her favorite charity. On *Iron Chef America,* chefs use the same ingredients to see who can create the most delicious gourmet dishes. *Worst Cooks in America* takes 12 of the worst cooks and puts them through culinary boot camp. Whoever can prove that they've learned the most culinary skills receives a cash prize.

Cooking shows have surged in popularity, and TV stations such as the Food Network, Bravo, and the Travel Channel can't create them fast enough, which is why many now say that we are now living in the "age of food TV."

Working from the start

School isn't for everyone. Many people learn better by doing rather than listening or watching. If you're one of those people who feels they'd be better off diving right into the industry — without going to culinary school — you should be prepared to work hard. As long as you're willing to start at the bottom and work your way up the ladder, you may not need to attend culinary school to achieve success. Many famous and renowned chefs, such as Rick Bayless and Mario Batali, never received culinary degrees.

Don't expect to walk into a restaurant and be granted the position of executive chef with no experience or education. Gaining the experience needed to run a kitchen and create menus takes years. If you're willing to take a lower position such as dishwasher and show that you're hard working, you may be able to quickly advance to other kitchen positions, and, with even more hard work, dedication, and perseverance, eventually advance to higher roles such as sous chef, kitchen manager, or executive chef.

You can gain a food education as well as experience in ways other than sitting in a classroom. You can secure an apprenticeship that will teach you skills similar to what you'd learn in a culinary school (see "Landing an apprenticeship" earlier in this chapter). Maybe you come from a family that owns a restaurant and can teach you everything they know about food and cooking. Or perhaps your family just loves to cook, and you can learn recipes and cooking skills that have been passed from generation to generation. You can (and should) also simply self-teach. If you have an interest in food and cooking, be sure to work on your self-education by reading a ton of cookbooks and manuals and watch numerous cooking programs or instructional videos. And don't be shy about trying new things in the kitchen. Keeping up on the latest food and cooking trends can give you a leg up when you're looking to land a job in the culinary field.

Some cooking jobs don't require education or even experience. Many family-style restaurants and institutions hire new employees with no experience and give them on-the-job training, but others may require at least some experience. It depends on the establishment and their hiring practices. The same goes for non-cooking culinary jobs. Positions such as food writers may not require a culinary degree (although one may be helpful), but they do require degrees in other fields, such as English or communications, as well as excellent writing skills.

Finding the Right Culinary Career

Think about the type of culinary job you would most like to land. Maybe the idea of working in a restaurant that offers customers a fine-dining experience most appeals to you. Perhaps your goal is to one day become head chef in such an establishment, creating menus and overseeing the cooks. The type of food an establishment serves might factor into your decision. If you're fond of Italian or Japanese cuisine, you may see yourself working in such a kitchen. If you bake desserts in your spare time, you may strive to become a pastry chef. Or perhaps you want to take the road less traveled and become a caterer or specialize in volume cooking at a hospital or school. Maybe cooking isn't your thing and you'd rather write about it at a newspaper or online magazine, or perhaps you enjoy photographing food. Whatever type of culinary career you decide you would most like to have, you'll need to try to land a job that will prepare for this career. (And you must realize that wherever you work, you'll start at the bottom.)

In this section, we provide a questionnaire and answer explanations that can help you find your fit in the culinary field.

Culinary career questionnaire

Jot down an answer to each of the following questions. There are no right or wrong answers, but your answers will help you determine what type of culinary job is right for you. Be sure to read the answer explanations in the next section.

1. Do you enjoy cooking? Why or why not?

2. What is your favorite food?

3. Do you prefer to rise early in the morning or work late at night? Or would you rather have normal working hours?

4. Do you like baking and eating desserts?

5. How do you feel about working under pressure?

6. Are you comfortable standing on your feet for hours at a time?

7. Do you like to cook for large groups of people, or do you prefer to cook for only a few people?

8. Do you enjoy preparing healthy meals, and are you concerned with nutrition when you cook?

9. Do you like teaching people new things?

10. Do you like to be in charge, or do you prefer to follow orders?

11. Are you a good writer?

12. Are you a good photographer?

13. Do you enjoy learning about wine or other beverages?

14. Do you dream of owning your own business one day?

15. Would you like to earn a commission instead of earning a flat salary?

16. Do you make a particular recipe that everyone goes crazy for?

Answer explanations

After responding to the questionnaire in the last section, read the following explanations and consider the answers you wrote down.

1. This question is a no-brainer: If you enjoy cooking, then a culinary career may be right for you. Not all culinary careers require cooking, however, so don't rule out a culinary career if you don't like to cook. A career in the culinary field requires a strong interest and knowledge in food, not just cooking skills. For more information on non-cooking professions, check out the chapters in Part IV.

2. Your favorite food may help you determine what type of restaurant you would like to work in. For example, if you wrote down that your favorite food was tacos, you may enjoy working in a Mexican restaurant, or if you wrote down fettuccine Alfredo, you may try to land a job in an Italian restaurant. If you wrote down something more vague, such as chicken, don't be discouraged. Think about some of the other foods and cuisines you enjoy. Many different restaurants exist that serve all types of cuisines to suit any taste.

3. If you prefer to begin your workday in the wee hours of the morning before the rooster crows, consider working as a pastry chef or a baker. These culinary professionals have very early hours. (Read Chapter 8 to learn more about these culinary jobs.) If you're a night owl, you're probably best suited to employment in a restaurant. (Turn ahead to Chapter 5 to learn more.) If you prefer to work typical 9-to-5 hours, consider a career in institutional cooking, such as in a school or hospital cafeteria. (To learn more about volume cooking, read Chapter 7.) Many nontraditional food jobs don't fit into any of these categories and allow you to set your own hours or work a variety of different shifts. For example, a caterer may only work on the weekends during a large event or a food writer may work only a few days a week. (See Chapters 7 and 12 for more information on these professions.)

4. If you like baking and eating desserts, you may enjoy working as a pastry chef or a baker. (To find out the difference between these two professions, see Chapter 8.)

5. Commercial kitchens, such as those in restaurants, are stressful places. If you thrive under pressure, then consider working in a restaurant or hotel. (See Chapters 5 and 6.) If working under pressure is not your thing, consider working in institutions, where the pace is usually slower. (See Chapter 7.) Because some nontraditional food positions allow you to work for yourself, such as food bloggers or food stylists, these positions tend to be less stressful. Not all non-cooking jobs are stress-free, though. Jobs such as those in restaurant supply sales or marketing positions may be just as stressful as working in a fast-paced kitchen.

6. Standing on your feet for many hours at a time is a drawback of many culinary careers — but a few options exist that let you sit down now and then. Turn to Chapter 12 for info on media jobs, Chapter 13 to find out about PR and marketing jobs, Chapter 14 to read about becoming a culinary instructor, food photographer, or food stylist, and Chapter 15 to read up on retail sales jobs.

7. If you like to cook for large groups of people, consider volume cooking such as catering. (Turn to Chapter 7.) If you prefer cooking only for a few people, you may enjoy life as a private or personal chef. (See Chapter 9.)

8. Culinary professionals who work in resorts and spas prepare healthy meals for guests. If you like considering nutrition and making tasty, but healthy meals, you can find out more about your options in Chapter 6.

9. If you like to cook and have the patience to show others, then you may one day choose to become a culinary instructor. (To learn about this career, turn to Chapter 14.)

10. Perhaps your past coworkers always turned to you for advice on how to solve work-related problems. If so, you may be the kind of person who prefers giving orders rather than taking them. Born leaders should strive to one day become executive chefs or managers or open businesses of their own. If you're more comfortable taking orders, you may prefer to be a sous chef, cook, or work in another type of non-cooking profession such as in restaurant supply sales. (To learn about the hierarchy of positions in a restaurant, read Chapter 5; to learn about culinary entrepreneurs, see Chapter 18; and for more information about jobs in sales, flip to Chapter 15.)

11. Great writers and food lovers may choose to write about food instead of cooking it. (Find out about the different food writing jobs in Chapter 12.)

12. Maybe you'd like to take pictures of food for advertisements, product labels, or magazine covers. If this sounds like fun to you, flip ahead to Chapters 12 and 14.

13. Some culinary professionals specialize solely in beverages, such as wine and beer, but these aren't the only beverages someone in this position may work with. Establishments serve an array of alcoholic and nonalcoholic beverages to suit everyone's tastes, from cocktails to milkshakes to herbal teas. If a career in beverages interests you, turn to Chapter 11.

14. If you dream of owning your own business one day, you may want to think about getting on track to open a restaurant or start a different type of culinary business. (Turn to Chapter 10 to learn more about the role of artisans or see Chapter 18 for more information about culinary careers.)

15. If you're the kind of person who is motivated by money and also loves food, consider a career in culinary sales. (Read Chapter 13 for information about PR and marketing, see Chapter 11 to find out more about beverage jobs, and see Chapter 15 for the details on retail purchasing and sales jobs.)

16. If you're known for making the best chutney around, maybe you should consider bottling and selling it. Food artisans make and distribute their own hand-crafted products to specialty shops and grocery stores, who in turn sell their products. (For more information about artisans, see Chapter 10.)

Grabbing the Job You Want

A love of food, a culinary degree, and terrific experience don't do you a whole lot of good if you don't have a job in which to strut your hard-earned skills. Part V details how to land a job (maybe even your dream job!), move up the culinary ladder, and perhaps even own your own business one day. Here, we discuss some of the basics of getting you to the job you want.

Seeking out the right job

Thanks to the questionnaire in the previous section, you know what you want to do, right? Well, it should at least have given you an idea. After you know what you want to do, start looking for a job that meets your needs and interests. You may ask yourself, "How do I even begin?" Start with what you know. Visit places that you frequent, such as the sandwich shop around the corner you grab lunch from each day or the bakery where you ordered that heavenly birthday cake last month. Consider whether you'd like to work at these types of places.

If you find that you don't want to work in any establishments where you live, you may want to consider moving. You should consider factors such as salary and cost of living when determining where you'd like to move, live, and work.

When you've determined the location of where you'd like to work, start the job search. Following are some ways to carry out your job hunt:

- ✔ Fill out an applications at establishments you'd like to work.
- ✔ Check the want ads in local publications and websites.
- ✔ Ask family or friends if they know of any opportunities, and tell them to look out for open positions that may suit you.
- ✔ Talk to past instructors about any job connections they may have.
- ✔ Use your school's career services.
- ✔ Attend a job fair.

Don't put all your eggs in one basket when looking for a job. The more applications you fill out at more establishments, the better your odds will be of landing a job.

Some jobs may require a cover letter and résumé as part of the application process. We take a more detailed look at writing these documents as well as the interview process in Chapter 16. After you submit this information to a potential employer, start preparing for an interview, which we touch on in the next section.

Preparing for an interview

Imagine that a prospective employer is interviewing you. Which do you think you should stress most: experience, education, or attitude? Most chefs confess that they consider applicants' attitudes more important than their experience and education. Be sure to convey a positive image during a job interview. Be upbeat, humble, and professional. Although discussing your experience and education is fine (and indeed recommended) if you're asked to do so, don't pretend to know more than the person interviewing you. Stress that you really want to work there and that you're willing to work hard to learn the needed skills. Before you leave, shake the interviewer's hand and thank him or her for taking the time to meet with you.

At any interview, be prepared to answer this question: "Why do you want to work here in particular?" Hint: Find out all you can about the restaurant (or store, or catering operation, and so on) beforehand. And eat there (if applicable).

What the heck is a toque, anyway?

Traditional attire for a chef consists of a double-breasted, long-sleeved white jacket, checkered or printed pants, a tall white hat, and, of course, at least one apron. Although such clothing may look strange, it's more practical than you'd think. The white cotton jacket actually repels heat and keeps the chef cooler in a steamy kitchen. The long sleeves protect the chef's arms from burns when reaching across stoves and into ovens. The jacket usually has knotted buttons because they don't fall off or break as easily as metal or plastic buttons. (Customers typically frown upon pieces of buttons in their food.) The double-breasted jacket can be reversed to hide stains. Checkered or patterned pants are practical in a kitchen because they hide stains, too.

The hat that chefs wear is called a *toque* (pronounced *toke*). This type of hat, which dates back to the 16th century, stands high and has no rim. The many folds in the top of the hat are said to represent the many ways that you can cook an egg. Some toques have exactly 101 folds, which are also called pleats. A toque designates a chef's rank — the higher the toque, the higher the rank. A toque also serves the general purpose of keeping hair and sweat out of food.

Today's chefs and cooks may wear many variations of this traditional attire. Some wear colored jackets and even shorts while they work. And some prefer to wrap a bandanna around their head instead of wearing a toque. Your place of employment will dictate what is acceptable to wear. Some employers may allow you to wear what you want or even provide you with a uniform.

Assessing the Culinary Job Outlook

According to the Bureau of Labor Statistics (BLS), the job outlook for culinary professionals who cook is good. The BLS predicts that many new positions will be created over the next decade. Additional job openings will be created by workers leaving the field, either to retire or pursue a different career.

Note that the BLS does not gather data on every culinary position discussed in this book. It only includes data on major categories.

Growth in culinary careers will occur largely because of the following factors:

- An increase in the population
- An increase in the demand for convenience
- An increase in the demand for more options when it comes to dining out

The head honchos

In the culinary world, chefs, head cooks, and supervisors are the cream of the crop. They earn the most money (see Table 1-1) but typically also need to have the most experience and the best education.

The Bureau of Labor Statistics (BLS) describes the outlook for chefs, head cooks, and supervisors over the next decade as good. (See Table 1-2.) Of the nearly 950,000 individuals in these positions in 2008, most (about 88 percent) were food-preparation and serving supervisors. Only about 12 percent worked as chefs and cooks.

Food-prep supervisors may work in full-service restaurants, which are restaurants offering table service, but they're more likely to work in fast-food and take-out restaurants and catering facilities. According to the BLS, of the individuals employed as food-prep supervisors and serving supervisors in 2008, nearly half worked at fast-food restaurants, cafeterias, and take-out restaurants. Only about 25 percent worked in full-service restaurants. The BLS expects the number of food-prep supervisors and serving supervisors to increase by 6 percent by 2018.

In 2008, most chefs and head cooks worked in full-service restaurants. About 20 percent worked in hotels or for caterers. A very small number worked as entrepreneurs, meaning they owned their own restaurant. The BLS predicts that the number of job openings for chefs and head cooks will increase only slightly by 2018.

If you're looking for a job in an upscale, white-tablecloth restaurant, expect to face the most competition. Why? This type of restaurant pays more than other establishments.

Table 1-1 shows the salary ranges and median salaries for supervisors and chefs and head cooks. Table 1-2 compares their job outlooks.

Table 1-1	Salaries for Chefs/Cooks and Supervisors	
Position	*Salary Range*	*Median Salary*
Chef, head cook	$22,120–$66,680 and up	$38,770
Food-prep and serving supervisors	$18,530–$46,810 and up	$28,970

Source: Bureau of Labor Statistics

Table 1-2	Job Outlook for Chefs/Cooks and Supervisors			
Position	*Number of Jobs in 2008*	*Projected Number of Jobs by 2018*	*Change from 2008–2018*	*Percent Increase*
Chef, head cook	108,300	108,500	+200	0%
Food-prep and serving supervisors	833,300	888,500	+55,200	7%

Source: Bureau of Labor Statistics

The worker bees

According to the Bureau of Labor Statistics (BLS), the outlook for culinary "worker bees" is better than for their supervisors. In 2008, about 3 million people in the United States worked as cooks and food-preparation workers in full-service restaurants, fast-food restaurants, institutions (schools, universities, hospitals, nursing homes, and correction centers), diners, private households, and hotels. (See Table 1-3 for the breakdown.)

Two-thirds of all cooks and food-prep workers worked in restaurants and about 16 percent worked in institutions. A smaller number worked in private households or other establishments such as hotels and grocery stores. You can check out salary data for different types of cooks and food-prep workers in Table 1-4.

Table 1-3   Distribution of Cooks and Food-Preparation Workers

Workplace	Number of Cooks and Food-Prep Workers
Full-service restaurants	914,200
Fast-food restaurants	566,000
Cafeterias and institutions	391,800
Diners	171,400
Private households	4,900
Other areas	18,000

Source: Bureau of Labor Statistics

Table 1-4   Salaries for Cooks and Food-Prep Workers

Position	Salary Range	Median Salary
Cooks in private households	$16,230–$56,280 and up	$24,070
Cooks in cafeterias and institutions	$15,220–$33,050 and up	$22,210
Cooks in full-service restaurants	$15,880–$31,330 and up	$21,990
Cooks in diners	$14,740–$27,639 and up	$19,260
Cooks in fast-food restaurants	$14,090–$22,080 and up	$16,880
Food-prep workers	$14,740–$27,440 and up	$18,630

Source: Bureau of Labor Statistics

Over the next few years, the number of jobs for cooks and food-preparation workers combined is predicted to increase by about 6 percent. The number of jobs with caterers and in institutions is expected to grow the fastest by 2018, about 10 percent. Jobs in fast-food restaurants are also expected to increase by about 8 percent. The job outlook is better for cooks than for lower-level food-prep workers. The number of food-prep jobs is expected to increase by only 4 percent. (See Table 1-5.)

Table 1-5	Job Outlook for Cooks and Food-Prep Workers			
Position	*Number of Jobs in 2008*	*Projected Number of Jobs by 2018*	*Change from 2008–2018*	*Percent Increase*
Cooks in full-service restaurants	914,200	984,400	70, 200	8%
Cooks in fast-food restaurants	566,000	608,400	42,400	7%
Cooks in cafeterias and institutions	391,800	429,700	37,900	10%
Cooks in diners	171,400	171,500	100	0%
Cooks in private households	4,900	5,100	200	4%
Cooks in other areas	18,000	20,900	2,900	16%
Food-prep workers	891,900	929,600	37,700	4%

Source: Bureau of Labor Statistics

Because people will always need to eat — whether at fast-food or fine-dining restaurants — the number of jobs in the culinary field will continue to grow. And because the culinary industry is filled with many opportunities, this industry is attractive to people with all levels of culinary training and experience.

Chapter 2

Finding the Jobs: Where Culinary Professionals Work

In This Chapter

▶ Finding out who fills culinary jobs in all kinds of locations

▶ Identifying traditional places where culinary professionals are employed

▶ Checking out the nontraditional places where cooks and chefs work

▶ Seeing where other people with a love of food may find employment

*T*hink back to the last time you dined at your favorite restaurant. Try to remember the many culinary professionals who worked there: the host, the wait staff, the bartender, and the chef. You may not have had an opportunity to see the employees working in the kitchen, but you can try to imagine how many were there. Culinary jobs abound in restaurants, and the United States has nearly 1 million restaurants.

Besides restaurants, culinary professionals also work in hotels, resorts, and spas. And many individuals work with food but don't cook for a living. Some culinary professionals choose to write about or photograph mouth-watering dishes. Others specialize in wine and other beverages, and still others work in food sales and marketing.

Because culinary professionals have so many options in terms of employment, some people describe the field as being wide open, and this is good news for you. When you're ready, you can look for work in many places — from upscale restaurants to cruise ships to correctional facilities. (We're not kidding! Volume cooks work in prisons, and it's more enjoyable than you may think.) We encourage you to pursue all culinary avenues to get your foot in the door and gain some experience working with food. In time, you can move into the job of your dreams.

Discovering Who Works in Culinary Arts

People who work in culinary arts are alike in that they all enjoy working with food. They enjoy the way food smells, feels, looks, and especially tastes. Culinary professionals who work in the kitchen of your favorite restaurant likely take pride in the dishes they prepare, just as food stylists and food photographers working at photo shoots take pride in their styling and photographs of food.

To be successful in this field, culinary professionals must be able to work with other people. The host in your favorite restaurant probably greeted you with a smile and led you to your table. Your server may have asked about your day and then was happy to answer your questions about the preparation of a particular dish. Even people working in the kitchen must function as a team to get their job done, so good people skills are a must.

Other than sharing a love of food and people, culinary professionals come in all shapes and sizes. People from all walks of life spend their days working in both traditional and nontraditional culinary environments. Some are young, inexperienced people who have just graduated high school or college and work as servers or bartenders in the hopes of one day making their way into the kitchen. Others are graduates of prestigious cooking schools and work as head chefs in famous kitchens. Still others are entrepreneurs who own their own businesses, such as pastry shops or catering companies. Food photographers, food writers, and beverage and wine professionals are culinary professionals with widely varying jobs, as well. Some culinary professionals have worked in the food business for most of their lives, whereas others are career changers who have decided to pursue their dream later in life.

Although many inexperienced people get entry-level work in culinary fields, culinary professionals in high-level positions such as chef typically have restaurant experience and some culinary schooling. If you want to hold such a position someday, even just taking a one-year certificate course and working somewhere that requires you to ask customers, "Do you want fries with that?" helps you get your foot in the door.

Checking Out Traditional Establishments in the Culinary Field

If you're interested in breaking into the world of culinary arts via a job in a kitchen or dining room, we advise you to hit the traditional establishments first — the places where people most often go to eat. Traditional establishments include (but are not limited to!) the following places: restaurants, hotels and resorts, pastry shops and bakeries, catering companies, and spas.

Restaurants

Scores of culinary jobs are in restaurants. (See the sidebar "The astounding number of restaurant jobs.") Americans love to eat in all kinds of restaurants, from white-tablecloth establishments to family-style chain restaurants to corner hot-dog stands. These restaurants all employ a staff to cook and serve food. Most serve meals *a la carte,* which means from a menu, but some restaurants offer buffets. In this section, we first discuss the types of culinary jobs you can find in restaurants, and then we give an overview of the different styles of restaurants where you may want to work.

Each restaurant is divided into two major sections: the back of the house and the front of the house. Workers employed in the back of the house — that is, the kitchen — prepare food. The employees in the front of the house care for customers. The number of employees a restaurant has depends on its size and the type of services it offers. (Think about it — if the restaurant doesn't have a bar, it doesn't need a bartender, which makes for a smaller staff and fewer available jobs.)

Following are some common positions in restaurant kitchens. To learn about the entire kitchen brigade, including their personality traits, salaries, education, training, and advancement prospects, flip ahead to Chapter 5.

- **Executive chef:** The executive chef is the kitchen's head honcho. The job responsibilities include planning menus, ordering and purchasing supplies from vendors, hiring and training new staff, and assigning tasks to the kitchen staff. Sometimes the executive chef may not actually cook food, but if he's needed and is available to help, he'll pick up a spot on the line or act as an expeditor, reading tickets and garnishing plates before they're set in the window. Executive chefs have significant restaurant experience and often formal schooling as well.

- **Sous chef:** The sous chef is the second-in-command in a kitchen. A sous chef assists the executive chef, oversees the kitchen staff, makes purchases for the kitchen, creates feature dishes, and assists in cooking. A sous chef also has many years of restaurant experience and often formal schooling.

- **Specialty chefs:** In a large kitchen, each cooking station may have its own chef, or supervisor. Specialty chefs include the fish chef, fry chef, grill chef, pasta chef, pizza chef, pantry chef, sauté chef, and vegetable chef. Specialty chefs usually have restaurant experience and training related to their specialty.

- **Pastry chef:** The pastry chef is a type of specialty chef who may work in a restaurant or in an establishment that sells desserts to restaurants. Pastry chefs have schooling related to their specialty and usually have restaurant experience as well.

✔ **Line cooks:** Most restaurants have at least a few line cooks. A line cook may work a particular station under a specialty chef or may work wherever needed at the moment. A line cook is an entry-level position. Line cooks sometimes work their way up the culinary ladder to other positions even if they don't have formal schooling.

✔ **Prep cooks:** Prep cooks prepare the food that line cooks make. They often come in earlier and make broths and soups and chop vegetables. This position is entry-level, and, similarly to line cooks, prep cooks may work their way up to other positions.

✔ **Roundsman:** A roundsman is also called a *swing cook*. This person is trained to work at any station in the kitchen and goes wherever needed. To become a roundsman, you'll need to have many years experience working every station in the kitchen. Kitchen supervisors expect their roundsmen to be able to perform well on every station and pick up the slack whenever necessary.

Following are some common positions in the front of the house:

✔ **General manager:** The general manager oversees the dining room and its staff. A general manager's tasks include scheduling events, hiring and training dining room staff, and developing the restaurant's budget.

The executive chef and the general manager must work closely together to ensure that the restaurant runs smoothly. If the executive chef is planning to have a special that will likely pull in many customers, the general manager needs to know to ensure that the dining room is adequately staffed.

✔ **Other positions:** Dining rooms also employ a wait staff, bartenders, bussers, hosts, and food runners. Larger restaurants may also have a head server, who supervises the wait staff in addition to seating guests and taking orders, and a sommelier, who creates wine lists and teaches customers about various kinds of wine.

In general, restaurants can be divided into the categories discussed in the following sections. (Chapter 5 explores these styles of restaurant in more detail.)

Keep in mind that many family-style, casual dining, and fast-food restaurants are chain restaurants. *Chain restaurants* are strings of restaurants that look similar and feature the same menu items and specials. They may be located across the country or only in specific regions. Fine-dining restaurants are not typically chain restaurants — being a unique establishment adds to their exclusivity and allows for higher menu prices.

The astounding number of restaurant jobs

The National Restaurant Association estimates that the 960,000 restaurants in the United States employ 13 million people — and this number is expected to grow to about 14.3 million by 2020. The employees within these restaurants comprise 10 percent of the U.S. workforce. The National Restaurant Association predicts that the restaurant industries in Texas and Florida will create the most jobs, followed by Arizona and Alabama.

Fine-dining restaurants

In the world of restaurants, fine dining is the top of the line. The food may be prepared by a well-known chef who uses rare and fresh ingredients. The table service is outstanding, and the price is high. Some fine-dining restaurants may have a full bar featuring top-shelf liquors, while others may only offer wine delivered by sommeliers and paired perfectly with menu items.

Because fine-dining restaurants usually pay more than other types of restaurants, the competition for jobs is tough. Culinary professionals working at fine-dining restaurants are less likely to leave for other opportunities and are more likely to have years of formal schooling and work-related experience under their belts.

Casual-dining restaurants

Like fine-dining restaurants, casual-dining restaurants offer table service, but the atmosphere and attire are more casual and the prices are not as steep. Casual restaurants usually have a full bar.

Landing a job at a casual-dining restaurant is easier than at an upscale restaurant, but you still have to be realistic: Without prior restaurant experience, you're going to have to start at the bottom of the culinary food chain (think line cook, dishwasher, or host).

Family-style restaurants

A family-style restaurant offers a casual dining experience that caters to children. Memorabilia typically covers the walls and customers may sit on benches or in booths. Family-style restaurants have a kids' menu and may offer crayons and placemats that kids can color on at the table. Soup and salad bars are commonplace at these establishments. Food is moderately priced.

It is fairly easy to land a job at a family-style restaurant, especially if you have some restaurant experience.

Diners

Most diners have a nostalgic theme that takes customers back to the 1940s and 1950s when life was simpler. Menus tend to be simple, with thick hamburgers, fries, and milk shakes. Some customers visit at a diner for a good cup of coffee and a slice of pie. Unlike other restaurants, diners are frequently busiest during breakfast and lunch. You won't find most members of the kitchen brigade at a diner. The number of cooks in the kitchen and types of food they prepare varies from diner to diner, but most diners have only a few short-order cooks in the kitchen, who prepare food that can be cooked quickly, such as sandwiches.

Working in the kitchen at a diner is a great way to enter the culinary field. Even though the menu items may not be as advanced as most restaurants, you'll still have a chance to learn the basics, work at a steady pace, and improve your skills.

Fast-food restaurants

As their name implies, fast-food restaurants serve food quickly. Table service is not offered at fast-food restaurants, and the food is much cheaper than at fine-dining, casual-dining, and family-style restaurants. Most fast-food joints are chains. In their kitchens, you won't find an executive or a sous chef; instead, many cooks are employed who prepare large quantities of only a few items. These cooks are supervised by managers who also oversee the staff working at the counter. Cooks at fast-food restaurants don't earn a high salary, but these jobs are fairly easy to get as the turnover is higher than at most other restaurants.

Hotels and resorts

Hotels and resorts usually have restaurants within them. The size and number of restaurants (and kitchens) depends on the size of the establishment. Smaller hotels or resorts may have one casual-dining restaurant and possibly a sandwich shop. Larger hotels may have an upscale restaurant with a famous chef, a smaller restaurant, a buffet, and a banquet hall. Many culinary professionals work in the kitchens at hotels and resorts.

The kitchen brigade in a hotel or resort is typical of that in any restaurant. Expect to find an executive chef, a sous chef, specialty chefs, line cooks, prep cooks, possibly a roundsman, and dishwashers in the back of the house. These culinary professionals must also prepare food for room-service orders in addition to orders from seated customers.

What's hot?

According to the National Restaurant Association, trends in restaurants include offering smaller portions for a smaller price, using locally grown produce and locally sourced meats and seafood, and offering nutritionally balanced children's meals and gluten-free/food-allergy conscious entrees. Other trends include simplicity, a back-to-the-basics approach to cooking; locally produced wine and beer; artisan cheeses; and ethnic-inspired breakfast items, such as Asian-flavored syrups. The way food is delivered to customers is also changing; for example, the popularity of food trucks and mobile food services is on the rise.

The front of the house at a hotel or resort restaurant typically employs a general manager, wait staff, bartenders, hosts, and bussers. If the hotel or resort has multiple restaurants, you may find some or all of these culinary professionals in each kitchen. The hotel or resort may also employ a hotel or resort manager to oversee the entire establishment. And if the hotel or resort has a banquet hall, it may have a banquet chef to oversee the separate banquet kitchen staff and a banquet manager to help plan and execute events.

If you live in or near a large city, you may have an advantage in finding a job due to the number of jobs available. However, because jobs in large hotel and resort restaurants pay more, expect some competition. Having restaurant experience and formal schooling can help you get your foot in the door. See Chapter 6 for more information about working in a hotel or resort.

Pastry shops and bakeries

Large restaurants may employ an executive pastry chef, which is a type of specialty chef, and possibly a pastry cook to assist in baking and creating desserts. Very large restaurants may also employ a baker, who takes care of making all the breads and other baked items, while the pastry chef concentrates on fine desserts that look as good as they taste. Although a baker's creations are delicious, they aren't as fancy as what a pastry chef makes. Turn to Chapter 8 to learn all about the duties of culinary professionals in pastry shops and bakeries.

In large restaurants, a pastry chef is a member of the kitchen brigade and head chef of the pastry department. Pastry chefs also work in pastry shops that sell desserts to restaurants and to the public. Bakeries are also another popular place of employment for pastry chefs. Some pastry chefs are self-employed and may specialize in an area, such as chocolate or wedding cakes. Pastry chefs usually have a combination of experience and formal education. Skills such as cake decorating are a plus.

Although large restaurants may employ a baker in the kitchen, most restaurants order bread from bakeries. Large bakeries have their own brigade and may include a head baker, an assistant baker, and other staff. Smaller bakeries may have only one baker and possibly an assistant or two. Like pastry chefs, most bakers have a combination of experience and formal schooling.

Catering companies

Catering is one of the fastest growing culinary professions in the United States. Culinary professionals also work at catering companies, which prepare supervise and prepare food for events such as: weddings, bridal showers, rehearsal dinners, bar mitzvahs, gallery openings, graduations, and corporate functions.

Culinary professionals interested in catering may choose to work for a banquet hall with its own catering staff or for a caterer serving the general public. Caterers also work in hotels and casinos. Some caterers are entrepreneurs with their own businesses.

Depending on the size of the catering firm, it may employ only one or two people and hire additional staff for the day of the event. Larger catering firms may employ catering managers, assistant managers, event planners, and food-service workers.

If you work for a caterer or become a caterer, expect to do much more than prepare and serve food. Chapter 7 explains catering in detail, but in general caterers perform these tasks:

- Meeting with clients to determine what a client wants and can afford.
- Preparing proposals that include information such as the type of event, the date, the number of guests expected, the price of catering the event, and ideas for the menu.
- Planning the event, which may involve working with managers of banquet halls, hiring and training staff, working with rental companies, and working with audio-visual companies. It also includes purchasing ingredients and supplies and testing recipes.
- Creating a schedule for the event, preferably down to the minute.
- Setting up on the day of the event, preparing and serving the food, and cleaning up after the event.

Creative culinary professionals in particular enjoy catering because they are involved in many tasks. A background in business in addition to culinary skills will help you land a job in catering. Understanding business management is especially helpful if you plan to one day operate your own catering business.

Spas

You won't find greasy cheeseburgers and fries at most spas, but you will find many culinary professionals cooking healthy and delicious meals for guests. Spas are places where guests go to feel healthy and refreshed, so they receive treatments such as massages and facials and dine on fine, nutritious cuisine.

The two main types of spas are destination spas and spas located in a hotel or resort or on a cruise ship.

- ✔ **Destination spa:** This type of spa is a vacation destination where guests may stay a few days, a week, or longer, enjoying spa cuisine and many relaxing activities. A destination spa may have a theme, such as fitness, health, or weight loss. At fitness spas, guests attend exercise classes with trainers. Health spas aim to improve guests' wellness. Weight-loss spas offer plenty of exercise and low-calorie cuisine. Culinary professionals, such as chefs, cooks, wait staff, and nutritionists are employed at destinations spas. The type of cuisine they prepare depends on the spa.

- ✔ **Hotel, resort, and cruise-ship spas:** These spas are located within a hotel or resort or aboard a cruise ship. Guests stay at these places to enjoy a vacation, so the trip is actually the main attraction, not the spa. Still, these spas are beautiful, enjoyable places that usually offer services such as exercise classes and facials. Most spas that are part of resorts, hotels, and cruise-ships do not have their own kitchen. Instead, a specific staff may be employed in one of the establishment's larger kitchens to prepare snacks, meals, and drinks for spa customers. These spas may, however, employ wait staff that cater to spa guests only. For more information on independent spas, see Chapter 6. For information on working for cruise ships, turn to Chapter 7.

Locating Other Popular Cooking Jobs in the Culinary Field

Most — but certainly not all — culinary professionals work in the traditional establishments discussed in the previous section. Many others work in places many people may consider nontraditional — places that you don't think of when someone says *culinary arts*. Working at a nontraditional establishment is a great way to get your foot in the door and gain some valuable experience. Following are some examples of nontraditional culinary establishments. These positions and more are discussed throughout Part II and Part III.

Private households

When you think of a personal or private chef, you may think of a famous chef cooking for a wealthy celebrity. Most personal and private chefs aren't famous, however, and landing such a job is easier than you may think. Today's households are busy places, often with adults working more than 40 hours each week. Individuals and families hire personal and private chefs to prepare the healthy, quality meals that they don't have time to prepare themselves.

A personal or private chef can also cater to an individual's needs. For example, if a customer is trying to lose weight, the chef can prepare low-calorie meals. These chefs are also great assets for customers with food allergies or other dietary restrictions.

Many personal and private chefs prepare meals in a customer's kitchen and then package, label, and freeze these meals for later use. A personal chef may perform the following tasks: meal planning, grocery shopping, meal preparation, and clean up.

Personal and private chefs almost always have formal schooling in their pocket as well as some restaurant experience. What's the difference between a personal and a private chef? Well, most personal chefs are self-employed. They may have multiple clients who they cook for on certain days of the week. Private chefs, on the other hand, typically live with one particular family. They travel with the family on vacation and may even be asked to perform duties unrelated to preparing meals, such as running errands or supervising children. To learn more about working as a personal or private chef, turn to Chapter 9.

Educational institutions

You may be surprised to learn that even your school cafeteria employed culinary professionals. Culinary professionals work in all kinds of educational institutions from elementary schools to trade schools to universities and colleges. Although this work isn't as prestigious as working in a white-tablecloth restaurant, it is certainly a good starting point. And *volume cooking,* cooking for many people, has its advantages. Many culinary professionals who work in schools enjoy better hours than restaurant workers — they may even be home for dinner at five. The culinary professionals who work in elementary and high-school cafeterias must have the ability to create meals that meet strict government regulations. To learn more about working in schools, turn ahead to Chapter 7.

Hospitals, nursing homes, and retirement homes

In addition to working in educational institutions, culinary professionals specializing in volume cooking also work in cafeterias in hospitals, nursing homes, and retirement homes. These institutions aren't prestigious, but many culinary jobs exist there. Working in this arena is a great way to gain experience and possibly even work your way up to kitchen manager.

Culinary professionals in hospitals, nursing homes, and retirement homes are adept at creating meals for patients with dietary restrictions. Making such meals taste great requires creativity. You never know — you may like it enough to stay. For more information, turn to Chapter 7.

Cruise ships

Working in the culinary industry may give you the chance to sail the seas. Cruise ships have large kitchens, called galleys, where many culinary professionals work. In most cruise ships, the galley is divided into two: the hot galley and the cold galley. Hot foods, such as steak and potatoes, are prepared in the hot galley and cold foods, such as salads, are prepared in the cold galley.

With some nautical modifications, cruise-ship kitchens employ the typical kitchen brigade (see Chapter 5). An executive chef oversees the kitchen and is assisted by the sous chef, who is second in command. Other cooks help prepare the food.

Landing a job in a cruise-ship galley may not be easy. You need some significant restaurant experience before you're even considered for a job in one of these kitchens. You need to prove that your talents as a chef will please hundreds of people during a voyage. When the ship sets sail, the only food options guests have are those that you've previously planned — so you better be sure that they'll love what you have to offer.

Airlines

People with a passion for culinary arts can even seek jobs on airlines. (Are you getting the impression that culinary professionals are everywhere? They are!) Airline chefs and cooks prepare meals for passengers taking long flights. Food-preparation workers, kitchen personnel, and culinary clean-up persons also work in airline kitchens. Some airline kitchens also have a supervisor. Food-service employees may be hired directly by an airline or through a catering company that has been hired by the airline. Among the many tasks airline culinary professionals perform are the following: planning menus, preparing food, and ensuring that food meets quality standards.

Most training for airline culinary professionals is on the job. However, working for a catering company for a few years will give you an extra edge. To work in a higher-level position, think of gaining some formal culinary training by taking courses or completing certification programs.

Correctional centers

When considering their futures in the culinary industry, many aspiring cooks and chefs don't see themselves in prison. However, working for a detention center or prison can be rewarding — chefs and cooks in prison kitchens learn to be creative and make quality food while adhering to a strict budget. Correctional centers may be one of the least attractive institutions to work for, but at least you'll always have job security — inmates need to eat, too. Learn the basics and show that you can follow the rules of the kitchen and you'll be on the line in no time.

Military bases and schools

Cooks and chefs at military bases and military schools prepare mass quantities of food on a daily basis. Not only do their meals need to be filling, but they must also be nutritious. The monotony of preparing pounds upon pounds of food for hungry soldiers is broken up many times each year when senior officers, politicians, and even members of Congress stop by the base. At this time, the executive chef — a coveted role in a military kitchen that requires nearly two decades of kitchen and managerial experience — must invent a menu that will impress visiting VIPs.

Test kitchens

You can find culinary professionals such as recipe developers, recipe testers, and research chefs in test kitchens. *Culinologists* (chefs from the Research Chefs Association who are able to successfully mix food with science) are employed by many test kitchens across the nation to develop new flavor pairings and recipes. Then, they follow the recipe over and over again, tweaking it until it's exactly the way they want it. If you're looking for a day job that enables you to be creative in the kitchen, test kitchens may be the place to look. Many people who work in test kitchens enjoy doing so because they can do what they love all day and still be home in time for dinner with their families.

Development kitchens

You'll more than likely find culinary scientists and chefs interested in the sciences in test kitchens. In research and development kitchens, however, you'll find quite a few food scientists. These scientists may be designing new packaging, creating new flavors, or even working on plans for new lines of cookware or baking equipment. Food scientists typically have college degrees in chemistry, biology, microbiology, engineering, or food science and safety. For more about food scientists, check out Chapter 10.

Commissary kitchens

If you're interested in preparing restaurant-quality food but don't want to experience the hustle and bustle of a restaurant kitchen, you may find that a job at a commissary kitchen suits you best. In commissary kitchens, cooks and chefs prepare food in large quantities that will be partially cooked, frozen, and then sent to restaurants or grocery stores. At the restaurant, the food is finished and then plated. Some restaurants, such as fast-food restaurants, may even request food that's ready to serve from commissary kitchens. Large food companies may own commissary kitchens, but you can also find them in large hotels, resorts, or casinos. Knowledge of the basics of food preparation and safety and a bit of kitchen experience should help you land a job in a commissary kitchen.

Wineries and breweries

If alcoholic beverages peak your interest more than food, you may be able to find a job at a winery or brewery. Here, you may or may not deal directly with the development of the beverage. Depending on your past experience in the industry, you may find a job as a tasting-room manager, brewer or brewmaster, lab technician, sommelier, winemaker, wine chemist, or wine-cellar worker. For more information on jobs in the beverage industry, see Chapter 11.

Working with Food in Nontraditional Settings

As strange as it may sound, some culinary professionals earn a living in their field without cooking food for customers. But just because these individuals don't cook food for a living doesn't mean that they don't know just about everything there is to know about food. They are simply skilled in more than one area.

You may still be able to work with food (yet not necessarily make or create it) if you're employed at places discussed in the following sections. (You can also check out the careers mentioned in Part IV for more information.)

Publications

If you're interested in photographing, designing, and styling food, but not so much in cooking it yourself, you may find a job at a newspaper, magazine, or catalogue. If you're interested in writing restaurant reviews, chef profiles or biographies, or cookbooks, you may also be able to find work at these publications, in addition to online blogs and websites. These are some of the most common food jobs you find at publications: cookbook writer/editor, food critic/reviewer, food photographer, food stylist, and recipe writer/editor.

Chapter 12 discusses food-writing options in more detail, and you can turn to Chapter 14 to find out more about food photographing and styling.

Television or radio programs

If you're interested in broadcasting television or radio programs about food, you're in luck — plenty of jobs exist that allow you to be part of the action. If you want to host your own radio show about food or perhaps direct episodes of a cooking show, this line of work may be for you. Some broadcast media food jobs include: host, producer, director, writer, and crew.

If you're a food stylist, recipe developer, or recipe tester, you may also be hired to work for television and radio shows. For more information about working with food in broadcast media, check out Chapter 12.

High schools, colleges, or technical schools

You can certainly prepare food for students to eat in the cafeterias of high schools, colleges/universities, and technical schools, but these educational establishments also have jobs that allow you to *teach* students how to prepare food for themselves. If you have extensive knowledge of the food industry, these institutions may hire you to teach students everything from boiling water to decorating elaborate wedding cakes.

If you're interested in teaching teenagers and young adults the basics of home economics, you should look into openings for home-ec teachers and cooking instructors at high schools and vocational schools. You'll need to have a squeaky clean background to be allowed to work with high school students, and you may even have to earn an education/teaching certificate for some schools.

Community colleges, four-year universities, and technical schools are also popular options if you want to teach others how to cook. Schools that offer associate's degrees, bachelor's degrees, technical degrees, and specialty certifications in baking, pastry arts, culinary arts, hospitality, or hotel and restaurant management offer various courses. A teaching job in these areas may require you to teach students about preparing soups and sauces, meats, cold foods, pastries, breads, cake decorating, and even chocolate and candy making. Depending on your background, you also have the option of teaching nutrition courses, hospitality, business management, and ServSafe courses. You'll need plenty of real-world kitchen experience to be considered for these positions, and a teaching or education certification could do nothing but benefit you, as well.

Grocery and specialty food stores

If you're interested in learning about food and selling it to others, but not in preparing it or serving it, you may want to look for a job in a specialty food store or even a grocery store. Managers in these stores typically meet with salespeople and speak with their most valued customers in order to make decisions about which foods their stores should sell. Managers may sample products and visit factories where items are made. They're also responsible for training their staff so that workers appear knowledgeable about the products they sell to their customers. The responsibilities of store managers differ from store to store, as do the requirements they must meet to secure the jobs.

For more information about working at a specialty-food store or grocery store, see Chapter 15.

Cookware and kitchen equipment stores

Managers of cookware and kitchen equipment stores (or even cookware or appliance departments) have jobs similar to grocery store and specialty-food store managers. They don't have a hand in developing or building the products, but they still need to know enough about them to secure sales. Whereas grocery store managers can describe the taste of a particular product, cookware store managers should be able to describe how a product works. They should be confident while they inform their customers about anything on the sales floor, from ice-cube trays to state-of-the-art backyard grills. You don't necessarily need a vast knowledge of food to become a cookware or kitchenware store manager; working a few years in retail will help you achieve this position.

For more information about working at cookware and kitchenware stores, see Chapter 15.

Restaurant supply distributors/companies

Many popular television cooking shows have created a boom in the culinary-product market. Chefs, as well as the general public, are on the lookout for new cooking tools as well as ingredients and other products to prepare new meals and desserts. Many culinary professionals work as sale representatives for food-service companies. They learn everything there is to know about their products and then they take them on the road, visiting restaurant chefs and owners, grocery and specialty food stores, and cookware and kitchen equipment stores. They may even attend trade shows and fairs to demonstrate how their newest products work or taste.

If you're interested in working for a restaurant supply distributor or sales company, you'll probably start at the bottom rung as an assistant salesperson or sales representative. You may then work your way up the ladder to an assistant buyer, regional buyer, national buyer, or district manager. You can find out more about careers in purchasing in Chapter 15.

Public relations and marketing firms

Some professionals work in public relations, a field in which they deal with the public, both in person and in writing. Marketing professionals work hard to prepare ads to sell a food company or a celebrity chef's products. They may also work specifically for a restaurant, promoting the restaurant's events, featured menu items, and VIP customers. Event planners that work for these firms find locations, hire entertainment and security, and work to make sure everyone knows where and when to show up for the festivities.

If you're looking for a job at a publication relations or marketing firm that deals with promoting food, chefs, and food-related events, you may end up with one of the following titles:

- Account executive
- Advertising manager
- Advertising sales director
- Communications specialist
- Event coordinator
- Market analyst
- Market researcher
- Media buyer

- Media coordinator
- Product development manager
- Public relations director
- Sales manager

Chapter 13 tells you more about how to find these jobs and what you'll need to do to obtain them.

Chapter 3

Culinary School Versus On-the-Job Training: Finding Your Fit

In This Chapter

▶ Evaluating your situation to determine whether culinary school is right for you

▶ Seeing what circumstances may make on-the-job training a better option

▶ Exploring the advantages of both choices

Deciding whether to go to culinary school is a personal decision. You have to do what's right for you. Many chefs and cooks, even famous ones (think Rachael Ray) never attended culinary school. These individuals started at the bottom, perhaps as food-preparation workers, and watched and learned. They honed their kitchen skills by working hard for many years. Yet, although on-the-job training is an undeniable asset, these same chefs and cooks will tell you not to solely go this route. They'll tell you to go to culinary school before entering the field. Why? Culinary school teaches you the basics: how to use a knife, how to move in a crowded kitchen, and how to sauté vegetables. In short, you're better able to jump in and help in a busy kitchen if you already know the basics and understand culinary terms. Completing a culinary program also shows that you're committed to working in the industry.

But we're realists. We know that not everyone can or wants to go to culinary school. In this chapter, we give you the pros and cons of both going to culinary school and learning what you need to know on the job so you can make the choice that's best for you.

Finding Out Whether You Should Go to Culinary School

Most chefs and cooks recommend that you go to culinary school before trying to land a job in a commercial kitchen. Going to culinary school is a good idea but not mandatory in most cases. However, culinary school is highly recommended in these instances:

- ✔ Your dream is to become a chef in a restaurant kitchen.
- ✔ You want to work in an upscale restaurant.
- ✔ You have a particular specialty in mind, such as sommelier.

You want to become a chef

If you have high aspirations and would like to one day be an executive chef (head chef) or a sous chef (second in command), you should go to culinary school. Although advancing in your career without a formal education is possible, climbing this far up the culinary ladder without it is really difficult. For example, taking a job as dishwasher and working your way up to a higher-level cook, such as a line cook, is fairly easy. But going from a line cook to an executive chef without a formal education is much more difficult. (To learn more about the various jobs in a restaurant kitchen, turn to Chapter 5.) The Bureau of Labor Statistics predicts that executive chef and sous chef jobs will be among the most competitive in the field over the next decade, so a solid culinary education and many years' experience is required to land these jobs.

You want to work in a fine-dining restaurant

Have you ever dined in a fine-dining restaurant? The experience is quite different from dinner at a local pizzeria. A fine-dining restaurant is also called a white tablecloth restaurant, and this type of restaurant offers diners first-class service in an intimate atmosphere. The pace is slow and relaxing. The food is almost always made from scratch and the staff is well trained to answer customers' questions about menu items. This means staff must have advanced culinary skills, usually received from a formal culinary education and years of experience. Because of this, the staff at a fine-dining restaurant is typically paid more than the staff at other types of restaurants, which makes the competition for such jobs stiff. If you'd ultimately like to work in a fine-dining establishment, you should go to culinary school.

You want to pursue a specialty

Some specialized culinary careers are difficult to break into without a culinary education. One of these careers is sommelier, or wine steward. A sommelier must be an expert in all things wine. Although there are always exceptions to the rule, the depth of knowledge to attain this position requires an extensive knowledge of wine and food, which can only be acquired with a formal education. The same holds true of a pastry chef; experience and education working with and creating pastries is most often required. Most personal and private chefs also have years of culinary experience in addition to culinary schooling because they need to be the best at what they do to beat out the competition for these types of jobs.

Contemplating When Learning on the Job Is Best

Culinary school is not for everyone. You may decide that you just don't want to go to school. You may be a working parent with three or four kids and the thought of adding one more thing to your "to-do" list makes you queasy. You should consider learning on the job instead of at culinary school in these instances:

- You don't have enough time to devote to school.
- You can't afford to attend school or stop working to attend.
- You're the kind of person who prefers hands-on training.
- The job you seek doesn't require a culinary education.

You should keep in mind that you may not be able to get the job you desire without attending culinary school. Someone who wants to be an executive chef at a four-star restaurant may not be able to obtain this position without a culinary education.

In the following sections, we explore how on-the-job training may be advantageous in another of these situations. If you're already sure that you don't want to go to culinary school, you can skip ahead to the end of this chapter and read the section "Considering the Advantages of Learning on the Job."

You don't have enough time

Depending on the program, a culinary education can take six months, two years, or four years to complete — and that's if you attend full time. In addition to day classes, most schools have evening classes for students who work. Still, if you work long hours and have a family, you just may not be able to find time for culinary school. Someone who doesn't have much time to devote to school may benefit from on-the-job training. Since most employers give their employees some type of training before throwing them right in to work, this is a great way to gain some culinary skills without having to go to school to learn them.

You lack the money

Unfortunately, culinary school isn't free — at least to those who live in the United States. (If you live in another country, however, you may qualify for a free or even low-cost culinary education.) The cost depends on how long you attend and the school that you choose. While a culinary certificate from a technical school or a community college may cost less than $5,000, a degree from a culinary institute or college is very expensive and can cost more than $30,000. And don't forget that other fees are involved: application fees, books and cooking supplies, and uniforms. If you attend a school away from home, you need to pay room and board as well as travel expenses.

Although a culinary education may help you land a job, it's not a sure thing. And paying back loans for a large amount of money may take you decades, even if you have a steady job in the culinary industry, so think hard about whether you can afford school.

Perhaps you're a career changer and you already paid to earn a different degree in the past. In this case, you may not want to invest in more schooling. (You may also want to consider choosing a culinary career that uses the degree you already have. For example, if you have an English degree, you may want to look into a career as a food writer, which typically doesn't require a culinary degree. For more information on careers such as this, see Part IV of this book.) You may be better off studying on your own and working as an apprentice. (We discuss this option more in the later section "Being taught by the pros as an apprentice.") If you choose to find employment instead of attending school, this saves you money in the long run since you usually receive on-the-job training while you're working (and getting paid), instead of having to pay for an education. This training usually gives you the basics you need for your job and doesn't require any further education.

You learn best in a different way

Consider your learning style when deciding whether to go to culinary school. Some people absolutely love the classroom and would stay in school forever if someone would foot the bill. But you may not be one of those people. You may be the kind of person who really dislikes the confines of a classroom and would much rather learn your craft while working. Learning on the job does have its advantages because you typically learn in a real-world setting rather than in a classroom. This teaches you skills such as how to work in a fast-paced setting, which requires you to be careful and patient. It also teaches you many different skill sets since you may have to learn how to work different stations and help others when they get too busy.

If you're independent and committed to learning all you can from reading culinary textbooks, cookbooks, and professional culinary publications, and watching instructional cooking shows and videos on television or online, you may be able to get by without going to culinary school. But if you're the kind of person who simply doesn't like to read or watch instructional programs or videos unless a teacher says you must, consider going to culinary school.

You want a different kind of job

Depending on the job you want to pursue, you may not need to go to culinary school. For example, if you want to work as a line cook or assistant in the kitchen — jobs that have relatively little responsibility or creative allowance — you don't need to invest in school. After you gain some restaurant experience, however, you may be able to land a job working in an institution such as a school or hospital. Restaurant experience and a high school diploma are usually all that are required for these jobs. You also don't need formal culinary schooling to work in retail food sales, equipment purchasing, or even public relations and marketing, but you may need a degree in marketing, public relations, or business plus at least some sales experience to obtain these positions.

When looking for an entry-level culinary job or an apprenticeship, many individuals shoot for the stars and try to land a job at the largest, most prestigious restaurants in their area. But although working in this type of establishment has its advantages, such as having the opportunity to work in different positions alongside well-known chefs, you may actually learn more at a smaller restaurant with only a chef and one or two cooks. If you're hired as a prep cook at this kind of restaurant, you'll be only one of a few entry-level employees and, therefore, will have a chance to perform many other duties. You'll also work more closely with the chef and cooks and have the opportunity to learn more skills. Furthermore, you may have an easier time getting hired at a smaller restaurant if you have little to no culinary education or training, because bigger and fancier restaurants tend to get more applicants with a culinary education and culinary experience.

Checking Out the Advantages of Culinary School

Having a certificate or a degree from a culinary school is almost always considered a good thing for the most obvious reason — it may help you get your foot in the door at a restaurant or other culinary establishment. But this isn't the only advantage of going to culinary school. The following sections explore some additional benefits.

The United States has literally hundreds of cooking schools, but not all these schools offer a certificate or degree. Schools that do are called *professional cooking* (or *culinary*) *schools.* If you're going to get a formal education, be sure to attend a professional school.

Training hands-on in a cooking-school kitchen

Some classes in culinary schools are held in a cooking-school kitchen, which simulates a restaurant kitchen. Most schools have a small class size, especially for this type of class. You get to work with others as you would in a real commercial kitchen, except you don't get fired for making a mistake. Culinary instructors in cooking-school kitchens take their time when teaching their students. Unlike chefs and cooks in restaurant kitchens, they're not rushed when explaining techniques. You'll learn about the following while in a cooking-school kitchen:

- Cooking with core methods using dry and moist heat
- Preparing and pairing meat, grains, and vegetables
- Mixing ingredients together in soups and sauces
- Baking and preparing pastries and desserts

Learning essential kitchen skills

Culinary instructors ensure that their students have a sound foundation in the basics: the parts of a chef's knife, basic knife cuts, seasoning and flavoring, cooking methods, sanitation methods, and food safety practices.

While home cooks may know how to use a knife to cut food such as fruits and vegetables, they may not know the proper way to use a knife. In culinary school, students will learn how to handle a knife safely and correctly, and learn how to chop, slice, dice, and cut. They will learn the difference between julienne, batonnet, allumette, and brunoise cuts. Home cooks may know how to use different cooking methods, but they may know why they use one method over another or why one differs from another. Culinary classes teach students cooking methods, such as braising, roasting, and poaching, and the differences between each, as well as when and how to apply these methods. The same goes for seasoning and flavoring. Home cooks may know about basic, everyday seasonings such as salt, pepper, and garlic, but may not possess the skill or knowledge to cook with exotic or foreign spices, such as cardamom or cumin, or even know how to blend spices.

Most home cooks also know the importance of food safety practices, such as not leaving meat on the counter to defrost, but they may not know proper sanitation methods, such as something as innocent as a sponge contains millions of germs and bacteria or that separate cutting boards should be used when cutting vegetables and meats to avoid cross contamination.

While many of these essential kitchen skills can be learned from books, television, or by watching cooking videos online, culinary school offers a hands-on experience. Students can get personalized attention from instructors, who can correct them and guide them along the way. This gives students an edge when they're looking for a culinary career.

Getting a broad experience

Perhaps the greatest advantage of attending culinary school is that your experience is much broader than if you opted to learn skills on the job. Because you take different classes taught by different chefs, you get a broad knowledge of cooking techniques using both common and rare ingredients. You learn to sauté, grill, pan-fry, deep-fry, braise, stew, steam, and poach. You learn to prepare many types of proteins, starches, and vegetables.

If you learn on the job while working in a restaurant, your training is limited to the type of cuisine the restaurant offers. If you work for an Italian restaurant, you're going to learn how to prepare Italian cuisine. Culinary school, on the other hand, gives you a chance to explore many types of cuisine in addition to Italian, including American (regional and nationwide), French, Asian, and Indian.

Taking classes in cooking theory and other important topics

Although you may not consider cooking-theory classes as much fun as the hands-on classes held in a cooking-school kitchen, they're important. In cooking-theory classes, you learn what happens to food when it cooks. These classes teach you about the chemistry of food, which helps you understand the purpose of certain ingredients, cooking methods, mixing methods, and even cooking times and temperatures. For example, you may learn that baking soda and baking powder have different effects on baked goods and can't be used interchangeably, which is something you may not have known unless you took cooking-theory classes. Following are a list of subjects you may also learn about in cooking-theory classes:

- ✔ Food cost control
- ✔ Sanitation methods
- ✔ Food safety practices
- ✔ Public health laws
- ✔ Nutrition
- ✔ Menu planning
- ✔ Purchasing and storage

Being given a chance to extern or intern

Many culinary schools require their students to complete an externship or an internship. During an externship, a student shadows a culinary professional, assisting and learning valuable skills along the way. This gives student a chance to determine if the particular line of work is right for them. Students completing an externship typically aren't paid and don't earn college credits for their time. Externships may last anywhere from a day to a few days. An internship is similar to an externship, but students usually earn college credit for their time and in some cases, they are paid for their work. Rather than shadowing an individual, students are given tasks to complete on their own and sometimes do the same work as employees. Internships can last from a few weeks to a semester or two and sometimes can lead to a permanent job.

Externships and internships aren't the only ways to gain real-world experience. A *stagiaire*, also called a *stage,* is another opportunity for students to learn more culinary skills from those already in the profession. A stagiaire is an informal, unpaid work experience that may last a shift, a few days, or a few weeks. During a stagiaire, students volunteer their time either to acquire new skills or to prove to a restaurant that they have what it takes to work there.

Meeting many people to network with

You meet many people when you go to culinary school. You get to know your instructors (chefs) as well as other students, all of whom may be able to help you find a job. Culinary schools also have a career services department, which can help you find work when you're ready. The career services department can also help you find externships, internships, and stagiaires that allow you to spend time in commercial kitchens following and working with the staff. These opportunities help students gain real-world experience as well help them decide if the atmosphere at a particular establishment is right for them.

Many chefs complain that graduates of culinary schools feel that they're entitled to higher-level kitchen jobs and aren't willing to start at the bottom. Be careful not to convey this attitude on job interviews or while you're completing a stagiaire. Keep in mind that culinary school teaches you basic skills. You still have much to learn.

Considering the Advantages of Learning on the Job

If culinary school is not a good option for you, you can learn what you need to know on the job. Starting your career without formal education usually means taking a lower-level job such as food-preparation worker or line cook in a commercial kitchen. Through hard work and determination, you'll learn what you need to know to advance in your career.

Being taught by the pros as an apprentice

If you know how to cook and can demonstrate some basic skills, you may get lucky and land an entry-level job in a commercial kitchen. Then all you have to do is work hard and learn, learn, learn. However, if you pound the pavement and can't seem to get your foot in the door of a commercial kitchen, consider completing an apprenticeship. Many of today's leading chefs got their starts by serving as apprentices.

An apprenticeship is very similar to an externship or internship that you may be required to complete if you go to culinary school. An apprenticeship typically allows you to gain experience by working alongside professionals in the field for weeks, months, or even years. During an apprenticeship, you may start slow and only be given small jobs to complete until you demonstrate mastery. Apprenticeships are occasionally paid and sometimes lead to full-time paid positions.

You may have to work hard to find a chef who is willing to take you in as an apprentice. Why? When chefs agree to give you an apprenticeship, they are committing some time to teach you in exchange for free or low-cost labor. Chefs are busy people. Many can't envision finding a few free minutes, let alone an hour here and there, to teach you. If you've even been in a busy restaurant kitchen, you understand why. Some apprenticeships only require you to work a few hours here and there, while others may demand full-time hours. You should take this into consideration if you have a full-time or part-time job in addition to your apprenticeship. For more information about apprenticeships, visit the American Culinary Federation's website at www. acfchefs.org.

Persistence is key in obtaining an apprenticeship. Try bringing the chef something you cooked or baked to show the chef what you can do. Mention that you're willing to apprentice for a long time and that you'll do whatever you can to help. (Humility counts here big time.) Keep approaching chefs and continue trying until one agrees to help you.

Getting first dibs on promotions

If you train on the job while working in a kitchen, you have a great advantage when you're ready to advance, because you're likely to know when a higher-level job becomes available. A restaurant may avoid having to interview new cooks if you're ready and willing to be trained. Chefs and cooks are also more likely to hire someone they know for a higher position rather than a stranger. And because they trained you, they know you've learned to perform the fundamentals the way that they want them performed. For example, you know what cutting techniques a particular chef prefers to be used when preparing a meal. You also know the menu, which is a huge plus. Familiarity will surely work in your favor.

Learning to cook — fast

Learning to cook in a commercial kitchen gives you a major advantage over someone who learned to prepare food in a culinary-school kitchen. You're familiar with the pace in a real kitchen where customers are impatiently waiting for their meals. At times, the pace may be so fast your head will spin. However, if you spend significant time in a commercial kitchen, you'll learn how to cook well — and cook fast. Recent culinary-school graduates are often unaccustomed to having to work so quickly.

If you learn to cook on the job, you'll also learn how to prepare multiple meals simultaneously so that all entrees at a table are ready at the same time.

Obtaining culinary certifications

Acquiring a culinary certification is one way to make yourself stand out from the pack and prove your culinary competency. The American Culinary Federation offers many culinary certifications. While a culinary education isn't required to obtain a few of these certifications, all of them require at least 30 hours of courses in nutrition, sanitation and safety, and supervisory management in addition to either a high school diploma or culinary education, and years of kitchen experience. They also require you to pass written and practical examinations.

For example, you can become a Certified Culinarian or Certified Pastry Culinarian without a complete culinary education. In addition to the 30 hours of coursework mentioned above, you'll need a high school diploma plus at least two of entry-level kitchen experience as well as a passing grade on the examinations. If you attended culinary school, you may only need to pass the written and practical examinations. For more detailed information about the different designations and the requirements for each, visit the ACF website at www.acfchefs.org. Following are brief descriptions of the different culinary certifications offered by the ACF:

- **Certified Culinarian (CC):** This certification is awarded to entry-level culinarians who work in commercial food-service operations where they prepare and cook food.

- **Certified Sous Chef (CSC):** Chefs who supervise a shift or stations within a food-service operation are eligible to test for this designation.

- **Certified Executive Chef (CEC):** The head chef within a food-service organization is eligible to test for this designation. In addition to culinary responsibilities, chefs who receive this designation must know how to prepare and maintain budgets, prepare payroll, control food costs, and maintain financial and inventory records.

- **Certified Master Chef (CMC):** A chef with this designation possesses the highest degree of professional culinary knowledge and mastery of cooking techniques. Before chefs can obtain this designation, they must already hold the designation of CEC or CEPC. The test for this designation takes eight days to complete.

- **Personal Certified Chef (PCC):** A chef who works as a "cook for hire" may choose to test for this designation. In addition to preparing, cooking, and serving food, a chef must have knowledge of menu planning, marketing, and financial management. A chef must have three years of cooking experience or one year of experience as a personal chef to apply and test for this designation.

- **Certified Pastry Culinarian (PCC):** This designation is awarded to entry-level culinarians within a pastry food-service operation who are responsible for preparing pies, cookies, cakes, breads, rolls, desserts, and other baked goods.

- **Certified Working Pastry Chef (CWPC):** This designation is available to pastry chefs who supervise a pastry section or a shift within a food-service organization.

- **Certified Executive Pastry Chef (CEPC):** A pastry chef who is a department head may seek this designation. A CEPC usually reports to an executive chef and displays outstanding administrative skills as well as culinary skills.

- **Certified Master Pastry Chef (CMPC):** Individuals with this designation possess the highest level of skills and mastery of pastry cooking and baking techniques. This test takes eight days to complete. Those applying for this designation must already hold the designation of CEC and CEPC.

Chapter 4

Ingredients for Success: Choosing a Culinary School

In This Chapter

▶ Finding the right approach to your culinary education

▶ Identifying top national and regional culinary schools

▶ Considering the study abroad option and hotel cooking schools

▶ Examining culinary programs at traditional colleges and universities

▶ Discovering ways to help pay for a culinary education

*Y*ou've decided that you want to become a culinary professional, but what's the next step in your recipe for success? As any chef will tell you, success in the kitchen starts with the right ingredients. For you, the key ingredient for a promising culinary career is choosing the right school or training program to sharpen your skills.

Choosing a school is not as easy as you may think. The choice depends largely on what you hope to gain from your culinary education. Among other questions, you need to ask yourself, what type of professional certification do I hope to achieve? Do I want to study at the local, regional, national, or international level? And how am I going to pay for it?

In this chapter, we help you answer these questions and more as we discuss some of the top culinary schools in the United States and around the globe. We also describe alternatives to schools that focus strictly on culinary arts, such as two- or four-year colleges and universities that offer various culinary programs. As the icing on the cake, we offer advice on finding scholarships and financial aid to help you pay for your culinary education.

Choosing the Right School for You

We'll be straight with you: We can't tell you what culinary school to choose. The types of schools and programs vary so much that the right school for one person may or may not be the right school for another. If you're a high school student who has worked in kitchens since the age of 16 and a career in the culinary arts is your passion, then a fully accredited culinary institute may be a perfect fit. If you're a professional in another field looking for a change mid-career, however, you may not want to devote another two to four years of study to a culinary school. Perhaps classes at a local community college or technical school or a short program that teaches a particular cooking style would work better for you. Knowing what you want to do, where you want to go, and what you can afford to spend are the keys to choosing the right school. It's also very important to visit the school you are interested in attending to get a sense of whether it's a good fit for you.

The Internet is a great resource for finding culinary schools. Websites dedicated to organizing information about culinary schools allow you to search by city or state (or nation, if you're looking for an international school), by major, by degree programs, and more. Following are just a few websites that may help in your search:

- ✔ CulinarySchools.org (www.culinaryschools.org)
- ✔ Culinary Schools U (www.culinaryschoolsu.com)
- ✔ Cooking Schools 101 (www.cookingschools101.com)

Knowing what you want to do

When choosing a culinary school or program, you should consider, first and foremost, what you want to do. Many professional cooking schools have three general tracks you can follow:

- ✔ **Culinary arts:** This track focuses on the art of cooking and displaying food and also on the science of food, food preparation skills, nutrition, and diet.
- ✔ **Baking and pastry arts:** This focus provides specialized training in baking and patisserie.
- ✔ **Hospitality management:** This path focuses on the business and leadership side of the hospitality industry, such as hotel or restaurant management.

The track you choose depends largely on your ultimate career goal. For example, if you want to be a sous chef in a fine dining establishment, you may choose to follow a culinary arts track, which provides instruction in cooking techniques, knife skills, and presentation. If your dream is to own your own bakery, however, pursing the bakery and pastry arts track, which includes instruction on cake decorating and bread making, is a better choice. If you want to own and operate a restaurant but don't want to actually prepare the food, pursuing the hospitality management track is probably the best choice.

Some schools strictly divide their curricula, whereas others may allow students to combine courses of study. Core classes may be common to all tracks, with students electing other classes based on the specialized training they want to receive.

In addition to knowing what you want to study — that is, choosing a track — you should determine what type of accreditation you want to receive — that is, choosing a culinary program. Following are the most common culinary programs:

- **Diploma or certificate programs:** Typically running from several weeks or months to a year, these programs usually offer basic training in a specific area of study, such as professional cooking or pastry arts. Such programs are ideal for students who want to get a taste of a career in culinary arts or for those with a high level of training who want to learn a specialized skill. Diploma or certificate programs are offered at culinary institutes, cooking schools, technical or vocational schools, community colleges, and some four-year colleges or universities.

- **Associate's degree programs:** Associate's degree programs, often offered at culinary institutes and community colleges, usually take two years to complete. These programs provide students with the basics of a culinary arts education. Students in these programs learn skills such as presentation, knife skills, and kitchen procedures.

- **Bachelor's degree programs:** Like associate's degree programs, bachelor's degree programs in the culinary arts, which take about four years to complete, help students hone their cooking skills but also provide a foundation in management and leadership. Such programs are typically found at culinary institutes and at four-year colleges or universities.

The amount of accreditation you should strive to achieve depends largely on your culinary goals. An executive chef needs far more training and credentials than someone who works part-time for a catering service. In addition, it's important to consider your salary aspirations. Those who earn a degree tend to earn more money, on average, than those who haven't earned a degree. In addition, many employers place a high value on education, and while you'll still be expected to pay your dues in the kitchen and prove your talent when you first start, a degree can help you quickly move through the ranks.

Choosing a career track and degree program can seem overwhelming. How do you know which track and program are right for your goals? One of the best things you can do is to visit the websites of a number of community colleges, culinary institutes, and four-year colleges and universities and evaluate their culinary arts curriculum. Find out what courses they offer and what degrees you can earn, and determine which ones align with your goals. Consider scheduling a meeting to see the campus and talk with an adviser. You can also go online to websites such as www.cookingschools.com, which offers information about culinary programs, degrees, and schools.

Earning a culinary certificate or degree can put you on the fast-track to attaining the position you want, but you shouldn't discount hands-on experience. Plenty of hands-on cooking experience can serve as a replacement for a formal culinary education.

Knowing where you want to go

In relation to the other questions you have to answer about your future career goals, you may think school location is an insignificant concern. However, knowing how far you're willing to travel to receive a culinary arts education is an important part of choosing a school. Choices vary from the community college five minutes from home to a culinary institute on the opposite side of the world. Chances are that if you're considering a career change, you may already have a family or a house that needs your care and attention, and you may not want to uproot your whole life so you can study in France or Italy. Taking classes at a local community college or technical school may be the best option for you. The same may be true if you're just graduating from high school and want to live at home while you decide if a culinary career is the right path for you.

If moving isn't a problem for you, you may consider studying at a renowned regional school or attending one of the top-notch culinary schools in the United States. Similarly, if you have your heart set on working at a restaurant that specializes in international cuisine, you may get a leg up by studying at an international culinary school (a school that focuses on international cuisines) either in the United States or abroad or studying at a culinary institution in a foreign country.

You may find Table 4-1 useful as you compare culinary school curriculums and hunt down the school that's right for you. This table represents many of the curriculums you'll see at schools across the nation.

Table 4-1   **Comparing Culinary School Curriculums**

Program	Year One	Year Two	Year Three	Year Four
Culinary arts certificate				
	Cooking Skills Fundamentals			
	Foodservice Sanitation			
	Baking Fundamentals			
	Quantity Food Production			
	Cooking Stock, Sauces and Soups			
	Cooking Meat, Fish, and Poultry			
	Nutrition			
Associate's degree in culinary arts				
	Food Prep I	Cost Control and Menu Planning		
	Foodservice Sanitation	Baking and Pastry		
	English Composition I	International Cuisine		
	Mathematics	Cooking Meat, Fish, and Poultry		
	Interpersonal Communications	Cooking Stock, Sauces and Soups		
	Garde Manger	Wines Studies		
	Technical Writing	Food Prep II		
	Nutrition	Formal Restaurant Cooking		
	Quantity Food Production	Hospitality and Service Management		

(continued)

Table 4-1 (continued)

Program	Year One	Year Two	Year Three	Year Four
Associate's degree in culinary arts				
	Cuisines of the Americas	Intro to Dining-Room Management		
	Summer: 18-week externship required			
Bachelor's degree in culinary arts				
	Food Prep 1	Fundamentals of Baking	Principles of Economics	Advanced Garde Manger
	Foodservice Sanitation	Service Operations Management	Quantity Food Production	Advanced Sauce and Fish
	English Composition	Introduction to Hospitality Management	Cuisines of the Americas	Advanced Sauce and Meat
	Introduction to Computers	Social Science/ Humanities	Mathematics	Culinary Internship
	English Composition 1	Nutrition	Interpersonal Communications	Composition II
	Garde Manger	Food Prep II	Cost Control and Menu Planning	Algebra
	Culinary Skills Lab	Classical Baking and Pastries	Wine Studies	Catering
	Principles of Accounting	International Cuisine	Human Resources Management	Restaurant Management
	Food and Beverage Purchasing and& Cost Control	Hospitality Law	Volume Cooking	Professional Development
		Introduction to Marketing	Food Science Chemistry Lab	Formal Restaurant Cooking

Knowing what you can afford to spend

When deciding where you'd like to pursue your education, be realistic. Diploma or certificate programs in the culinary arts may cost from a few hundred dollars to several thousand dollars, and the tuition at an esteemed culinary school may cost tens of thousands of dollars. Consider what you can afford to pay and how much of your education you're willing to finance through loans. Keep in mind that when you graduate, you'll have to start paying off any loans you take.

In addition to the cost of tuition or enrollment at a culinary school, college, university, technical school, or certificate program, you have to consider other expenses. Books, uniforms, and other supplies may be required. If you're leaving home for the first time or moving to a new city to attend school, remember to leave space in your budget for room-and-board fees at the school (if campus housing is available) or rent for an apartment.

Knowing what to look for when you visit

When deciding which culinary school, college or university, or technical school to attend, one of the best things you can do is pay a visit. Visiting the campus of your school of choice gives you a chance to view the facilities and equipment firsthand, learn more about the curriculum, and perhaps see the faculty in action. In addition, you can visit the financial aid office to get information about grants and scholarships and learn more about the school's accreditation. Following are some aspects to consider during your visit to any school:

- ✔ **Accreditation:** A school's accreditation (that is, official approval or recognition) depends largely on its ability to meet certain industry standards. When it comes time to get a job, a degree from an accredited school will likely carry more weight with an employer than a certificate from a non-accredited cooking class. Accreditation can even influence your eligibility for financial aid. For example, the U.S. Department of Education requires that students must attend an accredited institution to qualify for state or federal financial aid.

- ✔ **Admission requirements:** A good school usually requires students to have a high-school diploma or a GED.

- ✔ **Curriculum:** If your ultimate goal is to become an executive chef, make sure the curriculum (the material covered in classes) at the school you choose includes enough hands-on training to give you the experience you need to eventually learn more complex skills and run a kitchen. Ask how classes are taught. Do instructors demonstrate skills as students watch or do students get to work directly with the food?

Ask yourself if you can effectively learn from an observation-only standpoint or if you need that hands-on training. Also, you need to find out whether the school recommends (or even requires) working in the industry before attending classes there, so that you can plan accordingly.

Of course, you may want a career in the culinary arts industry that doesn't directly involve cooking. Whatever your culinary dream may be, make sure your school aligns with your goals and that you can earn the right degree or certification that you require to advance in your career.

✔ **Class size:** Determine the student-teacher ratio in the kitchen. Keep in mind that smaller is better and there should be no more than 15 students to one teacher, especially for classes taught in a kitchen.

✔ **Equipment and facilities:** When visiting a school, ask to take a tour of a kitchen so you can get a feel for where you'll be learning your skills. Cooking areas and appliances should appear clean, neat, and organized. Appliances should be in proper working order, and kitchens should be stocked with enough equipment for each student to be able to practice a new skill.

Check out the other facilities at the school, too. You may have to attend lectures, conduct research, or watch presentations, so you may want to get a look at classrooms, the library, and computer labs. Make sure the school has what you need to get a quality education.

✔ **Faculty and staff:** During your visit, ask about the faculty-to-student ratio. A smaller number of students per instructor, such as 15 to 1, means more time for individual students to ask questions and gain experience. Many schools hire full-time faculty who once worked in commercial kitchens. Check out what faculty members did before they began teaching. Instructors should be certified by the American Culinary Federation, hold a degree, and have significant industry experience.

✔ **Class schedule:** Make sure classes are offered at a time that is convenient for you. If you can't attend school full time because you work during the day, make sure the school offers the classes you need at night or on the weekends.

✔ **Current students:** While on campus, you may have the opportunity to talk with current students. Get their take on the equipment, facilities, faculty, and staff. Ask them what they like most about the school and what they like least. How many students are in each class? Is it difficult to get into the classes you need/want? Current students are in a unique position to give you a firsthand, unbiased perspective of the school, including its strengths and its weakness.

✔ **Financial aid:** Be sure to ask about available scholarships and grants. Depending on the school you choose, your culinary education may be quite expensive. Chances are that you'll need to finance at least part of it. Wouldn't some free money to put toward your education be nice? (For more information about financial aid, see "Paying for Culinary School: Scholarships and Financial Aid" later in this chapter.)

✔ **School's job placement rate:** Good schools work hard to find their students jobs. Note whether the school will assist you after graduation and how many students find jobs in the field after graduation.

✔ **Offered externships and internships:** Look for schools that offer or require students to complete externships and/or internships. Students completing an externship work in a culinary establishment such as a restaurant kitchen. They don't earn college credits for their time and aren't paid for their work. Students completing an internship earn college credits and are sometimes also paid.

✔ **Safety record:** The school's safety record should be available in the school's handbook, which you can often access online. You should want to feel safe on and around campus; knowing if the areas surrounding the school have high or low crime rates should influence your decision to go to that particular school. If you can't find this information, ask someone in the admissions office.

When compiling a list of potential culinary schools, visit each school's Web site. Note the financial-aid and student-loan options offered by the school. Jot down the tuition as well. Also locate the school's application and find out if there's a fee to apply. Some schools start at $100 just to submit the application; others don't charge you a penny.

Thinking Big: The Top Culinary Schools in the United States

You don't have to travel abroad to get a quality culinary arts education. The United States is home to some of the top culinary institutions in the world. Training at one of the schools in the following sections can put you on the road to success.

The Culinary Institute of America

The Culinary Institute of America is recognized as a world leader in culinary arts education. It was founded in 1946, though in its early years it was called the New Haven Restaurant Institute and the Restaurant Institute of Connecticut.

The CIA has four campuses: Hyde Park, New York; St. Helena, California; San Antonio, Texas; and Singapore. The CIA's educational programs include

✔ **Associate's degree programs:** Culinary arts, baking and pastry arts

✔ **Bachelor's degree programs:** Culinary arts management, baking and pastry arts management

In addition, the CIA offers programs on wine and beverages, courses for food enthusiasts, and professional development programs.

The Hyde Park campus of the CIA has four student-staffed restaurants, where culinary arts students prepare meals under the guidance of CIA faculty. The restaurants include American Bounty Restaurant, which offers foods of the Americas; Escoffier Restaurant, which offers French cuisine; Ristorante Caterina de'Medici, which prepares Italian cuisine; and St. Andrews Café, which relies on local ingredients in the preparation of meals. The Hyde Park campus is also home to the Apple Pie Bakery Café, which is staffed by students and faculty in the baking and pastry arts program.

The St. Helena campus in California boasts the Wine Spectator Greystone Restaurant, which is staffed by students and instructors. Here, students have the opportunity to interact with diners who watch them as they work.

The basic requirements to gain admission into the CIA include the following:

- ✔ A high school diploma or GED
- ✔ Recommendation letter(s)
- ✔ Placement tests
- ✔ Assessment tests (some campuses require math and writing assessments)
- ✔ Six months of experience in a kitchen or bakery for at least 10 to 15 hour per week

For more information about admission to the CIA, visit www.ciachef.edu. You can also e-mail the admissions office at admissions@culinary.edu or call 1-800-CULINARY or (845) 452-9430.

The International Culinary Schools at the Art Institutes

The International Culinary Schools at the Art Institutes touts itself as "North America's largest system of culinary programs." Programs are offered at more than 35 Art Institutes schools. Although programs may vary by location, chances are you can find an Art Institutes school in your neck of the woods. The following states and Canadian provinces are home to one or more Art Institutes schools that offer culinary programs: Arizona, California, Colorado, Florida, Georgia, Illinois, Indiana, Kansas, Massachusetts, Michigan, Minnesota, Nevada, New York, North Carolina, Ohio, Oregon, Pennsylvania, South Carolina, Tennessee, Texas, Utah, Virginia, Washington, Wisconsin, and British Columbia.

The degree offerings and areas of study at The International Culinary Schools at the Art Institutes can be broken down into the following categories:

✔ **Certificate programs:** Culinary arts, baking and pastry arts

✔ **Associate's degree programs:** Culinary arts; baking and pastry arts; wine, spirits, and beverage management

✔ **Bachelor's degree programs:** Culinary arts, culinary management, hospitality leadership management, hospitality food and beverage management

To gain admission to the International Culinary Schools at the Art Institutes, students need to submit an application, a high school transcript or GED scores, and an essay. In addition, students may be required to take an assessment test to confirm proficiency in English and math or provide recent ACT or SAT scores. To learn more about the programs available at each school and the admissions process, visit the website of The International Culinary Schools at the Art Institutes at www.artinstitutes.edu/culinary-degrees.aspx. The website allows you to search for program information by campus location and program of interest. You can also call 1-888-624-0300 for more information.

Le Cordon Bleu Schools North America

Le Cordon Bleu, which means *blue ribbon* in French, has a long and celebrated history. The culinary school began in Paris in 1895 and achieved rapid success. In the United States, Le Cordon Bleu Schools give students the chance to learn classical European techniques while using the latest technologies.

The United States is home to 16 Le Cordon Bleu campuses: Atlanta, Georgia; Austin, Texas; Boston, Massachusetts; Chicago, Illinois; Dallas, Texas; Las Vegas, Nevada; Los Angeles, California; Miami, Florida; Minneapolis, Minnesota; Orlando, Florida; Portland, Oregon; Sacramento, California; San Francisco, California; Scottsdale, Arizona; Seattle, Washington; and St. Louis, Missouri.

Following is a breakdown of the areas of study and degree offerings at Le Cordon Bleu Schools North America:

✔ **Certificate programs:** Culinary arts, bakery and pastry arts

✔ **Associate's degree:** Culinary arts, bakery and pastry arts, hospitality and restaurant management

To be admitted to one of the many Le Cordon Bleu Schools in North America, you have to submit an application along with a high school diploma or its equivalent. The admissions process also requires an interview with an admissions representative. Le Cordon Bleu Schools also offer nonprofessional cooking classes and online programs. To request more information, go online at www.chefs.edu or call toll-free at 1-800-736-6126.

The French Culinary Institute

Think you need to travel to France to learn the art of French cooking? Think again. The French Culinary Institute, which has campuses in New York and California, offers diploma programs in classic culinary arts and classic pastry arts as well as a variety of specialized training.

Students can study classic culinary arts, classic pastry arts, and the art of international bread baking. Offerings vary by campus, but options for specialized training include cake techniques and design, essential techniques for food styling, fundamentals of wine, new directions in school meal planning for culinary professionals, restaurant management; and *sous-vide* (a method of cooking food at low heat in air-tight containers for a specified length of time). Both campuses offer a number of amateur cooking classes, too.

For those pursuing a career in the culinary or pastry arts, the admissions process for the French Culinary Institute requires submission of an application and proof of high school graduation or its equivalent. Students who speak English as a second language must demonstrate English-language proficiency. To obtain admission to the Culinary Arts Honors Program, students must also include a short personal video and a letter of recommendation. The French Culinary Institute's website offers information about both campuses, the application process, tuition, financial aid, and more. Visit www.frenchculinary.com, or call 1-888-324-2433 for info on the New York campus and 1-866-318-2433 for info on the California campus.

The Italian Culinary Academy

The Italian Culinary Academy is the sister school of The French Culinary Institute. The Italian Culinary Academy offers the following two ways to learn about cooking Italian cuisine:

- **Italian Culinary Experience:** This option involves 10 weeks of training in New York City followed by 9 weeks of training at ALMA, The International School of Italian Cuisine in Parma, Italy. Students also spend time working at a top Italian restaurant. The Italian Culinary Experience is not an accredited program and is intended only for personal enrichment.

✔ **Essentials of Italian Cooking:** If you prefer to remain stateside, this track includes plenty of hands-on experience in a fast-paced learning environment. Students study eight units during weekend classes offered in five-hour blocks on Saturdays and Sundays over a one-month period. Essentials of Italian Cooking is an amateur course. It is not an accredited program and is intended only for personal enrichment.

The Italian Culinary Academy also offers several short courses that focus on Italian classics such as antipasti, carne, pasta, and more.

To gain admission to the Italian Culinary Academy, applicants must submit an online application and fee and later speak to an admissions representative. In addition, they must complete a signed Enrollment Agreement and provide proof of high school graduation or its equivalent. The Italian Culinary Academy's website (www.italianculinaryacademy.com) offers information about its courses, application process, tuition, financial aid, and more. You can also call 1-888-324-2433 for more info.

The French Pastry School

Yearly, more than 1,000 students at The French Pastry School in Chicago, Illinois, benefit from small classes (no more than 18 students per class), hands-on experience, and mentoring from renowned pastry chefs and cake artists. The school prides itself on its "superb instruction, superior equipment, and top quality ingredients." The French Pastry School offers two full-time certificate programs:

✔ *L'Art de la Pâtisserie:* A 24-week professional pastry and baking program

✔ *L'Art du Gâteau:* A 16-week professional cake decorating and baking program

The French Pastry School also offers *L'Art de la Boulangerie* — an 8-week artisanal bread baking course — and many continuing education courses for both food enthusiasts and professionals.

For admission into the French Pastry School, students must submit an application including three short essays. The following are also required;

✔ Two reference letters

✔ A resume

✔ A digital photo

✔ An official, sealed high school transcript

✔ An interview

✔ A copy of a valid state ID

For more information, contact The French Pastry School via phone at (312) 726-2419 or via e-mail at info@frenchpastryschool.com. You can also visit The French Pastry School on the web at www.frenchpastryschool.com.

National Center for Hospitality Studies

The National Center for Hospitality Studies (NCHS) is located at Sullivan University in Louisville, Kentucky. Its many renowned programs include culinary arts, professional catering, baking and pastry arts, hotel/restaurant management, and hospitality management. Culinary arts, professional catering, and baking and pastry arts students who train at the National Center for Hospitality Studies have the opportunity to work at three facilities located right on the Sullivan University campus as they complete their training: Winston's Restaurant, Juleps Catering, and The Bakery.

NCHS offers the following associate's degree programs:

- Baking & Pastry Arts
- Culinary Arts
- Culinary Arts/Baking & Pastry Arts
- Culinary Arts/Hotel & Restaurant Management
- Culinary Arts/Professional Catering
- Hotel & Restaurant Management
- Professional Catering
- Event Management & Tourism
- Beverage Management

NCHS offers the following diploma programs:

- Professional Baker
- Travel & Tourism
- Personal/Private Chef

In addition, NCHS offers a bachelor's degree in hospitality management. For more information, visit www.sullivan.edu/nchs.asp. You can also call (502) 456-6505 or 1-800-844-1354.

New England Culinary Institute

New England Culinary Institute (NECI) is a private culinary school located in Montpelier, Vermont. Dedicated to small class sizes, NECI ensures that students receive plenty of hands-on training in any of its nine production kitchens. Though it began with a class of just 7 students, NECI now instructs more than 500 students in a variety of programs.

Following is a breakdown of the degree offerings and areas of study at NECI:

- **Certificate programs:** Professional cooking, professional baking, and professional pastry
- **Associate's degree programs:** Culinary arts, baking and pastry arts, hospitality and restaurant management
- **Bachelor's degrees:** Culinary arts, hospitality and restaurant management

NECI's admissions process is quite stringent and requires the following:

- A completed application
- A high school diploma or its equivalent
- An interview
- Online learning readiness survey
- An essay
- A letter of recommendation from an instructor or counselor
- An application fee

NECI also recommends, but does not require, a campus tour before students apply. For more information about NECI's academic programs, admissions process, student life, and more, visit the website at www.neci.edu or call 1-877-223-NECI.

The Restaurant School at Walnut Hill College

Located in Philadelphia, Pennsylvania, The Restaurant School at Walnut Hill College boasts a low cost in comparison to other private hospitality and culinary institutions and emphasizes its dedication to student travel. At the end of both its associate's and bachelor's degree programs, students may travel to France, England, or Florida and the Bahamas, where they immerse themselves in "the art of true hospitality." Students at The Restaurant School can choose from four majors:

✔ **Associate's degree programs:** Culinary arts, pastry arts, hotel management, restaurant management

✔ **Bachelor's degree programs:** Culinary arts, pastry arts, hotel management, restaurant management

Professional, hands-on experience abounds at The Restaurant School, which features three student-run restaurants: The International Bistro, The Italian Trattoria, and The American Heartland.

To apply for admission to The Restaurant School, the following are required:

✔ A completed application ($50.00 application fee)

✔ A high school transcript or GED scores

✔ An interview

✔ A 250-word essay

✔ Two letters of recommendation

✔ Standardized test scores (SAT or ACT)

✔ A registration fee (upon completion of all other steps)

The Restaurant School also encourages students to gain some prior experience in restaurants or hospitality, but this is not a requirement for admission. For more information, visit The Restaurant School's website at www. walnuthillcollege.edu. You can also call (215) 222-4200.

The Institute of Culinary Education

Diploma programs at The Institute of Culinary Education (ICE) in New York City typically take between 8 and 13 months to complete. Students at ICE can receive diplomas in four areas: culinary arts, pastry and baking arts, culinary management, and hospitality management.

The culinary curriculum is grounded in classical French technique, but students are exposed to flavors and cooking styles from around the globe. Courses in the hospitality management program cover finances, marketing, hotel management, and more.

To apply to ICE, students need to go online or call admissions department to get started. ICE requires a completed application, a tour of the school, a signed enrollment agreement, and proof of a high school diploma, GED, or other degree (such as an associate's or bachelor's degree). To find out more about the ICE, visit the website at www.iceculinary.com. You can also call (212) 847-0700.

L'Academie de Cuisine

Located in Gaithersburg, Maryland, not far from Washington, D.C., L'Academie de Cuisine was founded on the idea that "simple technique and dedicated practice" lead to culinary achievement.

L'Academie de Cuisine offers programs for both professionals and recreational chefs. The two professional programs are Culinary Arts and Pastry Arts. The Culinary Arts program involves 1,800 hours of study stretched over a period of 50 to 62 weeks. The Pastry Arts program, which also requires 1,800 hours of study, lasts for 50 weeks.

Two continuing education classes, Culinary Techniques 101 and Pastry Techniques 101, are also offered. Recreational cooking classes include dinners, demonstrations, tastings, and participation classes.

To be considered for admission into L'Academie de Cuisine, applicants must provide the following:

- ✔ A completed application and $100 application fee
- ✔ A personal statement of 500+ words
- ✔ A resume
- ✔ A recommendation letter
- ✔ A high school transcript/diploma or college transcript or GED certificate
- ✔ Proof of U.S. citizenship

In addition, applicants must be interviewed by an admissions representative and take an entrance test. For information about classes, financial aid, and more, visit www.lacademie.com or call 1-800-664-CHEF.

Arizona Culinary Institute

Arizona Culinary Institute (ACI) prides itself on the fact that most of its graduates complete its certificate program in as little as nine months. In addition, it touts its small class sizes, moderate cost, and a hands-on approach to learning. ACI has five kitchens, each equipped to handle a specific type of cooking or baking, and a student-run restaurant called du Jour. Students who complete their studies at ACI will earn a diploma in culinary arts, baking, and restaurant management.

Admissions requirements for the Arizona Culinary Institute include an application, an application fee, and proof a high school diploma or GED. To learn more about the curriculum, admissions, and financial aid at ACI, visit `www.azculinary.com`, call 1-866-294-CHEF, or e-mail info@azculinary.com.

San Diego Culinary Institute

At the San Diego Culinary Institute, students learn the Commis Method, which focuses on culinary technique and flavor rather than on specific recipes. Students at the San Diego Culinary Institute benefit from small class sizes and a hands-on approach to learning — about 80 percent of the coursework involves working directly with food. In addition to earning a Diplome Professionnel du Commis de Cuisine, students at the San Diego Culinary Institute can earn a Diplome Professionnel du Commis de Patisserie/Boulangerie through the institute's baking and pastry program.

The San Diego Culinary Institute has very stringent admissions requirements, which include the following:

- A campus tour
- An enrollment application and $75 application fee
- A class sit-in
- A statement of purpose
- Two letters of recommendation
- A resume
- A high school diploma or its equivalent or college transcripts
- An entrance exam
- An interview

For more information about the available programs, visit `www.sdci-inc.com`, call (619) 644-2100, or e-mail info@sdci-inc.com.

Traveling Overseas: Studying Abroad

You may decide to take the plunge and move across the border (or an ocean) to attend culinary school. Although the United States has numerous first-rate culinary institutes, studying abroad provides an ideal opportunity to learn about a specific cuisine. If you want to specialize in french food, for example, what better place to study than France?

Studying in a foreign country can be an exciting, eye-opening adventure — but it also can be daunting. In addition to learning about different cuisines, you'll be exposed to other cultures, customs, people, and languages. These experiences can be invaluable throughout your lifetime. In this section, we walk you through the decision of whether to study abroad and give you an overview of some top schools in other countries.

Taking the leap, or not

The thought of traveling to a new country is exhilarating. When the excitement wears off, however, you must think about what living and attending school in a foreign country will be like. Are you ready to live on your own without family and friends nearby if you need them? Are you willing to learn another language? Can you afford to attend culinary school in another country?

If you answer yes to all those questions and decide that attending culinary school in another country is right for you, the next decision is where you'll attend school. France and Italy aren't the only countries with world-renowned cooking schools. For instance, Canada, England, India, China, and Australia boast interesting and exciting cuisines and are popular destinations to receive culinary training. So grab a globe and give it a spin or unroll a map and scope out a destination.

Another possible way to choose a location is to think about the type of cuisine you'd like to study or the type of restaurant you'd like to work in. If you want to immerse yourself in Pan-Asian cooking, you may look to Singapore, but if you're interested in gaining as much knowledge as you can on spices, perhaps India is the place for you. Matching your desire with its counterpart location is a good first step.

An important consideration when deciding where in the world to attend school is whether you know the language of the country you'll be calling home for the next few months or even years. If you're headed to Italy and can't communicate in Italian, you'd better start learning how to speak Italian — at least enough to get you by if needed. Although most international culinary schools teach their courses in English, knowing the language of the country you'll be living in is a practical necessity for everyday tasks. In addition to learning the language, you should learn about the country's culture and customs as a sign of your respect for the people you'll meet there and to avoid awkward and even embarrassing situations.

After you've decided where you'd like to study, you must find a school you'd like to apply to — just like in the United States. (We talk about some of the different international schools in the next section of this chapter.) You can find international culinary schools by doing a quick search on the Internet. You can also find information by talking to culinary instructors or others who've traveled this route.

When you're accepted, you're ready to hop a plane and start your culinary education abroad, right? Not so fast. You need to take care of a number of other concerns before you actually leave the country:

- ✔ Finalize financial decisions (determine how you'll pay for expenses such as tuition, housing, food, personal and medical needs, etc. Will you save money, borrow money, or obtain a part-time job while overseas?)
- ✔ Make living arrangements
- ✔ Arrange for healthcare coverage (determine what you'll need to do in case you need medical treatment while overseas)
- ✔ Get a passport
- ✔ Get a visa to the country, if necessary

If you're unsure what documents you'll need before you travel out of the country to your new destination, contact the school you'll be attending. They will most likely provide you with a detailed list of everything you'll need.

Checking out top-notch international culinary schools

Hundreds, if not thousands, of international culinary schools exist throughout the world. Though your choice of school will depends on where you want to go, we give you the scoop on some of the most popular international culinary schools in this section.

Academia Barilla (Italy)

Academia Barilla offers a range of cooking classes for both amateur and professional cooks. The advanced professional courses teach students not only technique and Italian gastronomic culture but also menu design, food pairings, and more. The amateur courses teach students basic cooking skills and technique and introduce them to Italian gastronomy. The facility, which is located in Parma, Italy, has 18 kitchens, including bread, pastry, and pizza kitchens, a tasting lab, and an extensive gastronomic library.

For more information about Academia Barilla, call +39-0521-26-40-60, e-mail info@academiabarilla.it, or visit www.academiabarilla.com.

Ecole Nationale Supérieure de la Pâtisserie (France)

The Ecole Nationale Supérieure de la Pâtisserie, located in Yssingeaux, France, is a French pastry and baking school. The school offers an intensive, five-month pastry program, which is taught in English and includes more than 500 hours working in state-of-the-art pastry laboratories. Students learn how to bake breads, cakes, and other pastries and make batters, doughs, ice creams, and chocolates. They also learn how to decorate cakes and pastries. Although most classes are taught in English, some classes at Ecole Nationale Supérieure de la Pâtisserie are taught solely in French.

For more information about the Ecole Nationale Supérieure de la Pâtisserie, call 04-71-65-7250 or visit www.ensp-adf.com.

Institut de tourisme et d'hôtellerie du Québec (ITHQ) (Canada)

The Institut de tourisme et d'hôtellerie du Québec (Quebec Tourism and Hotel Institute) offers training and research in the hotel, tourism, and food service industries. ITHQ has its own training hotel, where students learn how to take care of real-world hotel visitors. Students learn not only restaurant skills and kitchen operations but also all aspects of the hotel industry, including administrative duties, concierge services, and front desk operations. The hotel is home to numerous food labs; cooking, pastry, and chocolate classrooms; a sommellerie (wine cellar); a refrigerated classroom for catering training; and a multimedia center. All classes taught at the ITHQ are taught in French.

For more information about the Institut de tourisme et d'hôtellerie du Québec, call 1-800-361-5111, e-mail registrariat@ithq.qc.ca, or visit www.ithq.qc.ca.

Italian Institute for Advanced Culinary and Pastry Arts (Italy)

The Italian Institute for Advanced Culinary and Pastry Arts (ICI), one of Italy's top culinary academies, was founded in 1994. While at the institute, students are fully immersed in intensive culinary, baking, pastry, and gelato programs from as little as one week to three months. During the intensive training, students learn about Italian cuisine, pastry technique and decoration, and artisan and hearth baking. Students will also take trips to Italy's top restaurants and food markets. The courses include all room accommodations, meals, course materials, and travel accommodations.

The Italian Institute for Advanced Culinary and Pastry Arts has locations in Parma, Italy, and Calabria, Italy. For more information, call +39-334-333-2554, e-mail info@italianculinary.it, or visit www.italianculinary.it.

Le Cordon Bleu International (Multiple locations)

Le Cordon Bleu International is considered one of the world's best culinary institutes. The culinary institute, which emphasizes French cooking techniques, offers many different programs of culinary study. Students can gain their culinary arts diploma or certificate, hospitality management master's degree or bachelor's degree, or master's in gastronomy at campuses throughout the world, including Paris, France; London, England; Adelaide, Australia; Sydney, Australia; Melbourne, Australia; Tokyo, Japan; Kobe, Japan; Seoul, Korea; Ottawa, Canada; Mexico City, Mexico; and Lima, Peru.

For more information about Le Cordon Bleu International, call 1-800-457-2433 or visit www.cordonbleu.edu.

Adventures in cookery

More and more people are trading in beach vacations for gastronomy vacations filled with adventure, fine food, and wines. Instead of just sitting back and enjoying these luxuries, vacationers are spending their time learning about food and learning how to prepare these foods themselves. Many resorts throughout the world, including the following three, now offer intensive cooking classes.

Peggy Markel's Culinary Adventures

For more than 17 years, Peggy Markel traveled the world, learning about food from great chefs, winemakers, cheesemakers, and more. Today she teaches these experiences by offering tours to Tuscany, Sicily, Elba, Amalfi, Morocco, India, and Spain, where both amateurs and professionals can gain a hands-on education about food. Markel also offers custom and private tours as well as cooking classes. For more information about Peggy Markel's Culinary Adventures, call 1-800-988-2851, e-mail info@peggymarkel.com, or visit http://peggymarkel.com.

Philipkutty's Farm

Located in Kerala, South India, Philipkutty's Farm is a family-owned establishment that offers accommodations in waterfront villas on a farm island. While staying at the farm, vacationers can book a "cookery holiday" filled with cooking classes and lessons in Kerala cooking and cuisine. Vacationers will learn how to prepare dishes such as chutneys and curries with meats and fish as well as vegetarian meals. For more information about Philipkutty's Farm, e-mail mail@philipkuttysfarm.com or visit www.philipkuttysfarm.com.

Two Bordelais

Husband and wife duo Denise and Jean-Pierre Moullé use their experiences to offer Bordeaux tours filled with fine food and wine. Visitors staying at the Moullés's restored 17th-century barn, which is situated on a vineyard near St. Emilion, experience tours through numerous vineyards and culinary destinations, learning about cheesemaking, chocolates, charcuterie (butchery), organic vegetables, barrel making, and more. Visitors will also enjoy creative dishes prepared by Chef Jean-Pierre Moullé. For more information about Two Bordelais, e-mail info@twobordelais.com or visit www.twobordelais.com.

Booking a Class: Hotel Cooking Schools

If you're not the kind of person who sees yourself attending a traditional culinary school, then taking a few classes at a hotel cooking school may be right up your alley. Although you won't receive a formal education — meaning no certificate or degree — by taking these types of classes, you will receive hands-on training in the kitchen. These types of classes are perfect for someone who doesn't have time to complete a traditional culinary degree, but still wants some formal training, or someone who just wants to brush up on the basics. Hotels that offer cooking classes are also becoming popular destinations for vacationers who are interested in learning how to cook. One of the downfalls of taking a few classes at a hotel cooking school is that the hotel may require you to be a guest, which means you must stay at the hotel and pay lodging cost on top of the cost of the class.

Many hotels and resorts throughout the United States and the rest of the world now offer a variety of cooking classes that teach the basics and more advanced and specialized classes. The following sections introduce you to a few of the top hotel cooking schools.

Belle Isle Cookery School (Ireland)

Belle Isle Cookery School is located at the Bell Isle Castle at Duke of Abercorn's Belle Isle Estate in Northern Ireland. It offers classes for all skills levels from demonstrations to day-long, hands-on classes to a four-week diploma program. The kitchen at the Cookery features gas and electric stoves, an oil-fired Aga, as well as top-of-the line kitchen appliances and equipment. Students work with produce and herbs grown directly in the estate's garden and eggs from free-range chickens. For more information about Belle Isle Cookery School, call +44 (0)28-6638-7231, e-mail info@belle-isle.com, or visit www.belle-isle.com/cookery-school.htm.

Cavallo Point Lodge (United States)

Cavallo Point Lodge, which is located in Sausalito, California, offers its guests an array of ever-changing hands-on cooking classes and demonstrations in its top-of-the-line kitchen that boasts four workstations, cameras, and flat-screen televisions. The school is under the direction of Chef Jayne Reichert, who works with local organic farms, artisans, vineyards, and chefs. Cavallo Point Lodge was rated the No. 1 Hotel Culinary School by Gayot.com in October 2010. For more information about Cavallo Point Lodge, call 1-888-651-2003, e-mail cookingschool@cavallopoint.com, or visit www.cavallopoint.com.

Ritz Escoffier School (France)

Ritz Escoffier School is located at the most famous hotel in the world: Ritz Paris in France. The school was named after the hotel's first chef and the creator of the kitchen brigade (see Chapter 5), Georges Auguste Escoffier. The hotel school offers a variety of courses, including workshops and demonstrations that teach everything from French pastries and cuisine to molding chocolates to floral arrangements. Students can spend as little as a few hours at a workshop to as much as 19 weeks training for their master's in gastronomy at the Ritz Escoffier School. Classes are taught in French but are translated into English. For more information about Ritz Escoffier School, visit www.ritzparis.com.

Sazon Cookery School (Mexico)

The Sazon Cookery School is located at the Casa de Sierra Nevada in San Miguel de Allende, Guanajuato, Mexico. Guests and non-guests can partake in classes at the Sazon, which include tours of local Mexican markets, and learn about the different specialties of Mexican cuisine. For more information, call 1-800-701-1561, e-mail sazon@sazon.com, or visit www.casadesierra nevada.com.

Thorn Park by the Vines (Australia)

Guests at Thorn Park by the Vines, located in Seven Hill, Clare Valley, South Australia, can take part in cooking classes instructed by self-taught cook David Hay, co-owner of Thorn Park. Hay uses his personal cooking and travel experiences throughout Europe, Turkey, and Asia to offer fun and educational hands-on cooking classes and demonstrations. The classes, which feature local offerings, are held over several days and include wine pairings. For more information about Thorn Park by the Vines, call +61-8-8843-4304, e-mail david@thornpark.com.au, or visit www.thornpark.com.au.

Taking a Look at Traditional Schools

Studying at a school devoted specifically to the culinary and pastry arts may be advantageous and studying abroad may seem thrilling and exotic, but in some cases, these options just aren't possible. For example, if you're thinking of transitioning into a culinary career from another career, you may have to continue working while taking night classes after work instead of devoting a year or more to full-time study at a culinary school. Don't worry, however. Many two- and four-year colleges and universities and technical schools offer degrees, diplomas, and certificates in the culinary and pastry arts close to home.

Community college culinary degrees

Earning a culinary degree from a community college has its benefits. Community colleges typically have more affordable tuition than four-year colleges or universities or private culinary schools. As an added cost-saving bonus, community colleges are local. Students fresh out of high school don't have to worry about paying room-and-board charges or affording rent each month, because they can live right at home. Likewise, adults who are furthering their education with a culinary degree can take classes at night or on weekends while still maintaining another job or caring for family and home responsibilities.

Community colleges typically offer certificate or diploma programs, which you can usually earn within a few months to a year, or associate's degree programs, which typically take two years to complete. Keep in mind, however, that while a certificate or diploma program will likely focus only on culinary skills, an associate's degree in culinary arts at many community colleges requires additional coursework in accounting, math, and English.

Four-year colleges and universities

A common path of education is to follow high school graduation with attendance at a four-year college or university. Many of these learning institutions offer associate and bachelor's degrees in hospitality and restaurant management or food studies, and some even offer graduate degrees.

Attending a four-year college or university for your culinary education has both advantages and disadvantages. Students who attend a four-year college or university earn a well-rounded education. In addition, the earning potential for students who pursue higher degrees, such as a bachelor's or master's degree, is typically greater than it is for those who earn an associate's degree. However, tuition at a four-year college or university is typically higher than at a community college. Also, in comparison to culinary schools, which draw students from a diverse range of ages, four-year colleges and universities tend to attract recent high school graduates.

One of the most well-known names in culinary education is Johnson and Wales University. The original culinary school is located in Providence, Rhode Island, but the university boasts three satellite campuses including Charlotte, North Carolina; North Miami, Florida; and Denver, Colorado. Johnson and Wales has associate degree programs in culinary arts and baking and pastry arts at all its campuses. Students can also enroll in the following bachelor's degree programs, broken down by campus:

- ✔ **Providence:** Baking and pastry arts, culinary arts and food service management, culinary nutrition, food service entrepreneurship, baking and pastry arts food service management

- ✔ **North Miami:** Culinary arts and food service management, baking and pastry arts and food service management

- ✔ **Denver:** Culinary arts and food service management, culinary nutrition, baking and pastry arts and food service management

- ✔ **Charlotte:** Culinary arts and food service management, baking and pastry arts and food service management

If you complete a bachelor's degree and want to continue your formal culinary education, some schools offer graduate programs. For example, the Cornell School of Hotel Administration offers a master of management in hospitality (MMH) program as well as master's and doctoral degrees in hotel administration. Boston University is the only school in the United States to offer a master of liberal arts in gastronomy. Students here can earn their master's degree in combination with a culinary arts certificate.

Other schooling alternatives

If none of the other schooling options appeals to you, consider studying at one of the many vocational, technical, or trade schools located in cities across the country, where you can get competitive training targeted toward your ultimate career goal. Programs range in length from less than a year to two years. Those lasting for two years typically result in an associate's degree. At some technical schools, the programs involve externships that result in real-life experience and hands-on training. Studying at a vocational, technical, or trade school is often less expensive than studying at a private culinary arts college, but courses may cost more than they would at a community college.

Following are some of the programs of study available at vocational and technical schools:

- Professional Cooking, Baking, and Pastry Arts
- Commercial Cooking
- Baking Production
- Culinary Arts
- Casino Management
- Dietary Manager
- Food Service Aide
- Golf Course Management
- Hotel and Restaurant Management
- Hotel/Hospitality Management

One of the best ways to find vocational and technical schools near you is to go online. A number of websites are available to help you search for vocational and technical schools in your area. Some allow you to search by program, state, or zip code. Following are a few helpful sites:

- RWM Vocational Schools Database (www.rwm.org)
- Technical Schools Guide (www.technical-schools-guide.com)
- TechnicalSchool.org (www.technicalschool.org)

You can also visit a local One-Stop Career Center, which can provide you with information on various training programs as well as occupational trends, skills, and knowledge. To find a One-Stop Career Center near you, visit www.servicelocator.org. If you're still in high school, you can also talk to your school's guidance counselor for more information.

Paying for Culinary School: Scholarships and Financial Aid

When it comes to paying for culinary school, regardless of where you decide to go, research into financial aid is essential. Many schools offer grants, scholarships, and other financial aid to students who meet need- or merit-based qualifications. For example, the Culinary Institute of America offers 20 Cream of the Crop Scholarships to some of the best incoming students each year. You can also find scholarships and grants through industry organizations such as the International Dairy-Deli-Bakery Association, the National Restaurant Association Educational Foundation, and others.

Many people rely on various forms of financial aid to pay for their education. But what exactly are the different forms? Following is an overview of the most common types:

- ✔ **Scholarships:** These are financial gifts, often awarded based on merit (good grades, skilled in athletics), and do not have to be paid back.

- ✔ **Grants:** These, like scholarships, are financial awards and do not have to be paid back. Some grants are based on financial need. Those who award grants may place restrictions on how the money can be used — for example, only for tuition.

- ✔ **Student loans:** These, as you might have guessed, are borrowed money and have to be repaid. Federal student loans usually have a very low interest rate and usually are based on financial need, State and private student loans are also available.

- ✔ **Fellowships:** These often cover tuition, and sometimes other costs, usually in exchange for work, such as research. Many students pursuing graduate degrees receive fellowships.

If you're still in high school, one of the best places to find information about scholarships, grants, and student loans is your school's guidance office. High school students and others can also find information about scholarships and grants through online searches and by visiting websites such as FinAid (www.finaid.org) or Scholarships.com (www.scholarships.com). If you know where you want to attend school, visit the school's website. Most schools have web pages dedicated to information about financial aid, scholarships, and grants.

Consider the following tips when applying for scholarships or grants:

- ✔ **Pay attention to the details.** Read the fine print to make sure you're eligible. If you're already in college and looking to score a scholarship, you don't want to waste time filling out an application for a scholarship that is available only to high school students. To be eligible for some scholarships, you have to spend some time working in the industry before you apply, and you may even have to supply evidence of this work.

- ✔ **Follow directions.** Simple? Yes. Important? Definitely. If the application is supposed to be filled out in black ink, and you use blue, it may go right in the garbage upon receipt. So read the directions and make sure you understand exactly what you have to do.

- ✔ **Line up references.** For some scholarship or grant applications, you may have to supply a list of references who can vouch for your character. Before jotting down these names, check with each person you'd like to include and get his or her approval first. He or she will appreciate the heads-up and won't be caught off guard when someone calls to ask about you.

In addition to researching scholarships or grants, you should also fill out the Free Application for Federal Student Aid (FAFSA). Federal Student Aid, an office of the U.S. Department of Education, states that this form "ensures that all eligible individuals can benefit from federally funded financial assistance for education beyond high school." The government uses this form to determine how much money you can receive in grants and what your student loan eligibility is. After filing a FAFSA, you'll receive a Student Aid Report, which outlines the information you provided on your FAFSA and indicates your expected family contribution — that is, the amount the government expects you or your family to pay toward your education. This value is then used to determine your eligibility for federal student aid. For more information about the FAFSA and Federal Student Aid, visit http://studentaid.ed.gov.

Part II
Exploring Popular Career Paths and Profiles

The 5th Wave   By Rich Tennant

In this part . . .

*J*obs are plentiful in the culinary industry. Think about the many places where food is prepared and served and then envision the number of people needed to cook and serve this food.

In this part, we explore the popular career paths within the culinary industry. We give you the lowdown on working in restaurants, hotels, resorts, spas, catering companies, and institutions such as schools and hospitals. We also break down the major players inside and outside the kitchen as well as what is expected from food lovers working in these professions.

Chapter 5

Reservation for One: Working in Restaurants

In This Chapter

▶ Discovering the different types of restaurants

▶ Understanding the positions available in restaurant kitchens

▶ Identifying different roles in the front of the house

*P*eople dine at restaurants for many reasons — their meals may be in honor of a new job or a promotion, part of a romantic date, or just a more convenient option than cooking at home.

If you work in a restaurant, your main goal will be to prepare high-quality food for your customers. Of course, the definition of high-quality food varies depending on the restaurant in which you work. If you're a line cook in a restaurant with three Michelin stars (the highest rating given by the respected restaurant guide), customers may be smitten with super-small portions and an artistic presentation of food made with rare ingredients — and they won't mind paying a $700.95 bill. But if you're a cook in a chain restaurant, high-quality food may mean a delicious baked potato with sour cream, a cheeseburger with bacon, and an oversized portion of onion rings for under $20.

In this chapter, we discuss the different types of restaurants where you may one day work and what restaurant work is like in general. We also explain the different positions you may hold in the kitchen or dining room of a restaurant and what skills and experience you need to land such positions. As always, whether you're the busser or the executive chef, you need determination and a great work ethic to succeed.

Getting the Lowdown on Restaurants

Working in a restaurant can be challenging and yet simultaneously rewarding. The fast pace of restaurants always keeps you on your toes, which means you learn how to think — and move! — quickly. Restaurant jobs require you to multi-task and learn to work as part of a team. They also test your patience and your knowledge of food.

When you know that you want to work in a restaurant, you have to decide which style of restaurant best suits your personality and your skill set. In this section, we discuss the five main types of restaurants. Take note that not all restaurants fit into just one of these categories — some may be hybrids, combinations of two or more styles. After giving an overview of restaurant types, we discuss what a day working at a restaurant may be like.

Checking out different restaurant styles

The style of restaurants can vary widely. Items on the menu, processes for preparing dishes, and formality of service are all factors that determine what kind of restaurant an establishment is. In this section, we explore the most common styles of restaurants in which you may one day work.

Fine-dining restaurants

Sometimes referred to as *white-tablecloth restaurants,* these restaurants offer an intimate atmosphere, dishes that incorporate rare ingredients from around the world, and incredible, personalized service. Some fine-dining establishments offer service only on specific days of the week (in other words, perhaps they're closed for dinner Sunday through Tuesday). Others, like The French Laundry in California, close for weeks during the holiday season so staff can spend time with their families. Because of these restrictions, customers interested in fine-dining must make reservations sometimes months in advance.

The food offered at fine-dining restaurants is almost always made from scratch in house. In addition to dinner (and occasionally lunch) service, these restaurants also sometimes feature tasting menus, which are multiple-course dinner experiences the executive chef has designed to highlight the best dishes the restaurant offers. When customers order tasting menus, they simply have to sit back and wait for the courses (which are perfectly timed to allow the customer ample time to experience and enjoy each dish) to be brought to them. Sometimes, tasting menus also feature wine pairings, in which a sommelier or a member of the wait staff serves with each course a new glass of wine that complements the food. Tasting menus and wine pairings can be quite expensive.

Like the food, fine-dining service is stellar. The wait staff typically knows every ingredient in the dishes on the menu and can explain the techniques used to prepare each dish. Customers expect to have their chairs pushed in, their napkins placed in their laps, and their beverages refilled without request.

The pace at fine-dining restaurants is slower than the pace at other types of restaurants because exquisite food and mouth-watering presentations take longer to prepare and plate than your average burger and fries. Most customers who frequent fine-dining restaurants understand and expect the slower pace.

Between the cost of the food, wine, and the tip, the bill at fine-dining restaurants may seem overwhelming. To many customers, however, the adventure of trying new foods and the experience of being waited on to such an extreme is worth every penny!

Casual-dining restaurants

Casual-dining restaurants may be best defined as a combination of fine-dining and family-style restaurants (discussed in the following section). These restaurants have a casual atmosphere; you don't have to wear your best suit or little black dress to get a table. Compared to fine-dining establishments, casual-dining servers are more relaxed, the menu items are familiar, and the prices aren't as steep.

Many casual-dining restaurants also have a full bar and a happy hour. You may or may not find this feature at fine-dining restaurants because the chefs, in combination with the sommeliers, have previously decided which beverages you should drink to complement the flavors of the food they've laboriously prepared. At a casual-dining restaurant, the drink menu is less rigid — if you want an Alabama Slammer, Fuzzy Navel, or Screwdriver, you've got it!

The food at casual-dining restaurants isn't always as simple as burgers, fries, and pizza — but these options may certainly appear on the menu in one form or another. These restaurants offer small appetizers, salads, cheeses, full-sized entrees, and desserts. You may spot fresh seafood, homemade pastas, and a few upscale ingredients such as caviar on the menu. Chefs and cooks in the kitchen may prepare the food from scratch or they may use products previously prepared in commissary kitchens.

A *commissary kitchen* is also known as a *production kitchen*. These types of kitchens aren't located within restaurants, but the food prepared there is served in restaurants. Employees in commissary kitchens cook, bake, and prep thousands of meals and then package and freeze them. Some foods are semi-cooked, some just need reheating, and others are ready-to-eat. Ordering food prepared in commissary kitchens is sometimes easier and more affordable than hiring a butcher, pastry chef, and *garde-manger* (a chef who prepares cold dishes such as salads, pates, and terrines). If you want to prepare restaurant-style food but don't want to work under the pressure of a fast-paced kitchen, consider applying for a job in a commissary kitchen.

Family-style restaurants

As their name implies, family-style restaurants are kid-friendly places. The decor is typically cluttered with themed memorabilia, such as film items, and the servers have no problem kneeling at the side of your table to talk to your children. These restaurants typically offer younger customers their own menu and placemats that they can color on with crayons.

The food offered at family-style restaurants is typically not prepared completely in house. Much of it is prepared in commissary kitchens, frozen and packaged, and then shipped to restaurants. When an order is up, the cooks on the line open the package and place the contents on the grill, in the oven, or in the microwave. Clients don't often wait very long for their food at these establishments.

Family-style restaurants may also feature soup and salad bars, buffet lines, and dessert bars. This setup makes service simple and less stressful in both the back and the front of the house. Dining-room staff often only need to fetch drink refills, clear the tables of unused plates and silverware, and then bring the bill — which typically doesn't break the bank. Kitchen staff often prepare food in giant batches and watch that the temperature of the food is maintained. They only need to worry about making more food when they receive word that a particular item is running low. On occasion, they may receive a special request from a customer who has dietary needs or a picky eater on their hands.

Diners

Unlike fine-dining and family-style restaurants, diners make most of their profits in the morning and mid-afternoon, because they're more popular options for breakfast and lunch. They're also popular stops for hungry truckers and travelers in the middle of the night. Diner customers don't expect top-quality cuisine, nor do they expect fancy presentation or outstanding service. Instead, they'll part with a few bucks for simple food such as a bowl of oatmeal, muffin, burger with all the fixings, slice of meatloaf, cup of warm soup, or slice of turkey with a side of mashed potatoes drowning in homemade gravy. In a typical diner, food is typically made from scratch by a small staff of cooks with little to no formal culinary training.

Diners are normally small establishments located along busy roads. A diner is similar to a fast-food restaurant (addressed in the next section) in that management's goal is to serve as many people as possible as quickly as possible. Bar stools at diners don't have backs and tables don't have cloths, because customers don't need to be extremely comfortable for the short amount of time they stay.

Fast-food restaurants

Fast-food restaurants typically don't receive the *restaurant* label. In the food industry, they're often referred to as *stores* because the employees focus more on selling the food to customers rather than preparing it. Almost all food in fast-food restaurants is prepared in a commissary kitchen and shipped to the store, where it's either served as is or heated. You can occasionally find a shop that requires its kitchen employees to do more than throw a burger in the microwave or drop a pack of frozen fries in the fryer. Fast-food restaurants where employees grill the burgers, mix the chili, and even cut fresh vegetables for salads do exist. In the past years, fast food has stretched beyond burgers and fries to include tacos, chicken, fish, soups, sushi, and even healthier items such as wraps and salads.

Fast-food restaurants are favored by many Americans because they're quick and inexpensive, but service in these establishments is nearly non-existent. For the most part, customers serve themselves by gathering their own plastic utensils, straws, and condiments. They often even pour their own beverages. Some employees prepare the food and others punch the customers' orders into the computer. Management typically oversees the process and helps ensure that the food is ready quickly.

Many fast-food restaurants (as well as many casual-dining and family-style restaurants) in America are chain restaurants. *Chain restaurants* are strings of restaurants that look the same and feature similar menu items and specials. Some franchises, such as Pizza Hut or T.G.I. Friday's, are successful enough (and large enough) to have branches spanning the country. Others, such as In-N-Out Burger, are located only in a particular area of the country and are sometimes considered tourist destinations because of this exclusivity. In any case, most outlets of a chain restaurant are the same. The only difference between a McDonald's in North Carolina and a McDonald's in Las Vegas is the price of the food. Although they do exist, very few fine-dining restaurants are part of a chain. Fine-dining restaurants are considered "fine" because they're unique; if too many of them existed, they'd risk losing their charm.

Americans' increasing appetite for restaurant meals

In a 2010 survey, Restaurant.org discovered that during the previous year, the average family in the United States spent more than $2,600 on prepared food from restaurants and food carts. Approximately 74 percent of Americans agreed that they would rather eat at a restaurant with friends and family than cook a meal themselves and have to clean it up later. And really, who can blame them? Restaurants provide customers with a chance to have fun and socialize without worrying about burning the pot roast, undercooking the pasta, and eventually needing to scrub the growing pile of dishes, pots, and pans in the sink. Americans like eating in restaurants so much that researchers predict that restaurant sales in 2011 will reach $604.2 billion — $225 billion more than restaurant sales a decade earlier.

A day in the life of a restaurant employee

Regardless of whether you work in the front or the back of a restaurant, your work environment is going to be hectic. If you approach restaurant work with the right attitude — willing to work quickly, stay upbeat, and do your best — you should fit right in. But if you can't keep up and you're rude to your fellow staff members and customers, you won't last very long. Working in restaurants — especially those that cater to at least 500 patrons a night — is challenging. You want to be prepared before diving into the exhilarating and sometimes chaotic world of restaurant work, so in this section we tell you what you can expect the schedule, pace, teamwork, and responsibilities of restaurant employees to be.

Working nontraditional hours

Regardless of its type, a typical restaurant's busiest time of day is dinner — but because not all customers eat dinner at the same time, dinner service can last a long time. Beginning with early-bird specials at 4:00 p.m., restaurants typically see a steady increase in the number of diners they serve throughout the evening. Even as the cooks in the kitchen begin to lose steam as closing time approaches, customers continue to order food. Kitchen and dining-room employees in restaurants must be prepared to stay until the end of service — until the last customers pay their bills, put on their coats, and leave — and then some.

Even after all customers have left, restaurant employees must continue to work. Cooks and chefs clean the line and prep food for the next morning while dishwashers scrub piles upon piles of plates. Dining-room employees change table cloths, vacuum or sweep, fill condiments (salt, pepper, sugar, steak sauce, ketchup, and so on), and wipe down tables and chairs. Some dining-room employees may be responsible for tidying up the foyer, coat racks, and even the bathrooms.

A typical restaurant dinner shift may be from about 3:00 or 4:00 in the afternoon until roughly 11:00 at night (depending on the restaurant's hours of operation), but many employees don't leave work until closer to or past midnight. By the time most shifts end, friends and family members are asleep. Unless you're a night owl, nontraditional working hours are definitely the downside of working in a restaurant.

If you have a family, attend classes at night, or have prior commitments that don't allow you to work the dinner shift in a restaurant, you may still be able to land a job in a restaurant of your choosing. If the restaurant offers breakfast or lunch, you may be able to work earlier shifts. Typically, you receive fewer orders during breakfast and lunch and focus mostly on prepping for the dinner crew. However, if the restaurant is known for its breakfast deals or if it's located in a bustling downtown, you may find that working these earlier shifts is no cakewalk. If the establishment has a reputation for great food and is within distance of office buildings, it probably gets slammed at lunchtime.

Keeping up a fast pace

A restaurant's main goal is to make money — and, unless the restaurant is extremely expensive, the more customers it serves, the more money it makes. Many restaurant owners push their kitchen employees to get food out as fast as possible. Whether you cook in restaurants where everything is prepared from scratch or where some food comes premade from commissary kitchens, you're expected to hustle so diners can get their meals quickly and tables can be turned over.

If you work in a kitchen that requires you to do more than heat a chicken patty in a microwave for a few seconds, be prepared to encounter a fair amount of frustration. Microwave ovens and fast-food restaurant have conditioned customers to expect to receive food within minutes of ordering. Many customers don't stop to consider that you, as a chef or a cook, actually have to *cook* their food after you receive their order. Be prepared to receive inquiries about dishes you've just started working on from wait staff who have been asked by disgruntled customers to check on the food they have yet to receive. Keep your cool in these situations and (as politely as possible) give the server an estimate of when you think the dish will be ready so he or she can inform the customer.

Expect to work up quite a sweat as you hustle from station to station, weaving behind other employees holding hot pans and placing delicate garnishes on nearly finished plates. As the saying goes, if you can't stand the heat, get out of the kitchen. If you're not fast on your feet and you find multi-tasking difficult, working in a busy restaurant kitchen may not be right for you.

Although dining-room employees don't have to quickly produce meals requiring numerous ingredients that must be prepared in multiple pans, they must also move quickly. Servers have to hustle to take care of customers while also paying attention to when an order is ready so that it can be delivered to the customer before a perfectly cooked piece of fish or steak dries out or becomes cold. And if customers are waiting for tables, dining-room staff must change table settings right away when diners leave a table.

Working as a team

A restaurant can only achieve success when both the back and front of the house work together. The executive chef must work with the general manager, and the line cooks and chefs must work with the wait staff. (The later sections "Meeting All the Players in the Kitchen" and "Getting Acquainted with Staff in the Front of the House" fill you in on the responsibilities of these and other jobs.) In the kitchen, cooks and chefs must also work together to ensure that each part of every dish is ready to go at the same time and is of the highest quality. Cooks and chefs have to talk to each other and let one another know if they need help.

Communication is key to a smooth operation. If workers in the kitchen aren't aware of what's happening in the dining room, disaster may strike. If the kitchen staff isn't told that a 20-top (a group of 20 people) has made a last-minute reservation for 6:00 p.m. (a high-volume hour), they won't be ready to cook for an extra 20 people at that time. The result? Either meals will come out of the kitchen slower than usual, which will surely annoy customers, or multiple dishes will miss the mark because the cooks' time and attention were spread too thin.

Dining-room staff also suffer when communication isn't clear. If the chef has prepared a special for the night featuring unfamiliar ingredients and fails to explain the dish to the wait staff, they may encounter uncomfortable confusion when a customer asks a question about the special. To avoid this situation, the wait staff may skip stating the specials altogether which, in turn, means that a profit is not made from the dish. Instead, the restaurant pays for high-quality, possibly imported ingredients that will go to waste.

Working in a restaurant can be challenging and frustrating, no matter what position you hold. Remember that whether you work in the back or the front, your fellow staff members understand what you're feeling — and probably feel it, too. You need to be able to lean on each other for support when necessary, regardless of whether you wash dishes, chop vegetables, or carry a tray. And having a sense of humor helps.

Handling responsibilities

Your job responsibilities in a restaurant vary depending on the position you hold. To state the obvious, workers in the kitchen are responsible for different tasks related to preparing the food, and workers in the dining room are assigned responsibilities pertaining to serving the food.

The number of people in the kitchen of a restaurant depends on many factors, but one of the most important things executive chefs consider when making this decision is how busy the restaurant may be during its peak time. In large, hectic kitchens, one or two cooks or chefs may staff a single station. This means they're responsible for only the food prepared at that station.

Sometimes, small kitchens can get away with having only three or four cooks or chefs on the line. In this case, the chefs and cooks will have to multi-task and sometimes even cover other stations. If a cook is at the sauté station, he may also have to watch the fry station. If the cook at the pasta station doesn't have an order to fill, he may watch the fry station so the sauté cook can focus on finishing his dishes. These situations require kitchen employees to learn to balance their individual responsibilities and know how to step in for their teammates when necessary.

For the most part, back- and front-of-the-house positions don't overlap — workers in the front of the house stay with the customers, and staff in the back work with the food. Supervisors are the exception to this rule. They may work in both the front and the back of the house. For example, if you're a general manager, you may supervise the workers in both the front and the back of the house. If you're an executive chef, you may visit customers in the dining room to see if they're satisfied with their food or have any feedback for you.

Meeting All the Players in the Kitchen

Restaurants employ many people in different positions — in the front of the house (the dining room), the back of the house (the kitchen), and in the office. Some restaurant employees never actually prepare or come into contact with the food the restaurant serves. Some restaurant jobs require you to move fast, others require you to always smile, and still others require you to be good at managing money and creating marketing strategies.

Like all work environments, a chain of command or authority exists in the back of the house. This chain of command is often called the *kitchen brigade*. French chef Georges Auguste Escoffier came up with the idea of the kitchen brigade way back in the mid-19th century to eliminate confusion regarding responsibilities in the kitchen of the Savoy Hotel in London. Escoffier believed that if every man (or today, woman) in the kitchen knew his rightful place and responsibilities, fewer misunderstandings and accidents would occur.

Many employees work in the kitchen, from dishwashers to executive chefs. The executive chef heads the kitchen brigade. In most kitchens, the executive chef's right-hand man or woman is the *sous chef.* From there, chefs and cooks work various stations on the line, depending on their specialties and how many stations a particular restaurant features. If your restaurant happens to produce its own breads or pastries, you may also work with bakers, pastry chefs, and possibly even an executive pastry chef. Sometimes, even a butcher has a place within the kitchen.

Regardless of which style restaurant you may work in, the jobs of dishwashers, prep cooks, and line cooks are the same. The responsibilities of the sous chef, chef de cuisine, and executive chef may differ from kitchen to kitchen, however. Those roles are highly dependent on the presence of the executive chefs and which responsibilities they designate to others and which they fulfill themselves. In some kitchens, the executive chef does all the hiring and firing. In others, the chef de cuisine or sous chef may be asked to perform these tasks. Sometimes executive chefs cook on the line beside their kitchen staff, and other times they stay in their office, planning menus and working on budgets.

What's in a name? *Chef* versus *cook*

Although the terms *chef* and *cook* are often used interchangeably by people outside the industry, they really mean different things within the brigade system, mainly in terms of formal education and kitchen responsibilities.

Cooks prepare the ingredients and makes the dishes that a sous chef or executive chef creates. Cooks don't normally have authority over any areas in the kitchen, but if they prove their loyalty to their staff, they may be rewarded with a managerial position after a few years' work. You don't have to complete any coursework or attain any degrees to be a cook.

Chefs typically hold an authoritative position in which they may create menu items, take charge of purchasing, manage money, and supervise other cooks and chefs. A chef may also hold degrees or have received more formal culinary education. Many men and women interested in achieving the formal title of *chef* in America turn to the certification programs of the American Culinary Federation (ACF). These programs first require a particular number of hours in a kitchen or classroom. After these hours are recorded, candidates can apply to take the written test and the practical exam. During the practical exam, candidates complete specific tasks for a panel of judges and then prepare a dish. They're evaluated on safety and sanitation skills, organization, craftsmanship skills, and finished product skills. A grade of 70 percent or higher passes the written exam and 75 percent or higher is needed to successfully complete the practical exam. After both passing grades are attained, candidates then submit an application to the ACF for consideration.

Candidates can receive certifications for the following titles:

- Certified Culinarian (CC)
- Certified Sous Chef (CSC)
- Certified Chef de Cuisine (CCC)
- Certified Executive Chef (CEC)
- Certified Master Chef (CMC)
- Certified Pastry Culinarian (CPC)
- Certified Working Pastry Chef (CWPC)
- Certified Executive Pastry Chef (CEPC)
- Certified Master Pastry Chef (CMPC)

You don't have to hold a certification from the ACF to be referred to as a chef in the kitchen, but if you receive one of these certifications, you *always* hold the title of chef, regardless of the position you fill in any restaurant. For a complete list of ACF certifications and more information about the ACF tests, see Chapter 3 or visit www.ACFchefs.org.

As Escoffier originally envisioned, the executive chef has always been the person with the most authority in the kitchen of a restaurant. Executive chefs have the most responsibilities — and the most at stake if the restaurant fails. Sous chefs also play a huge role in every kitchen because they step in for the executive chef. They have more responsibilities than head line cooks, chefs de partie, and prep cooks. For these reasons, we provide in-depth information about the top roles on the follow pages.

Executive chef

The executive chef is the head honcho in the kitchen. In a restaurant, the executive chef's responsibilities include — but may go *way* beyond — planning menus, ordering and purchasing supplies from vendors, hiring and training new employees, assigning tasks, and motivating and managing kitchen staff.

If an executive chef owns the entire restaurant, then he is his own boss. If he works for a restaurant owned by someone else, then he must collaborate with the owner. Sometimes an executive chef may also have to answer to a general manager. At other times, he's free to make decisions without consulting either the general manager or the owner. It all depends on how the owner wishes to run the restaurant.

Every restaurant, regardless of its size or style, needs an executive chef. If the executive chef's presence is always required, he'll always be at the restaurant during times of service. Sometimes, however, an entire chain of restaurants will employ a single executive chef who travels from one restaurant in the chain to another. When the executive chef is not present, a sous chef or chef de cuisine may fulfill the duties of executive chef.

Depending on the size of the restaurant and how many cooks are working during a given shift, an executive chef may not have to cook in the kitchen alongside his staff. Instead, the executive chef may place garnishes, wipe finished plates clean, or fill the role of expediter by reading the tickets aloud and letting the staff know which dishes are needed.

On average, executive chefs work 10 to 12 hours each day, five to six days a week. If an executive chef is also the owner of the restaurant, he may even spend "off hours" in the restaurant's office, crunching numbers, examining marketing strategies, and scheduling events.

Personality traits

An executive chef must be confident and patient. Restaurant kitchens are fast-paced, stressful environments, so executive chefs must be able to keep control of their staff while simultaneously keeping their cool.

Executive chefs typically create or heavily influence the menu for their restaurant, so they must also be creative risk-takers. They must be personable and approachable, because creating eccentric and organized menus means working alongside other people in the business. Executive chefs may rely on sommeliers, pastry chefs, and specific vendors who supply ingredients to help them bring their menus together.

If the owner of the restaurant wants the executive chef to make frequent appearances in the dining room, the chef must be comfortable speaking to customers and receiving feedback. Polite, yet stern, communication skills are also necessary when working with all kitchen and dining-room staff members.

Executive chefs must also be good at math — beyond just the simple arithmetic and fractions used in recipe measurements, they must use math to determine if the restaurant is making a profit. They have to make sure that the kitchen isn't spending more to prepare dishes than customers are willing to pay to eat them. An organized executive chef knows exactly how much his kitchen is spending by keeping accurate records of costs and sales.

The best executive chefs are open-minded and understand that the industry is always changing. As restaurants continue to offer a growing number of meals using locally grown ingredients that are healthy and fresh, they'll most likely see an increase in the number of customers reserving seats in their dining rooms. In fact, 69 percent of people surveyed by Restaurant.org said they would rather dine at a restaurant that offers locally produced foods than at one that doesn't. More than half of the surveyed population also admitted that they decide where to dine in their area based on how involved restaurants are in their community. Executive chefs at restaurants (especially those who also own restaurants) need to be open to and aware of these trends so they can alter the ways they manage their businesses and pull in more customers. One of the best personality traits executive chefs can possess is the ability to be flexible.

Salaries

According to Salary.com, executive chefs of restaurants make approximately $58,000 to $88,000 annually. As always, this number depends on the location and size of the restaurant and which services the restaurant offers its clientele. Executive chefs at restaurants with two or three Michelin stars undoubtedly make more money than chefs at independently owned family-style restaurants. And chefs employed in large cities are more likely to earn the big bucks.

Aside from the characteristics of the restaurant itself, an executive chef's qualifications and experiences also affect his salary. The higher the degree or certification held and the more years spent working in and supervising kitchens, the more money a chef stands to make. The salary also increases with the amount of responsibility the job includes. For example, if the executive chef is also the general manager, the salary and benefits are better.

Education and training

Although working your way up to the position of executive chef without ever receiving any formal culinary training is possible, it's not the norm. Most chefs have some type of formal schooling in their back pocket. Many executive chefs at restaurants have bachelor's or associate's degrees in hotel and restaurant management, culinary arts, pastry arts, or hospitality. They may even hold degrees in nutrition. Many chefs have completed certifications, such as those offered by the American Culinary Federation (ACF). Other executive chefs completed courses in business management at technical schools that prepared them to work in an authoritative position in a kitchen.

Experience is also a major factor in landing a job as an executive chef. Most people in executive-chef positions have worked in supervisory kitchen positions for more than 10 years. The more experience you have in the field, the better your chances of becoming executive chef.

Advancement prospects

Even though executive chefs are at the top of the kitchen hierarchy, they still have room to advance within the restaurant industry. If they want to take a break from the line, they can certainly become general managers. If they have a willing partner or the financial capabilities, they also have the option to start their own restaurants and be their own bosses. See Chapter 18 for more information about becoming a culinary entrepreneur.

Executive chefs can also continue to achieve rankings based on the ACF certifications. As of 2009, fewer than 60 men and women in the United States had received the title of Master Chef. As executive chefs work their way up and earn higher titles, larger and better-known restaurants may welcome them. They may also choose to teach courses at culinary or technical schools and share their knowledge of the culinary field with incoming students. For more information about teaching culinary classes, check out Chapter 14.

Unions and associations

The larger the restaurant, the smaller the chances that it will belong to a workers union. Most restaurants belonging to unions are those situated in hotels that are unionized. Although most executive chefs aren't protected by unions due to their supervisory roles, they should still be familiar with the unions to which their employees belong. These may include the Hotel and Restaurant Employees Union (HERE) and the Service Employees International Union (SEIU).

Executive chefs can join many associations, however, including the American Culinary Federation (ACF), the Professional Chef's Association (PCA), National Restaurant Association (NRA), and the World Association of Chefs Societies (WACS). Executive chefs who belong to these associations are invited to conferences and trade shows that allow them to network and learn about the industry's newest trends.

Sous chef/chef de cuisine

In most restaurants kitchens, a *sous chef* is the second-in-command. The sous chef (pronounced *soo* chef) answers to the executive chef (the big boss), but everyone else in the kitchen answers to the sous chef. Whereas executive chefs may not always cook in the kitchen they command, sous chefs typically assist in cooking in restaurant kitchens. They often have a hand in creating feature dishes for special events and weekends. When the executive chef isn't in the kitchen, the sous chef steps in, performing many of the tasks the executive chef does on a daily basis. Sous chefs can make purchases for the kitchen, organize the pantry, and construct staff schedules when the executive chef isn't available.

In large kitchens, you may find an executive chef, a *chef de cuisine,* and a sous chef. The position of *chef de cuisine* doesn't exist in every kitchen, but when it does, this employee takes on a role similar to "ground-level commander." She makes sure the executive chef's orders are fulfilled and may serve as an expediter during service. She may also hire and fire staff — including sous chefs. The role of *chef de cuisine* is similar in some aspects to both executive chefs and sous chefs. When a *chef de cuisine* is not part of a restaurant's kitchen staff, the sous chef takes on these responsibilities and more. Because the personality traits, salary, and advancement prospects of a *chef de cuisine* are so similar to that of a sous chef, we include information about the *chef de cuisine* throughout this section.

Personality traits

A sous chef or *chef de cuisine* must have good leadership and communication skills. Because these chefs are the liaisons between the line cooks and the executive chef, they must be able to represent both sides and work well with everyone. To be a successful sous chef or *chef de cuisine,* you must be able to wear more than one hat — to take directions from the executive chef and then to be an effective leader for the line cooks. If mistakes or misunderstandings occur, you have to be able to step in and address these issues.

To fill these roles, you must also be a good listener. The executive chef will come to you when he needs something. You must be able to listen well to understand what you need to do, whether it's disciplining unruly staff members, explaining to the cooks on the line how to prepare a new dish, or locating a vendor of a specific ingredient.

Just like all other staff in a restaurant kitchen, these chefs must be able to multi-task. A sous chef must be able to cook a variety of foods at any given time while maintaining order on the line.

Salaries

Whether you want to be a sous chef or a *chef de cuisine,* the salary ranges from $33,000 to $55,000 in the United States, with the average restaurant sous chef making approximately $47,000 each year. This amount changes depending on the location and size of the restaurant and the roles the sous chef or *chef de cuisine* must play in the kitchen. Typically, the more responsibilities, the higher the pay.

Past experience in the food industry also influences salary. If you happen to make it to the rank of sous chef at your first job, congratulations! But don't expect a tremendous raise in salary. If you've been the sous chef, or even head line cook, at a few restaurants in the past, however, your new place of employment may offer you more money than it would if you were just starting out.

Education and training

Like an executive chef, a sous chef or *chef de cuisine* may have chosen the path of a formal education and attained an associate's degree or multiple certifications. But although having some formal schooling is helpful, you don't need a degree or have an ACF certification to get a job as a sous chef in a restaurant, and the majority of sous chefs and *chefs de cuisine* don't have bachelor's degrees.

In some restaurants, five or more years of working in kitchens as a line cook can help you become a sous chef. If you have any experience in supervisory roles as kitchen manager or even head line cook, you may also be a good candidate for the job.

Advancement opportunities

If you wish to advance in the food industry and stay in the kitchen, the next step is executive chef — unless you're a sous chef in a kitchen with an open *chef de cuisine* position. If this is the case, you'll have to tackle the responsibilities of *chef de cuisine* before you're considered for executive chef. In smaller kitchens, however, the sous chef may certainly be offered a job as executive chef at some point. Don't expect to work one or two years as a sous chef and then be offered full reign of the kitchen, however. You need to put your time in and prove that you can create dishes and manage a staff before you're put in charge.

If you decide that you no longer wish to work in the kitchen at a restaurant, you can always take your knowledge of food and restaurants and become a manager in the front of the house. Knowing the ins and outs of the kitchen definitely makes you attractive to someone looking to hire an assistant manager, dining-room manager, or even maybe a general manager. For more information about management in the front of the house, see "Getting Acquainted with Staff in the Front of the House" later in this chapter.

Unions and associations

Sous chefs and *chefs de cuisine* have a better chance of being part of a union than executive chefs, but depending on the restaurant, they may or may not be included in one. The Hotel and Restaurant Employees Union (HREU) and the Service Employees International Union (SEIU) are a sous chef's best bet if she wishes to be in a union.

Sous chefs and *chefs de cuisine* can also join associations. They can be members of associations such as the ACF, International Hotel & Restaurant Association (IHRA), the Professional Chef's Association (PCA), and the World Association of Chef Societies (WACS). Chefs that belong to these associations receive newsletters with information about new equipment and ingredients entering the culinary field. They're invited to meetings, trade shows, and conferences sponsored by these associations. These meetings allow them to network with other chefs and make valuable connections.

Other kitchen personnel

We cannot stress this enough: Every kitchen is different. We list a number of common kitchen positions in this section, but not all of them will necessarily exist in the restaurants where you work. The number of men and women working stations on the line depends on the size of the kitchen and the volume of food the restaurant puts out on any given night. On a Friday or Saturday night, you may find that so many cooks are in the kitchen that moving is nearly impossible. The following Tuesday, you may find just yourself and the sous chef working on a handful of tickets every half hour or so.

Specialty chefs

If the restaurant's kitchen is big and busy enough, you may find that each station has its own supervisor. This supervisor, otherwise known as a *chef de partie,* is in charge of that particular station and the one to two cooks (or sometimes more) that work on the station each night. Depending on what the restaurant offers, you may work in a kitchen featuring any of the following *chefs de partie:*

- ✔ **Fish chef:** The fish chef, or the *poissonier,* prepares all fish dishes, including fish stocks and sauces for fish. The fish chef understands the anatomy of numerous types of fish and knows how to butcher a fish in such a way that multiple parts of it can be used for various dishes. However, if the kitchen employs a butcher, he may cut, trim, and debone the fish before it reaches the fish chef's station. In smaller kitchens, the responsibilities of a fish chef may fall to the sauté chef or the grill chef.

- ✔ **Fry chef:** The fry chef, or the *friturier,* is — you guessed it — in charge of all fried foods, which may be anything from calamari to French fries. In smaller kitchens, any line cook stationed near the fryer may be responsible for overseeing what is battered and fried.

Most kitchen-related injuries occur when dealing with the fryer, which can cause hot-oil burns. If you're working with the fryer, be sure to gently lower any frozen or battered foods into the hot oil. Dropping from above can create splashes that can burn the skin on your hands, arms, and even face. Hot oil is one of the reasons chefs wear coats with long sleeves, long pants, and closed-toe shoes.

Although every restaurant chef carries the scent of the food they've prepared home with them on their clothes and in their hair, the cook stuck with fryer duty experiences this most often. If you have a date after a shift with the fryer (or even near it!), we suggest bringing clean clothes to change into (and possibly some cologne or perfume) if you don't have time to go home and shower.

✔ **Grill chef:** The grill chef, or *grillardin,* prepares all grilled and broiled menu items. The grill chef is also responsible for making sauces for the items they cook. Steaks and burgers are two of the most popular items on menus today and both are the sole responsibility of the grill chef. Because of the sheer number of orders a grill chef and crew must handle at one time, grill chefs must be especially adept at multi-tasking. And it's absolutely necessary that grill chefs be able to tell when meat is done to the customer's preference (well, medium-well, medium, medium-rare, or rare). A grill station, like a fry station, is present in nearly every restaurant.

✔ **Pasta chef:** Pasta is offered in many restaurants as a side dish, appetizer, or standard entrée. Because of pasta's frequent appearances, the staff who work this station need to be able to multi-task and rely on their memories to know which ingredients belong in which pasta dishes. At this station, the pasta chef is also responsible for making sauces for the pasta dishes.

✔ **Pastry chef:** If the restaurant where you work doesn't receive its desserts from private bakeries, shops, or commissary kitchens, it may have a separate station for the executive pastry chef, or *pâtissier,* and pastry cooks. At this station, the pastry chefs and cooks prepare cakes, pies, candies, and even frozen or cold desserts. If a baker isn't present in the kitchen, a pastry chef or cook may also need to make the bread for service. For more information on what pastry chefs and bakers do, see Chapter 8.

✔ **Pizza chef:** If one of the most popular ingredients on your restaurant's menu is pizza, you may find a pizza chef on the employment roster. Sometimes pizza chefs are put on display in restaurants so customers can watch them knead and toss their dough and then litter it with a variety of delicious toppings. Today, pizza chefs not only cook traditional pizzas for lunch and dinner but also occasionally produce breakfast pizzas featuring eggs, sausage, and bacon and dessert pizzas topped with ingredients like whipped cream, chocolate sauce, and cherries.

✔ **Sauté chef:** One of the most important positions on the line is that of the sauté chef, or *saucier,* who prepares sautéed items and many sauces for various dishes. It's one of the busiest, yet most sought-after positions in the kitchen, because your placement at the sauté station shows the rest of the kitchen that you're capable of taking responsibility for multiple dishes and sauces while working at an extremely fast pace. This position is also challenging because many of the sauces that sauté chefs make can be prepared only after the order is placed.

Although sauté stations appear in nearly every restaurant, sauté chefs do not. Because of the importance of the position, sometimes sous chefs or even executive chefs take responsibility for this station.

✔ **Vegetable chef:** Depending on the size of the restaurant and its kitchen, a vegetable chef and cooks may have their own station on the line. A vegetable chef, or *entremetier,* is often responsible for more than just preparing vegetables for service, however. In many kitchens, vegetable chefs also make hot appetizers and soups. In larger restaurants that are able to support a more numerous staff, these responsibilities are split between two separate chefs: the *légumier,* who works only with the vegetables, and the soup cook, or *potager,* who prepares soups and stews.

Additional kitchen staff

If you haven't yet acquired the skill or education needed to be one of the *chefs de partie* described in the preceding section and aren't part of the management staff described in the following section, you can still play an important role in the kitchen. Plenty of other jobs exist, although some require restaurant experience. At some restaurants you may the following positions:

✔ **Lead cook:** The lead cook, who may also be called the head line cook or chef, is typically the senior-most person on the line in a kitchen where *chefs de partie* aren't employed. Although the lead cook doesn't have the authority of a sous chef, he still supervises fellow line cooks. The lead cook may even help train new cooks. If the lead chef knows the kitchen well, he may also act as a roundsman (see the later bullet).

✔ **Line cook:** Every restaurant employs a handful of line cooks in the kitchen. Line cooks may be assigned to particular stations, where they are trained by specialty chefs, or they may simply go where they are needed. They help prepare and cook all types of foods, from appetizers to entrées, soups, and salads. A line cook is an easily attainable entry-level position in most kitchens. If you're interested in working in fine-dining, you may need a few years of experience as a prep cook to land a position on the line. Apprenticeships and formal education may also help you get a job as a line cook in a prestigious restaurant.

✔ **Pantry chef:** The pantry cook is also known as the *cold-foods chef,* or the *garde-manger.* This chef is a specialty chef who works with cold foods used in cold appetizers, salads, and pâtés at a separate station. The pantry chef creates dressings and marinades and prepares cold meats. The pantry chef may even have a hand in creating cold desserts. If a restaurant doesn't have a butcher (see the later bullet), occasionally the pantry chef breaks down meat for other stations.

✔ **Prep cook:** If you know how to hold a knife and dice an onion, you can be a prep cook. This position, like that of a line cook, is entry-level and can get you started on the path to a successful culinary career. Prep cooks start their shifts earlier than line cooks because they have to prepare the food for the line cooks to use later when cooking food to order. They may make broths and soups, chop and store vegetables, and even clean or pound meats. In smaller kitchens, line cooks act as prep cooks. They're required to come in early to prep the food and stay late to cook it.

✔ **Roundsman:** Also called a *tournant* or a *swing cook,* the roundsman has the skills to cover any station in the kitchen as needed. A roundsman is familiar with every station, from sauté to pasta, grill to pantry. This is a highly coveted position in the kitchen and what most cooks who have a desire to move upward aspire to be.

A common misconception of the roundsman's capabilities is that the person in this position will struggle when placed at the pastry or baking station. Because baking and making desserts is a specialized job, you may not encounter many chefs who also like to bake, but this doesn't mean they won't or can't bake if they're asked to. Today, many chefs take additional certification courses in baking and pastry arts so they can tackle any challenge that comes their way. Roundsmen are respected because know their way around the entire kitchen — including the pastry station.

✔ **Butcher:** If the restaurant is large enough, the owner may choose to employ a butcher, or *boucher.* The butcher is in charge of breaking down meat, poultry, and occasionally fish for the line cooks to work with. On a slow night — or if one or more butchers are employed in one restaurant — the butcher may assist the chefs in breading the meat, if needed. (In smaller operations where a butcher is not a position in the kitchen, sauté chefs, fish chefs, and grill chefs break down their own meat.)

✔ *Commis:* The *commis,* or apprentice, is typically a "green" employee, meaning he has no prior experience in the kitchen. The *commis* studies under a particular station chef to learn the ropes for that station and may eventually move to a new station to learn more. He may prepare food for the station, keep the station clean, or simply observe. A *commis* may or may not be paid, but the true benefit is that jobs are frequently offered when the apprenticeship is over. For more about finding an apprenticeship that's right for you, see Chapter 3.

✔ *Communard:* Three meals a day are important for everyone — even people who work in the kitchen who might otherwise nibble on bits and pieces of food all day. In large restaurants, a *communard* may be employed to make the staff a meal, which is sometimes called the family meal. The *communard* prepares a large batch of food for employees in the front and back of the house to eat quickly on their breaks. In smaller restaurants, line cooks take turns making the staff meal throughout the week.

✔ **Dishwasher:** If you're looking for entry-level employment in a restaurant, you should have no problem landing a job as a dishwasher. Sure, it's not the most glamorous position in the kitchen (*that* job belongs to the sauté chef!), but it's easy and it pays. Other than being sure to scrub each item you receive (or sort them into the correct machines, depending on the kitchen), the only real requirements of a dishwasher are to keep a steady, fast pace and be gentle with the glassware. Every restaurant needs dishwashers.

If your dream is to become a chef but culinary school is not in your future, you can certainly begin as a dishwasher and work your way up a few rungs. If you're a dishwasher and you express an interest in making food to your coworkers, they may let you help prep when they're short-staffed. From prep work, you can easily be promoted to a spot on the line. You just need to show an interest in learning to cook and demonstrate your dedication to the restaurant by being punctual and doing high-quality work.

✔ **Expediter:** The expediter is the first person to see tickets with customer's orders when they come in from the dining room and the last person to work with the dishes before they leave the kitchen. This staff member is sometimes referred to as the announcer, or *aboyeur.* When expediters receive the tickets, they read the items to the station chefs who must cook the food. After the food is plated, expediters may wipe and garnish the plates so they look perfect when the servers come to pick them up. In smaller kitchens, the lead cook, sous chef, *chef de cuisine,* or even executive chef may take charge of the expeditor's duties.

Some restaurants have a large back room or even a dining hall where they host large receptions, private parties, and community meetings and events. In this case, a special-events staff containing a banquet chef, banquet manager, or caterer may also be on the restaurant's payroll. If you're interested in cooking for a crowd, see Chapter 6, which addresses hotel and spa work, or see Chapter 7 for more information on becoming or working for a caterer.

Getting Acquainted with Staff in the Front of the House

Employees who work in the dining room of a restaurant are just as important as those who work in the kitchen. In fact, some people in the industry may argue that dining-room employees are so important they can make or break an entire restaurant. If your server isn't friendly, can't explain the specials, and forgets to look in on you, will you want to come back to that restaurant? Even if the food is the best you've ever eaten, horrible service can truly ruin your entire experience. Front of the house employees need to be friendly, efficient, and courteous at all times.

Even though they don't prepare the food, dining-room workers are still responsible for taking food orders, delivering the food, and receiving feedback about the food. Hosts, servers, bussers, and managers alike deserve credit for the jobs they do. No one ever said customer service was easy.

General manager

General managers (GM) are like the executive chefs of dining rooms, and occasionally they oversee entire restaurants. The GM is the face of the establishment, which means that the general manager represents the restaurant to the media and to the restaurant's guests. When customers want to complement the service or critique a dish, they do their best to hunt down the GM, who they believe will handle all their problems. A GM works with dining-room staff to ensure that customer service is the best it can be, which can only happen if the GM also works closely with the executive chef. If the kitchen is organized and its execution is flawless, then chances are service at the front of the house is also exceptional.

In a restaurant, a GM has a hand in scheduling events, hiring and firing dining-room staff (and sometimes even kitchen staff), training dining-room staff, and developing and sticking to a budget for the restaurant. Although the GM's role in overseeing the smooth operation of wait staff is pretty obvious, you may not know that the GM also works closely with sommeliers, bartenders, and even food and beverage directors (administrators who provide a link from the executive chef to food vendors and vice versa). When they aren't supervising dining-room operations, GMs may also help carry trays of food to large tables or may speak to customers about their dining experience.

Personality traits

Staying organized and being able to multi-task are two key characteristics possessed by successful GMs. Problem-solving ability is also key. A good GM knows what's going on in the kitchen and in the dining room at all times. If the window (where food ready to be served waits) is backed up, the GM must know why. If the dining-room manager can't resolve an issue with a customer, the GM needs to be able to offer a solution. If the executive chef ever needs to leave the kitchen for an emergency, the GM needs to be able to step in and help out the kitchen crew by expediting or possibly even placing the finishing garnishes on a few plates. In general, GMs need to be able to keep cool in stressful situations and handle any problems that may arise.

Whereas executive chefs track how much money is spent on kitchen items, GMs monitor how much money the dining room is spending and making. Because they establish and must adhere to strict budgets, GMs must be confident managing money. They're responsible for seeing that bills and staff are paid on time and that the operation stays afloat.

Salaries

According to PayScale.com, general manager salaries range from $32,000 to $85,000 per year, depending on the size and location of the restaurant. The more upscale the restaurant, the more money its GM makes. Also, the more management experience GMs have in their back pocket, the better their pay is. Similar to executive chefs, GMs earn a larger salary than most other employees in the restaurant business because they typically work 60 to 70 hours a week.

Education and training

To become a general manager, you don't necessarily have to go to school or obtain a degree — but it doesn't hurt. If you complete a program related to hotel and restaurant management at a two- or four-year school anywhere in the country, you may reach the top position of GM more quickly than if you don't attend school at all. Even a business or general-management degree may help you land a position faster.

If you don't complete a degree, the way to become a GM is by paying your dues. Positions in the dining room are similar to positions in the kitchen — room for advancement always exists when you gain enough experience. You can start as a member of the wait staff and receive a promotion to floor manager or dining-room manager. From there, if you show your dedication to the company, you may reach the position of assistant general manager. At that point, the position of GM is within your reach. All you have to do is prove yourself.

Advancement prospects

Unless you have plans to acquire ownership in a restaurant after you become a GM, you've pretty much hit the top of the ranks. Sometimes executive chefs may move out of the kitchen to become a GM, but not many GMs enroll in culinary school so they can be part of the kitchen staff. Instead, GMs may open their own restaurant or may apply for a position managing a hotel or bed and breakfast. They may also choose to leave food service and teach at a community college or vocational school. For more information on becoming a culinary instructor, see Chapter 14.

Unions and associations

Typically, general managers at restaurants don't belong to unions. Instead, they may manage a unionized staff. Although they don't work under the protection of unions, they may still join associations such as the Hospitality Asset Managers Association (HAMA) and the Hospitality Sales and Marketing Association International (HSMAI). GMs who join associations receive the latest information about developments in the food and beverage industry. They may be invited to attend events with other GMs from their region, which allows them to assess their competitors or work together to further their fields.

Dining-room manager

Imagine you're a server and one of your customers has been dissatisfied with his food and service all night. When you bring him his check, he doesn't approve of the amount and immediately asks to see your manager. Enter the dining-room manager.

If the GM is the "executive chef" of the dining room, then the dining-room manager is the sous chef in this analogy. Like the way the sous chef oversees the entire kitchen staff and worries about the quality of food, the dining-room manager, also called the *maître d'hôtel* or *maitre d'*, supervises the entire dining-room staff and focuses her attention on the quality of service.

Although the dining-room manager reports directly to the GM, she still has authority over the floor supervisors, servers, hosts, food runners, and bussers. The dining-room manager may also work with the bartenders. Depending on the restaurant, the dining-room manager may be responsible for hiring and firing, training, and creating schedules for the front-of-the-house staff. Even though dining-room managers may receive feedback about the quality of food coming from the kitchen, they don't typically have a say in what's going on in the back of the house.

Personality traits

To be a good dining-room manager, you must be organized and able to think on your feet. If an issue arises in the dining room, you must handle it respectfully. Aside from ensuring that service is nearly flawless, a dining-room manager's main goal should be to run the dining room without the GM's involvement whenever possible. The GM has bigger fish to fry and shouldn't be bothered about a customer at table 53 who says her fries are cold.

To maintain control over the staff, a dining-room manager has to be strong-willed and tough. She needs to be able to discipline staff members who break the rules or mistreat customers. But a dining-room manager also needs to be approachable so customers and wait staff who genuinely need her assistance aren't afraid to speak with her.

Salaries

Salaries for dining-room managers are typically between $32,000 and $45,000, according to PayScale.com, with the average being approximately $37,000. However, salary depends heavily on the type of restaurant. In a fine-dining restaurant, dining-room managers may stand to make double (or even triple) the average amount. In a family-style restaurant that's part of a nationwide chain, a dining-room manager probably makes less than the average salary for this position. The location and size of the restaurant also affect the dining-room manager's salary immensely.

Education and training

As always, the more experience you have, the easier it is to land a job near the top of the totem pole. You don't need to go to school to become a dining-room manager, but if you don't want to work your way up from busser or server, then you should consider formal schooling. A business degree, management degree, or even a hotel-and-restaurant degree can help you reach this position without spending years at the bottom of the ranks.

Although as a dining-room manager you don't necessarily have anything to do with the food in a restaurant, you should still understand how the kitchen works. A dining-room manager who is aware of how long it takes to cook a medium steak and who knows the ingredients in the weekend special is more valuable and helpful than one who doesn't.

Advancement prospects

After you prove yourself in the role of dining-room manager, you may be able to apply for positions such as assistant general manager or even general manager of a restaurant. To reach the position of GM, however, you have to put in a few years as a dining-room manager first.

Unions and associations

Depending on the restaurant, you may belong to UNITE HERE, a union for employees in the food service industry, along with employees who work in warehouses and casinos. Because the role of a dining-room manager is supervisory, however, you may find that you're not protected under a union. You can still join associations such as Hospitality Asset Managers Association (HAMA) and the Hospitality Sales and Marketing Association International (HSMAI). Joining an association ensures that dining-room managers always know about upcoming events in the industry, such as conferences and trade shows. They also receive updates about the industry's newest trends.

Working on the inside

If your dream is to work in the food industry but you don't necessarily want to cook or serve the food, you may consider trying to work your way into restaurant administration. In such a position, you may work in an office and manage a restaurant without actually setting foot in the dining room or in the kitchen. Of course, occasionally visiting these areas to witness the operation of the business for yourself is a good idea, but you won't ever have to boil water, fry onion rings, or refill a customer's glass.

Restaurant administration isn't considered entry-level. You most likely will have to work in a restaurant for a few years first, either in the kitchen or in the front of the house. After you demonstrate a clear understanding of how a restaurant works, you may be able to apply for an administrative position. Perhaps someday you may have the money to open your own restaurant, which would automatically make you part of the administration.

Administrative restaurant positions include, but are not limited to, the following:

- **Accountant:** This person records and inspects financial accounts for the restaurant.

- **Accounts receivable/payable staff:** This team keeps track of how much money the business owes and how much money they will receive.

- **Controller:** The controller is a senior member of the accounting staff who oversees all aspects of accounting, financial reporting, and payroll.

- **Director of purchasing:** This person manages the purchasing staff and is responsible for coordinating and purchasing needed inventory and supplies.

- **Facilities manager:** In large restaurants, the facilities manager deals with issues within the building or grounds that require maintenance.

- **Food and beverage director:** This person works with executive chefs and sommeliers to order/purchase the ingredients needed to create menu items. Food and beverage directors must be knowledgeable of wines, beers, spirits, and other beverages because they're normally tasked with purchasing these items for their restaurants. See Chapter 11 for more information about this position.

- **Human resources manager:** This person handles personnel matters such as hiring, position assignment, training, benefits, and compensation.

- **Public relations/marketing manager:** This person is in charge of all public relations, marketing, and advertising for the restaurant. They may design flyers, contact local media for coverage, book musical acts/guests, or plan events taking place at the restaurant. For more information about public relations and marketing professionals in the culinary industry, check out Chapter 13.

- **Restaurant consultant:** Consultants are hired by restaurant owners to advise on issues such as interior design, menu development, human resources, and operations management.

Other dining-room personnel

When famed French chef Escoffier created the kitchen brigade in the mid-1800s, he also kept dining-room service in mind. His solution to the hustle, bustle, and disorganization of the dining-room was a system called the *dining-room brigade*. Similar to the kitchen brigade, the dining-room brigade placed authoritative positions at the top of the rankings and then let the power trickle down to others. At the top, of course, is the general manager (GM), followed by the dining-room manager. Following are some of the other positions you may find in the dining-room brigade:

- ✔ **Floor manager/supervisor:** Depending on the size of the restaurant, you may find a floor manager/supervisor in the dining room. This person ranks below a dining-room manager and is only responsible for supervising the wait staff, which includes the head server, food runners, bussers, and servers. Sometimes a person in this position may be referred to as *assistant dining-room manager.*

- ✔ **Sommeliers:** At fine-dining restaurants, wine stewards, or *sommeliers,* work with the executive chef to create wine lists and select wines to pair with the courses on the menu. In some situations, a sommelier may teach customers about the wine they're drinking with their dinners. He typically gives customers a short history lesson about where the wine was made and how old it is as he pours the glasses. For more information about sommeliers, see Chapter 11.

- ✔ **Head server:** This position in the dining room is similar to the lead cook's position in the kitchen. The head server, or *chef de salle,* typically earns the position after many years of service. In larger restaurants, the head server is in charge of the dining room to some degree. Although he doesn't have authority equal to that of the dining-room manager or floor supervisor, he may still manage the staff. In smaller restaurants, this position may not exist.

- ✔ **Servers (wait staff):** Servers are the heart of the dining room, yet they're typically underappreciated by restaurant employees and customers alike. Without their service, every restaurant would be similar to a fast-food restaurant or a buffet: Customers would have to serve themselves, fetch their own beverages, and clean their own messes. They would also have to keep track of their own checks. Waiters are on the front lines of the battle between customers and staff — if a customer isn't happy, guess who gets to deal with it? Although the job may be challenging at times, it's an easily attainable entry-level position in family-style and some casual-dining restaurants. If you want to be a server in a fine-dining restaurant, however, you'll need many years of service experience under your belt.

✔ **Bartenders:** Restaurants employ bartenders who prepare alcoholic and nonalcoholic beverages for guests who may be waiting for a table, at the bar, or seated and having a meal. Sometimes bartenders may be required to help with after-hours cleaning.

✔ **Host:** The host is the first person customers see when they walk through the doors of a restaurant. The host greets the customers, lets them know if they will have to wait for a table, and then assigns a server and a table. Hosts may also be responsible for answering the restaurant's phones and taking reservations. Hosts are typically considered entry-level positions.

✔ **Food runner:** On a busy night, sometimes servers need assistance getting the food to the table before it dries out or becomes cold, which is where food runners come in handy. These employees simply take the food to the table when it's ready to go. This position is entry-level. In smaller restaurants, sometimes servers take additional shifts each week in which they solely move the food.

✔ **Bussers:** Also sometimes called *back waiters,* bussers are responsible for clearing tables after customers have finished dining and preparing them for the next guests. In some restaurants, bussers dress in uniforms similar to servers', refill glasses of wine and water, and remove finished plates between courses. You can typically get a job as a busser without any previous restaurant experience.

Chapter 6

Living the Good Life: Working in Hotels, Resorts, and Spas

In This Chapter

▶ Finding out what to expect in hotel and resort kitchens

▶ Distinguishing the many roles of kitchen and dining-room employees at hotels and resorts

▶ Discovering the different setup in spa kitchens

▶ Exploring the possibilities for work in a spa

Most people enjoy an occasional escape from their busy lives. They may visit a nearby spa or jet off to another country. Regardless of how far they trek, customers at hotels, resorts, and spas expect to be pampered. When it comes to food, they want the best of the best. If you work in a kitchen at such a place, it's your job to prepare food that meets their high expectations.

In this chapter, you find information on popular positions offered in kitchens or dining rooms at hotels, resorts, and spas. From executive chef to room-service staff, we cover all the bases so you know what to expect if you wish to enter this area of the industry. Because spas offer additional services — such as an abundance of healthy foods and personalized care — we discuss these work environments independently in the second half of this chapter.

Seeing What Working in a Hotel or Resort Is Like

Hotels and resorts range in size, depending on their location and the services they offer. Therefore, the kitchens in these arenas also fluctuate in size. If you work at a petite hotel that customers generally frequent for only a night or two, your kitchen is going to be quite small because the services offered are usually only room-service related. However, if you work in a very large hotel or one that is situated within a resort, you may find that your hotel has multiple dining facilities. These may include chain restaurants, banquet halls, and buffets. In this case, you may encounter one of two set ups: one very large kitchen, or multiple kitchens to suit each separate facility.

In hotels with one large kitchen, the kitchen must accommodate many cooks responsible for making food for the resort's restaurants, bars, banquet halls, buffet lines, and room service. The larger the hotel, the larger the kitchen and the more people needed to staff it.

You can typically find hotels and resorts that have multiple kitchens in larger cities, such as Miami or Las Vegas, where many popular hotels, casinos, and destination resorts are located. Depending on the hours of operation and the services offered at a specific hotel or resort (think blackjack tables, swimming pools, spas, and theaters), some of these kitchens may stay open to serve patrons round-the-clock. The pace of the kitchen may slow between 2 a.m. and 6 a.m. in some areas; however, if the city where you're employed never sleeps, you shouldn't expect to, either!

Because many hotels are open 24 hours a day, seven days a week, you should be prepared to work at night — and sometimes overnight — as well as on the weekends and on holidays. Although some restaurants in hotels close between 11:00 p.m. and 2:00 a.m., depending on the location, the hotel or resort's main kitchen remains open all night. Typically, hotel and resort kitchen and dining-room employees work 50 to 70 hours a week, sometimes up to 14 hours a day. So if you're hoping to land a culinary job in the hotel industry, buy comfy shoes. You'll need them.

Some resorts may be open for business seasonally, which allows for some flexibility in year-round work experience because you may work fewer days (or sometimes no days at all) when business slows. If you're interested in working 52 weeks a year but have your sights set on working at a destination resort, consider changing it up by season: Find a job at a tropical resort for the busy summer season and then head for the mountains and ski resorts for the winter.

Many large resorts rely on (or have their own!) commissary kitchens to produce large quantities of products that are commonly used in several kitchens in hotel or resorts, such as soups, sauces, and prepared vegetables. As we discuss in Chapter 5, commissary kitchens produce mass quantities of food that may be partially cooked and then frozen before being shipped to other kitchens where the cooking process is completed. For cooks in kitchens that receive commissary goods, this process makes life on the line much easier.

Making food for many people in many different areas

Your responsibilities as a cook or a chef at a hotel or a resort may range from simple room service to preparing thousands of dishes for banquets and wedding parties. Sometimes hotels have one large kitchen that enables the staff to simultaneously accomplish multiple feats; butchering, catering, and pastry and dessert production sometimes take place within the same kitchen at the same time. In these kitchens, cooks may prepare meals for the hotel or resort's restaurant, fill room-service requests, and make food for hungry bar patrons. And employees in these kitchens may occasionally need to fulfill responsibilities for two unrelated events. For example, the sous chef or executive chef may ask a prep cook to make 30 pounds of mashed potatoes for a private party in the banquet hall while cooks on the line continue to make the food requested on the tickets from the restaurant.

To avoid the hassle that comes with preparing all food items on-site, sometimes executive chefs make arrangements with commissary kitchens so the prep work is completed elsewhere. Bringing in foods that are already partially prepared allows the kitchen employees time to finish and plate each dish before service.

If you work in a restaurant in a hotel or casino in a city as popular as Las Vegas, however, you will likely work only for the restaurant that employs you. Hotels such as the MGM Grand and the Bellagio in Las Vegas house multiple kitchens for the numerous fine-dining restaurants, cafés, and specialty shops located within their vast floor plans. These hotels may also have separate kitchens where staff works to prepare food for meetings, banquets, buffets, and even room service. Depending on the hotel and the services it offers, you may never be asked to prepare food for events or parties in these different settings.

If you work in a hotel kitchen, one of your responsibilities may be to prepare food for the staff. Kitchens in these arenas are typically very stressful, fast-paced environments. Staff members need to be at their stations every minute, because you never know when or what a customer is going to order. Due to these high demands, kitchen staff and even dining-room staff sometimes find taking a break impossible. Being busy doesn't mean that they can't eat when they're hungry, however. Every day, a cook or chef on the line is assigned the task of making food that the staff can quickly eat when business lulls. This food may be referred to as staff meal, family meal, or *communard*. In many of today's fine-dining restaurants, cooks who are new to the kitchen or the profession in general are given this task to complete on a daily basis.

The history of hotel food service

In centuries past, hotels used to offer only *table d'hôtes,* or complete meals. Hotel customers couldn't change the menu or request other foods; instead, they ate what they received. Although cooks were making elaborate dishes in royal households at the time, many restaurant and hotel kitchens in the 1700s and 1800s didn't have the equipment or funds to offer intricate or personalized meals to their customers. Hotel cooks kept their approaches to preparing food for their customers simple and refined.

Everything changed when the Savoy Hotel opened in London in 1898. Under the supervision and direction of César Ritz and Georges-Auguste Escoffier, the Savoy altered its menus, switching from options set in stone to *á la carte,* or individually priced options.

The Savoy's new approach to food service was so well received that other hotels quickly followed suit, and the rest is history.

Understanding kitchen structure

The organization of kitchen staff in hotels and resorts is similar to that of restaurants (discussed in Chapter 5). The hierarchy is simple: Executive chefs run the show, the *chefs de cuisine* and sous chefs help them do so, and a variety of other chefs and cooks work the lines. As discussed in Chapter 5, these chefs may hold titles, such as *entremetier, tourant,* and *garde manger.* (In English, these terms respectively mean *vegetable prep cook, roundsman,* and *cold foods/pantry cook.*) If desserts and pastries are prepared in-house, you may find an executive pastry chef and pastry chefs and cooks in a designated area of your kitchen, as well.

People who land jobs in hotel and resort kitchens deal with hotel or resort managers in addition to the executive chef. Although managers don't have authority over the menu, the executive chef must consider their input, because they're in the front of the house and hear what their customers have to say firsthand. Managers at hotels or resorts have similar responsibilities to dining-room managers in restaurants and may be floor managers or supervisors who work closely with the dining-room staff (wait staff, runners, bussers, sommeliers, and so on), or they may be general managers who move between the kitchen and the front of the house with instructions, reminders, and demands.

Getting Acquainted with the Hotel and Resort Staff

Restaurant staffs comprise many different people fulfilling various responsibilities. At a hotel and resort featuring multiple kitchens for entirely different events, the number of people needed for the hotel or resort to successfully function is larger than that for a restaurant. Some hotels need more help than others. The positions listed in this section describe the head honchos employed in hotels and resorts around the world.

Every hotel and resort is different, so some of the positions discussed in this chapter may not exist at your particular establishment. In smaller operations, chefs often double as management and have complete authority over the kitchen and the dining-room staff. At larger venues, separate managers are more common. In addition, sometimes the general manager or executive chef is also the owner of the operation. In such a case, general managers have absolute control over their hotels or resorts.

Executive chef a la hotel

As you already know, every kitchen needs an executive chef. If a hotel has one kitchen, then the executive chef is in charge of all food production in that hotel. If the hotel has multiple kitchens, then each kitchen most likely has its own executive, or head, chef. On average, executive chefs work 10 to 12 hours each day, five to six (and sometimes seven!) days a week.

The executive chef's responsibilities when employed at a hotel or resort include planning meals and menus, ordering supplies, hiring and training staff, overseeing the quality of food leaving the kitchen, assigning tasks, and motivating and managing staff. Executive chefs' responsibilities are mainly managerial; they rarely cook in the kitchen alongside the staff. The executive chef may put finishing touches on the plates or play the role of expeditor, reading the tickets and managing what dishes are needed for which tables.

Personality traits

Executive chefs at hotels and resorts must be confident and patient if they are to handle an entire kitchen staff in a fast-paced and stressful environment. They must also be creative and unafraid to take risks, because they're the main men and women working on the menus for their hotels or resorts. Executive chefs must also know how to delegate responsibilities. To do this, they must be confident that the team they hire and train will perform to high standards.

Executive chefs who achieve success in the culinary industry are those men and women who have the ability to identify and admit their own weaknesses. After they recognize the techniques or cuisines where they may personally falter, executive chefs need to be smart enough to hire a team of people who can compensate for their shortcomings. This lineup helps balance or offset the executive chef's personality traits and abilities, or lack thereof.

If a hotel or resort doesn't have a general manager, the executive chef must also be personable, because he or she may often have to speak with not only the dining room staff but also the customers. Sometimes executive chefs who have control over the front of the house may also have a say in the decor or theme of the dining area; therefore, it would benefit these chefs to have an eye for style and an understanding of the types of customers their restaurants wish to attract.

The ability to speak with people is also important for executive chefs who place orders with vendors such as restaurant supply salespeople and local food artisans. These chefs must be easy to work with and speak to, because vendors who perceive chefs to be angry, difficult, or overwhelming may choose to break their partnership with the kitchen. Executive chefs need these vendors to work closely with and for them because occasionally chefs may need a particular item that only a specific vendor can offer.

Executive chefs should also be good at math — not only to know what measurements of ingredients are needed in recipes but also to be able to tell if the kitchen's costs are outweighing its profits. After all, kitchens are businesses, and executive chefs must be organized and able to keep accurate records of what they spend and where they spend it.

Salaries

According to a survey performed by the American Hotel and Lodging Association (AH&LA), executive chefs employed at hotels or resorts can make approximately $65,000 annually. Of course, this number depends on the location and size of the hotel. An executive chef at a standard hotel may make between $40,000 and $80,000 each year.

An executive chef whose responsibilities include many tasks that a hotel manager typically completes may earn a higher salary.

Education and training

Though many executive chefs at hotels and resorts across the nation have a bachelor's degree or higher, many others have completed certifications, attained associate's degrees, or taken courses at technical schools that similarly prepared them for their role. Men and women typically make it to the position of head or executive chef due to kitchen experience. Executive chefs in hotel and resort kitchens most often have prior experience working in hotels or at resorts before they apply for the top position. Depending on the size of the operation and its reputation, some hotels require more than ten years of experience for this position.

Having a basic understanding of word processing and spreadsheet applications and knowledge of hospitality accounting will also help you land a job as an executive chef. You should also know how to read profit and loss (income) statements.

Advancement prospects

Because executive chefs are at the top of the hierarchy, they don't have much room for advancement — in the kitchen, anyway. Some executive chefs may leave their responsibilities in the kitchen to become hotel managers. They may also become consultants, offer private culinary training, or land a job in a research and development kitchen. Others may leave the hotel industry altogether and open their own restaurant so they can be their own bosses. See Chapter 18 for more information about becoming a culinary entrepreneur.

Unions and associations

Depending on the location of the hotel or resort in which you work, executive chefs may or may not be part of a union. More than likely, when you reach the level of executive chef, you'll find that you cannot be represented by a union, because you're then considered part of the management team. As an executive chef, you are far more likely to be defending yourself and your practices against the union than being supported by one.

Although you may not be part of a union, you should still be familiar with what they do — after all, if you work in a large city like New York or Las Vegas, many of your employees will be unionized. If your workers come into conflict with their superiors, union representatives will fight on their behalf. Your employees may belong to the Hotel Employees and Restaurant Employees International Union (HEREIU) or the Service Employees International Union (SEIU).

Even though you may not be part of a union as an executive chef, you can still join many culinary associations. These include the American Culinary Federation (ACF), the International Association of Culinary Professionals (IACP), and the Women Chef and Restaurateurs (WCR). Joining these associations helps executive chefs promote their business, stay up-to-date with new advancements in the industry, and network with chefs from around the world.

General manager

A hotel restaurant's general manager (GM) has responsibilities that are similar to that of an executive chef's, except that a GM doesn't directly deal with the food. A GM schedules events, hires and fires, trains the front-of-the-house staff, and creates and adheres to a budget for the establishment.

A GM works with many people to ensure that customer service is top-notch. In most cases, the manager and the executive chef work hand-in-hand to ensure the kitchen and the front of the house are organized and that execution is nearly flawless. The GM oversees service in the dining room, while the executive chef takes responsibility for the kitchen staff. In these establishments, the GM and the executive chef stand on equal ground. Occasionally, a GM may supervise the entire hotel, including all restaurants and their employees in the dining room and the kitchen — even the executive chef. However, if the hotel or resort has multiple restaurants, each restaurant typically has its own GM. A GM also works closely with the sommeliers, bartenders, and food and beverage directors.

Personality traits

Unlike an executive chef, a GM doesn't necessarily need to know the ins and outs of food preparation. The GM must instead know how to read customers' reactions to food. They must also be able to perceive the morale of the entire establishment; if the staff members aren't happy with the food or the service, then chances are the customers won't be, either. GMs must be personable and open to new ideas and suggestions, because they'll surely receive many of them while on the job. Whereas the executive chef is the face of the kitchen, the GM typically represents the entire establishment. A GM moves about the dining-room floor with the wait staff, sometimes even carrying out a plate or two when the window is backed up.

GMs need to be organized and able to micromanage. Although they typically create shifts and schedules for only the dining-room staff, they may also be responsible for overseeing the scheduling of the kitchen staff. They may occasionally step in for the executive chef in emergency situations. This doesn't mean that they have to cook, however. Instead, they may oversee the quality of plates leaving the kitchen or even expedite in sticky and stressful situations. GMs need to be able to think on their toes and perform well under pressure. Beyond all else, the ability to stay calm, cool, and collected will help a person in this position find success.

GMs are part of the executive-management team at most hotels and resorts, so they also need to be confident in their money management. As previously mentioned, GMs typically work with budgets. Their budgets differ from those of executive chefs. An executive chef worries about the costs of food and labor, while a GM focuses on bill payment, staff payment, marketing, and the finances of the operation as a whole.

Salaries

According to PayScale.com, general managers' salaries range from $38,000 to $76,000 per year depending on the size and location of the hotel or resort. However, a GM working for a luxury hotel or resort with upscale restaurants or private clubs may earn up to $300,000 each year. And on average, GMs in larger hotels in big cities earn between $100,000 and $160,000 each year. GMs at smaller hotels that host chain restaurants and smaller kitchens may make up to $55,000 a year. Like executive chefs, GMs earn a large salary because they typically work 60 to 70 hours a week.

Education and training

To reach the position of GM at a hotel or resort, you may or may not need a formal education. Many GMs have worked their way up from wait staff to floor manager, maitre d' to assistant manager, and finally to GM. At some establishments, you need only a high-school diploma and many, many years of experience to reach the level of GM.

If you wish to start at (or as close as possible to) the top, consider formal schooling. Many two- and four-year schools across the country offer associate's and bachelor's degrees in hotel and restaurant management. You may also attain this role in a hotel or resort if you possess a business or general-management degree. Even with a degree, however, expect a lower salary if you enter the field as a manager-in-training — especially if you decide to work for a chain establishment. After you complete the training and prove yourself worthy, you should see an increase in funds and responsibilities.

Your best bet to landing a job as a GM is to have both education and experience. Go to school, build your résumé, and then show them what you can do.

Advancement prospects

As with executive chefs, few positions exist in a hotel or resort higher than GM. Although the executive chef may branch into management positions, very rarely do GMs decide to either return to or take a shot at a cooking position in a kitchen. Instead, GMs may choose to start their own restaurant, bed and breakfast, or hotel or leave the industry altogether to teach at community colleges or vocational schools. See Chapter 14 for more information about becoming a culinary instructor.

Unions and associations

Typically, hotel managers don't belong to unions. Instead, they may manage a unionized staff. However, they may join associations such as the American Hotel & Lodging Association (AH&LA), Hospitality Asset Managers Association (HAMA), and the Hospitality Sales and Marketing Association International (HSMAI). These associations allow managers to network and make connections to numerous hotels around the world. Associations also provide their members with information that keeps them up-to-date on the ever-evolving culinary world.

Head banquet chef

Hotels and resorts that host many conventions, wedding receptions, formal dances, meetings, awards dinners, and other functions often feature one or more banquet halls. These halls normally have their own kitchens, as well as their own dining-room staff and chefs. If you're interested in being in charge of feeding a large number of people an even larger amount of food, you may want to work toward becoming a head banquet chef.

If you're employed in a kitchen that serves only a small banquet hall, you'll find that the head banquet chef is the person in charge of nearly everything. Head banquet chefs meet with event planners and their clients, design and revise menus, and help their staff (in the kitchen and in the dining room) during prep and service.

Bigger banquet halls also have their own kitchens where head banquet chefs and their kitchen staff of chefs, cooks, and dishwashers work. If the hall is large enough and has the budget to do so, a banquet manager may also work there. The banquet manager splits the management responsibilities with the head banquet chef, just as a dining-room or general manager works with an executive chef in a hotel restaurant. The banquet manager meets with event planners and clients, takes their requests and ideas to the head banquet chef, and then presents a menu to the clients. Because the banquet manager works closely with the event planner and the dining-room staff, the head banquet chef has more time to work with the food and kitchen staff. For more information on banquet managers, see the "Banquet manager" section later in this chapter.

Things may get a bit confusing in the banquet world if you work in a large kitchen that handles food for restaurants and banquets at the same time. In cases where the banquet staff and the restaurant staff share a kitchen, the executive chef supervises the entire kitchen — including the head banquet chef and his staff. The head banquet chef is then ranked alongside *chefs de partie,* or station supervisors. The head banquet chef follows the executive chef's orders but also manages all the food needed for events in the banquet hall.

No matter where the head banquet chef and his staff are situated in a hotel or resort, their main priority is to produce high-quality food. From the get-go, banquet chefs may produce a list of standard items their clients can choose from to form the menus for their events. The dishes a banquet chef offers may depend on the season in which the event is taking place. These items must also be appropriate for banquet-style events — in other words, they need to be able to be produced in large batches and then chilled or kept warm until service. Most banquet chefs allow their clients to choose from particular meats, vegetables, and side dishes. They also work with their clients to ensure all dietary needs, if any, are met. If clients want particular items that aren't listed on the menu (such as something gourmet like truffles or relaxed and simple like cheeseburgers), chefs may choose to fulfill these wishes — but only for a price.

If you want to be a head banquet chef, you'll need to know when to bargain and when to put your foot down when working with your clients, event planners, banquet managers, and even banquet salespeople. These people are generally not trained in the culinary arts; therefore, they may not understand that selling events and menus may sometimes be implausible due to the seasonality, availability, and value of particular items.

Personality traits

Head banquet chefs have to be organized and able to multi-task. These qualities are extremely important because of the nature of banquet cooking. Large amounts of food need to be ready at the same time. In restaurants, several tickets for tables come in at a time. You have time to read the ticket, understand what is needed, and begin cooking. In a banquet hall, you know beforehand that every person at every table needs a plate for every course. If tickets were involved, you'd surely go insane.

Head banquet chefs, like executive chefs, must also have an eye for detail. They must make sure that every plate that leaves the kitchen should be perfect — in both appearance and taste. Sauces shouldn't be laid on the plate until they're tasted, and plates shouldn't leave the kitchen unless they're wiped clean and garnished appropriately.

Understanding how to best manage your time is another important trait to possess if you wish to be a head banquet chef. Banquet service should follow a timeline; each course has a designated time slot in which it should be served. It's up to banquet chefs to coordinate with the waiters and managers to ensure that the food is ready at the exact time it needs to be.

A head banquet chef, especially one who is also wearing the hat of the banquet manager, must also possess the skills to coordinate tasks between the kitchen and dining room staffs. Banquet chefs must be able to give orders to both staffs to ensure the food is ready when the wait staff arrives to take the plates. They must also stay up-to-date on the events in the dining room; as soon as one course is complete, the next course must be ready.

Like executive chefs, head banquet chefs must know how to crunch numbers and work within a budget. They must be aware of how many guests they must feed and how much food they must purchase and prepare for the event. They must also come up with a fair price for their services — they need to charge their customers enough that the banquet hall makes a profit, but not so much that customers refuse to return or sing the banquet hall's praises. Banquet chefs need to know how to buy in bulk and get the best deals so they can save money and feed the masses.

Head banquet chefs must also be personable, because they often meet the hosts of fundraisers, functions, and conventions before the event. They must listen to what the host wants and then consult their budgets and other resources to see if they can meet the host's demands.

Flexibility is a necessary trait for head banquet chefs, especially when they deal directly with their clients. When banquet chefs create a menu, they must be able to change it on the fly when their clients call and ask for additional vegetables or different colors on the cake. Banquet chefs must also be able to see into the future and prepare for any additions to the number of guests at the function.

Salaries

Because the job of a head banquet chef is not entry-level and requires experience and management skills, the average salary for this position is $52,000, but it can range generally from $40,000 to $60,000. Like an executive chef who doubles as a general manager, a banquet chef who also acts as banquet manager may receive a higher salary. The location and size of the hotel and resort may also affect your salary if you become a head banquet chef.

Education and training

In addition to leadership and organization skills, you need ample experience to land a job as a head banquet chef at a hotel or resort. This experience may come from a variety of areas, however. You may have worked for a small catering company, a country club, a restaurant with a private backroom, or really anywhere involving high-volume cooking. For information about volume cooking and catering, see Chapter 7.

Although volume cooking and managerial experience are important to land a job as a head banquet chef, you may also need some formal education. Associate's or bachelor's degrees in the culinary arts from any two- or four-year college are ideal. Completing a technical or vocational school program may also suffice. Sometimes, if you have enough experience, a high-school diploma may be acceptable.

Advancement prospects

After spending a few years as a head banquet chef, you may decide to shoot for a management position. Many banquet chefs become banquet managers or even assistant or general managers. If you work at a facility where the banquet staff and restaurant staff share a kitchen, you may be able to advance to executive chef so you could manage the entire kitchen staff, including banquet staff. If you're a head banquet chef of a dining hall but are interested in being an executive chef of a hotel kitchen, your experience as a leader in a banquet kitchen should assist you in attaining this position.

You may also opt to leave the hotel-and-resort industry and start your own banquet or catering company. The connections you make as a head banquet chef will surely help you get a new business off the ground. For more information on catering, see Chapter 7. If you think you're interested in starting your own business, turn ahead to Chapter 18.

Unions and associations

If you're employed as a banquet chef in a hotel or resort in a large city, your kitchen may be part of a union. If you hold a management position, however, you most likely won't be able to join a union. Like executive chefs, head banquet chefs should understand how unions work, because they manage employees who belong to these organizations. The most common unions for hotel-and-resort kitchen employees are the Service Employees International Union (SEIU) and the Hotel Employees and Restaurant Employees International Union (HEREIU). In the event of a serious disagreement with management, union representatives will stand by employees and fight with them to ensure fair treatment in the workplace.

As with all hotel employees, a head banquet chef at a hotel may also be a member of the American Hotel & Lodging Association (AH&LA). Because they're essentially caterers, banquet chefs may also join the International Caterers Association (ICA), the National Association of Catering Executives (NACE), and the Leading Caterers of America. These associations often hold functions that allow their members to network and learn about events and new techniques the industry is embracing.

Banquet manager

At a hotel or resort, a banquet manager's responsibilities are similar to a general manager's, except banquet managers deal only with the events in the banquet hall. They are the go-to between the kitchen staff and the dining-room staff. They are also the link between the banquet chef and the customers hosting events. Whereas a banquet chef deals directly with the menu and the food, the banquet manager spends more time supervising the dining room and organizing the event, sometimes with the help of an event planner.

Typically, banquet managers manage the front of the house or the dining room. They schedule the wait staff and bartenders. They have the final say on the set up of the room and oversee the construction of stages or dance floors. As a banquet manager, you may have to help set up and clean up, which can require lifting heavy tables, chairs, and displays. You may also hire, train, and fire banquet staff.

Depending on the size of the hotel or resort, banquet managers may also take on the role of event planners. They may be responsible for booking the dining hall, scheduling the event, developing a theme or planning decor, renting equipment (chairs, china, tables, and so on), booking a band, and ordering flowers or ice sculptures. If the event is a wedding, they may need to ensure that the colors of the banquet hall match the colors of the cake.

Much of a banquet manager's job is providing communication between the customers and the head banquet chef. These responsibilities include taking the chef's prepared menu to the customers, helping the customers choose which dishes they'd like, and then taking the customers' requests back to the chef to ensure the kitchen staff can produce the food the customer wants. Being a banquet manager is like being in sales — banquet managers spend much of their time listening to what their clients want, trying to understand what their chefs can do, and then putting both of these together to come up with a reasonably priced and easily executable menu.

If a hotel or resort is large enough to employ its own event planner, a banquet manager's responsibilities, along with salary, drastically decrease.

Personality traits

Organizational skills are key to a successful career as a banquet manager. You must be able to balance your time between guests, dining-room staff, and kitchen staff. You must have your eye on all events in the dining room. (Does every table have water? Are all the burners lit? Is the band too loud?) You must also be aware of the status of all food coming out of the kitchen.

Banquet managers must be friendly and enjoy communicating with people, especially customers, so curmudgeons need not apply. You have to understand what customers want and then find a way to give it to them (ever heard that saying, "The customer is always right"?). If an issue arises, you have to handle it. If a light bulb goes out above the stage, if the tables are too close to the buffet line, or if the tablecloths aren't the right shade of white, you need to fix the problem or find someone who can.

Like GMs, banquet managers must be responsible with money. If you're a banquet manager, part of your job is determining the cost of the event and collecting the money from your customers. You must keep track of how much was spent on rented equipment, food, and other supplies and be sure that the hotel or the kitchen has enough money to cover these costs.

Salaries

According to PayScale.com, a banquet manager's salary falls between $34,000 and $54,000. As with other positions at hotels and resorts, salary depends on the location and size of the venue and the number of people on staff. The more help you have, the more people you have to manage and the more stressful the job becomes. Banquet managers working at hotels in larger cities or private resorts that host national or international conventions have higher salaries than banquet managers in small towns. Salaries for these positions may reach more than $70,000.

Education and training

Many hotels and resorts require banquet managers to have an associate's or bachelor's degree in food service or hospitality management. A business degree may also help you attain a banquet manager job. Another option is to become a Certified Professional Catering Executive (CPCE), which requires the completion of at least a high-school diploma and a minimum number of hours working in a banquet hall or with a catering company.

Your experience in the hotel industry is sometimes more important than your education, however. If you (and your résumé) prove that you work well with large groups of people and can keep your cool and perform well under pressure, the type of degree you hold may become irrelevant.

Advancement prospects

As a banquet manager, you may advance to assistant manager or general manager of a hotel restaurant or of the hotel or resort as a whole. Another option is to begin your own catering or banquet business. If you hold a degree, you may also be able to teach hotel management to culinary students at a vocational or technical school. For more information on teaching culinary students, see Chapter 14.

Unions and associations

Most managers are not part of workers unions. Instead, they manage a unionized staff, which means the managers should be familiar with the unions to which their staff members belong so that they're prepared to handle any cases brought to them by their employees and union representatives.

Even though banquet managers don't typically belong to unions, they can still join organizations and associations. Common associations include the American Hotel & Lodging Association (AH&LA), Hospitality Asset Managers Association (HAMA), and the Hospitality Sales and Marketing Association International (HSMAI). They may also join the International Caterers Association (ICA), the National Association of Catering Executives (NACE), and the Leading Caterers of America. Banquet managers will learn about new trends in the industry and will be able to network (make connections) with other professionals in their industry.

Other culinary hotel and resort staff

Hotels and resorts employ many other types of culinary professionals, from room service cooks to food-and-beverage directors. Although not all the following positions deal directly with food, they're still important in the hotel-and-resort industry and may offer you an opportunity to gain relevant experience.

✔ **Room service staff:** When guests want room service, they call to place an order with a member of the room-service staff. The kitchen staff prepares the food and then places it on a cart or tray for a room-service staff member to deliver. Room-service staff ensure the food arrives at the correct room within a designated amount of time. If you deliver room service, you may also have to deliver laundry, collect supplies, press clothes, shine shoes, and change linens. This position is often entry-level, which means you don't necessarily need restaurant or hotel experience to land the job.

✔ **Wait staff:** The wait staff at a restaurant in a hotel or resort typically consists of hosts, servers, food runners, bussers, and floor managers or supervisors. The staff in banquet halls includes servers who help set up, serve the food, clear the tables, and clean. A position on the wait staff may be considered entry-level.

✔ **Bartenders:** Hotels and resorts typically employ many bartenders who prepare alcoholic and nonalcoholic beverages for guests. Occasionally, bartenders may be asked to take on duties similar to those of staff, such as clearing tables. In larger hotels, employers may require their bartenders to complete courses that help them learn about the effects of alcohol, the process of combining flavors, and performing tricks during service. Experience on a wait staff will also show employers that you know already how to serve customers.

✔ **Sommeliers:** At hotels and resorts with fine-dining restaurants, sommeliers (wine stewards) work hand-in-hand with the executive chef to create wine lists and select wines to pair with the courses on the menu. Sometimes they teach customers about the wine they're drinking with their meals; they typically give their guests a small history lesson as they pour the glasses. To be a sommelier, you need to be interested in history and geography and you should also know quite a bit about how and where wine is made. Consider attending wine making classes and tastings in your area. Flip ahead to Chapter 11 to learn more about becoming a sommelier.

✔ **Line cooks:** Every kitchen in a venue employs a handful of line cooks, who prepare and cook all food leaving the kitchen. Line cook, especially prep cook (which may be a separate position), is an easily attainable entry-level positions.

✔ **Event planners:** Event planners may be employed by hotels or resorts that host many events such as concerts, awards dinners, weddings, or fundraisers. These men and women provide a link between the front of the house, back of the house, and their customers. They know what their customers want, they understand what their employers can do, and then they put this information together to make the event possible. They may be in charge of altering the menu, booking musical acts, obtaining themed decor, or hiring security. Experience in public relations, sales, or business consulting may help you land a job as an event planner at a hotel or resort. A long list of connections to important people and organizations also can't hurt your chances of impressing a potential employer.

✔ **Sous chefs:** Every kitchen in a hotel or resort typically has a sous chef, or a second in command. The sous chef assists the executive chef in any way possible. These chefs take on management responsibilities as well as cook. They may assign tasks and train and discipline line cooks. In the absence of the executive chef, the sous chef takes command of the kitchen. Sous chefs typically work their way up the line, from prep cook to saucier. If your sights are set on the rank of sous chef, you'll need experience cooking in every position in the kitchen.

✔ **Assistant managers:** The assistant manager is equal to the sous chef but typically works outside the kitchen. The assistant manager generally assists the general manager. The assistant manager may supervise the dining-room staff and serve as a link between the front of the house and the kitchen. Like a sous chef, assistant managers typically need prior experience working in other dining-room positions, such as those positions offered on the wait staff. A degree in business management or hospitality may also help you land a job as an assistant manager in a hotel or resort.

✔ **Executive pastry chefs:** If breakfast and dessert pastries are made in house at a hotel or resort, each kitchen may employ a staff of pastry chefs. These chefs answer to executive pastry chefs, who have the same responsibilities as executive chefs, except they bake instead of cook. To become an executive pastry chef, you need ample experience making pastries, breads, and other plated desserts. Time spent in a bakery or a kitchen where these items are made from scratch will help you catch the eye of future employers. See Chapter 8 for more information about pastry chefs.

Exploring the Spa Scene

When people want to get away from their stressful lives, they may choose to spend a day or two (or three . . .) at a spa. Although hotels and resorts offer some luxuries, spas often take pampering to another level. After a day's or week's worth of hair and scalp treatments, facials, full-body massages, body wraps, mud baths, and even tooth whitening, spa customers leave their location feeling brand new. Because a trip to the spa is typically an all-day event, the time comes when guests must eat. If you're a spa chef, this is where you come in, offering healthy delicacies and tasty treats to help customers forget about the guilt they feel over eating fast food the day before or a piece of chocolate cake for breakfast.

Spas are the fastest-growing area of the hotel and resort industries. Between 1990 and 2010, the number of spas in the United States increased by more than 11,000. Twenty years ago, you had to travel if you wanted to enjoy the luxuries of a spa day. Today, a spa may be located right in your own neighborhood. In fact, the United States is home to approximately 14,000 spas and counting. More than 45 million people enjoy at least one spa day every year.

Enjoying a slower pace

Guests at spas are much more patient than those at restaurants, probably because their day is dedicated to taking deep breaths and relaxing. Yelling at wait staff and making impossible demands would simply ruin their *chi,* their positive life energy. Instead, they typically sit back, put up their feet, and enjoy the personalized service they receive from spa staff.

The slower pace of spas benefits you, as a spa chef, immensely. Although you certainly work hard to produce quality food, you don't have to worry about doing so while meeting seemingly impossible deadlines. The quality of work often suffers when a chef doesn't have adequate time to complete tasks, but you rarely face that issue in a spa. Because you don't have to worry about reading hundreds of tickets as quickly as possible and hurrying to put food on plates, you actually have time to make sure that the food going out looks and tastes the way it should. You can take the time to carefully apply garnishes and cater to special requests. Furthermore, this slower pace also means less stress, which creates a more enjoyable work environment.

Placing an emphasis on nutrition

Many spas are health spas, so they promote good nutrition. Spa chefs must keep this in mind, because many of their guests expect multiple courses of small, nutritious dishes. These dishes most likely don't contain butter, fatty oils, or too much red meat. Ingredients are healthy and fresh and are never fried or sautéed.

Other than the obvious fruits, vegetables, and salads, the most common dishes on spa menus include whole grains, fish, scallops, and small portions of lean meat, such as poultry and particular cuts of beef. Spa chefs rely on simple cooking techniques such as steaming, grilling, and roasting to create their dishes. They may also serve some raw foods, such as sushi. Beverages offered at spas are rarely caffeinated; instead, customers usually drink mineral water or herbal tea. If requested, staff will grind beans for decaffeinated coffee.

To cut the number of calories but ensure nutritious value in all their dishes, many spa chefs work hand-in-hand with nutritionists. The chef develops a menu and sends it to the nutritionist. The nutritionist evaluates what the chef is planning and then provides feedback as to why some dishes have too many (or, believe it or not, too few) calories or too much sugar or protein. With nutritionists' help, chefs can then revise their menus to offer guilt-free food to spa guests.

The best spas typically have the best chefs, regardless of whether these chefs ever intended to be in the spa business. Most of the time, high-end spas approach established, high-end chefs and ask them to create a healthy gourmet menu for their guests. At this point, chefs must decide whether they should attempt to convert their most famous, fat-filled dishes into smaller, healthier versions or start from scratch and develop brand-new dishes using a new set of nutritious ingredients and techniques. The decision is entirely up to the chef and the spa owner.

While working as a spa chef, sometimes you may get a request for foods that aren't high in nutritional value, such as desserts. You should always give the customers what they want; don't be afraid to fulfill these requests. However, try to make the requested item as healthy as possible. Substitute artificial sweeteners for natural sugars, incorporate seasonal fruits, and try offering a smaller portion size. Most of the time, the customer's sweet tooth is satisfied after a mere bite or two.

Gourmet cooking with high-end ingredients

Spa chefs use only fresh ingredients and natural flavors. To ensure that they know exactly what they're getting, they may choose to plant a few gardens on spa grounds. Depending on the size of a spa and its budget constraints, a spa owner may even hire a staff to manage a greenhouse or garden.

In addition to planting their own gardens, spa chefs may frequent farmers' markets to buy fresh foods grown throughout the regions surrounding the spa. If farmers' markets are hard to reach, spa chefs may develop relationships with the closest farmers and ask them to periodically ship their products to the kitchen. This arrangement not only ensures freshness but also helps local small businesses.

But spa chefs are also fans of rare, delicate ingredients from around the world. And due to the success of spas across the country, many spa chefs have large budgets that enable them to order specialty ingredients that cannot be found locally. They often place high-priority orders with international vendors for these products, which are flown in for use in the spa chef's kitchen.

Meeting the Spa Players

Like in any kitchen, line cooks, a sous chef, and an executive chef work in a spa kitchen. Depending on the spa, a pastry chef may even have a station. The typical hierarchy exists, both inside and outside the kitchen. The wait staff serves the food, clears the table, sets up for meetings and events, and is supervised by a floor manager. The processes of food production and service are often supervised by spa managers and directors who most likely aren't categorized as kitchen or dining-room employees. As always, the player with the most responsibility in the kitchen is the executive chef.

Executive spa chef

Similar to an executive chef at a hotel, resort, or restaurant, executive spa chefs run the kitchen. What they say goes. An executive spa chef's responsibilities include planning meals and menus, hiring and training staff, ordering supplies, assigning tasks, and overseeing the quality of food leaving the kitchen.

The hours the executive spa chef works throughout the week depend on the spa's hours of operation. If they are open in the morning and early afternoon, a chef's hours in the kitchen will be fewer than if the spa offers additional dining services in the evening. Spa chefs should expect to work at least 40 hours a week, depending on how big their staff is and when the spa is open for business. If the spa is closed on Sundays, for example, the executive chef may only come in for a few hours to work on the budget, purchasing, or paperwork.

Personality traits

If you want to be an executive chef at a spa, you need to be creative and innovative. You need to create healthy dishes that are appealing to the eye and taste great. You should also have a knack for identifying healthy foods and understanding why some foods are more nutritious than others.

You also need to be approachable and personable, because you have to work with many people in the development and execution of your menu, including the nutritionist, spa director or owner, and sous chef. With their input, you'll know what your budget looks like and what spa guests expect from your food. If you're open to ideas and honest with these people about your ability and desire to produce the dishes they suggest throughout the process, they will surely return the favor and respect your ideas and opinions, as well.

Salaries

Your salary as executive chef at a spa depends on what the spa can afford. If spa owners came to you and asked you to work for them, your salary will probably be higher than average, because the owners want *you* specifically. If the spa where you work is a high-end health spa specializing in week-long retreats, you may make more money than a chef at a day spa. Typically, an executive spa chef can expect to make between $30,000 and $60,000 annually. The more expensive and exclusive the spa, the higher your salary.

Education and training

Most executive chefs have either an associate's or a bachelor's degree or have completed certain certification tests that designate them as executive chefs. A degree in business or hotel and restaurant management may also help you attain this particular position.

On-the-job experience is more important than education, however. As we discuss in "Placing an emphasis on nutrition," a spa may approach a particular chef and ask him to design the spa's menus. If you establish yourself as a health-conscious gourmet chef, spas may be more apt to seek you out than if your restaurant offers fried foods, massive steaks, and burgers with all the fixings. As always, the longer you're in the business, the better the chances you'll become an executive chef.

Advancement prospects

Executive chefs at spas have many options for advancement, but this advancement typically doesn't happen in the kitchen. Executive spa chefs may move into management positions such as spa director. They may even decide to start their own spas. If they're already the owner or executive chef of one or more establishments, they may develop spa-inspired, healthy and light menus for their own restaurants.

Unions and associations

Although line cooks and even the sous chef may be union members, as an executive chef at a spa, you probably won't be protected under any union. Again, it depends on the location of the spa and the various requirements of particular unions. You can be part of many associations, however, including the International Spa Association (ISPA) and the Resort and Day Spa Association. You may also choose to attend events hosted by the American Dietetics Association (ADA), an organization concerned with nutrition. Joining associations allows executive spa chefs to speak with and learn from other professionals in the field. These organizations enable chefs to network and learn about growing trends in their industry.

Other culinary spa careers

Similar to hotels, resorts, and general restaurants, every kitchen and dining room at a spa needs a staff. This staff consists of line cooks, a sous chef, and sometimes a food-and-beverage coordinator, depending on which services the spa offers. See the earlier section "Other culinary hotel and resort staff" for details on some of the basic jobs. Also on the payroll are nutritionists and spa directors:

✔ **Nutritionist:** Many spas employ nutritionists or dietitians. These employees may meet with the kitchen staff to ensure that they're using the freshest and healthiest ingredients possible, but they may also meet with spa customers to teach them about healthy eating and dieting habits.

✔ **Spa director/manager:** The spa director or manager has many supervisory duties, including acting as the link between the kitchen and the dining room. The spa director receives all comments and suggestions from spa guests and then, if necessary, forwards these messages to the kitchen staff. The spa director is also responsible for budgeting, marketing, and working with the public relations team.

Chapter 7

Cooking for a Crowd: Volume Cooking

Chances are good that you have recently attended a graduation party, wedding, large luncheon, gallery opening, bridal shower, bar mitzvah, or anniversary party. Who cooked the food for this event? Possibly a caterer, either a cook (or cooks) from a catering company, or the staff at a banquet hall. Caterers strive to make food that is as elegant and delicious as food served in restaurants — but they make this food for a large number of people.

Volume cooking simply means cooking for a large group of people. Cooking for a crowd is no easy task. Volume cooks are perfectionists whose work is repetitious. How do you feel about making hundreds of stuffed mushrooms or thousands of éclairs? If repetition doesn't bother you, then a job in a volume-cooking setting may be right for you.

Caterers aren't the only ones who specialize in volume cooking. Cooks in institutions, such as schools and hospitals, also feed large groups of people. In this chapter, we discuss the ins and outs of volume cooking by caterers and cooks in various types of institutions.

Catering: It's a Party!

With thousands of catered events taking place each day, catering has become a multi-billion-dollar industry and one of the fastest-growing food-service segments in the United States. As long as couples get married and corporations host annual parties and conferences, good caterers will always be in demand.

Working in the catering field allows you to be part of many types of events. If you're the type of person who likes planning and cooking for elegant bridal showers and weddings, then a job as a caterer may be right for you. Or, if you enjoy putting together tailored corporate affairs or fun birthday parties, the catering business can fill that dream as well. Caterers work on small events such as intimate dinner parties with fewer than 20 guests and grand celebrations with hundreds of people.

Working for a catering company

If you choose to work for a catering company, whether through a banquet hall or with an independent business, be prepared to wear more than one hat. Although preparing mouth-watering food is paramount, caterers have other tasks as well. They are often involved in helping plan the food, which may include the following tasks:

- Designing a menu, perhaps around a theme
- Testing new recipes
- Choosing and purchasing supplies
- Setting prices

Caterers are also sometimes involved in planning and helping orchestrate the event, including these tasks:

- Drumming up business, working with clients, and handling contracts
- Arranging for a decorative food buffet, wait-staff service, or butler-style service
- Transporting and setting up food
- Decorating the venue, including setting up tables, chairs, linens, and flatware
- Serving food
- Cleaning up after the event

At most companies, you won't have to do all (or maybe even many) of these jobs. Most large catering companies employ a team of people to help. Event planners, waiters and waitresses, and bartenders may be on staff.

Preparing for the event

The food is without a doubt the star in a caterer's show. But before caterers can plan the menu for an event, they must meet with the client. Caterers must ask questions to determine the location of the event, the client's budget, and the kind of food the client desires.

A caterer offers menu ideas and suggestions to complement the theme of the event while keeping in mind the budget. A caterer also works with the client to determine how the food will be served at the event. Will the dinner be buffet style or plated? The way in which the food will be served determines the number of servers the caterer needs for the event.

After the menu is created and the event is planned, caterers really get down to business. They make a list of necessary food, supplies, and staff. Caterers at a banquet hall have an advantage here — they may already have on hand everything they need for an event, including the food, staff, tables, chairs, and linens. Although large catering businesses have their own staff and supplies, smaller ones may not, so they may have to rent or purchase supplies and hire staff in addition to preparing food.

Sometimes when creating a menu, a client may ask for ethnic foods (perhaps Polish pirogi or Italian gnocchi) that caterers are unfamiliar with. When given such a request, caterers may need to develop and test a new recipe prior to the event to please the client. They may even allow the client to taste the food before the big day.

Working the day of the event

Caterers prepare for an event in advance, so on the day of the event all they need to worry about is preparing and transporting the food, right? Wrong! A caterer is like the coach of a large sporting event. The caterer must decide who does what — who will set up and serve the food, who will serve drinks, who will clean up afterward, and so on. Only after these tasks are accomplished can the caterer focus intensely on preparing the food.

Food may be prepared at the site of the event if the necessary equipment is available, such as stoves and refrigerators. Otherwise, food is prepared at another location and then transported to the site. If all food preparation and cooking is being done on site, caterers must ensure that they bring everything they need. Forgotten items waste precious time and may even ruin an event, so good caterers knows they must make a list and, like Santa Claus, check it at least twice just to be sure. If a caterer is preparing everything off site, then food must be transported at safe temperatures. Caterers have proper equipment to ensure that hot foods stay hot and cold foods stay cold.

Now, on to the food. Caterers must be able to prepare large quantities of food, from appetizers to salads to main courses to desserts. This food must all look the same and be of the same quality. The last plate to come out of the kitchen must look identical to the first. The same goes for buffet lines. The food should be displayed in an appealing and easily accessible way — and caterers should never run out of an item. Caterers may serve foods in the following ways:

✔ **Buffet style:** Either guests or servers dish out food that is set up on decorative displays. (Servers are usually used to help with portion control to ensure there is enough food for the last person in the buffet line.)

✔ **Butler style:** Wait staff offer items such as hors d'oeuvres on trays to guests.

✔ **Family style:** Guests serve themselves from plated foods passed around the table.

✔ **Food stations:** Servers prepare foods to order, such as pasta or omelets, or slice meats.

✔ **Plated service:** Food is plated and then served to individual guests.

The timing of dessert service may vary at weddings where cutting the cake is part of the festivities. Immediately after the cake is cut, the cake should be whisked to the kitchen so staff can quickly cut and serve it.

After dessert is served and eaten, caterers may need to clean up. Some venues have cleaning services that come in after events. But if cleaning is in the catering company's contract, that staff cleans the kitchen, removes items such as dishes and glassware from tables, and washes them. After all guests leave, the caterers disassemble chairs and tables and clean the rest of the venue.

Locating where caterers work

Caterers may work at on-premise catering sites such as banquet halls or hotels or at off-premise catering sites such as independent catering kitchens (that transport food to where it's needed). Banquet halls or hotels usually have a large staff and don't need to hire additional employees for events. They usually employ a kitchen staff to be in charge of the food preparation; a wait staff to serve food, set up, and clean up; and a banquet manager, who is in charge of planning and managing the event. See Chapter 6 for more information about the roles of hotel kitchen employees.

Independent catering businesses are usually much smaller than on-premise catering sites and typically don't employ a large staff unless they need help with large events. They may also have to rent or purchase supplies such as tables, chairs, and linens for events and determine if they will prepare food at the venue or prepare it off-site and transport it to the venue.

In addition to working at banquet halls, hotels, and independent catering businesses, caterers may also find similar work at country clubs, restaurants, diners, and specialty shops.

Feeding the masses: Potbelly Sandwich Shop

Think about the different events that you've attended, from weddings to birthday parties to bridal showers. Most of these parties — whether they were lavish parties or simple get togethers — most likely had one common theme: food. And the food that wasn't prepared at home probably was purchased from a catering company that specializes in feeding a crowd.

Potbelly Sandwich Shop, based in Chicago, is one of these examples. Its success is an indication of the importance of catering companies. Started from the back of an antiques shop in 1977, the small sandwich shop has evolved into a catering franchise with more than 200 shops throughout the United States today. The company offers sandwiches with all the fixings, soups, and salads to feed any size crowd and some shops even offer delivery services.

Catering to your own needs

You may decide after working for a catering company for a while that you'd like to open your own business. (*Note:* We do suggest that you first spend some time working for a catering business before jumping in, to determine if this path is right for you.) Being your own boss can be exciting, but it can also be very stressful and require long hours and incredibly hard work. If you're the boss, you have to make many decisions. And plenty of those decisions will come before you ever open your doors for business.

Ask yourself the following questions when considering whether to open your own catering business:

- ✔ **Do you have a business plan?** A business plan is your blueprint for how you will run your business. Consider it the meat and potatoes of your business. It includes the name of your business, explains how your catering business will operate, and describes how it will be structured and managed. It should also include information about how it will be financed and how much profit the business expects to make.

- ✔ **Will you run the business out of your home or rent a space?** If you run your business out of your home, you may need special permits, licenses, and insurance, so you should check your local and state laws. You'll need an inspection of your kitchen and may also need special equipment. If you rent a space, you may not need equipment, but you'll still need permits, licenses, and insurance. Sometimes you'll be able to use a vendor's facilities for food preparation, but you shouldn't count on it for all events. Whether you work out of your home or rent a space, you'll need to know and follow strict safety regulations that must be observed at all times.

✔ **Do you have enough money for start-up costs?** You need a hefty chunk of money to get started. Do you have the funds to cover fees for permits and licensing? Do you have money to purchase equipment? How about enough money to pay staff and advertise your services? If not, you may want to consider borrowing money from a bank. If you go this route, remember you'll have to pay back the loan (with interest).

You may not make any profit during the first few years your business is open. Take that fact into consideration when determining your company's budget and operating costs.

✔ **Will you work alone or hire a staff?** You probably won't be able to do everything yourself, so you may need to hire some staff to help you, especially on the day of an event. For most events, you need a wait staff, staff to prepare food, someone to oversee the event (if that's not your job), and additional staff to set up and clean up. You may also need someone to help transport food if you're working off site.

When hiring employees or vendors, find out their work experience and check references to be sure they're hardworking and dependable. You should also look for people who are personable, punctual, and easygoing and who can work well under pressure.

Many metropolitan areas have agencies that specialize in temporary foodservice workers. Bartenders, wait staff, cooks, buffet carvers, and others are available on call or at very short notice. This also helps to increase your pool of staff without having to hire help yourself.

✔ **What type of foods will you offer?** Food is the most important part of a catering business. Although one bad dish won't ruin your business, word may get around and affect your client base, so make sure your food is delicious and of the best quality. Are you creative and able to come up with exciting and appealing menus? Do you have any specializations or make a signature dish that everyone loves? If you won't be the one doing the food preparation and cooking, will you hire a chef who specializes in a particular area?

Customers often prefer caterers who specialize in specific dietary needs, such as kosher or Italian food. Specialization is one way to make your business noticeable among the competition. The way you present a dish can also differentiate you from your competition.

✔ **Will you rent or buy items needed for events?** You may need to work with vendors to rent tables and chairs, linens, plates, glassware, flatware, decor and design elements. And if you're transporting food, you must adhere to safety regulations that require hot foods to stay hot and cold foods to stay cold, which requires special equipment.

✔ **Will you advertise?** Advertising is key to getting your name out there. Ads in newspapers, fliers, and brochures are great ways to let people know about your business. You may even want to hire someone who has sales and marketing experience to take care of your advertising needs and help you manage a client base.

> ✔ **What kind of schedule will you work?** Having weekends off is most desirable, but that schedule may not be feasible because most events are held on Saturdays or Sundays. Part of scheduling is also deciding how many clients you will take. You don't want to stretch yourself too thin and schedule too many events in one week, but you also want your business to make money, so you need to figure out a middle ground.

After you answer all these questions, you're ready to get the ball rolling and put all the pieces in place to open your own catering business. For a more detailed look at starting your own business, see Chapter 18.

Career profile

Whether you work for a catering company or own your own, the catering field is demanding and stressful. Caterers are required to make large quantities of food, sometimes for multiple events, and then plate this food in an aesthetically pleasing manner so that all plates look identical. They must also ensure that all plates are served at the same time and each guest is on the same course. Depending on the event, caterers may have to set up an attractive buffet to showcase the food they've just prepared. Either way, caterers have one shot to make an event perfect and they must ensure each and every event runs smoothly. Not everyone is cut out to work as a caterer, so read on to find out if you fit the profile.

Personality traits

Caterers must be able to work well in a fast-paced setting and be very detail-oriented to make sure that the special event they've been hired for goes well. Caterers should be good multi-taskers. They're responsible not only for preparing food but also for planning events. Because anything can go wrong at any time, caterers must be able keep a level head and think on their toes. They should be flexible enough to handle last-minute changes. What happens if it rains on the day of a catered event? What if they forget a needed ingredient or something as simple as Sternos (small canned burners placed under dishes to heat food and keep it warm)? Thinking about how you would react in these situations can help you determine if catering is right for you.

Caterers also need to have great organizational skills to be able to manage several events at once. They must also be good in math and measurements so they can follow recipes (and quickly double or even triple them for large volumes) and possibly calculate budgets.

Caterers need to be creative enough to develop menus and themes to suit their clients' tastes. They should be able to offer suggestions based on the event, the venue, and the client's budget. Successful caterers also have good customer-service skills and interpersonal skills. They listen carefully to clients' requests and offer ideas of their own when helping to plan a catered event. And caterers who run their own business must have good management skills to successfully manage their staff.

Salaries

As with any job in the culinary industry, a caterer's salary depends on factors such as experience and responsibilities. It also depends on the number of jobs you can handle at once. The more jobs you take on, the more money you make. If you're just starting out as a caterer, expect to be paid much less than someone who has been in the business for more than a decade. The type of business you work for also affects your salary. People who own their own catering businesses may have higher salaries than those who work for a catering business, but they also have more responsibilities.

According to Payscale.com, caterers who work for catering businesses make an average of $20,000 to $50,000 a year, whereas salaries of caterers who run their own business can range from $40,000 to $200,000. Remember, salary depends on factors such as size of an event, food costs, staff costs, transportation costs, and whether the caterer works full-time, part-time, or seasonally.

Education and training

Certain catering positions, such as serving, may not need any formal culinary education, but food-preparation positions such as cooks, however do require a formal culinary education. Banquet-manager or event-coordinator positions usually require a degree in hospitality or sales management in addition to training in banquet operations. If you're interested in running your own catering business, you should look into a Certified Professional Catering Executive (CPCE) designation, which is awarded by the National Association of Catering Executives (NACE) to people who have demonstrated their expertise in catering and event management.

Advancement prospects

Working in many different catering positions allows you to learn the overall job. You may be able to move up the catering hierarchy based on your experience and abilities after working at a banquet hall or independent catering business. If you first work for an independent catering business and learn the ropes, you'll be more prepared if you decide later that you want to run your own catering business. The more time you put in, the more experience and training you gain. Later, you can apply what you have learned to your own business.

Unions and associations

Caterers who work in banquet halls at hotels — especially at large hotels — may be required to be part of a union. Caterers who work for independent catering companies or who run their own catering businesses most likely won't be part of a union. Many associations and organizations exist for caterers or those interested in more information about catering. These associations provide caterers with certification information, networking opportunities, and support groups and include the Convenience Caterers and Food Manufacturers Association (CCFMA), the International Caterers Association (ICA), the Leading Caterers of America, the National Association of Catering Executives (NACE), and the National Restaurant Association (NRA).

Cooking for Institutions

What is an institution? The word *institution* has a negative connotation. It probably makes you envision a place that's, well, not so nice. However, an institution is simply an established organization or a corporation. Some institutions, such as hospitals, are large and deal with many individuals (in this case, patients, visitors, doctors, nurses, and other staff). These people need to be fed, some of them three meals a day, so many large institutions have numerous cooking positions. Institutional cooking may sound boring and bring images to mind such as long cafeteria lines and cooks wearing hairnets slapping unappetizing food on to trays. But there's much more to the job than this, and it's not as boring as you may think.

Considering institutional cooking

Cooking for an institution has its advantages and disadvantages. It may not seem as glamorous as working in a French bistro or top-notch restaurant, but the purpose is the same: to prepare and serve quality food to guests. Before you dismiss a job in an institutional setting, weigh the pros and cons in the following sections.

Evaluating the pros

The pros of working in an institutional setting include working regular and set hours. Institutions such as schools are not open on weekends or holidays or during summers, so you most likely won't be required to work during these times. The hours worked are usually during the day. This schedule is very attractive for someone with a family or for a student taking night classes.

Another pro to working in an institution is the opportunity to learn skill sets that can be useful outside the kitchen. A large organization must purchase enormous quantities of food. Such an organization usually employs a person to take care of this task, which requires great organizational and budgeting skills. These skills may prove handy in the long run, especially if you want to open your own business one day.

Because institutions are usually large and employ many people, they're able to offer attractive benefits packages that include paid time off, such as vacation, sick, and personal days, and insurance policies, such as medical, dental, optical, and life. Some companies even have 401(k) plans and profit-sharing plans, so if you're looking for a long-term job, a job in an institution may be the right path for you.

Although most institutions usually serve the same dishes on a rotating schedule, leaving little room for creativity, some (such as cruise ships) do require creativity. Vacationers usually expect the food on cruise ships to match that of a fine dining restaurant.

Considering the cons

Some institutions require you to work nights, holidays, and weekends. For example, because hospitals never close and serve three meals a day, they may require you to work a variety of shifts. This schedule may not appeal to someone who likes to work exclusively during the day or prefers to work set hours.

Another con to working in an institution is that room for personal growth as a cook may be limited. Many institutions serve the same rotating menu with little room for change or creativity. Institutional cooks usually prepare a large quantity of limited entrees, vegetables, and desserts, so someone who enjoys making something different every day may quickly get bored. Also, salaries for institutional cooks vary but are usually lower than salaries paid to chefs in top-notch restaurants.

Even though institutions may have a preplanned menu, you may still have opportunities to be creative. Prisons, which are another type of institution, have strict budgets and limited ingredients, so you may have to think outside the box to come up with meals using the ingredients you have available. Hospitals and nursing homes may require chefs to create recipes for people on strict diets, so you need to be able to adhere to strict guidelines while creating recipes that are interesting and delicious.

Contract feeding

Contract feeding is another area that caters or volume cooks turn to in the culinary field. Companies enter in to contracts with large businesses to provide food services for the large business's clients, patients, and employees. Think about the food needs for an institution such as a high school. High schools need large amounts of food to feed to their students and employees and usually turn to a food-service contractor to provide these services. Unlike caterers, contract feeders usually sign long-term contracts with a particular company to take care of all their food needs — from the cooking to the packaging to the delivering. An example of a contract feeding company is Aramark Corporation, which offers food services for more than 255,000 employees in 22 countries.

Looking at types of institutions

The following are some common volume-cooking institutions that employ cooks and chefs:

- **Airlines:** Airline cooking is a changing business. Virtually all meals served on airlines are no longer free, so airline chefs must come up with creative and appealing choices to pique an airline passenger's interest enough to buy a meal. Also, the types of meals served are changing from standard entrees to a la carte items such as sandwiches or salads. These meals must also be prepared with specific food safety regulations; for instance, they must be packaged individually and not require any additional preparation other than heating.

- **Armed forces:** Chefs at military bases and military schools are responsible for feeding large numbers of personnel. These chefs need to be able to produce large quantities of filling, nutritious meals to feed large numbers of people as well as prepare special dishes for occasional VIPs such as senior officers, the president, or members of Congress. Executive chef jobs within the military are coveted and require education and at least 15 years of culinary experience, with military service being a plus.

- **Commissary kitchens:** *Commissary kitchens* (also known as *production kitchens*) are kitchens where foods are prepared and then shipped to institutions or restaurants to be cooked and served. Commissary chefs are in charge of cooking, preparing, and packaging numerous meals in large volumes and then shipping these meals. Many different types of foods are prepared in commissary kitchens and are shipped to restaurants, food truck vendors, institutions, and more. Since these recipes are usually standard and specific recipes must be followed, commissary chefs may not have much room for personal growth or the opportunity to create new and exciting dishes.

- **Corporations:** Large companies and corporations usually have cafeterias or contracts with independent businesses to provide meals so employees don't have to leave their work site for lunch. Because most employees are required to pay out of their pockets for their meals, the options available must be tempting and appealing enough to keep employees from going elsewhere.

- **Correctional centers:** Detention centers and prisons are responsible for feeding inmates three meals a day, usually on strict budgets with limited ingredients, so prison chefs must be able to think on their toes. Prisons are probably the least attractive institutions to work for, but these jobs can be rewarding if you like thinking outside the box

- **Cruise ships:** The cruise-ship industry is perhaps one of the most exciting institutional cooking settings. Although these jobs are demanding, they're rewarding because you get to travel to many different countries throughout the world while working. Vacationers expect top-notch food comparable to what they'd find in restaurants, and they rate dining as one of the top reasons for choosing one cruise line over another, so cruise chefs have the opportunity to create gourmet foods. In addition to creating attractive and appealing dishes, cruise ship chefs must also adhere to strict food safety regulations and must have impeccable purchasing and organizational skills to be able to buy enough food to feed thousands of people, including the crew, during a voyage.

✔ **Hospitals, nursing homes, and retirement homes:** Hospitals used to be notorious for their horrible food, but that's a thing of the past. Now hospitals must offer creative and appealing choices for patients, staff, and visitors. Hospital and nursing-home chefs are also responsible for developing dishes for patients with special dietary restrictions due to heart conditions, diabetes, or other ailments. Chefs must be able to prepare meals that are not only healthy but also tasty. Although some residents of retirement homes may share some of the same dietary restrictions as patients in hospitals and nursing homes, most people living in a retirement home are relatively healthy and want dining choices similar to what they'd find in a restaurant, so chefs must be able to prepare creative meals worthy of being on menus of gourmet restaurants.

✔ **Schools:** Most educational institutions have cafeterias responsible for feeding students and staff. Meals in elementary schools and high schools usually have strict government regulations, so a school chef must be able to develop menus based on these regulations. Colleges and universities do not have these restrictions. Because college and university students and staff are free to leave campus for meals, these cafeterias have high competition from other restaurants — some of them are even located right on campus — so the school cafeterias must offer a variety of meal choices to keep students and staff from going elsewhere for their meals. Jobs in school settings are coveted because of the hours worked and time off, such as weekends and holidays.

Career profile

Cooking for multiple people is no easy task. Working in any type of volume-cooking setting takes great skill. Most jobs require you to make large quantities of food and either plate this food or set it up in a buffet line. Some volume-cooking settings may not be as exciting as others. Like any cooking job, though, you have to carefully consider the job and decide whether it's a good fit for you.

Personality traits

In volume-cooking settings, you need to be able to handle numerous tasks at once. You must have great organization skills and be able to follow directions to make and plate large amounts of food without error. You must have great skill and patience while being able to work at a fast pace. Sometimes you may have to serve the food you make, so you must have excellent communication and interpersonal skills.

Salaries

The salary for a position in a volume-cooking setting is typically lower than that of a caterer, but many organizations offer great benefits packages depending on the type of institution and your schedule. According to PayScale.com, the salary for volume cooking positions ranges from $15,000 to $50,000, with the average being about $28,000.

Education and training

Unlike many other jobs in the culinary field, some volume-cooking positions, such as those in schools or hospitals, don't require any formal culinary education or training beyond a high-school diploma. Others, such as a chef in the armed forces or on a cruise ship, may require you to have a formal culinary education as well as years of on-the-job training.

Advancement prospects

Because most institutional cooking jobs don't require any special training, most skills are learned on the job. You usually have to start at the bottom — say, as a dietary aid, who plates and passes out dishes in a hospital setting — and work your way up the ladder toward a chef position. After you acquire basic food handling, preparation, and cooking skills, you may be able to advance to other cooking positions with more responsibilities based on your capabilities.

Unions and associations

Your place of employment determines whether you must belong to a union. Many employees who work for large institutions such as airlines, hospitals, schools, and prisons belong to a union such as the United Food and Commercial Workers International Union (UFCW). Volume cooks may also belong to associations depending on their area of expertise. These organizations include the American School Food Service Association (ASFSA), the Association for Healthcare Foodservice (AHF), the Association of Correctional Food Service Associates (ACFSA), AMAMARK, the Cruise Line International Association (CLIA), LSG Sky Chefs, the Military Hospitality Alliance (MHA), and the School Nutrition Association (SNA).In addition, volume cooks can also belong to the American Culinary Federation (ACF) and the International Foodservice Executives Association (IFSEA).

Part III
Taking a Specialized Approach

The 5th Wave   By Rich Tennant

"What a wonderful swirled icing effect! How ever did you do it?"

In this part . . .

Many specializations exist in the culinary world. After you determine that you want to work in the culinary industry, you may want to explore a specific focus, be it breads or beer. From desserts to wine to food science, the possibilities are endless.

Part III explores the many specializations within the culinary world. Do you have a sweet tooth? Then maybe you'd like a career as a baker or pastry chef, baking and decorating cakes and preparing special desserts. Would you like to work on your own as a private or personal chef? How about a career in beverages, working with wine or beer? We explore the different career choices and help you determine which path is right for you. In this part we also explore some old and new food trends and look at the roles of food scientists and food artisans.

Chapter 8

How Sweet It Is! Becoming a Pastry Chef or Baker

o you love desserts? Do you like making desserts as much as eating them? If you answered yes to these questions, then you may want to consider becoming a pastry chef or baker. As a pastry chef or baker, you may get to spend your days creating and testing new recipes. You'll get to make foods you love every day, possibly including cakes, cupcakes, pies, cookies, delicately layered pastries, and maybe even beautiful and delicious chocolates and candies.

Pastry chefs and bakers usually have different roles, but they can work side by side in restaurants, large hotels, pastry shops, patisseries, bakeries, and even casinos. They can even open their own shops and be their own bosses. In this chapter, we get started by telling you how the jobs of baker and pastry chef differ from each other so you can decide which area appeals to you more. You find out what both jobs are like and what kind of specialization is possible in the pastry field. We tell you what tasks and responsibilities the various jobs include, what kind of person does well at them, and what background experience, education, and training is necessary or helpful to a successful career as a baker or pastry chef. If you have a sweet tooth and want to make it a professional asset, you'll devour all the info in this chapter.

Measuring the Difference Between Pastry Chefs and Bakers

A pastry chef, also known as a *pâtissier,* and a baker, also known as a *boulanger,* both bake, so they have the same job, right? Wrong! The key word is *chef,* which indicates someone who's in charge of a kitchen station and oversees staff. A pastry chef is therefore higher up on the food chain (pun intended!) than a baker, who usually isn't a boss. In fact, in a large hotel restaurant, a baker may even work for a pastry chef.

Another difference is in the kind of food they prepare. Pastry chefs mainly concentrate on pastries, such as *pâte à choux,* and stunning desserts such as tarts, although they may also bake bread. Bakers bake items such as breads, pies, cakes, muffins, rolls, and simple desserts and pastries.

Pastry chefs focus more than bakers do on designing desserts that are visually appealing and tantalizing to the taste buds. They want to make desserts look as perfect as they taste. The items bakers make also taste great, but they aren't as fancy. Bakers also usually produce greater quantities of baked items whereas pastry chefs work with chocolate or sugar and produce lavish tortes and desserts. Though some bakers decorate cakes and other pastries, pastry chefs usually are more skilled in design and can concentrate on finer details. Bakers have to spend most of their time working with dough and simply baking.

If you find you'd like to work with sweets every day, you'll have to decide which route is best for you. Do you have a great eye for detail and love the idea of developing recipes and designing desserts? Then a job as a pastry chef, described in the next section, may be your cup of tea. If you like the feeling of accomplishment you get when you pull a perfectly baked cake or loaf of bread from the oven, consider the route of baker (discussed in the later section "Sifting Through the Job of a Baker").

Edible Artistry: Understanding the Job of a Pastry Chef

A pastry chef is most often a member of the kitchen brigade and is the station chef of the pastry department. Pastry chefs in large restaurants may have an assistant within the department. In very large hotels, bakers may also work within the pastry department (but we discuss that arrangement later in this chapter). Regardless of the location, pastry chefs work under the supervision of the executive or head kitchen chef, who is in charge of the entire kitchen. In this section, we give you the scoop on the details of the job, places where pastry chefs work, and what kind of particulars are involved in working as a pastry chef.

Working as a pastry chef

A pastry chef's job is difficult because it's more exacting than other jobs in the kitchen brigade. Small changes in a dessert recipe can make a big difference in taste, so pastry chefs must pay great attention to detail or risk wasting time and ingredients. If they change a recipe by adding more of one ingredient and less of another and the dessert doesn't turn out as expected, they're back at square one. Because pastry chefs do most of their work by hand and spend most of their day on their feet, their job is very demanding.

Although it may seem difficult at times, the job is also creative and interesting. Much artistry goes into the desserts that pastry chefs create. Each dessert must *look* as good as it tastes. People dining at restaurants order entrées because they are hungry, but dessert is a completely different matter. It's something extra special, and it must entice a customer into ordering it. If it doesn't sound enticing, the customer is more likely to skip dessert and ask for the check, so pastry chefs must be creative enough to create desserts to pique a customer's interest.

For example, though a slice of chocolate cake may be delicious, it's not very exciting. Pastry chefs should be able to use their expertise to put a new spin on that boring chocolate cake. For example, a pastry chef can make a deconstructed chocolate cake that consists of a large plate containing a slice of decadent chocolate cake next to a mound of fresh raspberry compote, a dish of dark chocolate ganache, and a dollop of whipped cream that the customers use to construct their own dessert. This idea requires much more creativity than just being able to make a chocolate cake. It also makes the dining experience interactive and appealing — for once, customers won't be scolded for playing with their food!

Most pastry chefs have different hours than the rest of the kitchen brigade. Kitchen personnel usually come to work in the afternoon and then work throughout the evening, but pastry chefs typically begin their day in the wee hours of the morning, sometimes before the sun rises. Why must they rise before the rooster crows? Cakes, pies, and pastries may take hours to prepare and bake, and some gourmet recipes are so detailed and require so many steps that they take days to create. Pastry chefs do the work in advance so that customers don't have to wait for their dessert. Because pastry chefs' workday begins so early, they typically leave before a restaurant gets busy, so they don't often plate or serve the desserts they make. They instruct other kitchen personnel on how to properly plate the desserts.

Most pastry chefs perform at least some of the following tasks:

- Creating and testing new recipes
- Decorating desserts
- Ordering supplies from vendors

> ✔ Discussing upcoming menus and specials with other chefs so that they can prepare desserts that complement entrées
>
> ✔ Preparing and maintaining a budget for the pastry department
>
> ✔ Ensuring organization within the pastry department
>
> ✔ Hiring, training, and firing staff
>
> ✔ Representing their place of employment at business and media events

Finding out where pastry chefs work

In addition to restaurants and hotels, pastry chefs may also work in other establishments — some of which are off the beaten track such as a commissary kitchen.

Restaurants

A pastry chef in a larger restaurant is in charge of a station within the kitchen. He or she may have an assistant. Some smaller restaurants don't have a full-time pastry chef. They employ one part time or have another cook in the kitchen plate desserts that are brought in from a gourmet pastry shop, a commissary kitchen, or a commercial bakeshop.

Hotel restaurants

Hotel restaurants typically have a larger kitchen staff than other restaurants. Very large hotel restaurants may have several employees in the pastry department. In addition to the pastry chef, they may have a pastry sous chef (assistant) and a pastry cook. The pastry sous chef is the second in command under the pastry chef and usually assists the pastry chef in managing all aspects of the pastry department. The pastry cook prepares and bakes pastries and other desserts under the supervision of the pastry chef and/or pastry sous chef if necessary. They may also have specialized pastry chefs, who concentrate on specific items, such as a *confiseur,* who works with confections and candies; or a *décorateur,* who decorates cakes and pastries. Hotel restaurants may also have an onsite baker who prepares pastries and fresh bread included with entrées. (See Chapter 6 for more information about working in a hotel kitchen.)

Pastry shops

Pastry chefs may open their own pastry shops or work for other pastry chefs in such shops, preparing pastries and desserts for the general public and selling larger quantities of these desserts to local restaurants and caterers. Because stiff competition exists between pastry shops, pastry chefs must be experts in working with sugar and chocolate and do extremely detailed and precise work. They must ensure their pastries are the best of the best. Pastry shops usually offer intricate and diverse pastries such as tarts, tortes, petit fours, cream puffs, éclairs, and palmier pastries. They can also offer simple cakes as wells as cakes as high as five or six tiers featuring a variety of sugar-and-gum paste flowers, complicated piping, blown-sugar pieces, and impressive fondant work. You may even see cakes formed into various shapes, such as people, buildings, and animals. Because of the variety of interesting products made, pastry chefs tend to gravitate toward jobs at pastry shops rather than a bakery.

Commissary kitchens

Because more and more restaurants and hotels are choosing to purchase their desserts and baked goods rather than hire their own pastry chefs, pastry chefs are turning to jobs in commissary kitchens. Commissary kitchens prepare and package foods for establishments such as restaurants and hotels that don't have the time or staff to prepare their own. While restaurants and hotels demand desserts to be made at a quicker pace, commissary jobs allow pastry chefs to work at a much slower pace and perfect their desserts. This extra time leaves more room for pastry chefs to be more creative.

Banquet halls and catering companies

Banquet halls and caterers need numerous desserts for events, so they typically hire pastry chefs to create gorgeous and elegant desserts for many of their events. Pastry chefs may also be responsible for decorating tiered wedding or birthday cakes. Positions with banquet halls and caterers are usually part time because pastry chefs are typically only hired when needed.

Some pastry chefs who operate their own businesses specialize in the creation of exquisite cakes for weddings or other events. (Some pastry chefs in large hotels or banquet halls also may have the opportunity to create high-end cakes.) These cakes are made from scratch using only the highest-quality ingredients. See "Decorating specialty cakes" later in this chapter for more information about this line of work.

Career profile

Becoming a pastry chef is almost as demanding as working as a pastry chef. You need years of education and training and must be prepared to work long hours on detailed desserts or cakes. Because restaurants and hotels typically don't hire one more than one pastry chef, the competition for these types of jobs is high. If you want to become a pastry chef, you must strive to be the best of the best to make yourself stand out among the competition. In this section, we discuss what kind of person is a good fit for the job of a pastry chef and what the job entails.

Personality traits

Not everyone who wants to work in culinary arts has what it takes to be a pastry chef. Top-notch pastry chefs must be patient. In fact, patience is probably the most important personality trait of anyone wanting to be a pastry chef. Creating pastries is more precise than other types of cooking, and pastry chefs must carefully measure and weigh ingredients, often following extremely specific directions. Working with chocolate and sugar takes much practice. The job of a pastry chef can be repetitive, too. A pastry chef may be given a daily production schedule that involves the tedious job of making many of the same desserts.

A pastry chef must also be an early bird. Most pastry chefs begin their day in the wee hours of the morning while most people are still sleeping. Waking up so early is difficult and requires an early bedtime. Pastry chefs also spend most of their day on their feet and have to reach, lift, and mix by hand. And their work area in the kitchen may be quite cozy. (Read between the lines here: The workstation is small and cramped.)

Pastry chefs must have superior organizational skills and be able to quickly locate and retrieve countless ingredients and the many tools of their trade. Arranging so many items in a practical way takes great organizational skills.

Additionally, pastry chefs must have business and management skills to maintain the budget for the pastry department. They're the boss of their station. They may also have to manage an assistant along with other kitchen personnel. These skills are especially essential for the pastry chef who is thinking about starting his or her own business one day.

Salaries

The salaries for pastry chefs vary due to a number of different factors, such as the type of business you work for, the location of that business, the duties you perform, your education, and your work experience. Remember, every place of employment is different and has specific salary guidelines. A pastry chef working for a large restaurant may not necessarily make more money than a pastry chef working in a small pastry shop, but hotels and fine-dining restaurants in big cities tend to pay more. According to Payscale.com, the average salary for pastry chefs ranges from $25,000 to $70,000.

Education and training

Pastry chefs must be knowledgeable of their craft. Pastry chefs need to know how to combine ingredients in a way that tastes good and ensures safe food for their customers. They typically take courses in dough methods, pastry fillings, culinary theory and technique, nutrition and food science, food safety, baking cakes and cookies, and candy making and need to be able to recall all that information on the job.

To gain all that knowledge, most pastry chefs are educated at culinary schools. But education and training for pastry chefs varies (see "Gaining Education and Experience" later in this chapter). A pastry chef's salary is usually based on his or her worth, which increases with years of education and/or experience, so the more you have, the more attractive you are to employers and the more handsomely you'll be paid. A pastry chef who has experience decorating cakes is more valuable than a pastry chef who does not, and someone who was properly trained at a top-notch culinary school is often looked upon more highly than someone who has little formal culinary education and experience.

Advancement prospects

Advancement opportunities for pastry chefs depend on their training, work experience, and ability to perform more responsibilities in the kitchen. Usually, pastry chefs begin their career as a pastry sous chef or a pastry cook, assisting the pastry chef. After pastry cooks demonstrate they're capable of performing more duties, they may be able to advance to the pastry sous chef position and eventually become full-fledged executive pastry chefs, overseeing a staff. This career step may also be achieved by moving from one restaurant to another. They may also choose to work in one specialized field, such as decorating desserts or working with confections. Other times, pastry chefs use the experience and knowledge gained through working in a kitchen to open a business of their own.

Unions and associations

Pastry chefs can join many different associations, such as the American Culinary Federation (ACF), the International Association of Culinary Professionals (IACP), and the National Restaurant Association (NRA). These associations provide pastry chefs with resources that can help them find employment and stay up-to-date with culinary advancements within the culinary industry.

Where you're employed determines whether you belong to a union. Places of employment with unions, such as hotels and restaurants, usually pay better than places that don't have unions — but this is not always the case. Unions also protect pastry chefs' working conditions and prevent them from having to work long hours on their feet with no breaks. Two examples of such unions are the Service Employees International Union and the Hotel Employees and Restaurant Employees International Union.

Sifting Through the Job of a Baker

So if a pastry chef is a baker, but a baker is not a pastry chef, then what is a baker? Clearly put, a baker is in charge of baking. According to the *Chef's Companion,* 3rd Edition, when you bake something, you "cook food by surrounding it with hot, dry air in an oven or on hot stones in a dry metal pan." Bakers typically produce breads, cakes, pies, quiches, cookies, breakfast pastries, Danish, muffins, quick-breads, croissants, laminated dough products, and even crackers and tortillas.

In this section, we explore the tasks performed by bakers, the locations where they may work, and the skills required to be a professional baker.

Working as a baker

Are you an early riser? Are you alert in the morning? If so, a job as a baker may appeal to you. Bakers' duties vary according to where they work, but one thing is for sure: They begin their day very early in the morning — so early that they may be awake and on their way to work before some people are in bed for the night. Bakers need to begin their day way before dawn because some items that may need to be ready by breakfast or lunch take hours to prepare. When a baker makes a loaf of bread, he or she must first mix the ingredients to form dough. Then the baker must knead the dough and let it rise multiple times before the dough bakes into a loaf of bread. If the result burns or doesn't turn out as expected, the baker must repeat this process.

The number of bakers employed by a particular business usually determines a baker's main duties and responsibilities. A small business may only hire a head baker, who is in charge of running the bakery in addition to producing baked goods. Larger businesses may employ a head baker, an assistant baker, and additional staff. In an environment such as this, the head baker is usually in charge of the day-to-day production and oversees the rest of the staff. Sometimes larger bakeries have enough staff that bakers are assigned specific jobs each day, often on a rotating basis. One baker may be in charge of baking breads and cakes, while another may be in charge of decorating cakes or creating delectable pie fillings.

Depending on where you work as a baker, you can expect to perform at least some of these tasks:

- Weighing and measuring ingredients
- Mixing ingredients and preparing dough
- Baking breads, cakes, pies, pastries, and more
- Operating equipment such as commercial ovens and mixers
- Decorating desserts
- Ordering supplies from vendors
- Taking orders from customers
- Preparing and maintaining a budget for the bakery
- Hiring, training, and firing staff

Finding out where bakers work

Like pastry chefs, bakers can work in many different establishments, such as restaurants, hotels, grocery stores, bakeries, and pastry shops. Where bakers work depends heavily on what they want to do and what they are trained to do.

Some people who enjoy baking at home would like to sell baked goods out of their own homes. You should be careful if you choose to go this route, because many states have laws forbidding the sale of any foods from an unlicensed kitchen. For more information about licensing your home kitchen and opening a home-based business, see Chapter 18.

Pastry shops

In a pastry shop, a baker may make the cakes and products that pastry cooks and chefs decorate or fill, but unless the baker has experience in advanced decorating, he or she probably won't work with the product after it has finished baking. Of course, this is dependent on the size of the pastry shop and whether it employs a pastry chef. Bakers at pastry shops may bake and decorate simple cakes with icing flowers and phrases such as "Happy Birthday" piped on top. They may also bake more specialized pastries such as tarts, tortes, petit fours, cream puffs, éclairs, and palmier pastries, which are typically not found in bakeries.

Bakeries

Although some pastry shops employ bakers, most bakers work in bakeries. Many different types of bakeries exist, from commercial bakeries (that bake items to sell directly to businesses and restaurants) to privately owned bakeries (that sell to the public) to specialty bakeshops (that focus on specific items such as cakes, cupcakes, or breads). The role of bakers in these types of bakeries is usually the same: They are in charge of baking and distributing products for customers. In a bakery, you're more likely to find selections such as bagels, loafs of flavored breads, rolls, croissants, Danishes, simple cakes and cupcakes, pies, quiches, cookies, breakfast pastries, muffins, and laminated dough products. Bakers working in a bakery spend most of their day concentrating on baking items — usually in bulk — rather than decorating or creating artistic desserts. Because many bakeries typically offer lavishly decorated cakes for birthday and weddings, some bakers may take on the role of decorator as needed or hire someone to solely decorate cakes.

Restaurants and hotel restaurants

Bakers who work in a restaurant or hotel restaurant are typically responsible for all the baked goods, such as breads and rolls to be served with entrées and desserts such as cakes and pies. In addition to making foods for restaurant customers, a baker working in a hotel restaurant may also be responsible for items needed for room service. Bakers are usually at work in the early hours of the morning to prepare for breakfast, lunch, or dinner service — unlike most of the other restaurant employees — because preparing many baked goods takes a lot of time.

Banquet halls and catering companies

Because banquet halls and caterers provide food for events, they may rely on bakers to produce large quantities of breads and rolls, plus desserts such as cakes, pastries, or éclairs. A baker working at a banquet hall or for a caterer may also be required to decorate specialty cakes for events such as weddings, birthdays, or company parties. These types of jobs are usually part time or on an as-needed basis.

Grocery stores

Most grocery stores have their own bakery department stocked with numerous baked goods, including doughnuts, pastries, cookies, bagels, breads, rolls, pies, and specialty cakes made right in the store. Some stores even offer gourmet items similar to what's found in bakeries and pastry shops.

Grocery store bakery departments have a staff of bakers to produce these baked goods from scratch each day. In addition to preparing breads and other baked items, bakers are typically responsible for baking and decorating cakes for all occasions — including birthday and wedding cakes — so they should have at least some cake decorating skills and experience.

Career profile

Baking is sometimes called a science, and it requires specific traits and training that sets it apart from other cooking careers. In this section, we detail what it takes to be a baker, the necessary experience and education, salary expectations, advancement prospects, and union involvement expectations.

Personality traits

Not everyone who wants to work in culinary arts has what it takes to be a baker. Bakers usually share many of the same personality traits as pastry chefs, particularly patience, organization, and precision. They must spend ample time carefully measuring and weighing ingredients, because too much or too little of a particular ingredient can ruin an entire batch. Rushing the long process of mixing, rising, baking, and cooling the baked goods can make the product a failure and waste time and ingredients.

Although you can't rush the baking process, you should possess speed and accuracy. Think about how delicious warm pastries are right from the oven. Good bakers know how to time their baked goods for anxiously awaiting customers.

Finally — and we can't stress this enough — if you aren't the kind of person who can get up before the roosters, then you shouldn't pursue a job as a baker. Many baked goods are breakfast foods. You can't start preparing these foods even an hour or two behind schedule. If you're late, your products won't be ready for the morning commute, the time when many Americans eat their breakfast. Your bakery (or pastry shop or grocery store) may be a pit stop for people on their way to work and school. These people will depend on you to have fresh goods ready for them to purchase and eat as they board their subway trains, buses, and minivans to start their day.

Everyone knows that breakfast is the most important meal of the day. Because bakers prepare many breakfast foods, they are an important part of Americans' morning routine.

Salaries

Just as with pastry chefs, salaries for bakers vary depending on where you work, your employer's salary guidelines, the size of the business you work in, your duties, your experience, and your education. A baker working in a large commercial bakery may not make more money than a baker working in a privately owned bakeshop. The average salary for a baker in the United States ranges from $20,000 to $50,000, according to Payscale.com.

Education and training

The education and training bakers receive varies greatly. Some bakers train at top-notch culinary schools, whereas others learn what they need to know at home or by watching family members. Many bakeries are owned by generations of family members who have little or no formal baking education. Other places of employment are staffed by bakers with years of education and experience.

As a rule of thumb, the more education and training you have, the more valuable you are as a baker and the more likely you will be to land a good job. Other skills, such as the ability to decorate cakes, also influence your worth as an employee. Your education, experience, and skills also determine how much you'll be paid as a baker (see "Gaining Education and Experience" later in this chapter).

Advancement prospects

Advancement opportunities for bakers depend on their education, experience, and skills. Bakers typically start their careers at the bottom and work their way up the ladder. You may begin by baking breads and only breads, graduate to baking cakes, and then move on to also decorating cakes. You may eventually advance to head baker and oversee other bakers or open your own business.

Unions and associations

Many different bakers' associations, such as the American Bakers Association, the Retail Bakers of America, and the Independent Bakers Association, provide information and resources about the ever-changing culinary industry. Individual bakers do not typically join these associations. Instead, bakery owners enroll their entire business in these associations and pay depending on the total revenue of the business. Private bakeries that sell to the public don't pay as much as commercial bakeries that supply products for grocery stores across the country.

In addition to associations, unions for bakers exist to help protect and improve bakers' working conditions. The Bakery, Confectionery, Tobacco Workers, and Grain Millers International Union (BCTGM), the Bakers' Guild of America, and Bakers Food and Allied Workers Union (BFAWU) are examples of these types of unions. Typically, bakeries that are part of a union pay their bakers more and offer more benefits. Whether your bakery is part of a union may depend on your location and the size of the bakery.

Savoring Specialization

When entering the world of pastry arts, you may choose to go in a variety of directions. You can work with bread, cakes, or even candy. You may choose to work in a more traditional setting, such as a bakery or a restaurant, or you may choose to open your own shop and specialize in a particular area.

Plenty of pastry professionals around the world have started small specialty businesses that focus on producing one type of product — and producing it well. Sprinkles Cupcakes in Beverly Hills, for example, became America's first successful cupcake bakery in 2004. Since then, founder Candace Nelson has opened additional shops in some of the biggest and busiest cities in the country, including Chicago, Washington D.C., and New York. See Chapter 18 for more information about becoming a culinary entrepreneur.

Areas of specialization in the pastry arts may include large-scale showpieces, sugar work, confections, cake decorating, and chocolate work. If you choose to specialize in any of these areas, you may find the job you're looking for in a restaurant, hotel, casino, or privately owned shop. Today, the two most common areas of pastry-art specialization are chocolate work and cake decorating or designing.

Sweets get a shout-out on television

It's no secret that desserts are gaining popularity — and in a big way! Specialty cake, cupcake, and cookie shops are popping up across America and are the basis for many reality television shows. These reality shows range from profiles about specific businesses, such as *Ace of Cakes, Cake Boss,* and *D.C. Cupcakes,* to competitions such as *Cupcake Wars, Top Chef* *Just Desserts, Last Cake Standing,* and *Ultimate Cake Off. Amazing Wedding Cakes* showcases exquisite creations that are more like works of art than food. These television shows give us a glimpse into the world of desserts as pastry chefs and bakers demonstrate what it's like to work in this sweet industry.

Becoming a chocolatier

If you're a lifelong fan of chocolate and enjoy working with your hands, you may want to become a *chocolatier,* a chef who specializes in chocolate. Chocolatiers don't create chocolate using cacao beans — that's a chocolate maker — but they use the products created by chocolate makers to make tasty confections and build impressive showpieces.

You may not need a formal education to become a successful chocolatier, but a certificate or degree in the culinary or pastry arts will certainly open more doors for you. Typically, schools don't offer chocolatier degrees, but most pastry arts programs offer chocolate courses that teach you the basics of chocolate work. You can also learn many of the techniques chocolatiers use by reading books and surfing the Internet. You can perfect those techniques and receive hands-on training and experience if you attend chocolate classes and work alongside professionals in the business. Often, students interested in pursuing specialized careers in chocolate work look for apprenticeships working under Master Chocolatiers in specialty shops. The best way to find a chocolatier apprenticeship is to stop in chocolate shops and ask if they have any opportunities for someone wishing to learn about chocolate.

Regardless of how you want to incorporate chocolate into your career, working with chocolate is always challenging and demanding. One little mistake — perhaps an accidental drop of water in a chocolate mixture or an ill-advised adjustment to your heat source — can ruin an entire batch. Because chocolate is so temperamental and sensitive, chocolatiers must be patient, creative, skillful, and knowledgeable about the ingredients they work with. This means they should know how to work with equipment such as dehumidifiers and air filtration units to ensure harmonious working conditions. To successfully execute chocolate-based creations, chocolatiers must understand specific techniques such as tempering, molding, and sculpting.

Chocolatiers must also be familiar with the latest trends in flavor pairings in the culinary world. To be a culinary professional in chocolate, you must know the many types of chocolate beyond milk, white, and dark and understand the distinctions between semisweet, bittersweet, unsweetened, and even couverture and gianduja chocolates. You also have to know how to incorporate ingredients such as honey, lemongrass, raspberries, hazelnuts, oranges, mint, and even chili peppers into chocolate. Understanding which flavors work best with different types of chocolate is key to producing unique and tasty bonbons, candies, chocolate sculptures, and other confections.

Decorating specialty cakes

Pastry chefs who decorate cakes can be thought of as artists rather than cake decorators or designers. These professionals work with tools such as airbrushes, paints, knives, stencils (and sometimes even power tools!) to complete their products. Often times, intricate cakes, such as wedding cakes, are seen as stunning works of art.

Cake decorators or designers are in high demand around the world. Many people are ready and willing to pay big bucks to designers who find ways to turn their most cherished memories into cakes. If you can handle the pressure of producing a cake that will please even the pickiest customer — from the brattiest bridezilla who wants a wedding cake to match her dress to the overzealous mother looking for the perfect cake for her daughter's sweet 16 party — consider becoming a cake decorator or designer. But before you start taking cake orders, consider taking courses to learn the techniques you'll need to decorate these complex cakes.

Cake-decorating classes are not only offered at culinary schools. Many crafts stores offer classes that teach basic decorating skills from icing a smooth cake to making roses out of frosting. These classes are a good start for anyone wanting to learn the basics. If you're interested in learning how to bake and decorate professional-looking cakes, think about pursuing a pastry-arts degree. Pastry-arts classes teach you not only how to bake the perfect cake but also how to decorate it with intricate designs.

Cake decorators need to be creative, but they also need to be patient perfectionists. In addition to knowing the basics of baking cakes and making fillings, they must understand flavor pairings so the cake, filling, and frosting don't clash. Many cake decorators and designers are pushing aside simple buttercream icing to work with *fondant,* a matte-smooth icing. If the fondant becomes cracked, bumpy, or folded, wedding-cake decorators must know how to fix or mask the blemish. They must also possess the skills to pipe icing into elaborate patterns and create edible flowers out of frosting or gum paste.

These pastry-art professionals may work in restaurants, hotels, or casinos. They may work for private catering companies or small, privately owned shops. Large shops may have employees who bake and other employees who decorate, while smaller shops require employees to bake cakes and decorate them. Regardless of where they work, all cake decorators must possess strong customer-service skills. Specialty-cake designers or decorators must be able to listen to what their clients want and then produce it exactly. The cakes will be a staple and focal point at their customers' weddings, birthday parties, and bar mitzvahs, so it's extremely important that the product be professional and exceptional.

Gaining Education and Experience

Sure, you can teach yourself much of what you need to know to work in the pastry-arts industry. You can learn the basics of baking by reading instructional texts, watching videos online, and even tuning in to your favorite television shows. But you're more likely to find a job in your field if you have the proper education and experience necessary. To hone your skills and improve your techniques, look into some of the many educational options available to you.

As we discuss in Chapters 3 and 4, if you're looking to save a bit of cash while you pursue an education, a community college may be the best place to begin your search for programs that offer certifications or degrees in baking or pastry arts. Some community colleges offer associate's degrees and certification in pastry arts in addition to skilled certifications that prepare students to start their careers as assistant bakers.

Technical schools or vocational schools are next in line. Depending on the services offered and the location of the school, these credits may be more expensive than community-college credits, and you may need to take more of them. On the other hand, you can also find some technical-school programs that take a year or less to complete.

If you're looking to attend a top-notch school where the most successful culinary professionals in the world completed their education, you're going to have to dish out a few more bucks and definitely more time. These top schools include the Culinary Institute of America, the French Pastry School in Chicago, Illinois, and Le Cordon Bleu Schools. You even have the option to travel out of the country to schools such as Ecole Nationale Supérieure de la Pâtisserie in France or the Italian Institute for Advanced Culinary and Pastry Arts in Italy.

Of course, you don't have to enroll in a certification or degree program at all if you don't want to. Many successful pastry chefs and bakers taught themselves exactly what they needed to know, and others enrolled in an apprenticeship program. Apprenticeships are great ways to get a hands-on real-life education in the culinary field. They are inexpensive, but they do, however, require more time to complete than an externship or internship. Most importantly, apprenticeships can help you get your foot in the door when it's time to find employment.

Baking/pastry arts certificate

You can easily earn a certification in pastry arts or baking in less than two years. In fact, you can complete many programs offered in the United States in about a year at community colleges, technical schools, and culinary schools as well as through associations and organizations such as the American Culinary Federation. Taking courses to fulfill the requirements of this certificate enables you to learn about cakes, pies, breads, pastries, wedding cakes, and even showpieces. You'll learn how to flawlessly decorate cakes, mix dough, and temper chocolate. Some schools even offer courses in sugar work and centerpieces.

Completing the work required for a pastry arts and baking certificate is typically as easy as attending classes and producing quality work during labs. You don't normally have to complete any hours in a professional kitchen or bakery, nor do you typically have to take many business or math classes. The specific requirements depend on the school and the program, however. (Taking some seemingly unrelated courses is something you may have to do if you pursue a degree, which we discuss in the next section.)

Obtaining a certification doesn't require as much time or money as a degree and is a good way to get your foot in the door of any restaurant, bakery, or specialty store. Completing a certification program shows that you have a true interest in the culinary field and are willing to do a bit of extra work to attain your goals. You won't be able to take on the role of executive pastry chef right away with a certificate, but if you build on your education with experience, you can get there someday.

Degrees in baking/pastry arts

If you choose to pursue a baking or pastry arts associate's degree and are a full-time student, you should expect to complete the program in approximately two years. This degree requires you to complete nearly twice the number of courses needed to attain a pastry-arts or baking certificate. If you're interested in attaining a bachelor's degree, you may be enrolled in school for three or four years, depending on the requirements of the program.

Students who earn an associate's or bachelor's degree not only learn about breads, cakes, pies, and chocolate, but also learn about starting a business, budgeting, and purchasing/ordering. You may have to complete a few business, entrepreneurship, and basic mathematics or accounting courses if you choose to follow this path. These courses are important because they teach you what you need to know to operate or run a kitchen.

If you already know that you want to own your own pastry shop or bakery, or if you want to be an executive pastry chef, you may want to pursue a bachelor's degree that focuses on working in both the front and the back of the house. These degrees have names such as Baking/Pastry Arts and Food Service Management. Schools that offer these programs wish to ensure that graduates leave their classrooms with the knowledge required to open a business, run a kitchen, or both.

Unlike the work that goes into a baking or pastry-arts certificate, an associate's or bachelor's degree often requires you to spend a certain number of hours working in a kitchen or bakery. Some schools may require you to complete an internship where you work for credit hours (and occasionally money!). Others present you with options such as traveling abroad, interning, and even picking up a second concentration before you complete the program. The belief at many institutions is that a person who completes a degree program should graduate with both education and experience.

Your course load at colleges or universities that offer associate's or bachelor's degrees will most likely include courses not related to the culinary field. You may have to take environmental science, biology, English, history, psychology, and even gym classes to meet their graduation requirements. You may also have to participate in community-service learning, which means you'll volunteer at various organizations that work with or serve food, such as the local food bank. Although these courses and experiences may seem pointless, many colleges and universities agree that students who complete these classes are well-rounded and have a better understanding of the world than students who only learn what they're interested in. Research the schools you're interested in to find out what courses they require before paying a deposit and enrolling in classes.

Externships and apprenticeships

Regardless of whether you complete a certificate or a degree in pastry arts, you should apply for an externship or apprenticeship to gain more experience. Externships are similar to internships (supervised work assignments done by students), but they're typically shorter (some only last a few days) and can't normally be used toward college credits. Depending on the duration of the externship, you may not get any hands-on experience. Instead, you may simply shadow a person in your field for a set amount of time.

You don't need to complete, or even be enrolled in, a certification or degree program to attain an externship. But if you're not in the process of completing a program and you're competing for the externship with someone who is, the other person may get the opportunity instead of you simply because that person has shown a commitment of money and time to learn about the profession.

You'll rarely find a paid externship. Some apprenticeships, however, are paid. Though not as popular as culinary courses, apprenticeships are a great way to enter the world of culinary and pastry arts. Apprenticeships allow you to study your craft alongside successful members of your field. You may not do much at first (think dishwasher), but if you keep a positive attitude and show your chef that you truly wish to learn, your responsibilities will grow. Apprenticeships can last weeks, months, or even years. An apprentice is often asked to be a permanent member of the kitchen staff.

Externships and apprenticeships are easy to find, especially if you're in school or have recently graduated. Many culinary instructors have various connections in the field who accept externs and apprentices as a favor to their old friends or colleagues. If your instructor doesn't know someone who may be able to help you, your academic advisor or the people who work in the career development office of your school should be able to point you in the right direction.

If you choose to forego getting a certificate or degree and don't know any instructors who may be able to set you up with an externship or apprenticeship, don't be deterred you from applying for these opportunities. You can hunt for your own opportunities or even create your own. If you have a favorite bakery or pastry shop or you frequent a particular grocery store with a bakery that produces items you wish to learn about, don't be afraid to approach the managers of these places. Ask if they have ever offered externships or employed apprentices in the past. If they haven't, ask if they're interested in doing so. They can start with you!

Chapter 9

Life On the Inside: Personal and Private Chefs

In This Chapter

▶ Distinguishing between the jobs of personal and private chefs

▶ Discovering what makes a good personal or private chef and how to become one

*I*n the hustle and bustle of today's high-tech world, people often try to get more done in less time, and one thing that often takes a back seat in their busy lives is nutritious, delicious, home-cooked meals. After a long day at the office, many people want nothing more than to kick off their shoes and relax. As they drive home, however, a feeling of dread washes over them as they ponder one of life's toughest questions: "What's for dinner?" A bowl of cereal or takeout from a restaurant is the answer for many families settling for a quick, if unsatisfying, option.

How would you like to be the bright spot — the savior of dinner — for a busy, overbooked individual or family? If the thought of preparing delicious home-cooked meals for others sounds appealing to you, then you may want to consider a career as a personal or private chef.

Personal chefs cook meals in either their own space or their clients' kitchens and package the meals so that when the clients arrive home, all they have to do is heat and serve. Private chefs prepare meals right in a client's home and have them ready at a requested time each day. They also take care of after-dinner cleanup. In addition, personal and private chefs often do most — if not all — the grocery shopping, which saves busy people even more valuable time.

Contrary to popular belief, personal and private chefs are not only for the rich and famous. They're becoming more popular among busy individuals and families who simply don't have the desire or time to cook. We walk you through the details of both jobs in this chapter so you can decide if this growing industry is the right fit for you.

Personal Chefs: Making Meals Easier

A personal chef concocts delicious dishes and prepares them for multiple clients in either their clients' kitchens or in a rented space. Personal chefs usually do the grocery shopping for needed supplies; plan, store, and prepare meals; and then clean up afterward and leave.

If personal chefs cook from a space other than a client's kitchen, they must ensure the space is licensed. They can't cook out of their own kitchens unless they have a license. They can cook, however, from their clients' unlicensed kitchens because the food is prepared and eaten in the kitchen. The personal chef in not allowed to transport or sell food that was prepared in unlicensed kitchens.

While it varies from person to person, most personal chefs choose the menu based on their clients' likes and dislikes, although some personal chefs allow the client to dictate exactly what they want with little input. It all comes down to what the client prefers and how flexible the personal chef is.

All the meals they prepare are tailored to their clients' tastes, requests, and dietary restrictions, and they're prepared in such a way that clients can heat and eat at their convenience. Sometimes personal chefs cook and plan small dinner parties and special-occasion events such as birthday or anniversary dinners. They also may teach cooking classes in clients' homes. Personal chefs typically work for themselves, serving as many clients as they choose. They usually sign a contract with a client that spells out important terms such as how many meals will be prepared, when they will be prepared, and the fee for services.

Starting out as a personal chef is difficult in the beginning. Most personal chefs have years of education and experience and have worked in the industry for many years, honing their skills and expanding their repertoire. Some personal chefs may start out their careers working for a company that hires out personal chef services, while others may choose to go the route of self-employment. The best piece of advice for any personal chef is to get your name out there. Use past employers, family, friends, and instructors to help spread the word of your services as well as advertisements in local publications.

If you choose to go the route of opening your own business, make sure you have the proper licenses and insurance. For more information about these requirements, contact your local small business association, chamber of commerce, health department, and/or cooperative extension. Also, see Chapter 18.

Pros and cons

Like any job in the culinary field, working as a personal chef has its ups and downs. It's not for everybody, so make sure you weigh the advantages and disadvantages if you're thinking of becoming a personal chef.

Pros

As a personal chef, you have the luxury of picking and choosing your clients. You can choose to work only for clients who prefer the types of foods you like to cook, prepared the way you like to prepare them. Personal chefs usually don't work set hours, which means you also can work at your own pace. You can choose to cook for specific clients on a regular basis or take small jobs that require you to cook only for a special event. The slower pace allows you to be more creative and whip up new and exciting dishes.

Some personal chefs choose to cook in a rented space and transport the food to their clients' homes. This saves the hassle of lugging food and equipment around all day and allows personal chefs to work in one space all day until they have to transport the food. Others prefer to cook in their clients' homes when their clients aren't home. Both of these arrangements remove the pressure of someone watching your every move, which results in a less stressful working environment. Many chefs prefer this easygoing environment to the hustle and bustle of a restaurant or hotel kitchen, which can be very stressful at times. Another advantage to working in a rented space is getting to work in a comfortable space usually designed for cooking with top-of-the-line appliances, and, if you're lucky, air conditioning! Some private home kitchens may also provide a personal chef with such luxuries.

Cons

Though some personal chefs can pick and choose clients to please themselves, others have to worry about finding enough clients. Without a sufficient number of clients, you may need to find an additional job to supplement your income. So to gain customers, you must be skilled in advertising and be able to market yourself, which can be difficult and time consuming. You may even need to hire someone who can help you in these areas.

If you don't have enough potential customers to select only the ones you like best, you may find yourself working with picky eaters. Some clients can be very particular and request dishes made with certain ingredients or cooked in a specific way. Such restrictions may make some personal chefs feel stifled because they can't be as creative as they'd like. Because not all members of a client's family may like the same foods, personal chefs sometimes have to prepare multiple versions of one dish for a meal. For instance, if the parents in a family you work for enjoy broccoli but the children don't, you may be asked to make broccoli for the parents and a different vegetable for the children.

When working as a personal chef, the lack of a set schedule can sometimes make life difficult because you're unable to plan ahead for certain events or social functions.

Another disadvantage of working as a personal chef is lugging supplies and equipment from location to location and working in less-than-ideal spaces. Some rented spaces don't have updated appliances or tons of workspace. They may also be shared spaces and personal chefs may have to work around other people's schedules. These time constraints may lead to more stress and the inability to take on more clients. Kitchens in some private homes are modern, but others may be very outdated and not ideal work spaces (think of old — and possibly broken — appliances in shades of harvest gold or avocado!). Some kitchens may be small, cramped, and set up in a way that makes maneuvering difficult.

Working for multiple clients

Personal chefs work for all kinds of clients, from professionals who simply don't have the time (or the willingness) to cook for themselves to new parents who need a little extra help until their children are grown. Sometimes they work for older individuals who cannot handle chores such as cooking or grocery shopping. They also work for people who believe that having someone else tend to their cooking needs is more cost effective than actually doing the cooking, shopping, and dishwashing themselves.

Many personal chefs juggle a handful of clients. Sometimes you may cook for one client one day and a different client the next day. Other times you may cook for multiple clients in a single day. You can decide how to arrange your schedule based on the number of jobs you feel comfortable working each day and when your clients want their meals prepared.

It also depends on the types of clients you feel comfortable working with. If you enjoy cooking foods that most adults enjoy, you may tend to take on more clients without children, such as single professionals or older clients. Other personal chefs may enjoy cooking for children and take on clients that include families with multiple children. Some personal chefs like to take on clients who enjoy the types of foods they are accustomed to cooking and preparing, while others prefer more challenging clients who request dishes that allow them to be creative and think outside the box.

Sometimes personal chefs work for clients with dietary restrictions. Cooking for people with food allergies or restrictions is an important skill to add to your repertoire. It makes you more desirable and can help broaden your client base. You can include these skills on your résumé and in your advertisements, or ask your existing clients to spread the word.

You can learn how to cook for restricted diets by attending classes or by reading specialized books or cookbooks. Many people are lactose intolerant, for example, and cannot consume any dairy products. Others have diabetes and can't consume sugar. As a personal chef, you should be skilled at finding substitutes for certain ingredients that taste just as good and don't alter the final outcome of the recipe. Knowing how to correctly substitute ingredients in a recipe comes in handy in such cases.

Remember, the amount of money you make doesn't necessarily depend on the number of clients you have. You're better off having a smaller clientele who is pleased with your work than having numerous clients to whom you're unable to give 100 percent. Think of your clients and your schedule when you determine the number of clients you can serve. Don't take on more jobs than you can handle!

Finding out where personal chefs work

Personal chefs can either be self-employed or work for a large or small business that contract out personal chefs on an as-needed basis. They can also run their own businesses, employing other personal chefs. See Chapter 18 for more information about becoming a culinary entrepreneur.

Working for yourself

As a self-employed personal chef, you typically begin your day at a grocery or specialty store, purchasing needed supplies including food and packaging supplies for the finished meals. A good personal chef would have already planned out the week's — or even month's — meals in advance and wrote out lists of ingredients needed for particular meals.

After your trek to the store, you'll head to either a rented space or to a client's home to begin cooking. If you cook in a rented space, you may not have to lug all of your equipment and supplies with you, depending on if you have a storage area. After you finish cooking, you pack and label the meals, clean up, and transport the meals to your clients.

If you cook at a client's home, you typically have to transport all of your stuff to and from the client's home. After you finish cooking, you package, label, and store the meals; clean up, pack your supplies, and leave. If you're working for multiple clients in one day, you'll most likely head to your next job.

Working for a personal chef service

Personal chefs who work for a company that hires out personal chefs are not much different than self-employed personal chefs in terms of the type of work they do. If you work for a service that hires out personal chefs, a client will contact the company and it will contract you for particular jobs. You're typically paid by the client — not the company — and the client pays a fee to the company for the use of their services.

Depending on the service, they may have someone who shops for your supplies as well as a space provided for you to cook your meals before transporting them to your clients. If not, you'll do all your own shopping and cook meals in a client's home. You'll do everything at the client's home, including packaging and storing the meals, and cleaning up before you leave and possibly head to another job.

Although personal chefs usually set their own hours, they must remember to schedule extra time between jobs just in case something doesn't go as planned. A burned dish may need to be remade and can throw a wrench in the most perfectly timed schedule. A good personal chef must be able to remain flexible and roll with the punches.

Career profile

Working as a personal chef requires great organizational skills and years of experience to produce impressive and appealing dishes for numerous clients. Personal chefs not only have to come up with fresh meal plans each week but also must learn the needs and requests of each client. Not everyone has what it takes to become a personal chef.

Personal Chef Ellen Postolowski

Ellen Postolowski is a personal chef and self-proclaimed former Taco Bell lover. Now embarrassed about her previous unhealthy eating habits, Postolowski focuses on cooking healthy meals for both her clients and herself. She spent six years preparing healthy meals for actress and journalist Joumana Kidd and her three children. Prior to meeting Kidd, Postolowski operated a baking business called Sweet Surrender, which was a commercial bakery that supplied desserts to restaurants. Kidd, who was looking for a personal chef to prepare healthy meals for her and her family, contacted Postolowski after hearing about her by word of mouth. While working for Kidd, Postolowski involved her children in the cooking process and educated them about nutrition and healthy eating. Postolowski, who currently resides in Allendale, New Jersey, published her first book about eating healthy, *It's Just Personal,* in 2009.

Personality traits

Personal chefs work with numerous people and generally have to market themselves, so they should have good interpersonal skills. They should be outgoing and friendly and not afraid to network or talk to others because many personal chefs get work through recommendations and by word of mouth from their existing clients. You never know who will need a personal chef — or who knows someone else who does.

Another valuable skill personal chefs should possess is organization so that they can juggle more than one job and cook for more than one client. To be a successful personal chef, you must be able to pay attention to details, keep special requests straight, and know which clients have allergies or dietary restrictions. You also should be knowledgeable about nutrition and numerous cuisines. The more you know about these areas, the more attractive you'll be to potential employers.

Personal chefs should be flexible, easygoing, and open-minded. You should be willing to make new dishes that are outside your comfort zone if that's what a client wants. If you're unwilling to try something new, you may risk alienating potential clients. Creativity and the ability to go with the flow are also essential characteristics. If you make a soufflé that does not turn out as expected, you may have to make another one, modify the intended dish, or switch quickly to a backup plan.

Because personal chefs often work in other people's homes, they must be honest and trustworthy and have respect for personal property. When finding and working with new clients, keep a list of references who can vouch for you.

As a personal chef, you must also have a high standard of cleanliness and know how to follow proper sanitation practices. Remember, you should always leave a client's kitchen sparkling clean when you're finished with a job.

Salaries

The salaries of personal chefs can vary greatly. A personal chef with a long list of clients doesn't necessarily make more money than a personal chef with a smaller clientele. If you're just starting out as a personal chef, you may have to spend money to make money. You'll need to market and advertise yourself and your services, and you may even need the assistance of someone who has experience in this area. Also, more education and experience will almost guarantee you more money. The average salary for a personal chef depends on these factors and the types of services and foods you offer. If you offer high-end gourmet dinners and cleaning services, you can charge more than a personal chef who cooks casseroles or simpler dishes and just puts everything in the dishwasher after they are finished.

Self-employed personal chefs and personal chefs working for a chef service usually get paid by the hour or by the job, depending on the contract established between the personal chef and the client and/or the company. One day of cooking can net anywhere from $50 to more than $1,000, depending on factors such as the number of people they have to prepare food for and the types of dishes they're cooking.

Education and training

Education and expertise are the keys to landing a job as a personal chef. Many personal chefs attain a culinary degree and spend years in the kitchens of restaurants, hotels, or other establishments, honing their skills before deciding to pursue this line of work. In addition to attending culinary school, you can gain certification as either a Personal Certified Executive Chef (PCEC) or a Personal Certified Chef (PCC) through the American Culinary Federation or a Certified Personal Chef (CPC) through the United States Personal Chef Association. These certifications require years of experience, hours of training, in addition to a written exam and practical exam that test knowledge and abilities. See Chapter 3 for more information about the different certifications available.

Advancement prospects

Most personal chefs work for themselves, so room for growth doesn't really exist in this field — that is, unless you transition to becoming a private chef, which is similar to a personal chef and is discussed in the later section "What Is a Private Chef?" Personal chefs may also choose to open their own chef service and manage multiple personal chefs. Some may decide to change careers altogether and take jobs in restaurants or hotels, or they may decide to teach cooking classes. For more information about becoming a culinary instructor, see Chapter 14.

Unions and associations

Because personal chefs usually are employed by the hour or job or work for a personal chef service that contracts them out by the job, they typically don't belong to a union. Several associations for personal chefs do exist, however, including the American Personal & Private Chef Association (APPCA), Big City Chefs, and United States Personal Chef Association (USPCA). These associations provide personal chefs with training and education materials, certification prospects, networking opportunities, and information about finding work as a personal chef.

Private Chefs: Cooking for a Single Client

A private chef and a personal chef have similar job duties, but private chefs primarily work for a single client instead of multiple clients. Private chefs often live with their clients and prepare and serve all the clients' daily meals and snacks. The kitchen is their domain, and they usually take care of all aspects that pertain to it — cooking, grocery shopping, cleaning, and so on.

Private chefs prepare all the meal plans for their client. Some even accompany their clients on vacations. Some private chefs are permitted to eat and interact with their clients and clients' families, whereas others are not.

Private chefs may have special duties relating to cooking and the household in general. If you work for a client who's hosting a special event, you may be expected to manage the event even if you're not actually cooking for it. For example, for a large event, a private chef often hires a caterer and manages the menu and any additional staff for the event. As a private chef you may also teach cooking classes for your clients' friends. Your client may even ask you to perform additional duties that are unrelated to cooking, such as light cleaning, dog walking, and administrative work.

Pros and cons

Working as a private chef — as with any other culinary job — has its positives and negatives. It's not an ideal job for everyone, but it can be very rewarding and lucrative. If you choose to follow this path, make sure it's right for you.

Pros

Private chefs usually are paid handsomely and receive benefits such as 401(k) plans, health care, paid vacations, and sick time. Clients may even provide living quarters inside their home or in a nearby apartment plus the use of a car. Private chefs may also travel with their clients around the world.

Private chefs typically get to work in well-equipped kitchens with modern appliances. They get to be creative and develop menus that are interesting and new. They may even be asked to plan lavish dinner parties or teach cooking classes, which may present a fun opportunity to do something different. Depending on the client, private chefs may have the opportunity to cook for and meet famous or influential people.

Because you work for the same people, you get to know their likes and dislikes and this gives private chefs an opportunity to try new recipes without stressing over whether their clients will enjoy new dishes.

Cons

If you decide to pursue a career as a private chef, understand that it can be isolating because it involves working with the same people day after day. In restaurants, people come and go and you meet numerous people, but in a private home, you see the same people each day. Because your customers never change, you may have trouble keeping them excited with new and creative foods, and cooking may become repetitive if clients request the same meals over and over again. In addition, you may have to cook for picky clients and make more than one dish for different family members. Furthermore, the hours can be demanding and leave little room for a personal life. Some clients request private chefs to make all meals, including snacks — even in the middle of the night — so be sure you know what you're getting into before you commit to a job as a private chef.

Responsibilities, such as extra duties and hours worked, as well as time off, pay, and living arrangements, should be agreed upon between the client and the private chef and written down in a contract, prior to the private chef's first day of work.

Because private chefs may have to cook for special events involving numerous guests, you must know how to cook for a crowd or be able to hire and manage help for these types of affairs. Private chefs also may be responsible for making less glamorous meals, such as packing lunches for their clients' children. You'll have to stay within the limits of a budget and come up with new and creative dishes without breaking the bank.

Another con private chefs face is getting too close to their clients. Although clients may treat their private chefs as family members, chefs must remember that they're employees and can be dismissed at any time.

Sometimes the line between employer and employee gets blurred and you may find yourself in a difficult position. Make sure you establish firm boundaries about what your job entails from the start. For example, a client may ask you to perform a task that's not part of your normal job responsibilities, such as doing a load of laundry or walking the family dog. You may not know how to handle these requests. If you keep your relationship strictly professional, you should have no problem declining to perform a task. If you do decide to perform the task, you should inform your employer that you're making an exception and that it's not part of your normal responsibilities.

Working for one family

Working as a private chef is different from working as a personal chef because you typically work for — and live with — only one client or family. Although you may enjoy spending time getting to know and working with just one family, you may have difficulty keeping your personal life separate from your professional life. Remember, however, that you're an employee, not part of the family. You should have a clearly defined set of ground rules and understand what they expect from you before you take a job with a potential employer.

Speaking of employers, be sure that you mesh well with potential clients before agreeing to work for them. If you butt heads with your employer, your working (and living) environment will be tense and less than ideal. The bottom line is that even if you don't necessarily like your employer, you must be able to get along, because you'll be spending large chunks of time together, especially if you're living under the same roof.

Defining your job within the household

Some private chefs choose not to do any work — laundry, cleaning (except the kitchen), dog walking, babysitting, and so on — outside the kitchen. Other private chefs are more flexible, however, and may be willing to take on additional tasks. You can decide for yourself what you're willing to do and what you're not willing to do, but in any case you must make your policies known to any potential employers and should be stated clearly in a signed contract. Additionally, each employer is different and will have a set of rules for you to follow.

Making meals for the family

At first, integrating into the family and learning everyone's routines may be difficult. In addition to developing a schedule, you'll need to create meal plans and purchase needed ingredients and supplies. Try to learn the likes and dislikes of the family, as well as any allergies or dietary restrictions, as soon as you can.

After some time, you'll most likely know your clients' favorite meals, so you should exercise some creativity and come up with ways to spice up these meals to keep them fresh and exciting. You also want to keep a few tricks up your sleeve, because you never know whom to expect at dinner. If your client has a vegan guest, for example, you should know how to prepare meals without meat or dairy. If a family member is diagnosed with high cholesterol, you should do your homework and learn how to prepare heart-healthy meals. You should also know how to prepare healthy meals for children. Because most children are picky, their parents will be grateful to you if you try to make fruits and vegetables fun and exciting so that kids will expand their horizons and try new things. (Making fruits and vegetables interesting is good for picky adults, too!)

Living and traveling with your client

Most private chefs typically live with their employers because they work long hours and spend so much time at their employers' homes. Employers like to have their private chefs close in case they need them at a moment's notice. Private chefs may have a bedroom inside the main house or separate living quarters outside the house. Some employers may even pay for an apartment nearby. Not all private chefs live with their employers, though. Some live in houses of their own with their own families. The living arrangements vary drastically from employer to employer, so be sure to discuss them in detail with potential employers.

Sometimes clients like to bring their private chef along on vacation to take care of their cooking needs while they're away from home. Other times, private chefs receive this time off to do what they choose. Your employer will let you know what to expect.

Finding a job as a private chef

Landing a job as a private chef is more difficult than finding work as a personal chef, but it's not much different than landing any other type of job. Because private chefs have access to their clients' homes — and because sometimes these clients are high-profile actors, political figures, musicians, or otherwise well-known or powerful families — extra steps must be taken during the interview process, such as undergoing a background check.

The first step to finding a position as private chef is to put together a cover letter and résumé. See Chapter 16 for step-by-step instructions on how to write a cover letter and résumé. After you've written your résumé, create a sample menu for a typical week or even month to show to potential employers. Be sure to include substitutions for people with dietary restrictions such as diabetes or heart disease.

When your paperwork is ready, it's time to market yourself. Have family, friends, and former colleagues get your name out there and spread the word about your services. Take out advertisements in local publications. Leave your business card at establishments such as restaurants and grocery stores. Finding a career as a private chef takes legwork and networking. Many of these jobs are not advertised and are found by word of mouth, so the more people you know, the better off you'll be in your job search. Another way to find a job is through an agency such as Private Chefs, Inc. (PCI), which helps place private chefs in homes.

Career profile

More and more people depend on the expertise of private chefs and choose to hire them instead of cooking on their own or dining out. But not every chef is cut out to be a private chef. These positions are demanding and can require you to work long hours — even all hours of the night — depending on the client. In this section we let you know who's cut out to do the job and what particulars you can expect.

The Royal Chef: Darren McGrady

Private chef Darren McGrady has made meals for many important figures, such as Queen Elizabeth II, Princess Diana of Wales, and U.S. presidents Bill Clinton and Ronald Reagan. After training at the Savoy Hotel in London, England, from 1980 to 1982, he became a private chef at Buckingham Palace. For the next 11 years, he cooked meals for the Queen and the Duke of Edinburgh and catered banquets for many of the royal family's affairs. In addition to cooking, he traveled with the royal family to many destinations around the world. In 1993 he moved to Kensington Palace, where he became a private chef for Princess Diana of Wales and her family. While there, he prepared the family's meals and catered lavish dinner parties. In 1998 he and his family moved to the United States. He was the first private chef invited to cook at the James Beard House in New York, and in 2007 he released his first cookbook, *Eating Royally: Recipes and Remembrances from a Palace Kitchen.* McGrady currently works as a private chef in Dallas, Texas. In addition to cooking, he is a culinary instructor, an event planner, and a public speaker.

Personality traits

Private chefs must be honest and trustworthy. Clients have to be able to trust you not only to work and live in their home, among their children and belongings, but also to handle a budget and large amounts of money to purchase needed ingredients. You may also be privy to private conversations and see intimate things, such as clients in their pajamas. To be a private chef, you must be able to mind your own business and focus on the job, ignoring what's going on in the background.

Maturity is just as important as trustworthiness. Many clients may have famous or high-profile family members or friends who frequently visit their homes. Private chefs must treat these people with the utmost respect. Never ask for an autograph or ask to have a photograph taken with them — no matter how close you are to your client. If in doubt about what behavior is acceptable in these situations, err on the side of caution and don't do it.

Private chefs should also be very organized. You need to develop meal plans, shop for ingredients, and stick to a budget. You must know what foods your clients like and dislike and remember to accommodate any special requests or dietary restrictions.

Other important traits are creativity, flexibility, and adaptability. You will need to generate dishes that are new and exciting to your clients. Sometimes you will need to make meals for numerous guests, such as during dinner parties, or for unexpected guests, so you need to be able to easily adapt without getting stressed.

Salaries

Working as a private chef can be very lucrative, which means you face stiff competition for these much-sought-after positions. The salary for a private chef varies and usually is based on years of experience, hours worked, and duties performed. A private chef can typically make $25 to $50 per hour and up, depending on the employer. Private chefs who work for famous people don't necessarily make more money than those who work for normal families. Many private chefs receive generous benefits in addition to their regular pay.

Education and training

Education and experience are important for landing a job as a private chef. After all, you'll be the one doing all the cooking, menu planning, and food purchasing — without anyone to consult or fall back on — so knowing these important skills is imperative. We recommend attending a culinary institute to gain knowledge about all things food-related. In addition to food preparation and execution, you'll learn menu planning, knife skills, sanitation practices, and food purchasing — all areas in which you should excel as a private chef. You also may gain experience and hone your skills by working in a restaurant or hotel or by completing an internship or apprenticeship. You can gain certification through the American Personal and Private Chef Association, which offers certification options such as a home-study program or a live seminar training program, or through the American Culinary Federation, which offers two certifications for both private and personal chefs: Personal Certified Executive Chef (PCEC) or Personal Certified Chef (PCC). The United States Personal Chef Association also offers a Certified Personal Chef (CPC) designation. See Chapter 3 for more information about the different certifications available.

Advancement prospects

Private chefs are typically employed by private individuals or families, so room for advancement doesn't really exist in this industry. In addition to searching for another family to work for, private chefs looking for a change of scenery can turn to jobs such as teaching cooking classes for multiple clients or teaching culinary classes at a university or college. They may even choose to find work in a restaurant or hotel kitchen or open their own catering business. For more information on catering, see Chapter 7.

Unions and associations

Private chefs are usually privately employed, so they typically don't belong to a union. Several associations, including the American Personal & Private Chef Association (APPC), Big City Chefs, and Private Chefs, Inc., are resources for private chefs that provide information about the industry.

Chapter 10

Old and New Trends: Food Artisans and Scientists

In This Chapter

▶ Understanding what a food artisan does

▶ Familiarizing yourself with the world of food science

*I*n recent years, the culinary industry has seen an increase in the demand for artisanal foods by business owners and consumers alike. What does it mean to produce artisanal foods? The focus is on creating one type of item, using quality, seasonal ingredients, and producing it exceptionally well. Many consumers associate artisanal products with old-fashioned foods because many of the methods artisans use are traditional, proven to be successful by past generations.

On the other side of the spectrum, the industry has also seen increases in the sales of prepared or prepackaged dinners. How do commissary cooks know what needs to be added to dishes to ensure they'll freeze correctly or stay fresh? How do they know which approach to packaging they should use? These decisions are made by food scientists, who research how foods react to certain chemicals in specific environments. These researchers take part in designing everything from food packaging to the machinery and technology used to make it. They also have a hand in determining the flavor and composition of said foods. Because much of food scientists' work results in new technologies and processes designed to make life easier, many consumers imagine the job of a food scientist to be futuristic.

In this chapter, we discuss the culinary careers of both old and new worlds. While food artisans work to keep tradition in play, food scientists look toward the future in an attempt to predict changes in the types of foods people want to consume — and how they want to consume it.

Taking a Traditional Approach: Food Artisans

If you aren't already considering becoming a food artisan, you may not have a clue about what this job entails. But don't feel too bad. Unfortunately, many people overlook food artisans and their products. Instead of frequenting farmers' markets and roadside stands for cured meats, aged cheeses, jams and jellies, or homemade bread, consumers tend to shop for brand-name products at large grocery stores, examining labels for anything marked "fat free," "no sugar added," or — in recent years — "organic."

Despite these habits, the United States has been experiencing a slow artisanal movement since the 1970s. Many food enthusiasts have urged consumers to look around them for locally grown and handcrafted products before visiting their local superstores. The growing popularity of these artisanal products ensures that more shoppers are consuming fresh and natural goods that have gone unaltered by modern production methods. It also keeps smaller, local businesses out of the red.

In this section, you find out how you can join the artisanal-foods trend as a producer, not just a consumer. We explain what food artisans do and where they do it, and give you an overview of some career specifics.

Seeing what food artisans do

Successful food artisans are cooks and bakers who specialize in making premium products that they wish to sell commercially. Food artisans make, grow, or gather the following products, among others:

- Cheese
- Meats
- Oils, condiments, and dressings
- Pickles
- Jams, jellies, and marmalades
- Canned foods
- Mushrooms and berries
- Fish
- Bread
- Wine
- Beer

What makes these products different from the ones you find at your local supermarket? The time and effort that goes into producing them.

An *artisan* is someone who produces a limited quantity of select items, often with traditional methods. These traditional methods are typically taught to the artisan by family members, and many artisans are part of a small family business. Following these methods ensures that products are of the highest quality possible, but it also tends to take more time than modern methods, which limits the amount that can be produced. Limited quantities typically mean the demand for the products is quite high.

The work of food artisans is typically considered *handcrafted*. When you're dealing with food, however, this term doesn't (normally) mean the artisans mold your food into shapes with their bare hands. Instead, it means they're fully responsible for producing the food — from start to finish. They milk the cows, harvest and press the grapes, and raise and slaughter the pigs, steers, and chickens. They inspect the hops, grind the spices, and cultivate the lands before planting their seeds. They design the packaging, and they're normally in charge of their own marketing and sales. They're not afraid to get their hands dirty. In fact, most food artisans actually live for that opportunity.

Artisans don't make thousands upon thousands of their specialized products; instead, when the product is in season, they produce a limited number for their dedicated customers — and a little extra for small displays in local stores or at trade shows. You may also find these products at farmers' markets and roadside stands where local artisans can display their items without worrying about flashy signs, overcrowded store aisles, and salespeople who may be uneducated about the work that goes into producing their products.

The decision to venture into the world of food artisans is an important one — one that you should make only after you're well-informed. You need to attain the proper certifications and licenses before you start selling things you grow in your garden or bake in your oven. You also need to follow state-specific regulations put forth by the U.S. Food and Drug Administration (FDA), such as the Food Safety Modernization Act, which was signed into law in January 2011. Adhering to the FDA's rules ensures that your food or drink is prepared and packaged correctly and safe for people to consume. Be sure to do your research before you get into the business.

If you develop a product, technique, or method that no one else has ever seen or used before, you may apply for a patent. If you patent a product or technique, this means that you have exclusive rights to that product. If anyone else wants to use your ideas, the law requires them to get your permission first. To be granted a patent, your product or technique needs to be unprecedented — you have to be the first to come up with the idea and prove its success.

Many food artisans work alone or with their immediate families, whereas others have teams of 20 or 30 people working for them. Why the difference? The size of the staff depends on many things, but the success of the product is the key factor. If no one buys your product, then you can't afford to hire help. Many times, food artisans work alone or with a few close friends or family members to get the business off the ground. Then, when sales increase and they begin to make a profit (which can take years), they can choose to hire and expand. Of course, many artisanal foods are produced by small family companies that may not look to outsiders when hiring. So if you're looking to get into this line of work, you may need to create your own product to sell.

Finding out where food artisans work

Food artisans must work where they're able to grow, age, or manufacture their products. They must consider a variety of different factors when choosing an area of operation, such as the location's climate and ease of access. If they want to grow produce, they'll need to find fertile land in an area of the country that receives a good balance of sunlight and rainwater. If they plan on raising animals, they'll need a space with appropriate shelter and grazing room for their livestock that adheres to all federal, state, and county laws.

The size of the workspace may range from an eat-in kitchen to a large factory building. Their products may begin in a garden in the backyard or on acres of farmland and pastures. And after the product is ready to be shipped and sold, artisans must be ready to hit the road for the sake of sales.

Everyone and everything can be found online today — and that should include you and your products! Be sure to put some money toward a good (that is, functional and informative) website when you start selling your products. Include links to information that visitors may be looking for, such as descriptions of all the products you offer and your contact information for questions or orders. You can also use social networking sites and blogs to keep your business active online. On these types of sites, you can share recipes, photos, sound clips, and videos — and most of the time, it's free!

Working on the homestead

Artisans who have the means to produce their goods on their own property typically do so. Many artisans live on or near farms or pastures where they raise cows, steers, sheep, goats, buffalo, turkeys, chickens, or pigs. They use their land and greenhouses to grow fruits, vegetables, flowers, and grains.

If you own land and want to put it to use, first make sure that it can appropriately accommodate the number and size of the plants and animals you'd like to grow and raise. Today, artisans and farmers alike stress the importance of having enough room for animals to roam freely and for plants to grow without their roots, stems, and vines intertwining.

After artisans have the meat, cheese, or produce they need, they may then use their kitchens to finish the process. In their kitchens, they may prepare foods for pickling or canning, or they may concoct spice mixes to cure the meats. If the business is small enough, packaging and weighing may even be done in a standard home-kitchen.

Before you sell anything you make in your kitchen, you'll need to license the space for commercial development. This involves applying for and obtaining a business license, a food-handler permit, a food-preparation license, and sometimes a ServSafe certification. To learn more about which permits you would need (and why you need them!), check out Chapter 18.

Renting a space

If the business is too big to be contained within a licensed kitchen, the artisan may own a small farmhouse, factory building, or warehouse for production of their goods. If your home or yard isn't appropriate for your new business, you may choose to rent or lease a farming space, commercial kitchen, or storage facility. Here, artisans house all the equipment they need to make their product and may also store caskets of wine, wheels of cheese, freezers of meat, or dark coolers of home-brewed beer. Similar to the licensing of a kitchen, these areas must also meet state and federal food and beverage safety standards.

Hitting the road

Depending on the profits and size of the company, artisans may be able to hire other companies to pack and ship their products safely. If the company is small — especially if it's a one-man operation — the artisan hits the road himself to deliver the products and try to sell them to others.

One stop a food artisan may make is at local grocery stores. Although supermarkets are typically jam-packed with brand names, many carry a small supply of locally grown and produced items in an effort to show their support for local farmers and artisans.

Other places you may spot these premium products (and the artisans that crafted them!) are at farmers' markets or roadside stands. The handcrafted goods sold at these stands often come from farms or home kitchens a few miles from the location of the market. Artisans or their staff members work these stands.

Artisans also typically take their products on the road to appear at trade shows. They put their products on display there for members of the media, specialty food store buyers, restaurant supply buyers, and often the public. Trade shows give artisans the opportunity to show off their new products, offer samples, receive feedback, and gain customers. At most shows, awards are given in categories such as best product or best product design. An appearance at a trade show can be deemed a success if buyers show an interest in purchasing the product to use in their restaurants or sell in their stores. Be sure to hand out business cards with your website address to anyone who shows an interest in your product at trade shows and market-places.

Career profile

Food artisans are individuals dedicated to every part of their craft. They work on their products from beginning to end and they know these items like the backs of their hands. A successful food artisan is not always someone who makes an unthinkable amount of money selling a product, however. Rather, a food artisan is someone who, at the end of the day, has respect for his product and the people working to help make a dream become a reality.

Personality traits

The most important thing to possess as a food artisan is drive. This part of the food industry is not easy; you'll face many ups and downs, and you have to be able to stick it out through all of them. Anything and everything can — and probably will — affect your work as an artisan. You may lose customers due to a declining economy. You may lose products due to weather conditions such as droughts, heavy rains, or even wind storms. You may walk away from trade shows and farmers' markets having talked to no one about your product. For these reasons and more, being dedicated to what you do is important to your success.

If you own the business, you need to understand accounting and bookkeeping so you know whether you're making a profit. You also have to have a knack for marketing, public relations, and advertising. As the company grows, you can certainly hire someone to deal with those tasks, but at the beginning you may be on your own. You should also be organized and capable of keeping detailed records. For more information about starting your own business, see Chapter 18.

Finally, as with nearly every other job, food artisans and people who work for them must be tolerant of repetitiveness. Every day typically begins and ends in the same way. Animals need to be fed, plants need to be watered and trimmed, and products such as wine, beer, and cheese need to be inspected (and sometimes tasted!). Days at the market and visits to trade shows certainly break up the monotony, but ample time is still spent on the farm, in the kitchen, or in the factory.

Salaries

The amount of money food artisans make each year ranges from a mere $10,000 to hundreds of thousands of dollars. This range is largely dependent on the costs of producing your product and the demand for your product. For many artisans, making these high-quality goods is a hobby or a part-time (seasonal) job because making a living in this industry is difficult.

If you're looking for a full-time career and will stop at nothing until you achieve success working for an artisanal food company or as a food artisan, we do have some numbers for you. On average, a master cheese maker earns $48,000 each year, and a meat producer may make $58,000 with a college degree. If you work on the production line at a factory that makes artisanal condiments, you may make $15,000 a year. If you work your way up to a managerial position, however, you could see a salary in the range of $60,000 annually.

Winemakers and beer brewers typically make more money than cheese and meat producers. A winemaker may earn between $50,000 and $200,000 each year, and a vineyard manager may make up to $90,000 a year. Depending on the size of the brewery and the popularity of a specific beer, brewers may earn between $30,000 and $130,000 each year.

When asked about their jobs, many food artisans speak of inconsistent business and funds. The majority of small businesses don't actually make a profit for years after they open their doors or start offering their services to others. We don't want to deter you from this career; however, many successful food artisans do advise people who are considering this path to get involved slowly and have another source of income. Make artisanal foods your hobby or second job; don't sacrifice a steady paycheck to sit and wait for cheese to age.

Education and training

Education and experience are crucial to success in the food industry. As an artisan, both are important. If you know you want to start your own business producing premium food products in the future, consider pursuing an associate's or bachelor's degree in business management. Taking food courses related to the items with which you'll be working is a good idea, too.

If your father has dreams of you becoming a business partner in his artisanal business some day, you should probably look at both business and culinary classes. If you decide to major in business or entrepreneurship, think about adding a few courses about meat and food safety to your class schedule. If you understand how to prepare the food or drink you're selling and you know how to budget, market, and manage fellow employees, you should be in good shape to enter the industry.

If you simply want to work with an established food artisan, you may get lucky and find someone willing to take you on as an apprentice without any prior experience. In this kind of arrangement you probably won't earn much money, but the lessons will make up for the lack of funds. As an apprentice, you'll learn the tools of the trade, and you'll most likely advance to other positions when you're ready.

Perhaps you'd like to skip the apprentice step and start, for example, as an assistant cheese maker. In this case, you need to demonstrate that you know what it takes to work with cheese. Where can you get this experience without working at an artisanal cheese company first? You can always take a few courses at a technical school, community college, or culinary institute. You can also get a job in the deli department at a grocery store. These experiences will help you identify many of the most common types of cheese by appearance, texture, and taste.

Advancement prospects

As an apprentice, if you work hard to learn the trade and respect the traditional methods used by the company, you may see a promotion to an assistant position. After a few years of service, assistants often end up managing particular aspects of the business, such as processing orders or fulfilling shipments. As your responsibilities grow, your paychecks should, too. Once you feel confident in the business, you may choose to leave your place of employment to start your own artisanal company.

Successful food artisans are at the top of their game: They own their businesses, they're in charge of who they work with and how often they work, and they have the last say in what gets put into their products. However, they can take one more step to achieve complete success — a buyout.

As an artisan, you may one day face a situation in which a larger company likes your product so much that it's willing to pay you a great deal of money to learn your techniques and secret ingredients and to take your patents, if you have any, off your hands. At that time, you have an important decision to make. Do you sell everything you've worked for and retire early, like the founders of Ben & Jerry's did? Or do you decline the offer and continue to work on your products while relishing in the fact that you have something everyone else wants? You may even decide to sell part of your company, but keep yourself in the loop during the development or marketing processes. How much you're actually involved, however, depends on the contract you sign with the company you're selling to. Keep this in mind during negotiations.

Unions and associations

Every food artisan may not be able to experience the protection and comfort of belonging to a union. Many unions are specific as to who they'll cover. For example, if you're interested in producing cheese and want to be part of a union, you're in luck! Under the Teamsters Union, more than 35,000 cheese makers are represented. If you work with poultry, sausage, or ham, you'll be happy to know that the United Food and Commercial Workers Union will defend your rights. The Brewery, Winery, & Distillery Workers Union represents people who work at wineries or breweries and are not part of the managerial team. If you're a brewer, you also have the International Brotherhood of Teamsters on your side. Farmers may also belong to the American Farm Bureau and the National Farmers Union.

As a food artisan, you can join a number of associations as long as you can afford the fees. These associations often have booths at the trade shows you may frequent. Here, you're able to represent your product, promote your company, and assess your competitors' products. You will also learn about new trends in the industry.

You may join the American Homebrewers Association, the Sonoma Valley Vintage & Growers Alliance, the National Association for the Specialty Food Trade, the Biodynamic Farming and Gardening Association, the Farmers' Market Coalition, the Association of Food Industries, the Association for Dressings and Sauces, and the International Association of Culinary Professionals.

Looking to the Future: Food and Culinary Scientists

While food artisans typically produce rustic, traditional products using proven methods developed by past generations, food scientists play a part in ushering society away from these age-old customs as they develop ways to preserve food longer and cook it more quickly.

Food scientists also work to improve the quality of food by changing the flavors, consistency, or colors of current foods and by producing new foods and beverages with fewer calories, sugars, or trans fats.

Simply put, these people are typically scientists who specialize in food safety or production or culinarians who have developed interests in the biological and chemical compositions of foods. If you're interested in becoming a food scientist, you need a college degree and the ability to comprehend chemical reactions and processes.

Many colleges offer degrees in food science, but others also offer degrees in culinary science. What's the difference? According to Iowa State University's College of Human Sciences, *food science* involves applying the fundamentals of basic science to every step of the development process, "from harvest until consumption." On the other hand, *culinary science* is a combination of food science and culinary skill development. In other words, culinary scientists are food scientists who know how to cook!

In this section, we discuss different jobs that food scientists and culinary scientists may hold. As you see, food scientists are more concerned with the development and advancement of the technology and science used to make and store food than processes such as testing recipes and inventing new techniques. These are the jobs culinary scientists are interested in performing, however.

Culinary scientists typically have a passion for cooking or baking; they may have once worked in a restaurant or bakery before deciding to get involved in the scientific world. These professionals are known to be practicing *culinology*, which is a term the Research Chefs Association (RCA) created to mean "the blending of culinary arts and food science." The RCA believes culinologists should embrace food science and technology while respecting food tradition.

Checking out food and culinary science jobs

Cooking is a chemical process, so in order to really understand what happens in the kitchen, you need to know about molecules and reactions. With backgrounds in microbiology and organic chemistry, food scientists (and chefs interested in food science) understand these processes and use this knowledge to develop new techniques and tastes.

Food scientists

Like cooks and chefs, food scientists can choose to specialize in areas in which they have the most interest or with which they're most familiar. Following are some of these potential specialties:

- **Food safety:** Scientists specializing in food safety work to ensure that the bacteria that cause food-borne illnesses are not present in a company's products. Food-borne illnesses include salmonellosis, cholera, and campylobacteriosis, which are easily transferred to humans through consumption and inhalation.

- **Food chemistry:** Scientists who work as food chemists are concerned with the chemical components of food and the chemical reactions they undergo through processing, packaging, storage, and even digestion. In the past, food chemists have been responsible for developing food replacements, such as NutraSweet, which contain fewer calories, sugars, or fats than the original food.

- **Food engineering:** Scientists interested in the physical manufacturing of food and beverage products work as food engineers. These men and women play a part in designing machinery that produces and packages large amounts of food at a rapid pace.

✔ **Food microbiology:** According to the Institute of Food Technologies, scientists who study food microbiology focus on the "detection and quantification of pathogenic organisms, how they survive in food and processing environments, and how to characterize those that are emerging." Food microbiologists thoroughly understand the processes behind fermenting and spoiling, for example.

✔ **Food technology:** Since the early 1800s, food technologists have been changing the way food is stored, prepared, and eaten. Although they weren't called technologists at the time, people like Nicolas Appert (1749–1841) and Louis Pasteur (1822–1895) were responsible for the development of canning and pasteurization, respectively. Today's food technologists have aided in the development of instantized milk powder, the process of freeze drying, and the decaffeination of coffee and tea.

✔ **Food packaging:** Scientists who work with food packaging are responsible for developing containers, trays, boxes, cans, cartons, and wrappers that keep food fresh or preserve it for a set amount of time. These packages must include the product's net weight, serving size, nutritional information, and cooking instructions. Scientists must ensure that packages are secure but convenient.

✔ **Product development:** Many food scientists work alongside chefs to develop new foods or beverages. They're part of the entire process, which includes the following steps: idea generation, idea screening, concept development and testing, business analysis, beta and market testing, technical implementation, and commercialization.

✔ **Flavor chemistry:** Scientists in this field focus on developing new recipes or formulas for existing or new foods and beverages. They may work with processing companies, retail food chains, or colleges or universities.

Culinary scientists

As a culinary scientist, you may find jobs in any of the aforementioned areas, but since you'll probably be more familiar with cooking food than you are with dissecting it and evaluating its every molecule, you may think about applying to television networks, food magazines, and food production companies such as Kellogg's Company and Nestlé USA for one of the following jobs:

✔ **Recipe developer:** Cooks with a background in food science are often employed by large companies as recipe developers. These men and women work with the company's products to either improve existing items or create new ones. They must keep in mind the image of the company as they develop these recipes. For example, recipes for companies specializing in weight-loss products should be low in sugar, calories, and trans fats.

✓ **Recipe tester:** After a recipe is written and submitted to a company, recipe testers prepare the dish and provide feedback about the process and the result to their supervisors. If the ingredients are too difficult to obtain or if the taste or texture leaves something to be desired, recipe testers may have the authority to alter the recipe so it will work for commercial use or in publications.

✓ **Research chef:** Companies often employ chefs to share their opinions about their products. Sometimes these chefs don't develop the recipe or even test it. Instead, they taste it, evaluate it, and then voice their thoughts about the product as a whole. They may also comment on packaging and marketing for the product.

If you're an experienced cook or chef and are interested in one of these positions, but aren't sure if you'd like to make culinary science your life yet, look for freelance opportunities in food company test kitchens. Many times, companies look for cooks, chefs, or bakers with knowledge of how to prepare and cook food to test their products in various stages of development.

Like food artisans, food scientists of all kinds must adhere to health standards set forth by the Food and Drug Administration (FDA). Food scientists must follow regulations about product packaging and preparation. The FDA has released product-specific information that food scientists must keep in mind when working with cheese, eggs, milk, seafood, and even bottled water and canned goods. They must also be aware of contamination by non-food items such as metals, natural toxins, and pesticides.

Molecular gastronomists

According to Hervé This, author of *Molecular Gastronomy: Exploring the Science of Flavor,* "generally speaking it is correct to say that food science deals with the composition and structure of food, and molecular gastronomy deals with culinary transformations and the sensory phenomena associated with eating." Although molecular gastronomy can certainly be considered a subdivision of food science, it's not always identified as such, because food science is typically concerned with industrial food production rather than food made at home or in restaurants. Molecular gastronomy, on the other hand, can be practiced in both by educated molecular gastronomists or by classically trained chefs with an interest in chemistry.

Fine-dining restaurants such as Alinea in Chicago, wd~50 in New York, and Salt of the Earth in Pittsburgh include many ingredients on their menus that have been modified, manipulated, or altered to improve the dish in some way. Table 10-1 shows some of the most common ingredients of molecular gastronomy used in these restaurants.

Table 10-1   Ingredients Used in Molecular Gastronomy

Ingredient	Uses
Carbon dioxide	Producing bubbles and foams
Hydrocolloids (starch, gelatin, pectin, natural gums)	Thickening, gelling, foaming, film forming, emulsifying, and stabilizing foods
Lecithin	Emulsifying, foaming, or can be used as a non-stick agent
Liquid nitrogen	Freezing liquids immediately ("freeze frying")
Maltodextrin	Turning liquid fats and oils into powders for plating
Sodium alginate (in combination with calciumgluconate)	Spherifying (creating a spherical, gel membrane around liquids)
Transglutaminase ("meat glue")	Binding other ingredients together

In Table 10-2 you find some of the most common tools and techniques used by chefs who embrace molecular gastronomy in their kitchens.

Table 10-2   Tools Used in Today's Progressive Kitchens

Equipment/Tools	Uses
Anti-griddle	Flash freezing
Blender (industrial strength)	Effortlessly blending and mixing
Centrifuge	Separating solids from liquids
Distiller	Pulling flavors from solids to produce liquids
Immersion blender	Producing silky sauces, creams, and soups

(continued)

Table 10-2 *(continued)*	
Induction cook top	Using electromagnetic technology to induce heat directly to the pan, resulting in faster and safer heating
Pacojet	Pureeing and processing ice creams/sorbets
Siphon (or cream whipper)	Producing foams and combining unlikely items for flavor infusion
Smoking gun	Adding the flavor of smoke to a dish without flame
Thermal immersion circulator	Cooking sous-vide (slow cooking in a hot water bath over a period of time)
Vacuum machine	Compressing textures, marinating
Volcano vaporizer	Turning spices into aromatic vapors

Although the most recognized term for these approaches to cooking is *molecular gastronomy,* many chefs have shied away from this label. Instead, they may use adjectives such as *avant-garde, progressive, experimental, constructive,* or simply *new* to describe their food. If you're interested in applying for a job at a restaurant where chefs use these techniques, throw a few of these descriptive words in your résumé and cover letter to let your future employer know that you, too, are open to playing with your food.

Finding out where food and culinary scientists work

Depending on the company you work for and the part you play in the development process, you may find yourself working in labs, test kitchens, or product development kitchens. Food science is everywhere — even in restaurants.

What's the difference between a test kitchen and a product development kitchen? Food magazines, cookbook publishers, and television networks often have their own test kitchens where recipes are tested and tweaked, whereas large food corporations typically build product development kitchens where research is performed. In test kitchens, your task may be to follow the recipe in hand, make what's on the plate look professional and appetizing, and then hand the dish over to someone else to photograph or film. If you're employed in a product development kitchen, however, you may supervise the quality of production from the item's point of origin (perhaps at a slaughterhouse or on a farm) to the moment it's loaded onto a delivery truck. This production process may include recipe development, taste testing, marketing, and everything in-between.

Product development kitchens

Product development kitchens are similar to science laboratories in that the scientists conduct experiments and dissect dishes to see what works and what doesn't. They watch for chemical reactions within foods and predict how these reactions may affect the human body. In these kitchens, scientists decide how particular foods should be prepared, packaged, and served. They may also determine the nutritional content of a product.

A single product development kitchen may house many different types of scientists working on various products and processes. For example, Northwestern Foods, Inc., in Saint Paul, Minnesota, employs four food scientists, a microbiologist, two food technicians, and a research chef. At any point in time, they may be participating in one of the following laboratory services:

- Analytical and microbiological work
- Batch testing
- Cost containment
- Final product testing
- Kosher compliance
- New product formulation
- Product improvement
- Recipe commercialization

 As a result of many food scientists' hard work, half-cooked, frozen, and packaged foods can withstand days, weeks, and even months before going bad. Because of this accomplishment, commissary kitchens are possible. In commissary kitchens, or production kitchens, cooks and chefs prepare food in mass quantities and package it in appropriately designed containers for shipment to restaurants. Many times, this food is semi-cooked or ready to eat. When the food reaches the restaurant, cooks defrost or reheat it and then serve it to their guests. If you want to prepare restaurant-style food but don't want to work in a hot, fast-paced restaurant kitchen, consider applying for a job in a commissary kitchen.

Test kitchens

If you've ever watched a cooking show on television or flipped through a magazine that features recipes, chances are high that the food you've seen has been prepared over and over (and over) again in professional test kitchens. These kitchens typically employ recipe developers, recipe testers, and research chefs along with test-kitchen cooks and chefs.

While working in a test kitchen, you may receive a recipe that will appear with a magazine article, in a cookbook, or on a television show. You have to produce the recipe multiple times, each time taking note of the weight and volume of the dish, the temperature of the dish, and the cooking time. If each batch produces a different outcome, then your job is to figure out and remedy the cause of the inconsistencies so that every reader or viewer who tries the recipe (and follows it exactly) will end up with the same dish.

The equipment available in many test kitchens is equivalent to what's found in the average consumer's kitchen. The kitchens are equipped with standard stoves and microwaves, blenders and mixers, and pots and pans that would be familiar to and affordable for home cooks. This setup ensures that the people reading the recipe or watching the cooking show will have the means necessary to replicate the dish.

When applying for a job in a test kitchen, be sure you're familiar with the company who owns the kitchen. Test kitchens for publications written for professional or advanced cooks house more sophisticated and expensive equipment than those publications or television shows meant to attract the attention of home cooks. If you've never worked with professional-caliber equipment before but you want to work in a test kitchen that will develop recipes for professionals, spend some time in a professional restaurant kitchen before applying for this job.

Restaurants

Food scientists aren't present in restaurants in their traditional forms. You won't see microbiologists and flavor chemists sitting on stools and peering into microscopes while line cooks move to and fro around them.

Instead, restaurant chefs with interests in chemistry and microbiology bring new ingredients, such as natural gums and hydrocolloids, and new cooking techniques into their kitchens and incorporate them into their dishes. These "secret" ingredients and new-age methods manipulate the tastes, aromas, textures, shapes, colors, and temperatures of their dishes. These chefs are said to be interested in molecular gastronomy. As we discussed earlier, molecular gastronomy is an approach to food that brings both cooking (which many people consider a form of art) and food science together. Chefs use this approach to create new items for their menus that their customers (and visiting food critics!) have never before seen.

Career profile

Food and culinary scientists are intelligent individuals who understand how food is prepared and how molecules in food may affect the human body. They can describe the reactions that take place when you grill a steak or sauté an onion. They're also aware of the best processing and packaging techniques. If you enjoy working with food and have a strong background in chemistry, microbiology, or engineering, a job as a food scientist may suit you well.

Personality traits

To be a good food or culinary scientist, you need to be patient — and extremely familiar with the process of trial and error. Scientists interested in food safety may work on a particular product for months, testing it again and again to be sure that consumers won't get sick after eating it. Engineers may spend weeks designing and then building a machine that will package thousands of candy bars within minutes without ripping or leaving holes in the wrappers. Even flavor chemists deal with this repetitive routine, as they may work on a particular product for an extended period of time, trying to capture the essence of two flavors in the same product in such a way that both flavors are equally present. If you grow tired of working on the same project week after week, these jobs may not be for you.

Food scientists specifically must also possess the ability to work with people who are unfamiliar with chemistry, biology, or physics. They have to be able to use different words to describe a chemical reaction to a visiting chef or a marketing representative than they would to a fellow scientist. Although being familiar with proper scientific terms is important, it's even more important to know when those words will confuse or intimidate others. Basically, you need to know how to communicate your ideas and findings to your audience.

Salaries

The salary of a food scientist is dependent on so many factors that assigning a value to this career is nearly impossible. The amount you're offered to work in a research department at a university will undoubtedly differ from the amount offered to you by a large, successful food company or plant. If you're the only food scientist on staff, you may also be offered more than if you're part of a team consisting of five or more scientists. Senior scientists, lab managers, or kitchen supervisors generally earn more than junior scientists due to a wider range of responsibilities and skills. On average, we estimate that a food scientist may make approximately $50,000 per year.

On the culinary scientist side of things, research chefs may make between $80,000 and $120,000 each year, depending on the company for which they work. The annual salary of a full-time recipe developer employed by a test kitchen may fall between $25,000 and $70,000. Assistants to recipe developers may make $10 to $25 per hour for full- or part-time work. Because recipe testers aren't creating formulas from scratch, they're typically paid less than developers. A recipe tester may make $30,000 a year. If you're a freelance recipe tester who works at home, you may be able to charge between $10 and $15 an hour.

Executive chefs who use molecular gastronomy in their restaurants' kitchens may earn the same amount as executive chefs that don't embrace these progressive techniques. As we discuss in Chapter 5, executive chefs of restaurants make approximately $58,000 to $88,000 each year. This number depends heavily on the location and size of the restaurant and if the chef's new-age or avant-garde techniques catch on. If the approach does well, then the restaurant will achieve success and so will the executive chef and owner.

Education and training

Unlike many other culinary careers, you cannot land a job as a food scientist without a college degree. It doesn't matter how many hours you spend in product development kitchens job shadowing or volunteering — the hiring supervisor most likely will throw your application away if you don't have a degree in a related field.

Luckily, more than 50 four-year colleges and technical schools across the nation offer degrees in food science. You may be able to find a job as a food scientist (specializing in just about any area from microbiology to flavor chemistry) if you attain a bachelor's degree (or higher) in one of the following areas:

- Biochemistry
- Biology
- Chemical engineering
- Chemistry
- Consumer food science
- Food manufacturing
- Food science
- Food science and industry
- Food science and technology

You're more likely to find experienced restaurant or bakery chefs in test kitchens than in product development kitchens because test kitchens focus more on cooking. Therefore, you'll have to take more culinary and baking courses to become a culinary scientist than you would to become a food scientist. Culinary scientists learn the basics of cooking before they begin taking chemistry and biology courses.

If you're looking for a job in a test kitchen or if you want to become a recipe tester, recipe developer, or research chef, you may want to consider attaining degrees in the following areas:

- ✔ Baking and pastry arts
- ✔ Culinary arts technology
- ✔ Culinary science
- ✔ Hotel and restaurant management

Again, you may also get these jobs if you're a good cook and possess a degree from the list of food-science related majors. After you attain a degree, get a job in a restaurant or bakery to hone your skills. When you're confident in your cooking abilities and your knowledge of science, you may then apply for jobs developing or testing recipes for a large company or publication.

If you're not interested in pursuing a degree in chemistry, biology, or even food science but you want to mix scientific methods into your cooking, you may want to take molecular gastronomy courses. You may choose to attend workshops that you discover online or in food magazine advertisements. You may also take a course or two to learn the ropes or even get a degree in gastronomy. This avant-garde form of cooking is still new to the culinary world, so very few schools offer these opportunities at this time. Boston University, however, offers a master's degree in gastronomy with a concentration in food policy.

Advancement prospects

Working in a product development kitchen, you may set your sights on a position such as manager, senior scientist, or supervisor. The people in these positions typically do less repetitive work and more paperwork and presentations. They supervise other employees, purchase and order equipment for the kitchen, and assist in product development on every level.

In test kitchens, you may begin as a recipe tester and work your way up to assistant recipe developer or even head recipe developer. You may become a kitchen manager or, with the proper training, a research chef. Depending on the size of the company, many research chefs may be stationed in one kitchen. If a position similar to head research chef becomes available, show your employers that you have what it takes to be on top!

Unions and associations

Food scientists may be members of the International Union of Food Science and Technology (IUFoST). This nongovernmental organization was founded in the 1960s to support the advancement of food science and technology. You may also be able to join the Society of Flavor Chemists, the Research Chefs Association (RCA), or the Institute of Food Technologists (IFT).

If you work in a test kitchen, you may join the International Association of Culinary Professionals or the American Association of Family and Consumer Sciences. Both frequently hold conferences and meetings for members of the industry.

Chapter 11

Drink Up! Jobs in the Beverage Industry

In This Chapter

▶ Identifying different types of jobs at wineries

▶ Finding out what careers may await you in the brewing industry

▶ Exploring jobs related to serving beverages in restaurants

*W*hen diners go out to eat, they typically order a beverage with their meal — whether alcoholic, such as a glass of beer or wine, or nonalcoholic, such as a soft drink or coffee. Some restaurants offer so many beverage choices that they have their own beverage menu that may list types of beer and wine, margaritas, martinis, and other cocktails as well as specialty nonalcoholic beverages, including flavored coffee, hot chocolate, milkshakes, smoothies, ice tea, and juices to quench any diner's thirst.

Some culinary professionals seek careers in beverages and wine, an ever-growing industry. These professionals may select wines for a restaurant's menu, brew beer, bar tend, or find interesting teas for a café. Jobs in the beverage and wine industry tend to be less stressful than other culinary jobs that require you to work in fast-paced kitchens. Also, when the economy takes a nosedive, the beverage-and-wine industry seems to slide through unaffected. People tend to spend less money on dining out and allot their funds to having drinks out instead. They may even purchase a bottle of wine or liquor (although it may be a less expensive one) to enjoy at home. The somewhat more relaxed nature and resiliency of the beverage industry makes it a very attractive choice for some professionals. In this chapter, we explore some of the most common career options.

Working at a Winery

Although some of the best-known wines in the world come from France, Italy, Argentina, or Germany, the United States is the fourth largest wine producing country in the world. Wineries are popping up throughout the United

States and jobs in this field are expanding each year. If you want a career in wine, you must love to drink wine and be well educated about the industry. If you're interested in this field, you'll eventually need to be able to answer the following questions:

- ✔ What are the major varieties of grapes?
- ✔ Where are these varietals grown?
- ✔ What wines pair well with certain foods?
- ✔ How do harvest decisions impact the style and flavor of the wine?
- ✔ What role do barrels play in winemaking?
- ✔ What types of bottles, glasses, or corks are used for certain wines?

Positions at wineries

Many types of jobs exist at wineries — from winemaker to sommelier to tasting room manager. Individuals holding these positions must work well together because they're all important to the success of the winery. Larger wineries may also employ other positions, such as tour guides, marketers, and viticulturalists to help a winery with day-to-day business decisions.

Winery sommelier

To become a sommelier, or wine steward, you must know everything there is to know about wine and love wine. A sommelier is a trained wine professional who possesses a vast knowledge about all — and we mean all — things related to wine. We're not kidding; you must live and breathe wine. You must be able to describe the regions, grapes, vineyards, and vintages of an assortment of wines. Sommeliers take wine very seriously and are often certified (see the later section "Education and training" for more info).

Sommeliers should have superior palates that allow them to distinguish between the numerous wine varieties, determine which country or region a certain wine is produced, and identify which wines pair well with which foods. Because sommeliers must know about pairing, they should have a culinary background, which can include a culinary arts degree or some culinary courses, in addition to advanced wine and sommelier courses and/or certifications. It also couldn't hurt to have restaurant experience, working as a server, bartender, or even sommelier. See the later section "Restaurant sommelier" for more information about those job responsibilities.

Sommeliers working at wineries must be able to educate and advise customers about the different types of wine produced at the winery, because some customers may be overwhelmed, intimidated, or unfamiliar with the selections offered. A good sommelier should be able to determine which wines a customer may enjoy based on the customer's likes and budgets. Sommeliers should also be ready to educate customers about how to taste wine, encouraging them to swirl the wine and bury their noses deep into the glass before sipping it.

The title of *master sommelier* is the highest distinction you can attain in the beverage and wine industry. A total of 180 sommeliers hold the title of master sommelier worldwide, with 112 in North America. To become a master sommelier, you must pass four levels of intensive examinations offered by the Court of Master Sommeliers: Master Sommelier Introductory Sommelier Course & Exam, Certified Sommelier Examination, Advanced Sommelier Course and Examination, and the Master Sommelier Diploma Examination. The exams are offered at various times and locations throughout the United States and Canada. For more information, visit the Court of Master Sommeliers website at `www.mastersommeliers.org`.

Winemaker

The duties of a winemaker depend on the size of the winery. At a small winery, which is defined as a winery that produces fewer than 5,000 cases of wine a year, the winemaker is typically the owner and is responsible for all aspects of the winemaking process. (For more information on owning your own business, see Chapter 18.) The winemaker oversees the winery's vineyards, pruning the vines and picking the grapes. (Or sometimes winemakers purchase grapes from other vineyards.) The winemaker then crushes and presses the grapes and makes, ages, and bottles the wine. When the wine is ready to be sold, the winemaker distributes the wine.

At a large winery, the winemaker may be responsible for performing only a few of the functions discussed above, such as solely bottling wine or pressing grapes. A large winery usually employs a team of employees, such as cellar workers, who help wash bottles or bottle the wine; a winery cellar manager, who manages the wine cellar; an assistant winemaker, who works hand-in-hand with the winemaker; a viticulturalist, who is in charge of the winery's vineyards; a sales and marketing team, who is in charge of events at the winery and distributing the wine; a tour guide, who offers tours of the winery; a gift shop attendant, who serves customers at the gift shop; and a wine chemist, who determines when grapes are ready for harvest and tests the grapes during the winemaking process.

Wineries are typically family-owned businesses that are passed down from generation to generation and employ family members or close friends. At some of these establishments you may have trouble getting your foot in the door, but if you're persistent and have the necessary experience and know-how, you shouldn't be discouraged from seeking employment at a family-owned winery.

Meet Master Sommelier Laura Maniec

Laura Maniec is the youngest of only 18 women master sommeliers in the world. Maniec took an 18-week sommelier certification course in 2001 that inspired her to pursue a career in wine. When she turned 21 years old, the Blue Fin restaurant in New York City hired her as its sommelier. While working there, Maniec met master sommelier Greg Harrington, and he became her mentor. She left Blue Fin to become part of the wine team at B.R. Guest Restaurant, and when she turned 25, she was made a partner and the Wine and Spirits Director for the entire restaurant group. She left B.R. Guest Restaurant to open her own business.

In 2011, Maniec opened Corkbuzz Wine Studio in New York City to share her passion about wine with her customers. In addition to serving wine and food, Corkbuzz offers wine classes, tastings, and other special events.

Maniec sits on the board of directors for the Guild of Sommeliers and on the *New York Times* tasting panel. She writes for *Food & Wine* magazine and *Sommelier Journal* and teaches wine classes.

Like artisans (which we discuss in Chapter 10), small wineries should take steps to market their products. They can drop off a few bottles of wine at local restaurants and specialty shops (or possibly even grocery stores, but laws for selling alcohol vary from state to state) to persuade them to sell their wine. They can also attend trade shows, where they can display their products for the media, restaurants, and the public who would otherwise not be familiar with their products. Trade shows give wineries the opportunity to show off their new products, offer samples, receive feedback, and gain new customers. Remember to hand out business cards with your website, location, and contact information to anyone who shows an interest in your products.

Tasting room manager

A tasting room manager runs a winery's tasting room, which is the winery's hub to show off its wine selection. The tasting room should be a cozy and inviting place where customers gather to taste and purchase the winery's selections.

Like winemakers, tasting room managers' duties vary depending on the size of the winery. At a small winery, tasting room managers are in charge of enticing guests to sample and purchase wines. They must be friendly, personable, and have great sales skills. If the winery does not employ a sommelier, the tasting room manager may also be in charge of educating customers about the wine. A tasting room manager may also be in charge of organizing special events at the winery, such as dinners, festivals, and concerts.

Other winery positions

Most large (and sometimes small) wineries employ other staff to aid in the winemaking process, such as wine-cellar workers, wine-cellar managers, and assistant winemakers, who typically assist the winemaker with duties that range from making wine to bottling wine. In addition, wineries may hire some of the following positrons:

- ✔ **Sales and marketing staff:** The sales and marketing team is usually in charge of selling and marketing the winery and its products. They also organize special events such as tastings, festivals, and dinners and may even give tours of the winery. Sales and marketing staff usually work hand-in-hand with the tasting room manager, tour guide, and/or gift-shop attendant.

- ✔ **Wine chemists:** Wine chemists perform chemical analyses of each wine throughout each stage of the winemaking process. They also determine when grapes are ready for harvest and test the grapes during the wine-making process. Sometimes they may use their vast knowledge of chemistry to help develop and improve new products, such as blended wines.

- ✔ **Viticulturalists:** A viticulturalist is typically in charge of the winery's vineyards. Think of them as wine farmers. They are responsible for monitoring the vines, pruning, controlling pests, fertilizing, and irrigation. They typically work hand-in-hand with winemakers to determine when grapes are ready to be harvested.

Career profile

Wineries are located in just about every state throughout the United States. Although Napa Valley and Sonoma County in California and the Finger Lakes region in New York are the front-runners when it comes to U.S. wine, other notable wineries are popping up in states such as Oregon, Washington, Texas, Michigan, New Jersey, Virginia, and Pennsylvania. When looking for a job at a winery, keep in mind that although larger wineries usually pay more than smaller wineries, you can learn much more about the winemaking process at a smaller, more intimate winery.

Personality traits

In addition to being experts in everything related to wine, sommeliers must be outgoing and personable because they work closely with customers to educate them and persuade them into purchasing wines. They must be able to describe different wines and explain why they pair with foods.

The job of a winemaker is strenuous, and winemakers aren't afraid to get their hands dirty. Because winemakers have to spend time in the vineyards, work with the grapes, make the wine, bottle, and distribute, they need to be able to stay organized and multi-task while handling the stress that comes from doing a time-sensitive job. To keep the winery running and produce a good product, a winemaker must be well organized, have a great sense of taste and smell, and be an expert in the different wine varietals to make superior wine. At small wineries, winemakers are usually the heart and soul of the operation. In addition, they must be mechanically inclined so they can keep machinery running smoothly and be able to fix equipment if it breaks.

Tasting room managers must possess great social and communication skills and a passion for wine. Because they're salespeople and responsible for dealing with customers, they must be outgoing and charismatic. They must also be well educated in wine so they can pass along their knowledge and entice customers into purchasing the winery's products.

Salaries

Sommeliers' salaries vary according to the size of the winery and whether the individual is a full- or part-time employee. Full-time sommeliers can expect to make $35,000 to $100,000 a year. They may also receive bonuses based on wine sales.

Winemakers' salaries depend on whether they are employed at a small or large winery. Location and popularity of a winery is also a factor that influences salary. A winemaker working in a well-known Napa Valley winery can expect to make more money than a winemaker working at a smaller winery in a region lesser known for wine, such as in Pennsylvania. The median pay for a winemaker ranges from $50,000 to $200,000 a year, but the average can be much less in small, lesser-known wine regions.

A tasting room manager is typically paid a base salary plus commission on anything sold in the tasting room, from wine to glassware to accessories. A tasting room manager can expect to make $15,000 to $60,000 a year, depending on commission and the size and location of the winery.

Like tasting room managers, sales and marketing staff are typically paid a base salary plus commission. Because the sales and marketing team are a vital part of running a successful winery, they are typically paid well and can make $30,000 to $100,000 per year. It depends on factors such as commission and the size and location of the winery.

Most wine chemists working at smaller wineries are only hired on an as-needed basis, and therefore don't make as much money as a wine chemist employed full-time by a large winery. Wine chemists who work at large wineries can expect to make $35,000 to $60,000 per year, depending on the size and popularity of the winery.

Like wine chemists, most viticulturalists working at smaller wineries are only hired on an as-needed basis, typically working part-time. Viticulturalists who are employed full-time by a winery can expect to make $35,000 to $70,000 per year, depending on the winery and its location, size, and popularity.

Other staff, such as wine-cellar workers, tour guides, and gift-shop attendants, are usually paid by the hour and are only employed at larger wineries that need their services. These jobs are typically part-time and may be filled on an as-needed basis.

Education and training

To begin their education, would-be sommeliers should earn a culinary arts degree. Additionally, to be a sommelier, you should take wine-related courses and classes, either as part of your degree program or supplementally. Also think about taking a certification program. The Culinary Institute of America offers a certified wine professional certification; the International Sommelier Guild offers a master's degree program; the Wine & Spirit Education Trust (WSET) offers a variety of certification levels in wines, spirits, and others; and the International Wine Guild and Society of Wine Educators offers several wine certifications. Sommeliers may become master sommeliers by passing four levels of intensive examinations offered by the Court of Master Sommeliers.

Sommeliers looking to gain employment at a winery should be prepared to prove they live and breathe wine and that their expertise would be an asset to the winery. Certification and courses are one way to do this. If you want to work as a sommelier, you may have to start out in other positions at the winery, such as a tasting room manager or in the marketing department, and work your way up the ladder after you prove your competence.

Winemakers' educations vary, depending on the type of winery in which they're employed. A winemaker employed by family-owned wineries generally learns the ins and outs of the business by working as an apprentice and has little formal training — although it never hurts to attend culinary school or pursue a degree in business management. If you're interested in working at larger wineries, then you'll need to get a culinary education, experience with wine, and/or a wine certification. Winemakers may become a master of wine by passing an examination offered by the Institute of Masters of Wine or a senior winemaker by passing advanced oenology courses and examinations.

To become a tasting room manager, an education in wine is usually required, especially if you work at a smaller winery that doesn't employ a sommelier. In addition, tasting room managers should have a degree in marketing, communications, or hospitality so that they know how to deal with the public and sell the products.

Wine chemists typically have a degree in chemistry or microbiology, salespeople and marketers have a degree in communications or marketing, and viticulturalists have a degree in viticulture or oenology.

Advancement prospects

Sommeliers may choose to change careers and go to work in a restaurant that has a more extensive wine selection that can allow them to broaden their duties and responsibilities by working more with pairings. They can also find a job at larger restaurants as a beverage director, who's in charge of all of a restaurant's beverage needs, not just wines. Sommeliers may also offer freelance services, such as hosting tasting dinners or teaching wine-tasting classes in addition to their full- or part-time jobs. Others may work for catering companies or use their knowledge of wine to write for print publications such as *Food & Wine* or online publications such as *Wine Spectator*.

Advancement prospects for winemakers vary. At small wineries, winemakers are typically in charge of the entire winemaking process and are usually the owner of the winery, so advancement prospects in this capacity are slim. This vast knowledge, however, may allow the winemaker to gain employment at a larger winery, which may offer positions with higher salaries and fewer duties.

At larger wineries, people in different positions can advance within the organization. People who work in roles such as cellar worker can advance into a position such as assistant winemaker or cellar manager and then to winemaker or senior management. Other positions, such as tour guides or gift-shop attendants, may be able to advance into roles such as tasting room manager or join the sales and marketing team. With enough experience and after gaining vast knowledge about wine, tasting room managers can aspire to become sommeliers or even take part in the wine-making process.

Unions and associations

Few unions exist for employees of wineries, but some winery employees may be a part of the Brewery, Winery, and Distillery Workers' Union or the Distillery, Wine, and Allied Workers Division of the United Food and Commercial Workers International Union. People interested in the wine industry may join the following associations: American Institute of Wine and Food (AIWF), Society of Wine Educators, Institute of Masters of Wine, Sommelier Society of America, Sommelier Society of America, International Wine Guild, or the American Society for Enology and Viticulture (ASEV). These associations offer much information about the wine industry, including educational information, networking opportunities, and certification programs.

Tapping Into Breweries

Do you enjoy a nice, cold beer? Do you consider yourself a beer expert? Do you dabble in home brewing? If so, a career as a brewer may be the right career path for you. Beer is one of the world's oldest alcoholic beverages and the most widely consumed alcoholic beverage in the world. It's the third most popular drink overall, behind water and tea. Beer sales are four times higher than wine sales, even though wine is the second most popular alcoholic beverage. Because beer is so popular, jobs in this industry are plentiful, which is good news to someone interested in this profession.

Whereas wine is made at wineries, beer is typically made at large commercial breweries, at microbreweries, which are small-scale breweries that produce no more than 15,000 U.S. beer barrels, or in home breweries, which are typically very small operations spawned from a hobby in beer brewing. Brewers who work out of their homes can be considered artisans. For more information on artisans, see Chapter 10.

Just as with wine, more and more restaurants are working with local breweries or home breweries to sell their specialty brews in their restaurants. For more information about brewing your own beer at home, pick up a copy of *Homebrewing For Dummies* by Marty Nachel (John Wiley & Sons, Inc.).

If you want to work in the beer industry in a restaurant-type setting, you can choose to work in a brewpub. A *brewpub* is an establishment that brews and sells beer right on the premises and typically includes a restaurant.

Breaker Brewing Company

The idea for Breaker Brewing Company, a small home brewery located in Plains Township, Pennsylvania, began in 2005 when friends Chris Miller and Mark Lehman decided to turn their love of beer into a hobby.

After hours of research and countless trips to purchase beer-brewing equipment, Miller and Lehman began experimenting. At first, they brewed only 5 gallons of beer, but they soon began producing 12 gallons at a time. The men eventually created a small homemade system to brew their beer.

After perfecting the brewing process and their recipes, Miller and Lehman marketed their beer to local bars and restaurants. They named their business Breaker Brewing Company as homage to the coal breakers who were once a common sight throughout Northeastern Pennsylvania. Today, Miller and Lehman distribute their beer to more than 25 bars and restaurants throughout the Wyoming Valley and are in the process of moving their business from Miller's garage to a permanent site a few miles away. The new site will feature a tasting room and beer will be made available to the public for purchase by the bottle or case.

Positions at breweries and microbreweries

According to the Brewer's Association, more than 100,000 jobs exist at beer breweries and microbreweries throughout the United States. Although most positions at breweries don't require a culinary arts degree, some may require an education in food science, microbiology, or chemistry. Other brewery jobs may not even require a degree at all but may require physical demands such as being able to lift cases or kegs or knowing how to operate machinery such as a forklift.

Brewer

A beer brewer coordinates the beer-production process. A brewer's responsibilities vary depending on the size of the brewery. At a large brewery, the brewer may act as a manager and oversee all operations, including supervising brewery workers, hiring and training employees, and working with a sales and marketing team. At a smaller brewery or microbrewery, a brewer performs all these duties and also supervises the fermentation process, performs maintenance and quality-control checks, bottles and labels beer after it's produced, orders supplies, and develops recipes. A brewer may also coordinate special events such as festivals, dinners, and beer tastings.

Brewers must be experts about beer and the beer-making process. Like sommeliers, they should be knowledgeable about the many varieties of beers, such as lagers, pilsners, stouts, and ales. They must have excellent palates to distinguish between different ingredients such as hops, barley, and grains. They should also be able to pair beers with certain foods.

Brewmaster

In short, a brewmaster is responsible for the quality of the beer produced at a brewery or microbrewery. Brewmasters supervise the entire beer-brewing process and usually manage staff and finances. They can be in charge of selecting ingredients, developing recipes, and testing recipes. A brewer is called a brewmaster only after he or she has undergone intensive training and years of experience. It can take 5 to 15 years to become a brewmaster; however, no universal education requirements exist for brewmasters. The Siebel Institute of Technology & World Brewing Academy offers a 20-week Master Brewer Program for brewers with years of extensive experience brewing beer. Other training, certificates, and brewmaster programs are available at schools such as the American Brewers Guild or the Institute for Brewing Studies.

Other brewery positions

Although not all brewery positions are as exciting as brewer or brewmaster, many opportunities exist — especially for people who are trying to get their foot in the door.

✔ **Lab technician:** Lab technicians perform quality-control checks on every product a brewery produces. These checks include taste analyses, ingredient quality, sanitation practices, and data entry. Lab technicians are responsible for ensuring that every step of the beer-brewing process is safe and produces quality products for consumers.

✔ **Maintenance mechanic:** Breweries depend on machines to keep the beer flowing, so they must hire maintenance mechanics to ensure their machines are working at all times. Maintenance mechanics should have experience in mechanical, electrical, pneumatic (pressurized gas), and hydraulic repairs. They should also have HVAC experience and be able to troubleshoot a variety of machines, such as high-speed packaging and bottling equipment.

✔ **Sales and marketing team:** The sales and marketing team of the brewery is an integral part of the staff. These employees are responsible for selling and marketing the products at the brewery. They may also organize special events such as festivals, dinners, and beer tastings or work with tour guides during special events.

✔ **Tour guides:** Tour guides show visitors around the brewery. They must be knowledgeable about the beer-production process to educate visitors. People in these positions may also work in the brewery's gift shop or work closely with the sales and marketing team during special events.

✔ **Warehouse personnel:** Although people in warehouse positions don't typically work directly with the beer-brewing process, these jobs are easy to obtain. If you're willing to work hard and learn all that you can about the beer-brewing process, you may be able to work your way up the ladder and obtain other positions at a brewery. Duties include handling and storing finished products and may require the ability to lift heavy objects or drive a forklift.

Career profile

Many career opportunities exist at breweries and microbreweries, and you can find many opportunities for growth. Don't worry if you don't have a background in brewing beer; you can start at the bottom and work your way up the ladder.

Personality traits

Brewers and brewmasters must possess superior organizational and management skills to keep operations running smoothly at the brewery. Depending on the size of the brewery, brewers and brewmasters should be well organized and have the ability to delegate as well as multi-task. Because they may have to work with the public and organize events such as beer tastings, they should also possess good social and communication skills and be outgoing to help sell the brewery's products.

Lab technicians must be detail-oriented, because they're responsible for ensuring that every step of the beer-brewing process is safe and produces quality products for consumers. Maintenance mechanics must have an interest in mechanical work and have patience to keep machinery running smoothly and troubleshoot problems when needed. Warehouse personnel should be hardworking and able to multi-task. They should also be detail-oriented.

Tour guides, salespeople, and marketers must possess social and communication skills, have great personalities, and be outgoing, because they're usually responsible for dealing with visitors and customers. They're also responsible for selling a brewery's or microbrewery's products, so they must also be well educated in beer and the beer-making process and able to pass this knowledge on to customers so they will purchase the brewery's products.

Salaries

Just like in many other jobs in the culinary field, the position, the size of the brewery, and the location of the brewery all factor into salaries.

Because brewer and brewmaster positions usually include management responsibilities, they are typically the highest-paid positions at breweries. Even so, brewers and brewmasters in small breweries may make only around $27,000 a year, though they may earn up to $130,000 at larger and more successful breweries.

A lab technician working at a brewery earns a salary that is less than that of a brewer and brewmaster, depending on the size and location of the brewery and the duties performed. A smaller brewery may pay much less than a larger brewery and only employ a part-time lab technician.

Although you may earn less money working at a smaller brewery, you can usually gain more experience because positions at smaller breweries usually include more duties than those at larger breweries. However, larger breweries have more room for advancement. See the later section "Advancement prospects" for more information.

Employees in sales and marketing positions at breweries usually are paid a base salary that can range from $30,000 to $100,000 plus commission. These salaries vary from company to company with people working at smaller breweries and microbreweries typically earning much less than someone working at a large brewery. The average salary for a maintenance mechanic is about $40,000, but that too can vary according to the size and location of the brewery. Tour guides and warehouse personnel are typically paid minimum wage but can usually advance into higher-paid positions after a few years of experience and training.

Education and training

Although a culinary arts degree is not required for all jobs at a brewery, having at least some food knowledge under your belt can't hurt. In addition, you may help your career by attending classes at a school that specializes in the beer-brewing process. The American Brewers Guild offers an intensive brewing science and engineering program as well as a craftbrewers apprenticeship. The Siebel Institute of Technology & World Brewing Academy offers a professional brewers certificate program.

A brewer wishing to become a brewmaster must have years of experience as well as an extensive beer and brewing education. Classes for brewmasters are offered at the American Brewers Guild, Institute and Guild of Brewing (IGB), Institute for Brewing Studies, University of California at Davis, Siebel Institute of Technology & World Brewing Academy, and the University of Wisconsin, among others.

Lab technicians must have a degree in food science, biology, microbiology, chemistry, or biochemistry. They should also have experience working with beer or have some knowledge about the beer-brewing process.

Employees in sales and marketing should have a degree in a related field, such as advertising, marketing, public relations, journalism, or communications. It also doesn't hurt to take a few classes about the beer-brewing process. Jobs as tour guides or warehouse personnel don't usually require a degree; people who fill these positions are usually trained on the job.

Advancement prospects

With the proper education and years of experience, brewers can advance to brewmaster. Although brewmasters are considered the *crème de la crème* at a brewery or microbrewery, they may choose to take a job with a larger brewery or open businesses of their own.

Lab technicians can advance into the role of brewer, start their own beer-brewing business, or move into a science-related job in another industry. With years of experience and an extensive beer education under their belts, sales and marketing employees may be able to advance into the role of brewer. They can also work in almost any industry.

People employed as tour guides can advance into sales and marketing positions after a few years of on-the-job training. With the proper education and years of experience, they may even be able to advance into other brewery positions, such as brewer.

With experience and training, hard-working warehouse personnel may be promoted to maintenance mechanics and, with the proper training and education, may eventually be promoted into brewery positions such as brewer.

Unions and associations

The International Brotherhood of Teamsters usually represents brewery workers, aside from those in management positions. In addition, numerous associations exist for people interested in brewing beer, including the American Homebrewers Association, Brewers Association, North American Brewers Association, and the Master Brewers Association of the Americas.

Pouring Drinks at Restaurants and Hotels

Beverage sales play a major role in the revenue generated by a restaurant or hotel. Jobs in the beverage industry in either restaurants or hotels are necessary and in demand. Restaurants and hotels need experts in beverages so they can offer pairings of wine and beer with certain dishes on their menus — which allows them to educate consumers while increasing their beverage sales! Read on to find what beverage jobs are available in restaurants and hotels.

Positions at restaurants and hotels

Restaurants and hotels offer a handful of positions for employees who'd rather work with beverages and stay out of the kitchen. Although most people who work in the beverage industry start out as servers or hosts, more and more opportunities are cropping up in this field, from food and beverage directors to bartenders.

Food and beverage director

Restaurants and hotels employ food and beverage directors to oversee the restaurant's food and beverage needs. These directors must not only be experienced in food and beverages but also have hospitality experience so that they have the skills necessary to run the front of the house (which includes managing staff and dealing with customers) as well as the kitchen.

Food and beverage directors must be culinary experts and knowledgeable of wines, beers, spirits, and other beverages, because they're typically in charge of purchasing all the ingredients necessary to create menu items in addition to ordering all the beverages the restaurant serves. They work with chefs and sommeliers inside the restaurant and restaurant suppliers outside the restaurant to place regular orders. Food and beverage directors, along with chefs and sommeliers and/or bartenders, may also oversee purchasing, which means seeking out specialty products and ingredients. (See Chapter 15 to find out more information about purchasing.) To be able to handle ordering and purchasing, they should have knowledge of inventory control, food pairing, and more.

Because the food and beverage director is a management position, people in this role may also be responsible for hiring and terminating employees and overseeing training programs. And because they work closely with customers as well as restaurant suppliers, they should also possess marketing and sales skills so they can ensure they're acquiring the products required to meet the needs of their restaurant or hotel and guests.

Some larger establishments and upscale restaurants that offer significant wine and beverage selections employ separate beverage directors who are in charge of all beverage purchasing for the restaurant or hotel and work with beverage distributors, wineries, and breweries. These establishments also employ a separate food director who is in charge of all the food purchasing for the restaurant or hotel and work with the executive chef, distributors, and restaurant suppliers. If you're interested in solely the beverage or food part of the industry, look for jobs in larger establishments, which are more likely to offer positions such as these.

Restaurant sommelier

A sommelier employed by a restaurant or hotel manages the wine selection, purchases wines and supplies, and handles and stores wines. Sommeliers work closely with the executive chef to plan menus that are complemented by the restaurant's wine selections. They educate servers and bartenders about various wines and train them how to pour wine. A sommelier also educates customers about the restaurant's wines and makes recommendations. Just like sommeliers who work at wineries, sommeliers at restaurants must know everything there is to know about wine and be able to share this knowledge with their customers. They should also have impeccable palates that allow them to pair foods and wines.

Because restaurants often carry many brands and varieties of wine, a restaurant sommelier must be knowledgeable about many different kinds of wines, compared to a winery sommelier who only has to know about a winery's products. Because restaurant sommeliers must have an extensive knowledge about many different wines and are in charge of purchasing wine for the restaurant, they may spend some of their time visiting different wineries to pick out unique selections to please the restaurant's customers.

For more information about a career as a sommelier, see the earlier section "Winery sommelier."

Bartender

Restaurants and hotels employ many bartenders who prepare alcoholic and nonalcoholic beverages. Working as a bartender is a great way to gain knowledge of wines, beers, and other spirits, because you'll be working with all types of beverages. Bartenders must know how to make a large array of different drinks, alcoholic and nonalcoholic, using numerous ingredients. They should also know which wine, beer, or cocktail pairs well with a dish (though their wine knowledge isn't expected to compete with the sommelier's). Most bartenders learn what they need to know by on-the-job training or by working in other restaurant positions such as servers or hosts.

Not all restaurants expect newly hired bartenders to know how to make a vast majority of beverages or to know much about them. Chain restaurants and smaller family-style restaurants usually offer a limited bar menu, which doesn't require any previous experience working with beverages. Other restaurants, however, such as those located in big cities, may expect bartenders to know how to make an array of drinks before even being hired. You can gain this knowledge by working in various positions in a restaurant and by taking bartending classes and programs at local community colleges or universities.

Bartenders are typically responsible for making alcoholic drinks for all the patrons throughout an establishment, including customers seated at the bar, at tables in the bar area, and in the dining room. They may also wait on tables in the bar area and take on duties similar to those of wait staff such as after-hours cleaning.

In some states, bartenders are responsible for determining when a patron has had enough or too much to drink. By law, bartenders are obligated to refuse to serve these types of guests. Bartenders should also ensure that they are serving alcohol only to people of legal drinking age, which is 21 years in every state in the U.S. Remember, if you serve an already intoxicated guest or forget to ask a patron for ID, you can face consequences, which may include losing your job and having to pay steep fines. Each state has different laws about limits and penalties, so check where you're employed. Some restaurants may require bartenders to take part in alcohol certification programs such as the National Restaurant Association's (NRA) ServSafe Alcohol and Training for Intervention Procedures (TIPS).

Career profile

Restaurants and hotels serve a plethora of beverages, so if you're looking for a career in the beverage industry, then a position at a restaurant or hotel may be right for you. Read on to find out some particulars of this career field.

Personality traits

Food and beverage directors must be hard working and know the ins and outs of the restaurant business. They have to be willing to work under stressful conditions for long hours, even working nights, weekends, and holidays as needed.

Sommeliers must be outgoing and personable and be able to persuade customers to try and then purchase wine.

Because bartenders work very closely with customers, they should have charismatic personalities and excellent customer-service skills. They need to know how to make drinks but should also know about and be willing to chat with customers about local activities, sports, and movies as well as the local hot spots. They should also know the location of airports, police stations, or hospitals. They should be cheery, upbeat, and have a sense of humor when dealing with guests at the bar and be able to work in a faced-paced environment under stressful conditions.

Salaries

The salary for food and beverage directors varies according to where they're employed. They typically earn about $60,000 per year, with those working at larger establishments making as much as $120,000 per year.

Full-time sommeliers at restaurants can expect to earn $35,000 to $100,000 a year in addition to bonuses or commissions earned for wine sales. Sommeliers' salaries depend upon the size and location of the establishment in which they work as well as whether they're certified or hold a master sommelier designation.

Bartenders are usually paid a wage, which is most likely determined by a variety of factors such as the state they work in and an establishment's size and location, plus tips from customers. Their salaries are dependent on how many guests they serve, how many shifts they work, and the price of food and drinks. Full-time bartenders earn between $25,000 and $40,000 per year, with people working in large and fine establishments earning more money.

Education and training

Some food and beverage directors start at the bottom of the ladder, working various positions along the way (see "Advancement prospects" later) and learning as much as they can. A hotel and hospitality management degree can be beneficial if you wish to become a food and beverage director, and so are years of experience in the restaurant and hotel industry. Because a food and beverage manager needs to know about food as well as drinks, a culinary education also doesn't hurt. Other courses of study that may be helpful include human relations, business management, marketing, or sales.

A sommelier should take wine-related courses and become certified by passing a certification program such as that offered by the Culinary Institute of America, the International Sommelier Guild, or the International Wine Guild. Sommeliers may become master sommeliers by passing examinations offered by the Court of Master Sommeliers. Many sommeliers also have a culinary arts degree.

Bartenders typically aren't required to have culinary arts degrees, but they should be knowledgeable in making beverages and be familiar with local laws regarding serving alcohol. Some schools offer bartending classes and programs that teach customer service, alcohol awareness, how to mix all types of drinks properly, as well as how to pour beer and wine. These classes can be beneficial to someone who is looking for a bartending position and doesn't have much experience working with beers, wines, or spirits.

Advancement prospects

Food and beverage directors usually work their way up the ladder, holding various positions such as dishwasher, chef, server, or bartender, and learning as much as they can about all aspects of working in a restaurant. Food and beverage directors can advance into the role of any management position in a restaurant, such as general manager, dining-room manager, or kitchen manager. They can also choose to work at larger establishments, which may pay more and offer more prestige, or open their own restaurant.

A sommelier can advance into the role of master sommelier after passing examinations offered by the Court of Master Sommeliers. They can also advance into the role of beverage director and work not only with wine but also with different beverages served in an establishment. Sommeliers with proper culinary training and experience may choose to switch gears and work in a kitchen. They can work at wineries or catering companies, or they may offer freelance services such as teaching wine-tasting classes. Sommeliers may also use their wine expertise to write columns for newspapers or magazines.

Bartenders with experience can choose to work for more prestigious restaurants and hotels. With the proper education, such as a culinary arts, business management, or hospitality degree, in addition to years of experience, bartenders may be able to advance into the role of food and beverage director.

Unions and associations

Although workers in management positions most likely won't belong to any unions, food and beverage directors can join associations such as the American Culinary Federation (ACF), the International Association of Culinary Professionals, the American Hotel and Lodging Association, the American Institute of Wine and Food, the Food and Beverage Association of America, the Hospitality Asset Managers Association (HAMA), and the Hospitality Sales and Marketing Association International (HSMAI). These associations offer up-to-date information about food and beverage trends, networking opportunities, and educational and certification programs.

One union solely for bartenders exists in the United States: Bartenders and Dispensers Union Local 165, Las Vegas. Bartenders and sommeliers who work in restaurants can also be represented by unions such as UNITE HERE, the United Food and Commercial Workers International Union (UFCW), Hotel and Restaurant Employees Union (HREU), and the Service Employees

International Union (SEIU). Bartenders may belong to associations such as the International Bartenders Association, the American Culinary Federation (ACF), International Hotel and Restaurant Association (IHR), and the National Restaurant Association (NRA).

Sommeliers may join the following associations: Society of Wine Educators, Institute of Masters of Wine, Sommelier Society of America, International Wine Guild, and American Society for Enology and Viticulture (ASEV).

Part IV
Checking Out Non-Cooking Careers

The 5th Wave   By Rich Tennant

SOLAR GRILLING

©RICHTENNANT

"Burgers ready in 6 hours!"

In this part . . .

*J*ust because you want to work with food doesn't mean you have to work in a kitchen. Maybe you love food but prefer when other people do the cooking. Many culinary jobs exist for those who can't stand the heat and stress of the kitchen. These positions still allow you to work in the food industry but don't always require you to get your hands dirty.

In this part, we explore the culinary world that awaits you outside the kitchen. You can write about food in magazines or host your own food-related television show. If you're more interested in touting a company's services, then a job in public relations or marketing may be right up your alley. The culinary industry even has a place for stylists and photographers. Maybe you'd like to teach hungry students all that you've learned along the way. Or perhaps you're interested in purchasing all the tasty ingredients and useful equipment that a restaurant needs. Whatever non-cooking focus you're interested in, this part has the info you need.

Chapter 12

Culinary in a Media World: What It's All About

C ulinary jobs in the media are plentiful. The different forms of media typically break down into three categories: print, broadcast, and digital. Deciding which of these areas to pursue all depends on your interests. Do you like writing about food? You could be a cookbook author, a restaurant reviewer for a local newspaper, or a blogger on the Internet. Do you enjoy watching cooking shows and competitions and have an interest in working on television — whether in front of the camera or behind the scenes? You can aspire to host your own cooking show or at least get your start working behind the camera as part of the crew or in a test kitchen. Perhaps you're more comfortable in front of your computer in the comfort of your own home. Between podcasts, food blogs, and thousands of food-related websites, you can find your niche somewhere in cyberspace.

You have plenty of options for expressing creativity in the culinary field without cooking in a kitchen. In this chapter, we show you how to get your food fix in the media world.

Getting Your Love of Food in Print

Do you have a way with words? Do you like to write and read about food as much as you enjoy food itself? Do you have a collection of your own recipes that you'd like to turn into a cookbook? Maybe you have a knack for editing and would like to work in the publishing industry. If so, a job in print media may be right for you. Print is one of the few types of media within the culinary industry that doesn't necessarily require any formal culinary training.

Many journalists and English majors have turned their cooking hobbies into careers outside the kitchen.

Although a culinary degree is not necessary for many food-writing careers, you'll want to have at least some experience with food when delving into food writing. Having a few culinary classes under your belt or even completing a culinary degree can be a valuable asset and increase your chances of landing a job.

Types of food writing jobs

Many different print media jobs exist. You can write for a newspaper or magazine. You can design food pages in a magazine or journal. You can author your own cookbook. In this section, we discuss the many opportunities within this industry. (Some additional culinary-themed jobs that may be involved in print media publishing as well as broadcasting, including food stylist and test-kitchen cook, are discussed in the later section "Sounding Off on Food.")

Food critic/reviewer

A food critic/reviewer eats in an establishment and then writes about it, analyzing the food, atmosphere, staff, and overall experience. Some critics focus on local fare, whereas others travel throughout a particular region or country and write about their experiences. Food critics/reviewers dine everywhere from top-notch restaurants and hole-in-the-wall dives to bakeries, fairs and festivals, and even street vendors and food trucks. Food critics/reviewers write for publications such as newspapers and magazines and may even have their own recurring column. They can also be employed on reality television programs geared toward food such as cooking challenges and competitions as guest judges. (For more information about the different food careers in the broadcast media, see "Sounding Off on Food" later in this chapter.)

Many people think that food critics/reviewers have glamorous and easy positions, getting paid to dine at extravagant restaurants. To become a successful food critic/reviewer, however, you need to know how to write using descriptions that appeal to readers. You need to have a way with words to make a simple dish sing. Simply stating that a rib-eye steak is delicious isn't going to cut it. The key is to use words that describe the color, texture, juiciness, and flavor of a steak so well that you make readers hungry. Most food critics/reviewers have degrees in either English or journalism as well as a culinary degree because they must be able to write well and be knowledgeable about food. They should also have a basic understanding of how a restaurant is run, so they're able to give a fair and accurate review.

Newspaper or magazine writer/editor

Thousands of newspapers and magazines cover an array of different subjects. These publications may hire many types of food writers — for example, food critics/reviewers (discussed in the preceding section) or food columnists, who write recurring pieces that express a particular opinion or point of view — to write about food and cover food events.

Newspapers and magazines hire food editors and copy editors to edit the writers' stories, and they hire page designers and graphic artists to lay out and design aesthetically pleasing pages. Some of these duties may be combined at smaller publications.

Newspapers and magazines offer many opportunities for staff and freelance writers with a passion for food. They are a great start for people looking to break into a food-writing career. Many publications now have websites, so they even provide an avenue for a crossover to writing for digital media. (We discuss digital media later in this chapter.) Although newspapers typically employ only one or two food writers and editors, depending on their size, magazines generally contain more food-related content and, therefore, hire more food writers and editors. Following are some of the most popular food magazines:

- *Bon Appétit*
- *Cooking Light*
- *Cook's Illustrated*
- *Everyday Food*
- *Food & Wine*
- *Food Network Magazine*
- *Saveur*

Magazines dedicated solely to food aren't the only publications that contain food-related content, however. Magazines such as *Woman's Day, Ladies' Home Journal, Health, Self,* and *Glamour* also contain food-related content. Journals and consumer magazines, which contain reviews and product ratings, also serve as popular forums for food writers and editors.

While a degree in culinary arts is not mandatory for a career in food writing, a degree in journalism, communications, or English may be required. Prior writing experience may also be helpful.

Keep in mind that the future of print media remains unknown due to the variety of different ways in which people can choose to get their information today. Fewer people are choosing to get information from magazines, newspapers, and books and are turning instead to television or the Internet. One good example of the demise of the print media is *Gourmet* magazine, which was the first food magazine devoted solely to cooking and wine. First printed in 1941, the magazine ceased publication in 2009. (Back issues of the magazine, along with recipes and other food articles, can still be found online at www.gourmet.com.)

Recipe writer/editor

Recipe writing is a difficult style of food writing that takes time to perfect. You not only need to know how to write, but you also must have a strong background in food, be able to differentiate between measurements, and be extremely detail-oriented. Writing an incorrect measurement — something as minute as one teaspoon too little of baking powder — can seriously affect a recipe and ruin the outcome, so you must pay close attention when writing. Recipes also need to be written in simple, clear terms so they're easy to understand and follow. Because of all the different types of cookbooks available, recipe writers must be creative and be able to write in a way to grab readers, such as in a humorous way or with a touching story accompanying each recipe, rather than just stating the ingredients and cooking directions. Recipe writers can work for publications, such as newspapers and magazines, or a publishing company writing cookbooks. They can also write recipes for television programs.

Editors in this field must possess the same skills as recipe writers and must have an even keener attention to detail and be able to spot discrepancies in recipes such as wrong measurements, ingredients, or instructions. Food editors typically work for publications, such as newspapers and magazines, or a publishing company, editing cookbooks.

Some food writing/editing positions, such as those for newspapers, magazines, and publishing companies, are freelance positions, which means a writer is not employed on a full-time basis. Freelance writers and editors typically get paid by the piece and may work for more than one employer. The upside to freelance positions is the ability to choose one's own hours and decide which projects to work on or turn down.

Other book author/editor

Jobs as book authors or editors in the food industry are abundant because many types of books beyond cookbooks appeal to all sorts of foodies. Some of these books include memoirs; biographies about well-known celebrity chefs or others who have shaped the food industry; and nonfiction books about health and nutrition, historical culinary topics, food science, or travel. Even some fictional books center around characters involved in cooking or baking and include recipes and cooking tips between chapters. Authors and editors can either be employed by publishing companies or on a freelance basis.

Career profile

Careers within print media are very competitive, but they can be very rewarding and interesting. They may, however, be less about food and more about writing, so if you'd rather spend more time at a desk than in the kitchen, a job in the print media may be for you.

Personality traits

To write about food, you must have a passion for food. Food writers should be adventurous and willing to try any type of food and drink. They should be knowledgeable about the food industry, cooking techniques, and the latest trends. They should be well educated in locally grown foods and wines.

Food writers and editors must also have impeccable writing and editing skills and the ability to report on news and events. They should be detail-oriented and have the capability to adhere to strict deadlines and generate creative ideas that will engage readers.

Salaries

Salaries within print media vary. Freelance writers, food critics, and columnists working at newspapers or magazines usually get paid by the piece, so the more articles they write and publish, the more money they make. Freelance writers can make $25 to more than $500 per piece, depending on the size, location, and type of publication as well as the size and type of piece written.

The salary for a staff food writer at a newspaper or magazine varies according to location and experience. If you have years of experience and are employed at a large, well-known publication, you can expect to make more money than someone just starting out in the field at a small publication. Food writers can expect to make an average of $25,000 to $50,000 a year, while editors at these types of publications usually are paid $40,000 to $60,000 a year.

Salaries for people involved in book production vary greatly. Book authors and editors who are self-employed usually get paid in a fashion similar to that of a freelancer — by the piece or, in this case, by the book. Book authors are paid either in one lump sum or receive a percentage of the price of each book sold. Book editors are usually paid by the project. Authors, editors, and others employed by publishing companies usually receive an average salary of $50,000 a year.

Education and training

Food writing is one of the few culinary careers that doesn't require a culinary arts degree. It usually does, however, require at least a bachelor's degree in journalism, English, or communications and prior experience in writing — food-related writing is a plus. Writers can gain this experience by working at publications run by their school, such as a school newspaper, or by completing an internship with a publication, such as a magazine. Some small publications, such as community newsletters, will print writers' articles (mostly unpaid — of course).

If you're interested in writing about food, you must *know* about food. You can beef up your food knowledge by working in a restaurant, taking a few culinary classes, or completing a culinary arts degree.

Advancement prospects

Advancement within careers in print media varies. Food critics may be granted full-time employment with specific publications or may receive their own weekly (or daily) columns. Freelance writers for newspapers or magazines may work their way up to full-time staffers. From there, they may be able to ascend to the role of editor. Book production is a little different. You may have to start out as a fact checker or proofreader before you can advance to the role of editor. You may also start out as a book author and stay that way or choose to take on the duties of an editor.

Unions and associations

Employees at some newspapers may belong to a union, such as The Newspaper Guild Communications Workers of America. Freelance writers may join the National Writers Union UAW Local 1981, and book authors may belong to the Authors Guild.

Numerous associations for food writers and editors exist, including those specifically dedicated to food writers and editors, such as the Association of Food Journalists, Inc. (AFJ), the International Food Wine & Travel Writers Association, the American Institute of Food and Wine, the International, and the Association of Culinary Professionals. Other are dedicated to just writing and editing, such as the American Society of Journalists and Authors, the National Writers, and the American Copy Editors Society Association. These associations offer information about conferences and contests; what's hot in the culinary and writing industries; as well as networking opportunities.

Sounding Off on Food

Since the introduction of television channels dedicated solely to food and cooking, such as the Food Network and the Cooking Channel, interest in this type of programming has exploded. As a result, many other television channels, such as Bravo, TLC, and PBS, have added cooking and food-related shows to their lineups. Programs range from instructional shows that teach viewers how to prepare particular dishes, such as Julia Child's *The French Chef* and *Good Eats* with Alton Brown, to cooking competitions, such as *Iron Chef* and *Hell's Kitchen,* to travel shows, such as *Bizarre Foods with Andrew*

Zimmern and *Anthony Bourdain: No Reservations.* Television is home to many food programs and channels designed to pique any foodie's interest.

Foodies may also get their fill by turning on the radio during their commute to and from work each day. Radio cooking shows such as *The Splendid Table, A Chef's Table with Jim Coleman,* and *What's Cookin' Today,* which delve into all topics related to cooking and food, are gaining in popularity.

Broadcast opportunities

Do you dream of cameras watching your every move as you prepare a delectable pasta Bolognese? Maybe you'd like to test the foods prepared on cooking programs? Or how about styling the food for the cameras on a cooking show? Many different jobs within the various broadcast media exist. You can aspire to be a television host like Claire Robinson *(Food Network Challenge!),* Padma Lakshmi *(Top Chef),* or Martha Stewart or demonstrate how to prepare meals like Anne Burrell, Tyler Florence, or Jamie Oliver *(The Naked Chef).* And although they're not as glamorous, jobs behind the scenes are just as important — if not more important — and can be just as rewarding. In the following sections we explore a range of different broadcast opportunities within the culinary field.

Host

Not everyone has what it takes to be in front of the camera. In addition to cooking skills, hosts of television and radio cooking shows must have sizzling personalities that hold viewers' and listeners' attention. Hosts must be able to shine in front of the camera (or microphone) without appearing nervous. They also have to multitask, walking viewers though step-by-step instructions while cooking and entertaining. Radio hosts have it a little easier because they don't have to get all gussied up for the cameras, but they must have good voices. They also must choose their words carefully to describe foods that listeners can't see. A pie is just a pie, but an apple pie fresh out of the oven topped with a scoop of vanilla-bean ice cream is heaven!

While these jobs may be difficult to attain, this shouldn't discourage you from pursuing a job as a television or radio host. Be persistent and confident! (Which shouldn't be difficult for you, since you're looking for work in this field!) Submit a video or recording of yourself to television and radio networks, telling them why you would make a good fit for their company and any ideas you may have for television or radio programs. Some networks, such as the Food Network, run shows such as *The Next Food Network Star* and *The Next Iron Chef* to find new personalities for their network.

Cooking up some competition

Americans' interest in reality television has spawned a rise in cooking competition programming. Bravo's *Top Chef* was so popular that the network launched *Top Chef Just Desserts,* to satisfy any viewer's sweet tooth, and *Top Chef Masters,* in which world-renowned chefs compete with each other. The network has two more *Top Chef* spin-offs planned.

The Food Network is home to *The Next Food Network Star,* which is in its seventh season, and pits home cooks and chefs against each other to win a cooking show of his or her own. The network is also home to numerous other cooking challenges to pique any foodie's interest, such as *Iron Chef, The Next Iron Chef, Iron Chef America, The Great American Food Truck Race, Cupcake Wars, Throwdown with Bobby Flay, Food Network Challenge!, Chopped, Worst Cooks in America,* and *Best in Smoke.*

NBC also has gotten in on the action with *The Next Great Restaurant.* Fox has Gordon Ramsay's *Hell's Kitchen* and *MasterChef.* And, don't forget TLC, which is home to shows such as *BBQ Pitmasters, Cake Boss: Next Great Baker,* and *Ultimate Cake-Off.*

Producer

A producer's job is one of the most stressful, but also one of the most important, in broadcasting. The producer's role largely depends on the type of show, but most producers have a hand in controlling most — if not all — aspects of the production of a television or radio show. They wear many hats while on the set and may be responsible for writing, developing new program ideas, working with budgets and contracts, adhering to a schedule, hiring cast members, and aiding in set design and directing. Those wishing to get into this line of work can get experience by interning or obtaining employment at local television or radio stations to get their foot in the door.

Director

Like producers, directors also have many roles, depending on the type of program. They must be able to remain calm under pressure and be leaders because they're responsible for making decisions such as where to place cameras, lights, microphones, and other props. In addition, they work closely with the hosts and camera operators, giving them cues and directions. Directors also need to be creative and are typically the ones who develop a vision for a program. You can gain experience as a director the same way as a producer — by interning or obtaining employment at local television or radio stations and then moving your way up the ladder or to another station.

Crew

The crew on the set of a television or radio show includes camera operators, light and sound technicians, and set designers. People in these positions should be knowledgeable about food, because they need to understand how to correctly film a scene to capture the best shots. The crew is responsible for designing and lighting the set, capturing difficult shots (such as steaming food, which has only a small window of time before it cools and stops steaming) and ensuring that foods look great under the hot lights and don't crumble or melt. Sound technicians working for radio shows must be able to capture important sounds such as the cook chopping vegetables or foods sizzling in a frying pan to entice listeners. You can gain set experience by interning on a television or film set or by obtaining employment at local television or radio stations.

Test kitchen staff

A test kitchen is used for developing new foods and products and testing recipes. Television and radio networks use test kitchens to develop and refine recipes before demonstrating them on their television or radio programs. (Print publications also have test kitchens working on recipes before they're printed in magazines and books.) Test kitchens employ a chef or kitchen supervisor, cooks, and recipe and product developers/testers. A chef or kitchen supervisor in a test kitchen may prepare a recipe as many as a few dozen times until the ingredient list, measurements, cooking technique, cooking temperature, cooking time, and tools used are perfected. Cooks may also fill this role with the chef acting as supervisor. Recipe and product developers/testers assist the chefs and cooks in perfecting these recipes and can also rate non-food items, such as cookware, equipment, and brand-name products.

Many different types of companies have test kitchens, not just food-related ones, such as Kraft or Nabisco. Publications, such as Hearst and Meredith Corporation, use test kitchens to test recipes before they're printed in their publications. Food retailers such as Whole Foods and Trader Joe's, also have test kitchens, where the stores' prepared foods, including rotisserie chickens and apple pies, are developed and refined.

Food writer

A food writer can work not only in print media, as discussed in the earlier section "Types of food writing jobs," but also in broadcast media, writing scripts and recipes for television and radio shows. (Writers can also work in the digital media as bloggers, which we discuss later in this chapter.) Screenwriting and scriptwriting differ from regular writing because the writer must include technical jargon and describe stage directions in addition to the story line. Because television is a visual medium, screenwriters have to show their story, rather than just tell it. To write for radio, a writer must remember to write what listeners will hear, not see. This style of writing is more difficult and takes much practice. If you're interested in this style of writing, read, read, and read some more. By reading numerous screenplays, you'll get a feel for this style of writing. You can also take a class geared toward screenwriting as many colleges now offer these types of classes.

Food stylist

Making food look appetizing in pictures and video is a food stylist's main responsibility. Food stylists understand the textures, colors, aromas, and tastes of real food and use them to their advantage when working with food for magazine spreads, television shows, and websites. When real food won't work in these situations, you need to know what types of materials and non-food items can be used in their place. For example, ice cream is difficult to film since it melts very fast, so the food stylist should know how to manipulate other ingredients to look like real ice cream, such as shortening mixed with flour and food coloring and shaped into a perfect scoop.

The job of a food stylist may sound like a walk in the park, but working with a camera operator and his lights and angles can be extremely challenging. The food itself is also temperamental; it can quickly lose its shape, crumble, melt, break, or harden after large amounts of time under hot lights. Some films may require you to use food specific to a particular film. For example, a film set in Italy during the nineteenth century would require you to know which types of cuisine should be used in shots. For an in-depth look at food stylists, see Chapter 14.

Career profile

Many opportunities exist in broadcast media, especially if you don't mind working behind the scenes. Much work and planning go into a 30-minute television cooking program or a 90-minute radio show. If you're interested in a career in broadcast media, be prepared for repetition. Sometimes you'll have to shoot the same scene several times until you get it right, or sometimes you'll have to make the same recipe dozens of times until it's perfect. The monotony is worth it in the end, however, when you've created a successful cooking show or developed a recipe that yields the perfect oatmeal raisin cookie.

Personality traits

Television or radio hosts must love to talk and have stellar personalities that come to life on the air. They should have the ability to capture and keep an audience's attention. They should be cool, calm, and collected, because being on camera or on air is no easy task. In addition, hosts should be able to multitask, because they may be cooking while talking to the camera or into the microphone.

Producers and directors must be well-organized and have the ability to manage others. Crew members on set for either television or radio must be able to follow directions and have the ability to work independently or as part of a team.

Chefs and cooks working in a test kitchen should possess the same qualities as chefs working in a restaurant or hotel (see Chapters 5 and 6). They should also be patient because they usually have to make the same dish over and over again until it's flawless. They should also be unafraid to take risks and bend the rules to achieve winning results. They must be team players and work side by side with recipe and product developers/testers — who must also possess some of these same personality traits.

Food writers should, of course, have the ability to write — and write well. Food writers should be passionate and well-versed in food. They also need to be up-to-date on the latest food trends and have the ability to generate fresh and new ideas to engage viewers and listeners.

Food stylists should be perfectionists when working with food to achieve that integral shot for a television program or publication. Their work should be consistent, and they should be able to think on their toes when things don't work out as planned, such as food drying out or melting. Food stylists must have much patience as they concentrate on getting food camera-ready. Hours may be needed to get a simple bowl of cereal to look a certain way. In addition, food stylists should be able to work as part of a team, because they usually work hand-in-hand with camera operators, producers, and directors.

Salaries

Salaries within the broadcast media vary. Television and radio hosts, producers, directors, and crew members are sometimes paid on a job-to-job basis, whereas others sign contracts for a specified number of television or radio programs. The amount of money you make depends on your experience and the type of company in which you work.

Test kitchen staff usually receive salaries based on their experience and education. Test kitchen chefs, kitchen supervisors, and cooks can expect to make salaries similar to those of staff in restaurants or hotels. According to Payscale.com, the average salary for a test kitchen worker ranges from $15,000 to $60,000, depending on the position and experience. The salaries for recipe and product developers/testers vary depending on the place of employment.

Food writers and editors who work within broadcast media may be paid by the job or may work on the staff of a television or radio show for a specified number of programs. Like other jobs within the industry, the salary varies according to experience, education, and place of employment. Writers and editors just starting out in the business can expect to make an average of $35,000 a year, and those who have years of experience under their belts can make as much as $100,000.

Food stylists usually charge by the hour or day and get paid by the project, although some may work for large corporations. Because a food stylist can work for publications, television programs, and online media, we can't pinpoint an exact salary for a food stylist.

Education and training

If you're interested in working in broadcast media, consider getting a bachelor's degree in broadcast journalism or communications. These degrees will prepare you for working on a television or radio set that uses cameras and sound and lighting equipment.

If you want to work in a test kitchen, a culinary degree and relevant work experience are your best bet for getting hired. Although you'll most likely receive on-the-job training, having at least some experience working in a kitchen will help get you noticed and hit the ground running. In addition to a degree in culinary arts, a degree in food chemistry, food science, or nutrition may also be helpful if you want to work in a test kitchen.

A career in food writing — whether in print or broadcast media — usually requires a bachelor's degree in journalism, English, or communications and most likely prior experience in writing. You can gain this experience by working at a school newspaper, writing for a blog, or as an intern, writing scripts at a television station. Also, it's important that you're knowledgeable about food. You can gain this knowledge by working in a restaurant or by taking a few culinary classes.

A career as a food stylist is a little harder to come by unless you have experience and education. Because you must be knowledgeable about food, you should at least complete a culinary arts degree. In addition, a certification in food styling is another avenue to consider. For more information about food styling, see Chapter 14.

Advancement prospects

Television and radio hosts can leave their positions in front of the camera (or microphone) for positions behind the camera (and microphone) such as producer, director, or even writer. Crew members such as camera operators, sound and light technicians, and set designers can also switch sides and end up in front of the camera or advance into roles of producer or designer.

Food writers in the broadcast media can advance to positions such as producers and directors and work on television and radio sets on the production end. Their knowledge of recipes can even land them in a position as a recipe tester within a test kitchen.

Advancement in the test kitchen is similar to that of a restaurant or hotel, which usually includes positions such as head chef or kitchen supervisor, sous chef, and line cook. To advance in these positions, education, experience, and hard work are required. Sometimes chefs, kitchen supervisors, or cooks may choose to change careers and work in restaurants or hotels. With the proper training and education, recipe and product developers/testers may ascend into the roles of chef, kitchen supervisor, or cook, or may work for other types of test kitchens.

Because most food stylists usually freelance, one way to advance is to find a permanent job at a publication — whether print, online, or on the set of a television program. You can start as an assistant and then work your way up the ladder to become the head food stylist. Another option for advancement is to become a culinary or art instructor, a food photographer, or a prop stylist, or you can even work in a restaurant kitchen.

Unions and associations

Many unions exist for broadcast media employees. Television or radio hosts may belong to the American Federation of Television & Radio Artists or the Screen Actors Guild. Crew members may belong to the International Brotherhood of Electrical Workers or the National Association of Broadcast Employees and Technicians. Producers and directors can join the Producers Guild of America or the Directors Guild of America.

Test kitchen staff, such as recipe and product developers/testers, usually don't belong to unions, but they may belong to the International Association of Culinary Professionals. Cooks and chefs within test kitchens may be protected under the Hotel Employees and Restaurant Employees International Union and the Service Employees International Union.

Writers in the broadcast media may belong to the Writers Guild of America, West and the Writers Guild of America, East.

Food stylists aren't generally protected under unions, but they may join associations such as the Association of Stylists and Coordinators, the New York Women's Culinary Alliance, and International Association of Culinary Professionals.

Taking Food Online

The World Wide Web is home to a wealth of information — so much information that you'd never be able to digest everything the Internet has to offer. Virtually everything that you can find in print and broadcast media you can also find online. Because more and more people are turning to the Internet for information, digital media are quickly overtaking print and broadcast media. The Internet allows viewers to read their favorite publications, watch their favorite television shows, and listen to their favorite radio programs. Because of this, many jobs in the print and broadcast mediums overlap those in the digital media, such as food writer.

Jobs within the digital media industry

Many companies have noticed that consumers are now turning to digital media for information. As a result, they have begun to package digital media with their other products. Most newspapers and magazines now have online versions that contain the same news and information as their print counterparts along with up-to-date headlines and other features. The online versions not only allow printed publications to compete with broadcast and digital media, but also open up more jobs across the various media.

Blogger

Food bloggers combine print media and digital media by writing for the Internet. A blog is defined as a website that contains personal reflections, comments, and sometimes photographs about a particular topic of interest. Known for their witty banter, mouthwatering photographs, and recipes, food blogs are receiving widespread attention across the Internet. Starting a blog is as easy as obtaining a web address and designing a webpage. Many sites such as Blogger and WordPress offer free blogging services and tutorials to help beginners.

Although blogging pays little — or nothing — bloggers can make big names for themselves, which can lead to other lucrative opportunities, such as employment opportunities, book deals, television shows, movies, and more. Bloggers who aren't so lucky can rely on money from donations from their followers or advertisers who pay a small fee to place ads on their sites. They also may write product reviews for companies that offer a small commission for reviewing and recommending their products.

Following are a few popular food blogs:

- 101 Cookbooks (www.101cookbooks.com)
- Baking Bites (http://bakingbites.com)
- Chocolate & Zucchini (http://chocolateandzucchini.com)
- David Lebovitz (www.davidlebovitz.com)
- Joy the Baker (www.joythebaker.com)
- Orangette (http://orangette.blogspot.com)
- Serious Eats (www.seriouseats.com)
- Smitten Kitchen (http://smittenkitchen.com)
- Tartelette (www.tarteletteblog.com)
- Use Real Butter (http://userealbutter.com)

The Pioneer Woman

Ree Drummond, a former city gal from Los Angeles who calls herself an "accidental country girl," started her blog *The Pioneer Woman* in 2006 as a way to share pictures and stories about her life on an Oklahoma ranch with her cowboy husband and four children. *The Pioneer Woman* contains a mix of recipes, musings, photos, and home-schooling information and a forum where readers can post their own kitchen stories and recipes.

To Drummond's surprise, her blog took off, and at the 2007 Bloggie Awards, it was named Best Kept Secret Blog. In 2008, she won the Best Writing and Best Food Blog awards, and in 2009 her blog was named Weblog of the Year.

A year later, she hit No. 22 on *Forbes*' 2010 Web Celeb 25.

Drummond published recipes from her blog in her first cookbook, *The Pioneer Woman Cooks,* in 2009. She appeared on a special Thanksgiving episode of *Throwdown with Bobby Flay* in 2010, during which she beat Flay. In 2011 she released *The Pioneer Woman: Black Heels to Tractor Wheels — A Love Story,* a memoir about her marriage, which is in movie production. She also released a children's book called *Charlie the Ranch Dog* in 2011. She is currently working on her second cookbook and will star in a cooking show in August 2011 on the Food Network.

Podcaster

A podcast is an audio or video file on the Internet that web surfers can listen to or watch at any time. These files differ from other Internet video or audio files because they're not live and they're portable, which means you can either listen or watch them directly on a computer or transfer them to a portable audio/video device such as an iPod or MP3 player to listen to or watch at your convenience.

Food and cooking podcasts are becoming popular ways to get information about food on the Internet. `Food-dining.podcast.com` offers numerous podcasts about cooking techniques, nutrition, restaurant reviews, recipes, sustainable farming practices, wine, and so on. Like blogging, however, podcasting is usually done more as a hobby than as a way to make money. A few ways to make money as a podcaster are by asking for donations, finding sponsors or advertisers, or charging to view/listen to the podcast. Someone getting into this field must be able to express strong opinions and be able to get their point across in a creative and interesting way to pull in more viewer/listeners. For example, they may use a niche such as "Locally Sourced Ingredients" to draw in those who are interested in using local foods.

Following are a few popular food podcasts:

- ✔ Crimes Against Food
- ✔ Edible Radio
- ✔ Farming Today (BBC)
- ✔ Food Programme (BBC)
- ✔ NPR: Food
- ✔ Nutrition Diva
- ✔ The Restaurant Guys
- ✔ Spilled Milk

E-zine writer/editor

Thousands of publications exist for people interested in food writing. If you're interested in writing or editing for print publications, you can cross over into digital media, because more and more publications now offer *e-zines,* or online versions of their publications. Some of these publications are offered only online, such as `Slate.com` or `BetterBaking.com`, whereas others, such as *Saveur* or *Food & Wine,* offer both print and digital versions. Food writers — whether they work for a print or digital media — should have strong writing skills. Working for an e-zine isn't much different from working at a magazine. For more information about food writing and editing, see the "Newspaper or magazine writer/editor" and "Food writer" sections earlier in this chapter.

Social media director/webmaster

Are you an Internet junkie who enjoys networking sites such as Facebook or Twitter? Are you interested in making websites for companies? Today all businesses — including culinary businesses — *need* presence on the Internet. Businesses such as wineries, restaurants, caterers, artisans, food distributors, farmers, and cooking schools need a way to advertise their services without paying for large advertising campaigns. The creation of a website, combined with Twitter and Facebook accounts, is a great way for a business to advertise. Through these sites, businesses can connect with potential customers and network with other similar businesses. A culinary degree is not essential to a job as a social media director/webmaster, but a degree in communications, computer science, or graphic design is usually required. A strong interest in food can't hurt, either! Those wishing to work as a social media director or webmaster should create sample websites to show prospective employers.

Social media director/webmaster positions may also require knowledge of advanced computer programs and graphic arts programs, and a proficiency in HTML coding. Just because you're crafty on the computer and love food doesn't mean you have what it takes to become a social media director/webmaster for a food-related company.

Career profile

Although digital media is constantly growing, limited (paying) opportunities exist. The good news is the World Wide Web is huge and offers a wealth of opportunities, so if you're interested in this type of career, chances are you may be able to find something — even if it's low-paying or even unpaid — to suit your interests and needs.

Personality traits

Most careers in digital media require you to work alone, so if you decide to go into this field, you should feel comfortable working independently. In addition to excellent computer skills, you should also have a keen eye for graphic arts, layout, and design. You should feel comfortable researching competitors within the culinary field and be able to keep up with the newest trends. You should also have great interpersonal skills and much patience when dealing with others who may not be as Net-savvy as you are.

Salaries

Bloggers and podcasters usually make very small salaries — usually from donations or by hosting advertising — of a couple of hundred dollars to a couple of thousand dollars a year. Successful, established bloggers and podcasters can make a decent salary, but if you're just starting out, don't count on it.

A writer/editor for an e-zine can expect to make a salary similar to that of a writer/editor for a publication such as a newspaper or magazine (see the earlier sections "Newspaper or magazine writer/editor" and "Food writer."

A social media director/webmaster can either freelance for multiple clients or work full time for a specific company. Freelancers' salaries vary by the job or hour. A social media director/webmaster who is employed full time by a specific employer can expect to make anywhere from $30,000 to $150,000, depending on the services offered and the size of the company.

Education and training

Bloggers and podcasters usually don't require any education or training to start and run a blog or podcast. Many resources on the Internet, including www.blogger.com or http://wordpress.com, have step-by-step tutorials that can help you start your own blog or podcast.

That being said, all writers and editors in digital media should have an excellent command of the English language and a vast knowledge of food. A career in food writing or editing usually requires a bachelor's degree in journalism, English, or communications. Prior writing experience and some culinary arts training are a plus.

A social media director/webmaster should have a degree in computer science, communications, or graphic design and knowledge of HTML coding. While not required, a few culinary courses could give social media directors/ webmasters the edge they need when looking for employment.

Advancement prospects

Some bloggers use their writing skills and knowledge of food to write for magazines or newspapers or even to become cookbook authors or recipe developers. Others may be sought after for their cooking skills and personalities and land roles as hosts of their own television or radio cooking show. Bloggers with a desire to create websites can advance into positions such as social media directors/webmasters or can offer their services on a freelance basis.

A podcaster can use his or her knowledge and personality to break into broadcast media as a radio or television host, producer, director, or technician.

Social media directors/webmasters who freelance can aspire to work in full-time positions at large corporations.

Unions and associations

Although bloggers have been trying to form a guild dedicated to bloggers for years, no such union exists — as of yet. Many associations for bloggers do exist, however, such as the Media Bloggers Association, Association of Food Bloggers, Internet Food Association, Food Blog Alliance, and Food Bloggers Unite! These associations offer a forum for bloggers to communicate with other bloggers and exchange information. They also offer legal support, blogging trends, links to meet-ups, and more.

No unions exist for podcasters, however, there are numerous associations, but most are geared toward regional groups or specific interests such as the Hawaii Association of Podcasters or the Association of Poetry Podcasting.

Writers and editors in digital media may belong to the Writers Guild of America, West and the Writers Guild of America, East. They also may join associations such as the Association of Food Journalists, Inc., the International Food Wine & Travel Writers Association, the American Institute of Food and Wine, the International Association of Culinary Professionals, the American Society of Journalists and Authors, the National Writers Union, and the American Copy Editors Society Association.

Social media directors/webmasters may belong to a union such as the HTML Writers Guild or associations such as the Web Design and Development Association and AIGA.

Chapter 13

The Star Makers: Public Relations and Marketing

In This Chapter

▶ Identifying the responsibilities of public relations and marketing professionals

▶ Knowing where public relations and marketing professionals work

▶ Finding out what careers in PR and marketing may be like

*B*elieve it or not, you can work in the culinary industry and never step foot in a kitchen (at least not while on the job). If you love food but don't want to work in a hot, cramped kitchen, you can look to become a public relations (PR) or marketing professional specializing in the culinary industry.

Culinary businesses, just like all businesses, need to spread the word about their services or they won't do well. Think about it: If you open a new business and no one knows about it, how can your business succeed and make a profit? It won't unless you advertise.

Why don't culinary businesses rely on word of mouth to attract new business? They do, but that free advertising is not enough to land the number of customers you need to succeed in today's economy. The owners of culinary businesses turn to PR and marketing experts to help them attract business.

Although some culinary businesses are large enough to be able to afford PR and marketing professionals on staff, most can't support such a luxury. Smaller culinary companies may hire PR and marketing professionals on an as-needed basis to help them announce big events such as grand openings, anniversary sales, or new product lines.

PR and marketing professionals are a great asset to any culinary business because they enable the business owners to spend less time worrying about advertising and more time running the business.

Taking a Look at What Culinary PR and Marketing Professionals Do

Public relations (PR) and marketing are both related to sales, but the two fields are distinct. PR deals with maintaining a company's image. For example, one of the tasks of a PR agent for a large restaurant may be to write press releases about the restaurant's involvement in a charitable event. The PR person then sends out the press releases to various contacts at newspapers, magazines, and websites in hopes of having them published so the public can read a positive story about the restaurant.

Marketing is the process of promoting, selling, and distributing a product or service. Marketing works hand-in-hand with advertising, though sometimes the two are separate entities. Some marketing and PR people, especially those employed at smaller establishments, may take care of a business's advertising needs, while larger establishments may hire someone who is solely in charge of advertising. Marketing professionals may help a restaurant owner create a menu that appeals to customers so that they are more likely to want to order appetizers, entrées, and desserts from the menu. They may also design newspaper advertisements, making customers aware of upcoming specials.

PR and marketing professionals work together to promote a business, getting the business's name out there so it's well known, helping it sell products or services. They run announcements and advertisements in various media outlets such as newspapers, magazines, journals, and television and radio stations. They also promote businesses by creating websites, blogs, and social network sites. They may also create flyers, mailings, brochures, and business cards for a business.

These professionals may even suggest and host charitable events, hold contests and giveaways, and attend and purchase booths at tradeshows, local bazaars, or festivals, all to generate a buzz about a business to stimulate sales.

Some very talented public relations (PR) professionals work for some exclusive names in the culinary world. They maintain the images of large culinary businesses, such as Kraft Foods; celebrity chefs, such as Bobby Flay; or exclusive restaurants, such as the French Laundry in California.

Playing the name game

Individuals who are involved in PR and marketing sometimes have titles other than PR specialist or marketing specialist. The following job titles all relate to PR and marketing:

- ✔ Account coordinator
- ✔ Account executive
- ✔ Advertising manager
- ✔ Advertising sales director
- ✔ Brand manager
- ✔ Communications specialist
- ✔ Event coordinator
- ✔ Market analyst
- ✔ Marketing director
- ✔ Market researcher
- ✔ Media buyer
- ✔ Media coordinator
- ✔ Media director
- ✔ Media specialist
- ✔ Product development manager
- ✔ Public relations director
- ✔ Public relations specialist
- ✔ Sales manager

A PR person's duties and a marketing person's duties sometimes overlap. For example, a PR media specialist may have some of the same duties as a marketing media specialist.

Some business owners take it upon themselves to manage their company's public relations and marketing needs. Since business owners are typically stretched too thin as it is, these services may suffer and in turn cause the business's sales to lag as well. Freelance PR and marketing professionals can approach such business owners and offer their services. Who knows? They may become so indispensible to a business owner that they may eventually be offered a full-time, permanent job.

Contemplating the pros and cons

As with any career, a job as a culinary PR or marketing person has its pros and cons. On the plus side, if you work as a culinary PR or marketing professional, you get to meet many new people by networking and socializing with clients and prospective clients. You may also get to host special events, such as a chili cook-off, which can be exciting and fun.

You also get to infuse a creative flair into your work. You may design advertising campaigns and even come up with ideas for events to get your company noticed. If you enjoy writing, you'll love a career as a PR or marketing professional, because you get to write articles and press releases about your client.

Now, on to the cons. You must be outgoing, cheery, upbeat, and smiling. Why is this a con, you ask? Being positive and friendly isn't easy to do all the time. You have to work hard to avoid hurting anyone's feelings.

Another con is the schedule. Like most culinary careers, you have to work long hours. Expect to work nights and weekends and even some holidays. Your hours may also be irregular. For example, you may have to promote an event in the morning and then have a huge gap in the afternoon because your next event isn't scheduled until the evening. This type of schedule makes having a personal life outside of work difficult.

The biggest con about working in the PR and marketing field is the sales aspect. You must to be able to sell, sell, sell. Whether you're selling a company's image or its products, you're selling. If you're not good at selling, you're not going to make it in this field.

Spending a day in the life of a PR and marketing professional

If you work as a PR or marketing professional, your job duties depend on your place of employment. For example, a PR person employed by a restaurant chain has different daily tasks than a PR person who works for a frozen food company. The following are some duties of a PR or marketing professional.

- ✔ **Looking for opportunities for free publicity:** PR and marketing professionals spend a good deal of their time writing and sending press releases about a their clients to different media in hopes the material is printed either in publications or on websites or broadcast over the radio or television. (For more information about food writing and the media, see Chapter 12.) They may call various publications before or after sending a press release.

  Creating a page on a social networking site such as Facebook or Twitter is an easy and free way to market a company. Social networking sites allow culinary business owners to interact with their customers without paying for expensive advertising campaigns. Customers can visit a business's pages to learn of drink and menu specials and special events and even access reviews and feedback about a business's services and products.

✔ **Coordinating paid publicity:** PR and marketing professionals are also in charge of paid publicity, such as advertisements, and work closely with advertising sales representatives to take care of the company's advertising needs. At smaller companies, PR and marketing professionals may act as sales representatives and even create and design an entire restaurant's advertising campaign and ensure that ads appear in media that reaches the greatest number of consumers, such as newspapers, magazines, and local television and radio stations. They are also in charge of updating their client's website and social media pages on sites such as Facebook and Twitter. They may post important details on these sites such specials or even events the company is hosting.

✔ **Planning special events:** PR and marketing professionals also plan special events to promote a company's services or products. For example, they may rent a booth at a local festival to give out samples or sell the client's products to attendees. Marketing and PR personnel may even be in charge of coordinating an entire event from beginning to end as well as representing the company during the event. For example, a PR or marketing person may plan a restaurant's chicken wing competition for charity. The PR or marketing person must make sure that the event gets adequate media coverage so the hosting company looks good.

Some culinary PR professionals specialize in the promotion of cookbook authors/chefs such as Mario Batali, Emeril Lagasse, and Marcella Hazen. These PR professionals create nationwide publicity campaigns and schedule book tours to expose the book and author to audiences who may become buyers.

✔ **Conducting market research:** PR and marketing professionals are also in charge of doing market research — keeping tabs on a client's competitors by reading newspapers and other publications and comparing advertisements. They must also keep up with the latest trends in the business. This duty is ongoing, attended to on a daily or weekly basis.

✔ **Attending trade shows:** PR and marketing professionals usually attend industry trade shows, whether to showcase their client's products or scope out other competitors within the industry. It's important for PR and marketing professionals to attend trade shows because they're an effective vehicle to market a company's products and services to a large group of prospective customers in a short amount of time. Most trade shows have hundreds of exhibits and thousands of attendees. Think about how many sales calls you can make in one day. This number can't even compare to the amount of contacts you can make in a few hours at a trade show.

Spotting Where PR and Marketing Professionals Work

The food industry, which is growing and very competitive, has many opportunities for PR and marketing professionals. They can either work for an agency that outsources their services to other companies or work directly for a company, handling all its marketing needs. They may also work as independent contractors, or freelancers, which means they work for themselves.

The following food-service-related companies utilize the services of PR and marking professionals:

- ✔ Airlines and cruise ships
- ✔ Artisans and home-based businesses
- ✔ Bakeries and pastry shops
- ✔ Casinos
- ✔ Catering companies
- ✔ Food stylists and photographers
- ✔ Hospitals, nursing homes, and retirement homes
- ✔ Hotels, resorts, and spas
- ✔ Party planning companies
- ✔ Personal, private, and famous chefs
- ✔ Restaurants
- ✔ Retail outlets and restaurant supply companies and shops
- ✔ Schools and colleges
- ✔ Wineries, breweries, and microbreweries

Companies such as wineries, breweries, and microbreweries often hire tour guides to give tours of their facilities. Tour guides must be knowledgeable about the company's products, be able to educate visitors, and be able to sell the company's services and products. These positions are great for people looking to get their feet wet in public relations and marketing. For more information about wineries and breweries, see Chapter 11.

Career Profile

Whether it's a job at an agency that specializes in PR and marketing services for food-related businesses or a celebrity chef, or a position with a high-end restaurant, numerous jobs exist for those interested in a career in PR and marketing within the culinary industry.

Excellent communication and writing skills as well as an interest in food are musts for someone interested in working in the food industry as a public relations and marketing specialist.

Personality traits

Think of someone who you know who is a "people person." This person can likely start a conversation with just about anyone, has many friends, and probably smiles often and is a good listener. A people person is just the right kind of individual for a marketing or PR job.

To do well in PR and marketing, you must be charismatic. You must be outgoing, have superior networking skills, and exude self-confidence. You must also be a great communicator, both verbally and in writing, and be creative, reliable, and ready to grab the bull by the horns. And to be a successful PR or marketing professional, you need to be an outstanding salesperson because, in essence, you're selling a company's image along with its goods and services.

PR and marketing professions in the culinary business should love food and have knowledge of the culinary industry. If they work for a restaurant, they need to be very familiar with the restaurant's menu and wine list.

PR and marketing professionals should be honest with their bosses and not afraid to give criticism when it's due, such as telling their employers when something they're doing isn't working and should be done another way. They should also work well under pressure and be able to adhere to strict deadlines.

Salaries

The salary for PR and marketing professionals varies according to where they're employed and their job duties. Most PR and marketing professionals working for a company receive a base salary in addition to commission, which is based on sales numbers, and a bonus for meeting or exceeding these numbers. They may earn as little as $20,000 to as much as $120,000 per year, including benefits and commissions.

The salaries for freelance PR and marketing professionals vary because they usually set their own pay scale, negotiating rates with prospective clients. Those who work for a firm that contracts them out on an as-needed basis are usually paid per job by the client, sometimes with a percentage going to the firm that contracted out their services.

Education and training

PR and marketing professionals working in the culinary industry typically don't have culinary degrees but do have knowledge of food. They may have gained this knowledge by taking culinary classes or through working in the industry, though some professionals have actually completed a culinary or hospitality degree.

Most marketing and PR professionals hold a degree in public relations, journalism, English, communications, marketing, business, or advertising. Sales experience and business management courses are especially helpful, as well as computer experience and knowledge of web design and graphic arts.

Advancement prospects

Advancement prospects vary according to the type of work and place of employment. PR and marketing professionals who start out at the bottom, such as event coordinators or account executives, are usually able to work their way up into management and supervisory positions, such as sales managers or marketing directors, with hard work and determination. They may be rewarded with clients that are more important and/or duties that require more responsibility, such as coordinating special events.

Unions and associations

Although no unions for PR and marketing professionals exist, these professionals can belong to culinary associations such as the National Restaurant Association and the American Institute of Food and Wine as well as more general associations such as the Public Relations Society of America or the American Marketing Association. The associations offer information about job prospects, industry news, and networking opportunities.

Chapter 14

Showcasing Food for Others

In This Chapter

▶ Teaching culinary techniques and methods to others

▶ Familiarizing yourself with food (and materials that look like food) for styling

▶ Capturing perfect images of food as a food photographer

*W*orking in nontraditional settings allows you to be creative and, in many cases, to work at your own pace. Nontraditional culinary jobs are found in settings where most people who work with food wouldn't typically think to look, such as classrooms or even art studios. Food photographers, food stylists, and culinary instructors often find themselves in positions of authority — they're the experts in their classrooms or on their sets, and they're looked to for instruction and guidance. If you're interested in teaching others what you know or in being creative with food, you may want to look into what it takes to be a culinary instructor or a food stylist or photographer.

Although many people are enthusiastic learners who strive to know everything about the subjects for which they have a true passion, others consider attending classes and working to gain experience to be extra, aggravating work. If you're looking for a job that you can immediately jump into with little or no experience or training, culinary instruction and styling may not be for you. You may be able to get by photographing food if you have an impressive portfolio, but without knowing a bit about technique and taste, you'll have difficulty finding a paying job as a stylist or instructor.

An Apple for the Teacher: Culinary Instructor

If you enjoy both cooking and teaching, you may logically be interested in pursuing a career in culinary instruction. If you know quite a bit about food and wish to share that knowledge with others, you may want to look into teaching small workshops or demonstrations at restaurants, in specialty stores, or even at a technical school or culinary institute. To be a truly influential culinary instructor, you must be knowledgeable about a variety of foods — you should know where hundreds of ingredients come from, what they're most commonly used with, how they taste and smell, and how they may be integrated into many different dishes.

Getting the basics on culinary instruction

Culinary instructors teach culinary students about food. Instructors may teach students about the history and background of foods, flavor pairings, or how to present food in ways that make each ingredient shine. They also teach students how to prepare, cook, bake, and decorate food.

If you're interested in pursuing a career as a culinary instructor, you'll most likely have to specialize in one particular type of food. If your strengths are in baking or pastry arts, you may teach nearly all the courses in these areas at one particular technical school. If you're interested solely in chocolate work, you may teach specialized courses about chocolate at multiple schools or programs simultaneously. If you would rather teach about sanitizing the work place or running a kitchen, you may find yourself teaching more business-related courses than soup-and-sauce or meat courses.

As you've probably noticed, teaching culinary courses doesn't necessarily mean you work with food directly — for 15 years, you may teach students how to start a restaurant or manage a kitchen, and never have to demonstrate how to dice an onion or make a successful soufflé. However, you still need to be knowledgeable about the food your students are interested in cooking. Whether you choose to teach specialized courses about carving meats, baking cakes, or purchasing items for a future kitchen, you should be knowledgeable about the culinary industry as a whole so you can point your students in the right direction when they come to you with general questions about the culinary field as a whole.

Finding out who culinary instructors are

The majority of culinary instructors were active in the culinary industry at some point in their professional lives. They may have culinary or hospitality degrees. Many times, culinary instructors are chefs who previously ran their own kitchens or even owned their own restaurants. They may even be active in the business as the owner of a bakery or catering company or chef of a seasonal restaurant, only teaching culinary courses part time in the morning, evening, or during the off-season. You even may encounter teachers who are also food writers and contribute restaurant reviews and recipes to local magazines and newspapers.

As cooks and chefs grow older, standing in a kitchen for more than ten hours a day, working 60 hours each week, and managing a staff become increasingly difficult. In an attempt to stay involved in the culinary industry and to share their experiences and wealth of knowledge with newcomers, chefs often decide to retire from the kitchen and take up work in the classroom. This line of work ensures that they get to spend holidays with their families and work very few weekends (if any).

Not all culinary instructors are aging chefs with aching joints, however. Many instructors have only five to ten years' worth of experience in the field. Although teaching culinary or pastry courses is often an afterthought for many experienced chefs and bakers, younger instructors you meet may have gone to culinary school with the intention of becoming culinary instructors. Their plans may have been to attain their degrees, work in a few kitchens or bakeries to learn certain skills well enough to teach them to others, and then find a vocational, technical, or culinary school where they could teach other culinarians about cakes, pies, poultry, nutrition, diets, or hospitality management.

Seeing where culinary instructors work

If you're interested in becoming a culinary instructor, you have to not only figure out your specialty but also determine who and where you'd like to teach. Sometimes choosing a specialty or determining who you'd like to teach is as easy as figuring out what you're passionate about. Following are a variety of options from which you can choose:

✔ **Vocational schools:** Many high school students opt to attend their high schools for half the day and then travel to vocational schools to take hands-on courses related to the careers they wish to pursue. If you're interested in teaching younger students (and occasionally adult learners) the basics of cooking, you may look to see if opportunities are available at local vocational schools. Vocational culinary teachers lecture and perform cooking demonstrations for their students.

- ✔ **Technical schools:** Instead of pursuing an academic degree, many students who wish to find careers in the culinary or hospitality industries may choose to attain a technical degree. These students are typically young adults who want to finish their schooling in one to two years. This training is hands-on, which means you'll be expected to demonstrate cooking techniques as well as lecture your students, so be prepared to be cooking alongside your students.

- ✔ **Community colleges:** Many students who can't afford expensive institutions take the community college route. These students are often pursuing associate degrees or certifications in specialized areas taught by instructors with experience in these particular areas. Community colleges offer basic courses in cooking, baking, purchasing, nutrition, and management. These courses are typically half lecture and half lab. The school may also offer an advanced course in cake decorating or fruit and vegetable preparation if they have enough students interested in enrolling and an instructor to teach it. After attaining their degree or certificate, students will head out into the workforce.

- ✔ **Four-year colleges:** Four-year colleges typically offer a wider variety of programs than community colleges or technical schools. If you're interested in teaching food science, agriculture, hospitality management, food in media (writing about or filming food), or molecular gastronomy, you may find a position at a four-year college. These colleges also offer advanced courses in baking, pastry arts, and cooking.

- ✔ **Culinary institutions:** If you have the degrees and experience necessary, you may be able to land a job at an impressive culinary institution, such as the Culinary Institute of America, Le Cordon Bleu, or even Johnson and Wales University. The students who attend these schools expect a first-class education, and you must be prepared to give it to them. They may choose to take courses such as food safety, introduction to gastronomy, culinary math, meat/seafood identification, world cuisine studies, and controlling costs and purchasing. If you're an instructor at a culinary institution, you'll most likely teach courses in areas where you have the most experience. Top-notch schools will ask accomplished bakers to teach baking courses, formal restaurant chefs to teach formal restaurant courses, and caterers or banquet chefs to teach volume cooking courses.

- ✔ **Distance-education schools:** If you can easily explain processes using words and short podcasts, you may look into teaching for a distance-education school. These online schools allow students the freedom to learn at times that are convenient for them. All you have to do is prepare the lesson, make sure students can access it, and then be available to answer questions and assign grades. Most students who enroll in online culinary courses are either home cooks who wish to learn more about the basics of cooking and get an associate's degree or certification in the process. Baking or culinary students who have previously attained their associate's degree and want to complete the courses necessary to finish their bachelor's.

Culinary programs are among the least popular for online schools, because teaching students how to cook or bake when you're not alongside them is difficult. How are you supposed to tell a confused student that he should be using a melon baller instead of an ice cream scoop if you can't see the tool he's holding?

✔ **Seminars and workshops:** If you don't want to work for a school or college but would still like to teach people how to cook, you may look into teaching a seminar or weekend workshop at a hotel, a restaurant, or even an arts-and-crafts store. These types of gigs allow you the freedom of booking workshops to fit your schedule, making connections with restaurant and store owners, and teaching courses about foods with which you're most familiar.

✔ **Private lessons:** If you develop a positive reputation as a good cook and teacher, you may find that people will seek you out to help them prepare food for special events such as romantic anniversary or birthday dinners. They may even ask you to come to their homes and teach them the basics so that they can start making meals on their own. Full-time chefs who wish to make some money on the side often favor this route because they can choose their clients.

For more information about different kinds of culinary schools and programs, see Chapter 4. Although that chapter is designed to help students choose the school that's right for them, it may also help you decide which type of program or school you'd like to work for.

Career profile

The path to teaching isn't necessarily one every person should follow — especially if you get frustrated easily, fear public speaking, and dislike demonstrating and explaining the same techniques over and over again every semester. However, if these things don't bother you and you know enough about food, you may want to look into a career as a culinary instructor.

Personality traits

To be a culinary instructor that students and other faculty members respect, you must first and foremost be knowledgeable about the food and techniques you're discussing. You should also be patient, because many students you teach are new to the industry and don't yet understand how to create roses from icing or take the scales and bones off fish. You may need to show your students these processes again and again; therefore, you must be able to keep your cool, no matter how frustrated you become.

To help your students understand both how and why particular methods and techniques must be followed and embraced, you have to be able to speak clearly and use simple language. You must also be approachable so that students can ask you questions about your material and methods. Even though you want students to feel like they can talk to you regarding any issues they may encounter, you must also be tough enough to make them behave in class and listen when you speak. To be a culinary instructor, you have to be able to find the proper balance between intimidation and friendliness.

Salaries

Culinary instructors can make anywhere between $40,000 and $100,000 annually. Salary depends on the institute where they teach, of course. Common sense tells you that an instructor teaching two night classes a week at a community college is going to make less than an instructor at a world-renowned institute with a full course load.

As with nearly all professions, your salary can rise and fall depending on the prior experience you bring with you to a new job. If you've completed higher-level academic degrees or have spent decades in kitchens all over the world, the salary a college or institution offers you will most likely be higher than one it would offer a college graduate with absolutely no experience in a real-life kitchen.

Education and training

The education and training you're required to complete before getting a teaching job differs depending on the program for which you'd like to work. Some schools are more impressed with experience within the industry itself (holding a position as a sous chef or executive chef, running your own restaurant, consistently writing a food column for the local newspaper, hosting a cooking show on television, or similar) than they are with the degree you hold. On the other hand, some schools require that you at least hold an associate's degree or higher to even set foot in the classroom as an instructor.

If your goal is to become a culinary instructor from the start, then you may increase your chances at becoming a young instructor by completing an additional certification in teaching or higher education while you attend culinary or pastry arts school. You'll most likely still need to complete a few years in a kitchen or bakery before you can teach others how to cook or bake, but when the time comes, your employers will know you're serious about teaching because you went the extra mile to learn how to teach as well as cook.

Advancement prospects

For culinary instructors who wish to remain in the academic world until retirement, attaining positions within the educational system such as those of tenured faculty members, department chairs, or even deans of a particular school or college may be within reach. A dean of a culinary school is equal to an executive chef in a kitchen. You're not in charge of the entire college, but you've got free reign over what happens in the culinary school, which courses will be offered, and who will teach those courses.

If you end up teaching a few courses a year but miss the hustle and heat of the kitchen, then perhaps you can take your newfound teaching experience and apply for higher-level positions in the kitchen or dining room of a restaurant. By holding an instructor's position at a college or technical school, you demonstrate to employers that you can give directions or orders and can supervise a room full of students and staff members. You may find yourself in a position of a general manager of a restaurant or hotel or a sous chef or executive chef of a kitchen.

Unions and associations

Public schools are the only arena that culinary teachers can work in and belong to a union. Those unions are general unions that protect all teachers, not just culinary instructors. Unfortunately, unions don't exist for culinary instructors at community colleges, universities, and culinary intuitions.

As a culinary instructor, you may join the National Restaurant Association Education Foundation, which funds and focuses on areas such as food safety and restaurant management in the classroom. You may also join the International Association of Culinary Professionals, which supports anyone in the food industry who benefits the food industry in some way. You may also want to look into memberships with the Association of Cooking Schools and the Council on Hotel, Restaurant, and Institutional Education.

Giving Food the "Wow" Factor: Food Stylist

Similar to becoming a culinary instructor, becoming a food stylist requires that you actually have some experience working with food. Although a background in art and design can definitely help you achieve your food-styling goals, this experience is not the only type you need. The best food stylists are the ones most familiar with food; they understand the natural textures, colors, aromas, and even tastes of real food. Food stylists often work with food photographers (which we discuss in the later section "Say 'Cheese!' Working as a Food Photographer"), but the responsibilities of these two professionals differ drastically.

Clarifying the food stylist job

Nothing is more satisfying to a food stylist than seeing a consumer catch a glimpse of the food on the front cover of a cookbook, stop in his tracks, and pick up the book to inspect the mouth-watering image more closely. Making food (or in some cases, other materials) look appetizing in print, on television, and online is a food stylist's main responsibility. This task may seem simple, but we can assure you it's not — working with a photographer and his lights and angles can be extremely challenging. The food itself is also temperamental, because it can quickly lose shape, crumble, melt, break, and harden.

A food stylist doesn't only style food; she also styles materials that resemble food. The "food" must be visually appealing and realistic. Ice cream must appear to melt slowly, hot soup must be steamy, and the skin on the Thanksgiving turkey must look crispy and cooked to perfection. For these tasks, food stylists must be well-versed in tricking the eye by using other foods and materials. When shooting ice cream, for example, many food stylists use scoops of mashed potatoes instead of ice cream. They then paint or dye the potatoes and add a misting of water to make it appear cold and wet. When styling that Thanksgiving turkey, food stylists work with a raw turkey, a blowtorch, and oftentimes a can of dark paint and a brush. And that bowl of steaming hot soup? It was never hot to begin with — dry ice can be a food stylist's best friend.

If you're interested in landing a job as a food stylist, start looking for everyday items that resemble your favorite foods. Shaving cream, for example, is often used as a substitute for whipped cream on the sets of photo shoots. Pieces of Styrofoam are often used to delineate layers in cake and are then covered with a bit of icing. Many food stylists also use marbles in their work, specifically when working with soups and chili. The marbles sink to the bottom, thus allowing vegetables and other ingredients to rest on top of the broth so they can be seen in the photograph. You can learn these styling tips and more by reading books, researching credible online sites, and experimenting in your free time. Being aware of tricks like these when applying for food styling jobs will certainly impress your future employer — as long as you aren't interviewing with an advertising agency! See "Where food stylists work" for more information on this topic.

In addition to designing food and other materials to be so appetizing that consumers want to buy the product or try the recipe on their own, food stylists must also work with food photographers and prop stylists to make the rest of the photograph look good. They must stand by as photographers adjust lighting and alter shadows, because the smallest modifications on the set can change the appearance of the food in the photograph. As time passes, beads of water may evaporate, foods may melt, and colors may become dull. Food stylists must be prepared to either fix or substitute their materials so the photographer can get the best shot possible.

What's the difference? Food vs. prop stylists

People frequently confuse food stylists for prop stylists because budget restrictions on the set of a photo shoot sometimes require both jobs to be done by the same person. On smaller shoots, where the focus is on the food, the company may not be able to pay a prop stylist to arrange tables, chairs, napkins, picnic baskets, and basically anything in the background of the image. Instead, this responsibility falls to the food stylist, who, on larger sets, is typically in charge of styling only the food.

Aside from having different responsibilities on the set of a photo shoot, food and prop stylists also differ in their training. Prop stylists normally have a background in interior design, whereas food stylists may have prior experience as chefs, bakers, nutritionists, or food journalists. These professions allow future food stylists to become familiar with food before they begin designing and styling it.

Exploring food stylists' workplaces

Food stylists often work as freelancers, applying for or bidding on random jobs that may last a few hours to a few days. Full-time food stylist jobs are hard to find, but companies that frequently require food styling services and may have a stylist or two on staff. Following are some of the types of workplaces where you may be able to find full-time work:

- **Advertising agencies:** Advertising agencies are hired by restaurants, bakeries, caterers, and food production companies of every size to help promote the company's services, events, and products. The agencies create advertisements for television, radio, and print media. (See Chapter 13 for more information on working for marketing, advertising, and public relations firms.). Larger companies, such as Kraft or Weight Watchers, may have their own internal marketing and public relations staff, but they typically hire several small advertising agencies to work closely with marketing personnel to promote the business.

  U.S. law, dubbed the "truth in advertising law," requires food stylists who work for all advertising agencies to ensure that the food being advertised in the photographs is exactly what consumers will receive when they buy the product. Stylists can't use marbles, dry ice, or motor oil (a perfect substitute for maple syrup!) when styling the food being advertised. They also can't include more food in the photograph than the consumer will receive in the package.

  The food being advertised must be true to form, taste, texture, and size, but any additional food in the shot can be altered or fixed. If the focus is on chicken tenders, the sides of broccoli and white rice and a glass of milk supplementing the dish can all be modified to make the meal as a whole appear more appealing.

✔ **Magazines:** As you can probably guess, food magazines employ food stylists. Because the majority of their pages are filled with photographs of food and people preparing food, they frequently rely on food stylists' expertise during photo shoots. If the food doesn't look attractive, readers won't read or try the recipe that goes with it.

✔ **Large newspapers:** In editions of newspapers (specifically Sunday editions) that contain "Food" or "Taste" sections, you'll often find large photographs of featured recipes. You may also see photographs of featured chefs or food professionals surrounded by their signature dishes or ingredients. Larger newspapers can typically afford to hire food stylists for these shoots so the food can look its best.

✔ **Cookbook publishers:** Companies that publish a large number of cookbooks each year definitely have food stylists on staff. Like magazines, the parts of cookbooks that catch the reader's eye first are the pictures. If a dish looks irresistible, the reader may want to try to buy the book and follow the recipe. Smaller publishing companies that occasionally publish cookbooks may hire food stylists on a freelance basis.

✔ **Digital media:** Food blogs have become incredibly popular in recent years. People share their experiences about dining out, cooking, baking, and developing their own creations. High-profile cooks and bakers often have blogs that supplement their television shows and specials, cookbooks, or restaurants. These blogs don't only feature images of completed recipes or techniques, however. Occasionally, they may also include podcasts.

✔ **Cooking shows:** When Tyler Florence prepares a dish on set, the food he's making may be real, but the items placed throughout his "kitchen" aren't. Any food on a television set that appears in the shot but isn't part of the day's cooking lesson has most likely been altered to look appetizing to television viewers and to withstand long hours (and possibly weeks) on the set. Food stylists are an important part of almost every quality cooking show.

Consider this: The photo and video shoots that food stylists are preparing food for may take place at nearly any physical location, including beaches, parks, kitchens, offices, test kitchens, living rooms, and even strange destinations such as at the top of a mountain or in the middle of a cranberry bog. (Think about the commercials and advertisements you see for grape juices, granola bars, and some fruits.) Food stylists need to be prepared to work in many different environments and locations. For more information on opportunities to work for cooking shows, magazines, cookbook publishers, newspapers, and digital media, see Chapter 12.

Career profile

By now, you probably figured out that to be a food stylist, you need to be familiar with food, and you need to be creative. To do this, you need experience working with food and quite a bit of patience. A food stylist is a valuable member of any team that produces photographs or videos featuring food.

Personality traits

Above all else, food stylists need to be perfectionists. They can't settle for three sloppy scoops of ice cream of all different sizes, nor will they stop cutting a block of cheese until they produce a slice that is straight on all sides and has the same thickness throughout. Nothing can be chipped if it's not supposed to be, nor can any part of the food melt or slide into a different position.

Food stylists should also be intelligent and crafty. They need to recognize materials that look like the foods they're working with and invent ways to make those materials look both edible and appetizing. Food stylists should be familiar with chemicals that alter color, shine, and texture, as well.

Patience is also a key factor in food styling. Sometimes the brunt of a food stylist's job is to sit for two hours, forming one quenelle after another until the exact look required for the photograph is achieved. Often photo shoots require multiple, identical models of the same items, because materials may collapse, melt, or change shape and color throughout the day. Stylists are responsible for creating these duplicates.

Finally, food stylists must work well with others. They can't simply walk onto the set and start barking orders. The success of their work depends on the cooperation of the food photographer, the prop stylist, and the product's representatives. If the people running the show don't like the stylist's concept, the stylist will need to switch gears. If the photographer thinks a shot from a different angle or with different lighting will better the image, then the stylist must consider these options and adjust the food to the photographer's liking. The stylist must get along with everyone to help the day run smoothly.

Salaries

Declaring an average salary for a food stylist is difficult because stylists typically work freelance and name their own price. They may charge by the hour or by the day. If they're on set as just food stylists, they receive less money than if they are acting as both food and prop stylist (and occasionally photographer, too).

Typically, print media jobs for newspapers and magazines pay around $500 a day, whereas work on satellite media tours or digital media projects may result in about $900 a day. According to CookingSchools.com, however, the average salary for a food stylist is $56,000.

Education and training

You can't simply wake up one morning and decide to be a food stylist. You need a substantial amount of experience — and typically education — before you can make this career your own.

Although schools such as the Culinary Institute of America offer food styling certification, just about any food-related career can put you on the path to becoming a food stylist. You can pursue an associate's or bachelor's degree in hospitality, home economics, or hotel and restaurant management. You can go to school to become a nutritionist or dietician. You can even take courses in food writing. Anything that helps you become familiar with food will help you achieve your goal of becoming a food stylist.

If you know you want to be a food stylist when you start taking courses, make yourself more marketable by completing art and photography courses. They'll teach you about lighting, shadows, painting, sculpting, and just about any other technique you may use. If you take these courses throughout your college or technical school career, you'll stay up to date with new techniques in the food industry as they evolve and will be able to impress your future employers with your modern methods.

In addition to finding the right educational program, you also need a few years of experience before your individual services will be requested at a photo or video shoot. The best way to get experience is to find work in a kitchen or bakery or with a catering company and become familiar with the way food is prepared and presented. When you feel you understand the techniques used by professional chefs and cooks, you can try to spend some time with a food stylist who is already successful in the field. You may be able to complete an apprenticeship or internship or work part-time with the stylist, which means you'll be asked to come along on photo shoots and assist the stylist. You'll surely pick up tricks of the trade while watching a skilled artist work.

Advancement prospects

If you work as a freelance food stylist, your next step may be finding a permanent gig at a magazine, newspaper, or publishing house. If working for someone else isn't your idea of a good time, you can even start your own food styling business. Create a name, print business cards, and market yourself as a business owner. Hire assistants, advertise, and get your name out there. For more information about becoming a culinary entrepreneur, see Chapter 18.

If you're lucky enough to come across a full-time position with a large company, you may want to try to work your way up the company's managerial ladder. You may begin as an assistant food stylist and then become the company's main go-to on all things food-related. From there (and if the possibility and position exists), you may work to become the company's art director or photo editor. Your eye for detail — which is a necessary skill for every food stylist — will open many doors for you in the culinary arts industry.

Other advancement options for food stylists include becoming culinary instructors, art instructors, food photographers, prop stylists, and even cooks and bakers. If you decide you no longer want to style fake food and would rather work with real dishes again, you can easily return to the kitchen.

Unions and associations

Even though food stylists — especially freelancers — aren't protected under unions, they can still join associations related to their field. These groups include the Association of Stylists and Coordinators, the New York Women's Culinary Alliance, and International Association of Culinary Professionals. Belonging to an association keeps will keep you in the loop; you'll learn about emerging techniques and trends in your field and you'll be able to attend conferences and meetings that will keep you in touch with other culinary professionals.

Say "Cheese!" Working as a Food Photographer

Food photographers are as valuable as (if not more valuable than) food stylists on set. After all, without the photographer, a photo of the product wouldn't exist. Food photographers, like food stylists, typically work freelance jobs and therefore set their hours and choose their clients.

At a photo shoot, the photographer is normally the one calling all the shots (no pun intended) unless a disagreement with the client arises. At this point, the photographer must cooperate with the client and other workers on the set to produce the highest-quality image possible.

Discovering what it's like to be a food photographer

Food photographers work with food stylists and prop stylists to produce mouth-watering images to pair with restaurant reviews, product advertisements, magazine articles, and recipes in cookbooks. Food photographers use their knowledge of lighting, set design, and camera operations to produce these images.

How photographers do their jobs depends on the directions they receive from their clients. If clients have certain visions for shoots, photographers will find ways to make these visions come to life. If clients give photographers freedom on the set, then photographers typically present their best ideas to the client or the client's art director for feedback before beginning the shoot. The creativity and skill of photographers is usually conveyed through the directions they give to stylists and set designers, and how the photo is actually shot.

Photographers have the most control over what they shoot when they're hired to take process shots. *Process shots* are simply photographs that document a technique or procedure (think step-by-step instructions). On these sets, photographers adjust lighting and switch angles to get the shot that best shows the process being captured.

After arriving on set, the photographer reviews his vision of the final photographs with the client and the rest of the crew. If the client did not provide the photographer with equipment such as lighting, the photographer and his staff set up for the shoot. Many publishing companies and ad agencies will hire photographers who are charged with procuring their own staff of food stylists, assistants, hand models, and so on. This makes things easier for the company, as there's only one contract to draw up in this case. Food magazines or magazines with a dedicated food section may have some of these staff members on their payroll, however.

As a photographer shoots from different angles, he asks for adjustments in lighting of the set and positioning of the food. Whether he's shooting in a private studio, at a public park, in a test kitchen, or even on a beach, the photographer's job is to make sure the focus is on the product (the food) and that the other details included in the image make the food look even more appetizing.

After shooting has wrapped, the photographer develops or prints the photographs (depending on whether he shoots with film or digital) and chooses the best few of the bunch to present to his client. The client ultimately has the final say on which image best represents their products. If necessary, photographers may edit the photos before or after meeting with the clients.

Finding out what kinds of places hire food photographers

A food photographer should be prepared to work in any environment, regardless of how difficult it may be to shoot there. As a food photographer, you may be asked to do shoots in green parks, on sandy beaches, on breezy mountains, in wet rain forests, in dark basements, and in busy kitchens. No matter the location, you must work with the environment's natural elements and produce the best possible picture.

Similar to food stylists, food photographers often work as freelancers; however, full-time jobs in food photography do exist. If you're looking for full-time work as a food photographer, you may want to check listings for the following types of companies:

- ✔ **Advertising agencies/departments:** Food photographers are often on staff at advertising agencies or large food companies with marketing departments that put images of food on packaging, on billboards, or in circulars or magazines. Similar to the job of a food stylist employed by an advertising agency, food photographers must ensure that everything being advertised in their photographs is true to form. They cannot fix the photograph (on the set or by editing digitally afterward) to make the advertised product more attractive than it is.

- ✔ **Magazines:** Magazines that often feature recipes, cooking tips, and even decorating tips sometimes employ a full-time food photographer. These photographers are responsible for making all the food in the magazine look edible and attractive. When the photograph accompanies an article, the photographer may have to read the article and work with the writer to capture the exact essence of the food.

- ✔ **Large newspapers:** Food photographers are often called on by large newspapers that run "Food" or "Taste" sections filled with recipes, how-to articles, reviews, and even chef/baker biographies. If the newspaper isn't large enough to afford the work of a photographer who specializes in food, however, it may ask its staff photographers to simply work with an affordable food stylist to get the job done.

- ✔ **Cookbook publishers:** Unlike newspapers, publishing companies that produce cookbooks always want photographers who specialize in taking photographs of food. Because cookbooks are all about food and the chefs and bakers who prepare it, the person producing the images for them need to be familiar with the subject area.

- ✔ **Digital media:** Similar to food stylists, food photographers may be called on to take images for blogs or websites. Food photographers who understand the difference between shooting for print media (lower quality) and online media (high quality) and who stay up to date on trends in digital media are in demand for these projects.

Refer to Chapter 12 for more information on working with food for magazines, cookbook publishers, newspapers, and digital media.

Career profile

The path to becoming a food photographer is similar to the path to becoming a food stylist: With a bit of knowledge about food and the proper training, you'll be in good shape to enter the field. Keep reading to find out what traits make a good photographer and what you can expect in this career path.

Personality traits

Like any other position in the culinary arts industry, the best food photographers are patient and cooperative. With confidence, they express their visions for their projects but then work with the clients, stylists, and all others on the set to get the job done. Sometimes bargaining is involved on set when the client's wishes and the photographer's ideas aren't in line — food photographers may be experts in taking photographs, but they aren't necessarily in charge of the food itself. If the client has a different vision or the food stylist simply can't find a way to make a particular material stand upright or appear fresh, the photographer may need to develop a new approach when shooting the object, so she must be flexible and adaptive.

Salaries

Most food photographers pick their own clients and hunt down their own work, so annual salaries have a very broad range. Depending on your expertise and how many jobs you work each year, you can make anywhere between $18,000 and $500,000 in a single year.

Food photographers can charge by the hour, the day, or the project as a whole. Shooting for a magazine can bring in $500 to $1,000, whereas shooting for an entire book can earn you up to (and sometimes well past, depending on the publisher's budget) $5,000. Many photographers find the most money on advertising assignments for consumer products. Advertising work can range from $3,000 to $20,000 per day.

Finding jobs that can pay thousands of dollars for a single day's work is extremely difficult; however, the more experience you gain, the more connections you'll make. Connections are key in this industry. If clients like your work and your personality, they're going to bring up your name in conversation. Be sure to print business cards and hand a few of them to your clients (and others on the set, if you wish). The more people you impress, the more work will come your way.

Education and training

This should be obvious to you already, but to be successful in this field, photographers should know how to work a camera. They should understand concepts such as depth of field measurements, focal lengths, aperture settings, shutter speeds, and exposure. They should be confident in their ability to light a set and find a good camera angle. Photography, specifically food photography, involves more than pointing a camera at an object and pressing a button. A degree or certificate in photography or the arts can definitely help you find work as a food photographer.

If you want to beef up your résumé by attaining a degree or certificate of some kind and you know you want to make a career out of food photography, you may want to take a few culinary or baking courses in addition to art and photography classes. Photographers who work with food often become familiar with what fresh fruits, vegetables, and cuts of meat should look like. They know which dishes should be served on ice, piping hot, or at room temperature. They also understand the difference between textures and tastes. To sum it up: They know about food! If you're reading this book, you're obviously fascinated by food, so becoming familiar with techniques, methods, and appearances of raw and cooked (and overdone!) foods is most likely an interest to you already.

With this combination of food knowledge and photography skills, potential employers will clearly see that you took the steps necessary to educate yourself about the profession and all it entails.

However, degrees and certificates aren't strictly necessary in this line of work. Many photography programs emphasize developing your skills by getting out of the classroom and taking thousands of photographs. If school's not your cup of tea, you can certainly teach yourself photography by doing some reading and getting lots of practice.

To get started, think about picking up a book that explains basic techniques and concepts to you. After reading a book such as *Photography For Dummies* (John Wiley & Sons, Inc.) by Russell Hart and Dan Richards, you can grab your camera, focus it on your object, and snap away. As in most other industries, practice makes perfect when learning how to take photographs. Save your best pictures and place them in a portfolio so you can show your future employers what you're capable of.

Experience is possibly the most crucial factor in food photography — you can never have enough of it. In school, volunteer to take photographs of anything and everything, even if it's not food. Take photographs for the school newspaper, the yearbook, and newsletters. Keep copies of your best work and start a portfolio. Look around town — do any new businesses (specifically restaurants, pastry shops, bakeries, or grocery stores) need a few photographs for advertisements, flyers, or up-and-coming websites? Offer your services to those closest to you, because these clients can become references for future jobs.

When you're ready to break into the food industry, do some research and try to find an internship or part-time work with a successful food photographer. Whether you help to take the actual photographs or simply hold the tripod and fetch coffee, you'll still learn a thing or two about the business. The longer you stick it out, the better your chances will be of getting the opportunity to shoot your own photographs.

Even if you can't get much practice taking pictures of food or can't find a food photographer to shadow, keep working at your general photography skills. If you know enough about photography as a whole, you can probably find a few businesses that will settle for a general professional photographer rather than one who specifically works with food at all times.

Advancement prospects

Food photographers have many options: They can freelance, start their own photography business, or attempt to work for a company such as a publishing house or newspaper. If employed by larger companies with available positions and higher budgets, food photographers can work their way up through the company to hold positions similar to those of photo editor or art director.

Because photographers work closely with food and prop stylists, they can always take a stab at those jobs if they tire of taking photographs. They can be set designers, too. If you're a food photographer and you think you may be interested in styling food or props in the future, pay close attention to the methods used by those around you. Take notes and give it a try if the opportunity arises.

Another option for food photographers is to return to the field of general photography. Just because you're a food photographer doesn't mean you should always limit yourself to taking photographs of food. You can respond to calls for photographs of buildings, people, and places. Even if melting mounds of ice cream and taco shells stuffed to the max with beef, cheese, and salsa are your favorite subjects, sometimes throwing a bridge, politician, or sunset into the mix to keep your portfolio diverse is a good idea.

Unions and associations

If you're freelancing or are a business owner, your chances of being part of a union are zero to none. However, you can still join associations such as the International Association of Culinary Professionals, the National Press Photographers Association, and the Association of Food Journalists. These associations help you stay up to date with industry advancements, such as the newest pieces of equipment. They also allow you to network and meet other photographers in your field.

Chapter 15

Careers in Purchasing: Specialty Foods, Cookware, and More

*I*n every restaurant, bakery, culinary classroom, or food store you visit, you're surrounded by items that have been sold to each space by talented buyers and salespeople working in the culinary field. When chefs are looking for industrial-strength equipment for their kitchens, when grocery store managers are thinking of expanding their international offerings, or when bakers need to buy bags of sugar and flour in bulk, they turn to these professionals to get them the best deals on items for their dining rooms, kitchens, display windows, and shelves.

In this chapter, you find out what it takes to be one of these behind-the-scenes people in the culinary world. We mainly discuss two different approaches to purchasing careers: the buying and the selling. If you're interested in traveling to stores and restaurants and earning a living off the products you sell, then you may want to look into a career as a restaurant-supply salesperson. If you want to acquire products for your company (restaurant-supply companies, grocery stores, restaurants) to sell to others, you may want to learn more about becoming a restaurant-supply buyer, specialty-foods store buyer or manager, or even a grocery store manager. We discuss these professions and more throughout this chapter.

Getting the Lowdown on Purchasing

The men and women who buy and sell foods and equipment may sometimes be referred to as *purchasers.* Typically, the term *purchasing* means paying for an item or service. There's more to this business than this definition lets on, however. To be more specific, purchasers effectively transfer products from their source of origin to retail outlets or restaurants that later make the product available to customers. Purchasers buy the products for their companies and then resell them to stores, restaurants, or sometimes even directly to public consumers. To understand this process better, we break down the buying aspect of purchasing into two parts: selection and procurement.

According to *Purchasing,* by Andrew Hale Feinstein and John M. Stefanelli (John Wiley & Sons, Inc.), *selection* is "choosing from among various alternatives on various levels." Purchasers choose between different brands, qualities, and suppliers based on the type of product they're looking to obtain.

After buyers select products, they can procure, or acquire, them. According to the same book, *procurement* is "an orderly, systematic exchange between a seller and a buyer. It is the process of obtaining goods and services, including all the activities associated with determining the types of products needed, making purchases, receiving and storing shipments, and administering purchase contracts."

After buying products, purchasers get them to retail stores or restaurants that want to use or resell the products. Purchasers may work directly for a specialty store, grocery store, cookware and appliance store, or restaurant, in which case they buy the products on the store or restaurant's behalf. Alternatively, they may work independently or for purchasing vendors and resell the products to stores and restaurants.

Buying and Selling Specialty Foods

Have you ever walked through a grocery store's international section and wondered where the products on the shelves came from? Why *those* products? Why so little of one item, but so many of another? Who decides which items the store should carry? And why does Bobby's Family Market on Hanover Street have five kinds of rice and the Bobby's on George Avenue only have two?

The presence of specialty items in grocery stores isn't random — companies such as specialty-food stores or grocery stores employ special purchasers (who may also be called simply *buyers* or *managers*) to ensure these sections are stocked with items that shoppers want. If a grocery store doesn't employ a specific person for purchasing specialty foods, grocery store managers generally play active roles in deciding which specialty items make it onto the stores' shelves.

Regardless of whether managers work for specialty-foods stores or grocery stores, they typically take part in (and thus must understand) both the buying and the selling that occur during the purchasing process. They may be in charge of buying the items, which makes them purchasers, but they also have to think like salespeople. Will the items they're interested in grab the attention of consumers? Will the items successfully sell?

What's so special about specialty foods?

According to the National Association for the Specialty Food Trade (NASFT), *specialty foods* are "foods and beverages that exemplify quality, innovation and style in their category. They are often known for their authenticity, ethnic or cultural origin, commitment to specific processing rules or traditions, superior ingredients, limited supply, or extraordinary packaging."

Examples of specialty foods may include types of:

- Herbs and spices
- Processed meats
- Pastas
- Fresh wild fish
- Organic vegetables
- Basmati rice
- Whole grains
- Artisanal cheeses
- Functional beverages
- Condiments

Chips, pretzels, salsas, dips, and other refrigerated sauces can also be added to this list if specialty foods companies produce them.

Throughout the years, the demand for specialty foods has increased. In fact, specialty food sales accounted for more than 13 percent of all retail food sales in 2010. The industry made more than $70 billion that year. In the State of the Specialty Food Industry 2011, the NASFT found that the average specialty food manufacturer produces more than 50 different items and brings in more than $2 million in sales each year. They also discovered that Mediterranean and Indian products were becoming more popular in restaurants, cafés, and grocery stores.

This increase will certainly keep specialty food manufacturers, buyers, and store owners busy for a while, which is great news for you as a purchaser. The better the business, the better your chances become at finding success within the industry.

Purchasing for specialty food stores

Dedicated specialty-food purchasers, who are more commonly referred to as *buyers* or *managers,* can usually be found in specialty food stores or at grocery stores with large international, gourmet, or specialty foods departments. Specialty-food store buyers and managers are in charge of buying certain kinds of items from manufacturers to sell in their own stores at a higher value.

This process sounds like a simple exchange of goods, but buyers will tell you the job's not that easy. Being a specialty-food store buyer is similar to being a scout for a college sports team: You quietly watch a few players to see how they do on the field or court and then you decide which ones are right for your team. You negotiate to get the ones you want into your school and then you hope they bring their A-game when they put on your uniform. This same approach can be used when purchasing specialty foods.

First, specialty food buyers watch the market to see which products are selling well. They may sign up for newsletters, watch the stocks, or even attend trade shows to find new products they'd like to place on their shelves.

Then they have to do a bit of research to figure out which products their customers want. Some buyers speak directly to their customers — they approach them in the store and ask them which products they'd like to see the store stock. They may suggest a few products and ask customers if they would purchase the items in the future. Other ways to gather this information are by mailing surveys that customers can fill out and return and by making phone calls to preferred customers to find out their opinions. Online polls are also a quick, easy, and cheap way of attaining these details.

When buyers think they know which products will sell in their stores, they strike a deal with the manufacturers. When the product is delivered, the buyers are then in charge of ensuring customers know the product is available. To spread the news, they may set up displays at the ends of aisles and teach employees about the products so they can answer customer inquiries.

Many specialty food store buyers and managers offer sample tables in stores where customers can taste new products. Behind the table is an employee who is knowledgeable about the item and can easily answer the customers' questions. Buyers often have the products placed on or near the sample table so customers can easily find the items if they enjoy the sample. The buyer may also have coupons designed for the product to help the sale.

If your goal is to own a small specialty food store, you'll probably have to wear two (or more) hats. Not only will you have to run the store, but you'll also have to act as the specialty food buyer. Procuring the specialty items, setting up the displays, and then seeing that the food remains fresh until it sells will all be up to you. As your business grows, however, you may be able to afford to bring in someone to assist you in either running the store or purchasing specialty items.

Purchasing specialty foods for the grocery store

Grocery store managers are in charge of purchasing all food in the store. After examining which items sold and need to be replenished, the grocery store manager orders a long list of food to be shipped to her store for the following week. If the store doesn't employ a specialty-food store buyer or manager, obtaining items for the store's international, gourmet, or other specialty food departments or aisles is one of the grocery store manager's tasks.

To find these specialty items, grocery store managers can do the same things specialty-food store managers do — if they have time. Because they're responsible for the entire store and not just the specialty-foods department, they may not have time to attend trade shows, personally survey customers, or teach their staff about each item. So if they don't have the budget to hire someone to manage the specialty food department and they don't have the time to give the department the attention it deserves, what do they do?

Simple answer — they wait for the products to come to them. Many times, manufacturers and distributors employ salespeople to take their products on the road and make deals with store owners and management staff. They visit the stores with a sample of their products, allow the managers to taste it and inspect it, and then wait for the managers to decide to carry it.

Food artisans (which we discuss in Chapter 10) sometimes take the same approach to selling their goods. With a case of their finest products, artisans visit local stores to see if management will consider selling their artisanal cheeses, sauces, canned goods, meats, or whatever else they make.

The responsibilities of the store manager depend on many factors, including the size of the store and whether the store is privately owned or part of a chain. Sometimes the owners are responsible for ordering the specialty foods while the grocery managers are in charge of the rest. Other times, the store owners take control of all of the purchasing and ordering. Also, in larger stores, each department (deli, frozen foods, dairy, grocery, produce, international, and so on) may have its own manager who does the ordering for his particular department. If you're interested in being a grocery store manager who is responsible for purchasing and sales, do some research on the store and the responsibilities of its employees before you apply.

If you're responsible for buying international and ethnic foods for a grocery store and work in an area that's populated by a particular ethnic group, you can improve sales by finding out about the group's interests. Learn some of the language, speak to the locals, and find out which foods they miss the most from their native countries. If you can find those spices, sauces, meats, or other rare items, you can most likely secure future business from those customers and members of their extended families.

Career profile

Specialty-food store buyers/managers have many responsibilities — and sometimes grocery store managers have even more! Between supervising employees, setting up displays, managing stock levels, purchasing and receiving, and dealing with disgruntled customers, these managers often have quite a bit on their plates. To fill either one of these positions, you need to show potential employers that you can keep your cool under pressure.

Personality traits

The most successful specialty-food store buyers/managers and grocery store managers are those who are approachable, trustworthy, and intelligent. These qualities are important because salespeople, employees, and customers alike won't want to associate with a buyer/manager if they don't feel as though they can ask them a question and expect an honest, thoughtful, and informed response. Having an abrasive or apathetic personality may cost your store sales. You also need to have extraordinary organizational skills, because you'll often have to receive and sort products when they come in and then give employees clear directions on building displays.

If you want to see yourself in either of these positions in a few years, you need to work on your ability to communicate with others. These jobs require you to speak to store customers, employees, and owners in addition to product salespeople, distributors, and local businesspersons. You need to be friendly yet serious. Salespeople should know that they can speak with you about their products but that they won't be able to take advantage of you or coax you into purchasing something you don't really want. Grocery store managers need to be capable of being the authority figure in the store, but they also must be available to employees if they have disagreements with customers or even other employees.

Salaries

Although grocery store managers in smaller stores with specialty departments perform the tasks of specialty-food store buyers/managers along with responsibilities of managing the entire store, they make less money each year than specialty-food store buyers. Specialty-food store buyers tend to work for bigger stores owned by wealthier companies, so their employers can afford to pay more. These workplaces also tend to offer better benefits and commissions. Both positions may receive annual bonuses, but grocery store managers are normally paid by the hour and specialty-food store buyers receive a salary.

In one year, the average grocery store manager makes approximately $50,000, although salaries range from $24,000 to approximately $80,000. Of course, the amount depends on the size of the grocery store, benefits, and the responsibilities of the store manager.

As a specialty food store buyer/manager, you may earn between $34,000 and $110,000 each year. Again, it depends on the company you work for, the qualifications and experience you have going into the job, and the location of the store.

Education and training

You can't wake up in the morning, having spent absolutely no time working in grocery stores or with specialty foods and apply for a job as a specialty-food store buyer/manager or a grocery store manager. These are two positions that you'll have to earn through hard work and dedication to the business.

After working a few years in a supermarket or grocery store as a bagger, cashier, or stockroom worker, you may be promoted to assistant manager of a single department or of the entire store, depending on the size of the store. When you're an assistant manager, you'll have to decide which path you want to take: specialty foods (if your store offers them and has a large department) or store management.

If your interests lie in specialty foods, show the current store manager or owners that you're good at finding gourmet or international products that customers want. Forming connections with local artisans, farmers, and businesspersons also helps you bring specialty products into the store. Let your employers know that you understand the local culture and are certain that stocking items that will interest native Asians, Mexicans, or Russians, for example, will draw in a range of customers.

Be careful not to get caught up in one certain type of specialty item. Sure, some large stores may employ assistants to specialty store buyers or managers who know the ins and outs of coffees, beans, breads, cheeses, or produce. This focused knowledge is helpful, but these narrow interests can only take you so far. Educating yourself in all things specialty food will help you climb the ranks, and eventually you may become knowledgeable enough to be the company's head buyer.

You obviously need experience in the industry to land these jobs — and an education doesn't hurt, either. Although you can probably get to the position of grocery store manager with a high school diploma, you can achieve that goal faster if you receive an associate's degree or higher from a community college or four-year university. You may choose to attain a degree in business, human resources, or even marketing.

Make sure your computer skills are adequate for the job you want. They will come in handy when filling the position of grocery store managers or specialty-food store buyers, because food ordering may be done online or through computer programs.

To become a manager at a grocery store, you don't need experience cooking food. However, experience working with food will benefit you if you apply for a specialty-food store buyer position. If you have a strong ethnic culinary background or if you've completed courses at a cooking school, you'll have an easier time getting a job that deals with specialty foods. Completing business, marketing, or food chemistry courses can also help you land a job as a specialty-food store buyer or assistant specialty food buyer.

Advancement prospects

Many specialty food store buyers go on to become grocery store managers who oversee the progress of the entire store. Others leave the grocery store to open their own specialty-food stores. These stores may carry a variety of gourmet products, artisanal items, or international ingredients. Owners may also offer items used for a particular cuisine, such as Japanese, Thai, or Mexican food.

With enough experience, grocery store managers can advance to positions such as district supervisor. In that job they oversee the work done by employees in multiple stores. If the possibility exists, grocery store managers may even have the chance to buy the business from its current owners and make it their own.

Unions and associations

Because specialty-food store buyers/managers and grocery store managers are clearly part of the management team, they cannot belong to any unions. However, they should still be familiar with how unions work because their employees may be part of the United Food and Commercial Workers International Union.

Although they can't join unions, grocery store managers and specialty-food store buyers/managers can become part of the National Association for Specialty Food Trade. Members of this association are invited to attend and participate in the Fancy Food Show, which is held twice a year. In the past, more than 24,000 people attended and more than 180,000 products were on display from 80 different countries.

Purchasing Cookware and Kitchen Equipment

Purchasing and selling cookware, kitchen equipment, and other essentials is similar to buying and selling specialty foods. Finding the best products for your store is difficult, but ensuring those items sell is even harder.

Think of the items you use in your kitchen everyday. Pots and pans; kitchen utensils such as forks, melon ballers, and whisks; casserole dishes; measuring cups; and mixing bowls all fall under the category of *cookware.* In stores where you find cookware, you'll most likely also find glassware, flatware, and bakeware. Items such as aprons, placemats, tablecloths and table settings, and dishtowels may also be identified as cookware.

The word *equipment,* on the other hand, is used to describe appliances such as refrigerators, blenders, microwaves, stovetops, toaster ovens, and convection ovens. In progressive kitchens, Anti-Griddles, thermal immersion circulators, smoking guns, and centrifuges are also popular pieces of equipment.

Cookware and kitchen equipment can be purchased in cookware stores, such as Williams Sonoma or Sur La Table, or in specified sections of department stores. In stores like Restaurant Depot, which are aimed at commercial kitchens in restaurants, hotels, and bakeries, industrial-strength equipment is sold. Some electronics stores even house sections that feature technologically advanced refrigerators, stovetops, ovens, and blenders. (Picture refrigerators with televisions in them, ovens with touch screens, and stovetops that boil water in 90 seconds.)

Similar to specialty food stores and grocery stores, the bigger the store, the more specialized a manager's job. If the store is large enough to employ both a cookware store buyer and a cookware store manager, then the buyer most likely will only buy the products for the store and the manager will help sell them. If the store is small and can only employ a manager, then the manager will most likely also be tasked with buying the products in addition to selling them. In these stores, it's important that cookware store managers not only know which products are popular, but they also need to understand and be able to explain how each product works. Whereas specialty-food store buyers may be able to offer a taste of their featured ingredient to coax their customers into buying the item, cookware store buyers and managers have only their word and the description of the product to work with. Their reputations as fair and trustworthy salespeople are as important as (if not more important than) the types of products they're selling.

Cookware store buyers and managers need to keep abreast of relevant changes in their area at all times. They need to know which types of restaurants, bakeries, and food stores are offered in his area. If restaurants open nearby with executive chefs who sometimes create avant-garde menus requiring flash freezing and flavored smoke, you need to be sure to stock Anti-Griddles and smoking guns to sell in your store. Buyers and managers also need to know how to shop for the appropriate season. If flakes are falling from the sky and kids are walking home from school in snow boots, you should know that any picnic baskets and ice cube trays you stock probably won't sell until late spring or early summer.

If you're applying for a job as a cookware store buyer or manager, be sure to check out the area surrounding the store. Are there restaurants? Bakeries? What kind of food do they offer and what type of equipment do they use? If you have the time, chat up the employees and find out how old their equipment is and if they ever run out of particular supplies, such as airbrushes, measuring cups, or spatulas. Before your interview, look at the products on the market and then go in with a business plan. You know which products are available and you've made connections with business owners who will purchase them — if you can guarantee paying customers, you'll most likely get the job. Even if you don't find anyone interested in shopping at the store, your research will help you learn about the area. This knowledge will also impress your future employer.

Working as a purchaser for cookware stores

A cookware store buyer has responsibilities similar to a specialty-food store buyer (see the earlier section "Purchasing for specialty food stores"). The only real difference is that cookware store buyers purchase cookware and kitchen equipment instead of food and beverages.

Cookware store buyers may work for small, privately owned stores, or they may be employed by large companies. In most cases, if buyers work for a small store, they work right in the stores. They set up displays, meet with salespeople, and speak directly with customers who have questions about the products. Buyers may even act as managers of cookware sections if the stores where they work sell other products.

A buyer who works for a large company that owns multiple stores in an area or region is more likely to be spotted in an office or conference room at the company's headquarters than roaming the aisles or straightening the racks in a single store. These buyers may be responsible for finding merchandise to sell in stores across the nation or in one specific area.

How do buyers know which items to purchase? They read newsletters and scan brochures, magazines, and catalogues. They keep track of recent trends, and they read performance reviews of the newest products. They may even attend trade shows like the annual International Housewares Show in Chicago. Like specialty-food store buyers, they may also gather data about the types of products their customers are looking for via mail or online surveys. Buyers also meet with salespeople who represent companies that produce cookware and kitchen equipment. If they like what the salespeople show them, they make a deal with the manufacturer to carry the product.

If your goal is to own a store that carries cookware or kitchen equipment, know that in the early years you'll most likely be the person in charge of researching the products, finding good deals, and then marketing the items you choose. Instead of supervising employees who set up window displays, assemble floor models, and show customers how to work the products for sale, you'll be performing these tasks. After the ball gets rolling, however, you may be able to hire other employees so you can focus on running the store.

Managing a cookware store

Cookware store managers' jobs are similar to grocery store managers' jobs (discussed in "Purchasing specialty foods for the grocery"), except cookware store managers supervise employees who stock and sell cookware and kitchen equipment instead of employees who work with food and beverages. Cookware store managers also keep track of inventory, set up displays, and speak with customers. They know how to use the registers, the computer programs, and machinery in the storage areas and back rooms so they can help other employees when they're in a pinch.

Sometimes cookware store managers take on the duties of cookware store buyers, which we cover in the preceding section. They may spend time doing market research, gathering opinions from customers, and perusing magazines and online catalogues for products and manufacturers who are new to the business. They meet with cookware product salespeople and, upon the owners' approval, agree to sell the products in their stores.

In addition to purchasing, receiving, and then marketing and selling cookware and kitchen equipment, cookware store managers may also hire, train, discipline, and fire staff.

Career profile

As long as people continue to cook — be it in their home kitchens or in restaurant kitchens — jobs with cookware will exist. And because everyone needs to eat, we're betting these jobs will be around for quite some time. Becoming a cookware store manager or cookware store buyer will take you a few years upon entering the industry, but these positions are attainable with a bit of experience and the right skill sets.

Personality traits

Whether you want to be a cookware store buyer or manager, you need to have good communication skills. Both of these positions require you to speak to people — your customers and employees, salespeople, and store owners. You need to be able to describe processes well and give clear instructions because you'll often need to teach employees how products work so they can turn around and clearly explain the products' functions to their customers. You also need to be friendly but firm to work well with customers and vendors.

To be a cookware purchaser, you also need to be organized and be able to multitask to handle the many responsibilities of the jobs and keep track of product details.

Salaries

Cookware store buyers may make between $40,000 and $100,000 annually, whereas cookware store managers may make up to $80,000 each year. Salary depends on the size of the store, the number of duties you must fulfill, and your rank within the company. If you're one of many buyers or managers, your salary may be less than if you were the head manager or the only buyer. Whether you receive benefits and work on commission is also dependent on the size of the company.

Education and training

Completing courses in business management, marketing, culinary arts, or public relations will help you get a job as a cookware store buyer or manager. However, college degrees aren't necessarily required in this field.

Although any educational accomplishment is impressive, employers often look for people with experience in sales to fill these roles. Therefore, you'll typically need to work in retail for a few years before being promoted to either of these positions. You can start as a cashier and then move to the position of a floor supervisor. From there, you may prove yourself worthy of the position of assistant manager. When you reach this spot, show that you're interested in and familiar with cookware or kitchen equipment and perhaps a job will become available for you as a buyer or a store manager.

Having experience with computers can also be helpful in this career path. Much of the work you do will be through computer programs designed to keep track of and order inventory. As a manager, you'll need to understand these programs well enough to train other employees to use them.

Advancement prospects

If employed by small or privately owned stores, cookware store buyers may become store managers after a few years of service. They may also choose to open their own cookware or kitchen equipment store. If employed by a larger company, they may be asked to manage multiple accounts or buy for more regions, or they may be promoted to a position such as purchasing manager.

One option available to a cookware store manager in department stores is to become manager of the entire store. After he's a general manager, he can then advance to district manager. Cookware store managers also have the option to open their own cookware store. If they don't want to go out on their own, however, they may be able to buy into the company that currently employs them.

Unions and associations

Because cookware store buyers and managers are considered part of the management team, they don't normally belong to trade unions. Their employees, however, may be part of the United Food and Commercial Workers International Union.

Associations for people who work with cookware or kitchen equipment include the International Housewares Association, the Commercial Food Equipment Service Association, and the Association of Food Industries. Becoming a member of an association will allow you to receive up-to-date information about growing trends in the industry. It will also help you network with other professionals in your field.

Buying for and Selling to Restaurant Owners and Chefs

When restaurant owners need flatware for their dining rooms and executive chefs need a particular blend of spices for their award-winning dishes, they may make a trip to the grocery store or restaurant-supply store. However, restaurant owners, chefs, and even general managers are always so busy that leisurely trips to the supermarket are rarely possible. When they can't get away from the restaurant, a call to a friendly restaurant-supply salesperson, who works in conjunction with a buyer, will get them what they need.

Although their job title implies that these men and women work solely with restaurants in mind, they have other clients as well. Restaurant-supply buyers and salespeople provide services for the owners of restaurants, bakeries, specialty food stores, delis, hotels, schools and universities, and institutions. Salespeople can and will find whatever is requested of them and, with approval from their company supervisors or buyers, will offer these products to owners at affordable prices.

Buying restaurant supplies

Distribution companies and restaurant-supply companies typically employ restaurant-supply buyers. The job of a restaurant-supply buyer is similar to that of a cookware store buyer or a specialty food store buyer (discussed in the preceding sections of this chapter): Find the best products for your company to sell.

The difference between a buyer for a restaurant-supply company and a buyer for a specialty food store or cookware store lies in what the buyer for the supply company does with the product. Buyers don't give it to someone to place on the shelf or highlight in a display. Instead, buyers learn everything there is to know about products and then teach their salespeople how to use them. When these salespeople are trained, buyers expect them to sell the products. (Salespeople are addressed in the following section.)

How do buyers know which products to buy for their company? They spend hours researching new foods, beverages, cookware, and equipment. They subscribe to hundreds of magazines and catalogues, they read blogs and online forums, and they attend trade shows like the Fancy Foods Show and the International Housewares Show. Much of a buyer's time is also spent meeting with or speaking on the phone with product representatives.

When buyers decide they're interested in an item, they may bring in the product's inventor, manufacturer, or a representative from the company for an interview. In the interview, the rep demonstrates to the buyer how the product works or allows the buyer to taste the product.

After this meeting, buyers may ask if they can tour the facility or farm where the item is produced. Here, buyers will make sure that the factory or farms are clean and meet all government regulations and requirements. They may check the storage area, ask to see the animals, and speak to the employees. If everything checks out, buyers may strike a deal with the company.

Restaurant-supply buyers aren't looking for random products that simply interest them and *may* sell in the future; instead, they watch for new items on the market that they're certain *will* sell. How do they know? They talk to their customers. They call on chefs, bakers, and restaurant owners in the area to see which items they need or have always wanted. With this information in mind, they begin their search. If you want to be a restaurant-supply buyer, one of the best things you can do is become familiar with your area's restaurants, bakeries, pastry shops, and grocery store kitchens. Find out what kind of equipment they use, which ingredients they use the most, and if they're going to need to contact a buyer to help them in the near future.

Selling restaurant supplies

To work as a restaurant-supply salesperson, you need to know your company's products like the back of your hand. You should know which metals items are made of, how quickly they transfer heat or freeze water, and where and how they're grown. You should know how to use the equipment and cookware you sell, and you should be able to describe the taste of the foods and beverages you push.

Restaurant-supply salespeople know which items to learn about and sell because their company's buyers assign them the products. Product representatives and the supply buyers explain to salespeople how to use the items and provide them with accurate and appealing words and phrases that will help peak their clients' interests. After the salespeople get the scoop from these higher-ups and learn everything there is to know about the product, the only part of the sale left to figure out is *who* to sell their products to.

Although buyers can certainly point their salespeople in a general direction (and they occasionally may be able to provide specific names), restaurant-supply salespeople typically find their own clients. Therefore, you need connections to professionals in the business and knowledge of the culinary arts to find success in this field. Clients may be friends in the food industry, friends of friends, or even friends of friends of friends. They may be restaurant chefs, cooks at local schools, pastry chefs, or spa chefs. How you track down potential customers (we recommend the door-to-door approach!) and who they are is irrelevant — convincing those customers to buy a product from you is the important part.

The sales pitch is where your shining personality and knowledge of the culinary field come into play. If you appear overconfident or desperate, if you don't understand how the products should work or taste, or if you can't answer your clients' questions, we can guarantee you'll leave without a sale. If you fail to make the sale, not only will your distribution company not make any money, but your paycheck may be smaller, as well, because salespeople often work on commission.

Although one sale to a new client is nice, a restaurant-supply salesperson's main goal is to secure repeat sales. Return customers may not show up in the first few weeks of partnership, but as the clients begin to trust that the salesperson is getting them good deals and can find what they need, the clients may call the salesperson multiple times a month or week. After a year or two working with the same reliable salesperson, sometimes clients allow the salesperson to reorder the ingredients, products, and equipment they need automatically at the end of a certain period. This arrangement guarantees products for the clients and profit for the salesperson and his distributing company.

Career profile

The best way to become a restaurant-supply buyer or salesperson is to start as an assistant. Assistants help their superiors with menial tasks, but as they prove their worth, they're given more responsibilities. Oftentimes, they shadow buyers and salespeople so they can model their superiors' approaches and techniques in the future. Working as an assistant will also show you what it takes to be successful in a business that oftentimes feels like it's based primarily on luck.

Personality traits

Salespeople and buyers need to have strong interpersonal skills, which means they have to be able to talk to people. Buyers must know how to ask questions and barter, because these are two tasks they perform daily when meeting with product representatives. Salespeople need to be able to show confidence in the items they're selling, but they also have to know where to draw the line between enthusiastic and overzealous, or they'll scare away potential customers. They need to know when using flattery and fluff in a conversation are appropriate and when they should simply get down to business.

Salespeople should also be good at interpreting nonverbal cues from their customers. These cues may include avoiding eye contact, wringing the hands, crossing the arms, stammering, and sweating, and they may indicate that the client is uncomfortable with the sale. If this is the case, the salesperson must be able to alter his approach and work to build trust.

A salesperson must always be able to interact with customers in a way that makes business with him a pleasure. Always remember that any product you sell is most likely available elsewhere. Customers don't have to make purchases through your company; instead, they may decide to avoid all contact with "pesky" salespeople and place orders through magazines, catalogues, or websites. This cuts out the middleman and cuts down on your income. To win customers' business, you must offer reasonable deals while being friendly but not overbearing. Quality customer service can set you apart from non-personal ordering sites. Just remember: A gentle push may get you a sale, but a hard shove may get you banned from the restaurant.

Salaries

A restaurant-supply buyer may earn between $35,000 and $100,000 each year, depending on the size of the distribution company that employs him. A restaurant-supply salesperson, on the other hand, will most likely earn less than this in his first year or so. As time passes, salespeople are normally moved from salary-based pay to commission-based pay. Depending on how many sales a salesperson makes in a year, he may then earn between $50,000 and $200,000 through commissions.

Education and training

Although there aren't any formal degrees or courses you can take to become a certified buyer or salesperson, taking courses in business management and marketing can teach you many secrets to selling products. In addition, knowledge of the culinary arts and kitchen equipment will help you thrive in this field because you'll be able to speak with first-hand experience and knowledge about using and understanding the products you sell, so taking a few culinary courses may also help you land a better paying job.

The best way to attain a job as a restaurant-supply buyer or salesperson, however, is to gain on-the-job experience. Time spent working in a kitchen, a dining room, or in a cookware store or department will help you become familiar with kitchen equipment and food. This kind of experience will aid you in entering this business as an assistant. What you learn on the job paired with what you may learn in a classroom will help you climb the ranks at a steady pace.

While working on getting the experience you need, be sure to develop your computer skills so that you understand how to operate text documents, spreadsheets, and e-mail. Knowing how to put together a presentation or design flyers may also put you ahead of the game. For information about working with computer programs such as the most recent version of Microsoft Office, check out *Office 2010 For Dummies* (John Wiley & Sons, Inc.) by Wallace Wang.

Advancement prospects

If you're an assistant to a buyer, which is an entry-level position in this field, your goal is probably to become a full-time buyer. Naturally, assistants to salespeople want to become full-time salespeople. But after you secure these positions, where can you go?

Most buyers working for distributors are in charge of buying for one region or area. As you advance in the company, you may be given the responsibilities of training other employees to buy for smaller areas while you serve larger ones. Eventually, you may be promoted to a position similar to purchasing manager, in which case your responsibilities will include handling complicated purchases and supervising teams of buyers.

Salespeople seeking advancement have a choice to make: They can switch gears and become buyers, or they can apply for positions as district managers. These managers oversee the salespeople in their district. They keep track of trends and they may discipline salespeople who aren't meeting their goals.

Unions and associations

Unions don't exist for restaurant-supply buyers and salespeople. However, they can connect with many associations that print newsletters, host events, and run trade shows. These include the Association of Food Industries, the Snack Food Association, the Food Processing Supplies Association, the Prepared Foods Association, the Commercial Food Equipment Service Association, the Foodservice Consultants Society International, the Manufacturers' Agents for the Food Service Industry, and the National Association of Wholesale-Distributors.

Noting Other Careers in Purchasing

If you don't want to work for a specialty food store, a grocery store, a distributor, or a cookware store, you can still find a job connected to purchasing. The following is a list of jobs that may be right for you if you have experience in areas such as web design, graphic design, architecture, construction, fashion design, and marketing. Although you may not be the person buying or selling your product, many of these jobs allow you to be part of the process in that you're designing or constructing the product that buyers are selling to restaurants and retail outlets.

In many cases, you present a draft of you idea to the buyer, who then sells your idea to their clients. If the client is interested, the buyer comes back to you and places an order (the client may tweak your design or have particular demands that you must meet). Depending on your contract with the buyer, you would then produce the work they need. The buyer would pay you for your services and then resell your items to their clients.

It may be a good idea to go through a restaurant-supply buyer when you're first beginning your career, but as you develop a name and reputation for yourself, you may want to consider cutting out the middleman. Working directly with the people who require your services (restaurant and possibly retail outlet owners) means that you won't have to split your profits with the buyer. The clients, or purchasers, will then purchase your product directly from you. Keep in mind, however, that without a buyer and his salespeople on your side, you'll need to take care of making the sales yourself. Be prepared to seek out clients, pitch your products, and barter on your own.

Additional careers in the food industry related to purchasing include, but are not limited to:

- ✔ **Kitchen designer:** Kitchen designers are typically employed by a design firm and know quite a bit about different kinds of cabinetry, countertops, and appliances. These people may work on designs for restaurant remodels or brand new kitchens. Their work may appear in completed restaurant kitchens in addition to showrooms in retail outlets.

- ✔ **Restaurant designer:** Restaurant designers work with their clients to design entire restaurants — not just the kitchen. They may help restaurant owners build from the ground up or renovate an existing space. These people design every part of a restaurant from its storage and freezers to its dining room and foyer.

- ✔ **Catalogue designer:** Catalogue designers in the culinary industry are often tasked with taking images of products such as appliances, cabinetry, and cookware and placing them (along with descriptions and product information) in a printed or online catalogue that clients can examine. Clients may choose to purchase products after seeing them in the catalogue.

✔ **Table top buyer:** Table top buyers work with chefs, restaurant owners, and even food photographers and food stylists to bring the best china, silver, and glassware to the table. After consulting with their clients, table top buyers go to warehouses, flip through catalogues, and choose multiple options to present. Once the client makes a decision, the table top buyer makes the purchase and the clients receive their new products.

✔ **Uniform designer:** Uniform designers may work for retail outlets that sell kitchen and restaurant uniforms or they may work directly for a restaurant owner. Like kitchen designers, they work on designs to present to their clients and if the client likes the design, they then manufacture the number of uniforms needed in the sizes and fabrics requested.

✔ **Menu designer:** Although many executive chefs at smaller restaurants designer and print their own menus, large chain restaurants and established, fine-dining restaurants work with professional menu designers when constructing the look and feel of their menus. These designers know how to work with graphics and layout and some of them will even write the descriptions of the dishes after receiving information from chefs about ingredients in the dish and the cooking process.

Part V

Landing the Job, Moving Up the Ladder, and More

The 5th Wave   By Rich Tennant

FREELANCE PEPPERIER

©RICHTENNANT

I just got tired of the 9 to 5 grind. Say when...

SOUP 'N SALAD

In this part . . .

You've decided what you want to do and completed your education. Now comes the hard part: Finding a job to suit your wants and needs. Your first job in the culinary industry may not be your first choice, but don't let that deter you. Getting your foot in the door is only the beginning, and whatever your first job may be, it can lead to bigger and better possibilities, such as owning your own business.

After you finish your education and decide what you want to do, you need to write that résumé and land a job! Or maybe you've been working in a different career field and think now's the time to pursue a new career in a new culinary direction. Have you ever dreamed about owning your own business? In this part we provide you with the basics so you can get started.

Chapter 16

Landing a Culinary Job

In This Chapter

▶ Figuring out what culinary direction you want to head in

▶ Discovering where and how to look for work at restaurants and other establishments

▶ Marketing yourself to impress future employers

▶ Understanding how to interview well

*O*kay, you've received your culinary arts certificate or finished an apprenticeship at a resort or earned your dues working the line at a local restaurant (whatever training you got your hands on), so now it's time to find a culinary job that you can really sink your teeth into!

The culinary industry has a plethora of jobs to whet your appetite! While you probably won't be hired as an executive chef right off the bat, you shouldn't let this discourage you during your job search. The more jobs you apply for, the better your chance that you'll land a job that may get you closer to your dream job.

In this chapter, we help you determine what type for culinary work is right for you and give you the basics to landing a job in this field. We walk you through creating a résumé and cover letter, correctly filling out a job application, and acing a job interview.

Realistically, you may have to start on the bottom rung of the culinary ladder. You may be able to reach for the stars (that is, your culinary goal) after many years (or even decades) of on-the-job training. We're here to teach you how to find the job that's best for you *right now*. If your ultimate goal is to become an executive chef of a five-diamond restaurant in Chicago, you may need to begin by putting in a few years on the line at a chain restaurant in Scranton, Pennsylvania.

Starting Your Search: Where Do You See Yourself?

Many opportunities exist in the culinary world — the possibilities are endless. Before you can even begin looking for a job, you need to narrow your search by determining *what* you eventually want to do. A lot of factors such as personal preferences, location, and schedule can affect this decision. You shouldn't let one factor alone such as the hours you'll work, however, sway your decision if you're set on working at a particular establishment. You just have to determine which factors are most important to you. In the next section, we take a closer look at these factors.

After you have determined the type of job that you would ultimately like to have, you can look for jobs that may lead to that job. For example, if you know that you one day want to start your own catering business, try to land a job working for a caterer or in a banquet hall. First jobs in the culinary industry are most likely to be entry-level positions, far from your dream job. If your first job isn't the work you really want to do and doesn't have the hours you'd prefer to work, keep in mind that it's just a stepping stone to the career you really want. You should treat your first job as a way to gain on-the-job experience and learn as much as you can along the way.

Figuring out what's right for you

You have to consider lots of preferences when trying to find your fit in the culinary field. The first area to contemplate is what general specialization you're interested in. To get started, ask yourself these questions:

- Do I prefer to bake or cook cuisine?
- If I prefer to cook cuisine, what type do I most enjoy cooking?
- If I like to bake, do I prefer baking bread or working with cakes and pastries?

You can turn to Part II of this book for details on general cooking as well as Chapter 8 for information on baking jobs. If you decide that your general area of focus is along these lines, next consider the type of work environment you might like.

- Would I most enjoy working in a restaurant, hotel, or spa?
- Does volume cooking for an institution interest me most?
- Do I eventually want to be a personal or private chef?
- Would I prefer to specialize in beverage and wine?
- Do I eventually want to start my own business?

For information on restaurant work, turn to Chapter 5. Chapter 6 provides details about working in hotels and spas. Chapter 7 contains information about volume cooking jobs. For the lowdown on working as a personal or private chef, see Chapter 9. If a career in beverages quenches your thirst, see Chapter 11. And if you want to explore your options for running a culinary business, turn to Chapter 18.

If you aren't sure whether cooking or baking is the route for you, you may want to consider other culinary fields. Ask yourself the following questions:

- ✔ Would I rather work out of the kitchen and write about food or style food? Would I rather photograph food?
- ✔ Do I want to be a culinary instructor one day?
- ✔ Would I rather hold a retail sales or food-purchasing position?
- ✔ Do I have a knack for touting a business's services and products?

The chapters in Part IV address culinary careers such as these that are off the beaten path.

In any case, you should also think about the following practical aspects when choosing your future career:

- ✔ What type of employment has my previous training best prepared me for?
- ✔ What job am I best suited for based on my personality traits?
- ✔ How much money do I need to earn? How much money would I like to earn one day?

The answers to these questions can help you narrow down your focus and help you decide what type of culinary career you'd be best suited for — either today or in the future.

Keep in mind that the atmosphere and working conditions differ from place to place, so check out a few jobs before making a decision. One of the easiest ways is to visit establishments where you think you may like to work. Do you a have a favorite restaurant? How about the bakery you stop at every morning for bagels? Can you see yourself working at any of these places?

Considering schedules

The hours during which you would like to work is a very important factor to consider when trying to decide where to apply for a culinary job.

✔ **Weekday, daytime jobs:** If you have a family, then working 9 to 5 may be ideal — but harder to find. Institutional settings usually have the most coveted daytime schedules. If you work in a school cafeteria, you'll get to follow a school's schedule, meaning you work during the day and have nights, weekends, and holidays free. Other positions such as instructors, retail sales and purchasing positions, and public relations and marketing professionals may have 9 to 5 schedules, but these jobs also may require you to work other shifts as well.

✔ **Weekend work:** Caterers typically schedule their work around events that frequently take place on weekends, so many catering jobs are part-time and leave you free time during the week. Restaurants are typically the busiest on the weekends, so these establishments may require you to work these shifts. Also, institutions such as hospitals and correctional facilities never close, so they need employees willing to work on weekends. Wineries and breweries are typically busier on weekends, so this line of work may require someone available during these times.

✔ **Work for early birds:** Job in bakeries and pastry shops require you to report to work very early in the morning, so if you typically wake up early, this type of work may be right for you. Restaurants that specialize in breakfast and lunch, and institutional settings such as schools, hospitals, and correctional facilities that serve breakfast, are other types of establishments that would require early morning hours.

✔ **Evening and night jobs:** If you're a night owl, then working in a restaurant or hotel during the dinner rush may be more your style, because many jobs in restaurant kitchens allow you to stay up late and sleep through the mornings. This type of schedule is the most common in the culinary field and many other culinary jobs have hours that fall into this category. Food writers and editors working at publications such as newspapers may work at night to meet deadlines. Public relations and marketing professionals may have to attend events held in the evening. Culinary instructors may teach night classes. Catered events, such as wedding receptions, are typically held in the evenings, and therefore, would require caterers to work during the evenings. Those working at wineries and breweries that are open during the evening may be required to work this type of schedule. The list goes on and on.

Keep in mind that hospitals, correctional facilities, nursing homes, and many hotels are open every day and around the clock, and many restaurants are open on holidays and weekends. These types of jobs require you to work a variety of shifts, so you probably won't have a set schedule. If you're scheduled to begin work at 4 p.m., chances are that your shift may not end until a few hours after the restaurant closes, because you may be required to help clean and get the kitchen ready for the next day.

Deciding on location

Location is another factor that affects where you may look for work. Big cities typically have numerous restaurants, hotels, casinos, schools, and hospitals, which offer more employment opportunities, whereas smaller cities and towns usually only have a handful, if any, of these businesses. If you reside in an area that doesn't offer many opportunities for employment, then you may consider moving to where the types of opportunities you want exist.

Another consideration of location is salary and cost of living. Businesses in large cities may offer higher salaries compared to those in small cities; however, the cost of living — what you pay in rent or housing, groceries, parking, or public transportation, and so on — in large cities may also be higher. In the excitement of starting a new career, don't forget to weigh the opportunities and advancement possibilities with what type of living conditions you would like to have now and down the road.

Putting Yourself Out There: Finding a Job You Want to Apply For

After you determine what type of culinary position you're interested in, it's time to seek an actual job.

Make sure you look presentable when you're job hunting. Being unshaven and looking like you've just rolled out of bed doesn't make a good impression on the person who's hiring. Take a shower, iron your clothes, and run a comb through your hair, because you want to look your best to impress potential employers when dropping off job applications.

Checking out where to job hunt

Your job hunt can begin in any number of places. The more approaches you take in searching for a job, the more opportunities will be available to you. Here are some great places to begin:

✓ **Talk to employees:** The easiest way to express interest in a job and get your name in the running for a position you want is to stop in and talk to the establishment's employees. Next time you're enjoying dinner at your favorite bistro, casually mention to your server or the host that you'd be interested in working there and don't forget to include the position you'd like to secure as well. The server most likely knows whether the establishment is hiring and may be able to introduce you to the manager or executive chef. This can improve your chances of landing a job or at least get your name out there.

✔ **Fill out an application:** Many establishments have applications you can fill out to apply for an open position or to put your name in the pool for future openings. If you can get an application for a place you'd like to work, fill it out at home. When you return it, ask to talk to the hiring manager if that's possible to further discuss the position and to show that you're interested.

Also, make sure you bring your résumé and cover letter with you when returning applications. Not all places of employment require résumés and cover letters (or even require you to fill out a formal application), but you should be prepared. For more information about résumés and cover letters, see the "Creating a Résumé and Cover Letter" section of this chapter.

✔ **Use the careers services department:** If you're still enrolled in school or are a recent graduate, use the career services department at your school. Its main function is to help students find employment after graduation. The department typically offers free services such as résumé and cover-letter writing workshops, career and job search programs, and personality assessments. Counselors in this department usually work with local employers who are recruiting students to fill internships, apprenticeships, and part- and full-time jobs.

✔ **Consult with past and/or present professors:** Another great resource is your former and/or current professors or instructors, who have many associates within the culinary industry who can give tips on where to find job opportunities.

✔ **Check the classifieds in print and online:** The classifieds section of local newspapers is another route to follow, as well as blogs and online job websites such as Monster.com and CareerBuilder.com. In addition to browsing thousands of job listings across the country, you can upload your résumé directly to these websites so employers can find you.

Many places of employment, such as restaurants or bakeries, may have a section on their website titled "Career Opportunities" that provides you with job postings for that particular establishment.

✔ **Attend a job fair:** You should also look for postings about job fairs, which are frequently advertised on local television and radio stations and in newspapers and other publications. Job fairs are a common way for numerous employers to collect résumés from potential employees. They also give you a chance to network — you get to meet company representatives from corporations of all sizes during a short time. If you decide to attend a job fair, make sure you dress your best and bring several copies of your résumé and cover letter to hand out to potential employers.

Putting experience to work

Before you can write your résumé and cover letter and land your first interview, you need to gain some experience in the culinary industry. While most employers offer training, most jobs in the culinary field require you to have some experience. You can gain this experience in a multitude of ways:

- ✔ **At home:** If you're interested in the culinary field, chances are you cook and/or bake at home. You most likely learned some skills by reading cookbooks or cooking blogs and watching cooking shows on television or instructional videos on websites such as YouTube. You may have learned to cook simply by watching family. Don't discount the skills you learn at home. Many famous cooks got their start this way including The Food Network's Southern belle Paula Deen or Rick Bayless, owner of Frontera Grill in Chicago and winner of Bravo's *Top Chef Masters*. While home experience is typically not relevant on a résumé, you can incorporate these experiences as interests on your cover letter.

- ✔ **Culinary school:** Attending culinary school is another way to gain experience. You can take the skills you've taught yourself at home and build on them by attending and participating in classes that teach you to cook along with other important skill such as the correct way to use a knife, sanitation practices, food purchasing, and kitchen management. The skills you learn in class and during internships, externships, and apprenticeships prepare you for a job in the culinary industry. The type of culinary school you attend isn't really relevant to most jobs, but some employers, however, may look to hire those who have completed degrees or courses at a prestigious culinary school such as the Culinary Institute of America or Le Cordon Bleu.

- ✔ **Externship:** An externship is typically unpaid and not completed for academic credit. During an externship, which usually lasts a day or a few days, you shadow someone and watch rather than participate. For example, you may spend a few days observing a pastry chef design desserts and then decide whether this line of work is right for you.

- ✔ **Internship:** An internship is a hands-on work experience. Rather than shadowing an individual, you'll actually be given tasks to complete on your own. It can be paid or unpaid and frequently is completed for academic credit as a requirement for a degree. Interns sometimes do the same work as the official employees. Internships can last from a few weeks to a semester or two and sometimes can lead to a permanent job.

- ✔ **Apprenticeship:** Apprenticeships typically allow you to gain experience by working alongside professionals in the field for weeks, months, or even years. When completing an apprenticeship, you may start slow and begin by completing small jobs such as peeling carrots or potatoes. After you demonstrate mastery in one skill, you're given more responsibilities. Apprenticeships, which are occasionally paid work, sometimes lead to full-time paid positions.

- ✔ **Stagiaire:** A *stagiaire*, also called a *stage,* is another opportunity to learn more culinary skills from those already in the profession. A stagiaire is an informal, unpaid work experience that may last a shift, or a few weeks. Basically, you volunteer your time to either acquire new skills or to prove to a restaurant that you have what it takes to work there. Top restaurants such as The French Laundry (Yountville, California), Alinia (Chicago), and Daniel (New York City) offer stagiaires.

Building your contact list

Networking, exchanging information or services among individuals or groups, is an important tool to use when you're looking for a job. Because many jobs aren't advertised, you need to surround yourself with a number of contacts who can aid you in your job search by keeping their ears to the ground for career possibilities.

You may already be networking and not even know it. When you drop off your résumé and talk to potential employers, you're networking. When you attend job fairs or ask your school instructors for help in your job search, you're networking. Even if the contacts you make can't help you directly, they may be able to put you in touch with someone who can, so it never hurts to put yourself out there. Every time you make a connection within the culinary field, either directly or indirectly, you're networking. You can increase your collection of contacts in the culinary industry by

- Attending job fairs, conferences, or conventions
- Joining clubs, groups, or social networking websites such as Facebook
- Seeking out former co-workers, professors, or instructors
- Striking up conversations with acquaintances or strangers
- Talking to family, friends, or neighbors
- Volunteering with local charities

Putting Your Best Foot Forward: Marketing Yourself

Think of yourself as a product on a shelf among other brand-name competitors. Your goal is to attract the customer's attention and have that customer purchase you. When you walk into an interview with potential employers, you are selling yourself as the product and the employers take on the role of customer. If you can't perform the tasks necessary to the job the employers' are offering, then they have no reason to "purchase" you. If your packaging (your appearance and your attitude) displeases employers, they aren't going to offer you the job. Your cover letter, résumé, and job applications are part of the packaging as well. If they aren't neat and concise, or if they neglect to include information about your skill sets and past experiences, they'll be tossed aside. Your customer will continue down the aisle, looking for another product.

The only way potential employers are going to learn about your skills, past experiences, career goals, and interest in the field is if you tell employers about yourself via your résumé, cover letter, and job application. Market yourself in a way that makes you seem like a candidate the employer simply can't overlook. Of course, doing so is more difficult than it sounds. Selling yourself without appearing cocky or arrogant (or misleading employers) is hard to accomplish on paper, but that's why we're here! In this section we walk you through the basics of your product packaging: creating an impressive résumé and cover letter and filling out job applications well.

Creating a résumé and a cover letter

When you begin your job hunt, you may discover that the documents you must submit differ from place to place. One restaurant may require you to submit only a job application, whereas the chef next door may want a cover letter, résumé, and job application. Smaller specialty places may not even have job applications available, so your résumé and cover letter should suffice. No matter what's required, though, have both your résumé and cover letter ready to go when you begin your job search, just in case you need them.

For more detailed information about writing a résumé and cover letter than we provide in this section, pick up a copy of *Resumes For Dummies* (John Wiley & Sons, Inc.) and *Cover Letters For Dummies* (John Wiley & Sons, Inc.) both by Joyce Lain Kennedy.

Writing a résumé

Basically, your résumé is the first chance your employer has to meet you. It's an introduction of sorts. It's a one-page document that gives potential employers a brief overview of your work history, education, and relevant skills. A résumé should be in the form of a bulleted list and should not include many (if any) large blocks of text.

Begin writing your résumé by creating a list of the places where you have worked in the past and the positions you held. Be sure to include any internships, externships, apprenticeships, or stagiaires in addition to full-time and part-time jobs. At this point, don't worry if these positions are related to culinary arts. Note the dates during which you were employed at each place, as well. The dates don't have to be as specific as the day you started, but months and years are important. Within this list, jot down the responsibilities you held in these positions.

Make yourself more marketable by using action words when describing your responsibilities at past jobs. Use words and phrases such as *created, responsible for, directed, assisted, supervised, provided,* and *maintained* to provide your potential employer with impressive details about your past work. Also, include numbers where possible. If you were a floor supervisor who created a schedule for a dining room staff of 25 hosts, servers, and busboys, include this information. If you were an apprentice for a specialty cake shop and assisted in baking and decorating up to five cakes a week, say exactly that.

When you've compiled your list of work experiences, place the information that's relevant to your career in the culinary field on your resume under a bold heading that reads "Professional Experience" or "Related Experience." If you have information that's not related to cooking or baking — say you baby-sat for six years, worked as a clerk in a grocery store, or drove a delivery truck — you can still list this information under a heading such as "Other Employment," especially if you need to fill white space on the page. If you can't fit all your past experience onto a one-page résumé, include only jobs that helped you develop particular abilities, such as leadership or communication skills, and that show that you're reliable and dedicated to your work. Even though you may not have received culinary training while fulfilling your responsibilities at these jobs, you still gleaned *something* from them.

After you complete the work experience sections of your résumé, list your education information under the heading, "Education." List the schools you attended, the degrees or certificates you completed, and the years you completed them. If you attended weekend workshops that are related to the job you're applying for, you can even include that information. Include the name of your high school only if you didn't go to college or technical school and haven't received any formal culinary training. In that case, including your high school graduation date is a good move.

If you have room to do so, include a short list of references on the bottom of your résumé. Include the names of people you've worked with who can provide unbiased information about your work ethic and your attitude or character. Don't list your family members or best friends here; instead, use the names of employers or supervisors you got along with and teachers who know you well. Make sure you ask for permission before listing someone as a reference, so they're not blindsided if they're contacted by a potential employer. If you cannot fit your references on your résumé, include a line that reads "References Available Upon Request" and then supply them when asked.

Try to keep your résumé to one page, especially at the beginning of your career. If the information you list doesn't fit, scale it down. Get rid of unnecessary words, don't include details that aren't related to the job you're applying for, and use fragments instead of complete sentences. Don't make the font size or margins smaller; just keep hacking away at the words until you can fit them on a single page. Fewer words on the page will help your résumé look neat and organized.

When you think you're done writing your résumé, read it over to make sure it still makes sense. Remember the product packaging idea: Your résumé is an introduction to you, the product, which must attract the customer. Your potential employer will likely cast aside your résumé if it's written in a teeny-tiny or massive font, contains large blocks of text or small lines that don't provide enough details, or has irregular margins (stick to one inch all the way around).

Your finished résumé may look similar to the example in Figure 16-1.

Michael H. Smithson
12345 Kennedy Boulevard
White Plains, NY 14621
(585) 555-0417
mikesmithson@yahoo.com

PROFESSIONAL EXPERIENCE

Head Line Cotok (August 20— to April 20—)
CiCi's Italian Bistro and Banquet Hall
White Plains, NY

- Created recipes for menu items and weekend specials
- Simultaneously provided food for banquets and dinner service in restaurant
- Directed up to six fellow cooks on the line and supervised food production
- Assisted in preparation, execution, and occasionally purchasing/ordering
- Maintained organization and stock of pantry

Prep Cook (September 20— to August 20—)
White Plains Country Club and Resort
White Plains, NY

- Responsible for ensuring fresh items are available and ready for lunch and dinner production
- Occasionally assisted in making salads and other cold appetizers

ADDITIONAL EXPERIENCE

Various Positions (November 20— to September 20—)
Little Timmy's Diner
White Plains, NY

- Fulfilled responsibilities of bus boy, host, wait staff, and performed occasional food prep
- Assisted in tasks such as balancing the money drawer, answering phones, and cleaning

EDUCATION

Associate's Degree in Hotel and Restaurant Management (May 20—)
White Plains Community College

Certification in Baking/Pastry Arts (January 20—)
White Plains Community College

PROFESSIONAL ORGANIZATIONS

Figure 16-1:
A résumé
example.

Member of the American Culinary Federation

References Available Upon Request

Composing a cover letter

If your résumé is like your introduction to a potential employer, then your cover letter is like your handshake with this employer. Your cover letter should be strong and polite, just like an impressive handshake. Like your résumé, your cover letter should be brief and to the point. However, you should use complete sentences and paragraphs in your cover letter.

Writing an effective cover letter is challenging. You need to tell a potential employer about some of your impressive accomplishments, but you only have three or four paragraphs in which to do this. You want to sound professional but not bigheaded and arrogant. Don't brag about yourself in your cover letter, just inform. Spend some time drafting your cover letter to make sure you present yourself well. Explain your accomplishments in detail. For example, revise the sentence "I cooked at Mantione's Family Restaurant for four years and really enjoyed the experience" so it reads, "For four years, I held the position of head line cook at Mantione's Family Restaurant, an Italian restaurant that seats 150 people. Here, I was responsible for prepping, cooking, and expediting. On the weekends, I frequently created feature dishes or specials." See the difference?

Include your name and contact information at the top of the letter. If the job posting includes a contact name, address the letter to that person. If not, call the establishment and ask for the name of the hiring manager and then address the cover letter to that person.

The body of your cover letter can be broken into three parts:

- **Introduction:** In the first paragraph, state which position you're applying for, where you heard about the job (on a particular job website, in a newspaper classified ad, from someone you know who is employed there and who recommended the job to you, and so on), and briefly state why you think you would be right for the job.

- **Your accomplishments:** In the second paragraph, expand upon what you've stated in the first paragraph. If you have a lot to say, this section can be two paragraphs long, but don't ramble on just to take up more room. Tell employers why they should hire you. Use words and phrases such as *dedicated, determined, hard-working, leadership, attention to detail*, and *teamwork*. Examine the requirements for the job in the employment ad and see if you can work some of those words into your letter. If the job requires five years' experience and you've got it, write that. If the job requires you to create schedules for the kitchen or dining room staff, work with vendors, and order supplies and you have experience with each of these tasks, say so. Try not to regurgitate everything you've already mentioned in your résumé, though. Cover letters are specific and can be used to expand upon parts of your résumé that are relevant to the job for which you're applying.

✔ **Closing:** In the last paragraph, let employers know how and where they can reach you. If you work or go to school during the day, explain that you're available at night. Thank potential employers for taking the time to consider your application and mention that you look forward to hearing from them. If you plan on following up (sending an e-mail, making a phone call, or even dropping by), let them know.

What do you say in your cover letter if you're applying for a position that you're hoping will open in the future? Mention something about the place to which you're applying and then explain your intentions. For example, you may say "I have dined at Medicco's Bistro many times, and it is one of my favorite restaurants. I would really like to work as a line cook there if you have an opening now or in the future." Then go on to explain your qualifications and accomplishments.

Your completed cover letter may look similar to the one in Figure 16-2.

Filling out a job application

Some places may not require you to fill out a job application, whereas others may require *only* a job application. As you're moving from restaurant to bakery to pastry shop (or clicking around on different employment websites) picking up applications for available jobs, you'll find that many job applications look the same. They generally ask for the same type of information and are easy to complete. A job application usually asks for very specific information that you would not include on a resume, such as your Social Security number.

Carry the following information with you whenever you think you may be asked to complete a job application:

✔ Social Security card

✔ Driver's license

✔ Name and addresses of the schools or programs you attended, along with the dates of graduation or completion

✔ Names, addresses, and telephone numbers of past employers, along with the dates you were employed

✔ Names, telephone numbers, and e-mail addresses of at least three references

Michael H. Smithson
12345 Kennedy Boulevard
White Plains, NY 14621
(585) 555-0417
mikesmithson@yahoo.com

May 17, 20—

Mr. Matthew Davis
Mia Bella Bistro
129 Broadway
New York City, NY 14621

Dear Mr. Davis:

As a graduate of White Plains Community College with a certificate in baking/pastry arts and an associate's degree in hotel and restaurant management, I am very interested in joining the kitchen staff at Mia Bella Bistro. My friend and your sous chef, Frank Lundy, told me about the open position of kitchen manager and suggested I apply. I believe that my formal training in the culinary arts and my experience working in Italian restaurants will help me fulfill the responsibilities of this position.

In the past, I was the head line cook at CiCi's Italian Bistro and Banquet Hall for roughly three years. CiCi's is a family-owned restaurant that seats approximately 150 customers in the dining room and upwards of 200 in the banquet hall. At CiCi's, I supervised the cooks on the line while I helped cook and prep food. I also had a hand in keeping the kitchen neat and orderly, organizing and stocking the pantry, and occasionally I helped my executive chef with ordering and purchasing. I understand that you are looking for a kitchen manager who can cook and supervise the kitchen, as well as handle purchasing responsibilities and form relationships with vendors. I believe the training I received at CiCi's, specifically, has prepared me for the responsibilities of this position. I also look forward to creating seasonal dishes for the menu and encouraging the staff to develop new menu items and think outside the box to create specials and features.

As a kitchen manager, I understand that I would frequently have to interact and cooperate with the manager of the front of the house. As you can see from my resume, I once worked the front of the house at a small diner in my hometown. My previous experience working a variety of positions at the diner has helped me understand the functions and responsibilities of the dining room staff.

Please contact me at any time for an interview. I can be reached via e-mail or phone, and I look forward to meeting with you personally to discuss this opportunity further.

Sincerely,

Michael H. Smithson

Michael H. Smithson

Figure 16-2:
A cover letter example.

Most job applications look similar to the example in Figure 16-3. Reviewing this example before you start applying will help you know what to expect.

Application for Employment

Personal Employment

Last Name	First	Middle	Date
Street Address			Home Phone ( ) -
City, State, Zip			
Business Phone ( ) -			Email Address:

Are you over 18 years of age? ☐ Yes ☐ No If not, employment is subject to verification of minimum legal age.

	Social Security No.
Have you ever applied for employment with us? ☐ Yes ☐ No If Yes: Month and Year _____ Location _____	- -

How did you learn of our organization?
Are you legally eligible for employment in the United States? If no, when will you be able to work?
Are you employed now? If so, may we inquire of your present employer?
Have you ever been convicted of a crime in the past ten years, excluding misdemeanors and summary offenses, which has not been annulled, expunged or sealed by the court? ☐ Yes ☐ No
Are there any reasons for which you might not be able to perform the job duties (with a reasonable accommodation)? ☐ Yes ☐ No   If yes, please explain.

Drivers License # State	Certifications/Professional Memberships

Figure 16-3: A job application example.

Education

School	Name and location of school	Course of study	No. of years completed	Did you graduate?	Degree or diploma
College/ Technical				☐ Yes ☐ No	
High School				☐ Yes ☐ No	

Employment History

Please give accurate, complete full-time and part-time employment record.
Start with the present or most recent employer.

1.	Company Name	Telephone ( ) -
	Address	Employed (Start Mo. & Yr.) From To
	Name of Supervisor	Hourly Rate Start Last
	Starting Job Title and Describe Your Work	Reason for Leaving
2.	Company Name	Telephone ( ) -
	Address	Employed (Start Mo. & Yr.) From To
	Name of Supervisor	Hourly Rate Start Last
	Starting Job Title and Describe Your Work	Reason for Leaving

References: Give below the names of three persons not related to you, whom you have known at least one year.

Name	Address	Business	Years Acquainted
1.			
2.			

The information provided in this Application for Employment is true, correct, and complete. If employed, any misstatements or omissions of fact on this application may result in my dismissal. I understand that acceptance of an offer of employment does not create a contractual obligation upon the employer to continue to employ me in the future.

Date - 2 - Signature

How you submit your job application (and résumé and cover letter) is crucial, because it shows your employer that you know how to follow directions. If you come across a job advertisement online that says to submit your information via e-mail, send your information in an e-mail. If it says to send it through the U.S. Postal Service, then go buy postage. If you're making phone calls or personal visits when the job advertisement specifically states not to, you're already showing the person you want to work with that you don't pay attention to details or that you don't like to follow directions. Read a job posting carefully and take note of how the employer would like you to submit information.

Acing a Job Interview

After potential employers reviews your résumé, cover letter, and/or job application, they may conclude that you're a good fit for the position advertised. They'll then contact you via phone or e-mail and ask you to come in for an interview — which is a great sign!

We don't need to tell you how important a job interview is. You already know that if you don't present yourself well during a job interview, you probably won't get the job. During a job interview, a potential employer will likely ask you more about what you say in your cover letter and résumé and ask you to answer questions that reveal a bit about your work ethic and attitude. For example, you may be asked how you would handle the stress of a busy kitchen or how you would go about preparing a signature dish.

To further help with the job interviewing process, check out *Job Interviews For Dummies* (John Wiley & Sons, Inc.) by Joyce Lain Kennedy.

Presenting yourself professionally during a job interview requires more than just dressing nice. (Although this point is extremely important! See the "Dress for Success" sidebar in this chapter for more information on what to wear and when to wear it.) You need to act and speak professionally as well. Appearing interested, educated, and enthusiastic is extremely important. To be as professional as possible, you should prepare for the meeting ahead of time.

Before the interview

Preparation should start as soon as you receive a request for an interview. Before you hang up the phone or when you respond to the e-mail, ask for and record the time and location of the interview and the name of the person you will be speaking with. If you're unsure of the location, ask for directions and the phone number of a person you can contact in case you get lost.

If you're interviewing for a position in a kitchen, ask the person scheduling your interview if you'll be expected to prepare a dish or demonstrate any knife skills during the interview. If so, ask if it would be appropriate to wear your chef's gear to the interview. If you'll be dicing an onion, breaking down a chicken, or creating your signature brown sugar cream cheese frosting, you may not want to complete these tasks in business attire.

After you have information about the location, date, and time of the interview, start researching the company, regardless of whether it's a restaurant, spa, food magazine, or technical college. If the place where you want to work has a website, click around until you find information about the company's history and news of its recent accomplishments. If biographies about the chefs, editors, teachers, or food researchers and developers appear on the page, read those as well. If a menu is available, examine it closely and see if you notice an underlying theme. Is it seasonal? Is it low in calories or carbs? Do many of the dishes incorporate the same ingredients? If you're unfamiliar with any ingredients, do a bit of research on those, too.

After you become familiar with the company, get to know *yourself* better so that you're ready to answer open-ended interview questions about you and your experiences. An open-ended question requires more than a simple yes or no response. Expect to answer questions about your educational background, employment history, and other training. Be prepared to answer questions similar to the following:

- ✔ Why did you stop your college education after earning a certification? Do you have plans to go back to school to attain a degree?

- ✔ How did you get into cooking/baking? Do you have a niche?

- ✔ What were some of your responsibilities at your last job?

- ✔ Why do you want to leave your current job?

- ✔ Have you ever held a supervisory role? Describe a challenging situation you experienced in the past during which you needed to take charge.

- ✔ What would you say is the most important skill you learned while working for Company A?

Aside from asking questions about the time you spent in school and working for other companies, your potential employer will also ask you personal questions that you should answer honestly. Employers ask these types of questions to get an idea of the type of employee you are. Remember, an employer wants to hire someone who is devoted to the craft, knowledgeable of the food industry, and willing to work well with others. Following are some examples of the type of personal questions you may be asked during a job interview:

✔ What do you like to eat?

✔ What is your favorite dish or item to prepare?

✔ Would you say that you're a team player?

✔ What do you do in your spare time? What are some of your hobbies?

✔ What are your strengths and weaknesses?

✔ What cookbooks are you currently reading?

✔ Where do you see yourself in five to ten years?

✔ How do you handle stress?

✔ What do you know about our company? Why do you want to work here?

Before any interview, be prepared to respond to the statement "Tell me about yourself." Your response can make or break an interview. As in your cover letter, you need to speak about yourself in a way that sounds impressive but not arrogant. Keep in mind that the interviewer does not want to hear your life story, so don't respond with an answer like this: "Well, I grew up in Ohio but moved to Pennsylvania when I was 16." The interviewer also doesn't want to know about your personal life, so don't respond by saying, "I am a mother of three who lives in Glen Lyon." A good rule of thumb when responding to "tell me about yourself" is to state what makes you qualified for the position at hand. If you're applying for the job of pastry chef, you might say, "As you can see from my résumé, I am a recent graduate of [insert school]. While I have always enjoyed baking cakes, cupcakes, and pies, I decided to make this a career when [insert experience]."

Write out your answer to "tell me about yourself" and other interview questions. Then have someone pretend to interview you so you can practice your responses.

In addition to practicing what you will say and do during your interview, you should also take the time to create a portfolio of your best work to show to your potential employer. If you want to be a food writer, stylist, or photographer, your portfolio should contain your best previously published work. If you're applying for a job in a kitchen that requires you to create menus and feature dishes, create a mock menu (or, if you've had experience designing menus in the past, bring in one you used in another restaurant) and take pictures of your signature dishes. If you ever appeared in your local newspaper or were featured in a restaurant review published in a magazine, also place a copy in your portfolio. Be sure to include only the work that's most impressive — your potential employer won't want to sit for hours flipping through photographs of food and recipes you wrote in high school.

Dress for success

Choosing what to wear to an interview is not easy. You may wonder if you should wear a skirt, a tie, a suit, jeans, or a chef coat and pants. When you're really unsure, know that being overdressed is better than underdressed.

When scheduling your interview, asking what will be expected of you during the interview process is a perfectly acceptable way to determine what you should wear. If you're told that you'll be tested on certain skills such as chopping an onion or preparing a dish during the interview, you can bet that a chef coat and pants are appropriate. If the interview process is a standard face-to-face meeting, then stick to these guidelines for appropriate dress:

✔ A solid-colored suit (or suit jacket with nice slacks) with a matching or coordi-

nating long-sleeved, button-down shirt underneath

✔ A simple tie (no characters or crazy patterns or colors)

✔ Neutral hosiery or dark socks

✔ Dress shoes (no sneakers or stilettos)

If you're unsure what to wear, ask. No matter what you wear, however, your clothes should be clean, ironed, and fit you well. And this advice should go without saying: Take a shower, trim your nails, and brush your teeth! Men should also shave. Don't go crazy with the aftershave, though. And women, don't wear much makeup or perfume.

During the interview

During the interview, listen carefully to the questions that are being asked. Before you answer a question, make sure you understand it completely. If you need the interviewer to explain something, ask. Asking for clarification is better than misunderstanding the question and providing an irrelevant answer to a question.

Asking questions throughout the interview (at any time just as long as you don't interrupt the interviewer) is always a good idea. This shows that you're not afraid to ask for clarification when you're confused or need help. This quality is important to have when you're working in a kitchen because you'll be expected to multitask, which can get confusing.

Before answering questions, take a deep breath and think about what you want to say. When you take a few seconds to collect your thoughts, you steer clear of tripping over your words or even rambling. When your responses are organized and to the point, your potential employer will surely be impressed.

If you prepared a portfolio for your interview, be sure to mention that you have it with you and ask if you can show it to the interviewer. As you flip through the pages, explain each page and why you included it.

If you're applying for a job in the kitchen, you may have to show off your basic knife skills or even make one of your signature dishes. If you're applying for a job in a bakery or pastry shop, you may have to make an icing flower or perhaps apply fondant to a previously baked cake. Every executive chef is different — you never know what the one who is interviewing you will ask. Sometimes interviews can last all day. Some executive chefs believe they won't know if potential employees are a good fit until they see them in action in the kitchen. They may ask you to shadow a line cook for a few hours and then take the reins on a station to show them what you've learned. This trial period is extremely important, so be sure to show that you're paying attention, that you're able to work with the other employees on the line, and that you want this job.

When the interview concludes, shake hands with the interviewers and thank them for meeting with you. Reiterate that you're very interested in the job, but be careful not to sound too desperate. Don't tell interviewers that you need the job or you won't be able to pay next month's rent.

After the interview

To help you stand out among other job candidates, write a brief thank-you note (Remember, handwritten is perfectly acceptable and helps you stand out!) to the person who interviewed you and either mail or e-mail it. This gesture shows your potential employer that you're well-mannered and courteous.

While you wait for the phone call (or e-mail) with the job offer to come, you're probably going to get antsy. You may want to call and ask if they have filled the position yet, but resist the urge to dial that number if your interviewer didn't tell you to. If the interview ended with "We'll be in touch," or "We'll call you," then the interviewer doesn't want you to call. Refrain from calling to show that you can listen to and follow directions.

Chapter 17

Moving Up the Ladder — or Switching Gears!

*W*hat makes the culinary arts industry so intriguing is the fact that you don't necessarily need traditional training or schooling to find success. You can own a restaurant without ever having to cook in its kitchen, for example. Sure, food knowledge will always be helpful in the long run, but sometimes understanding the ins and outs of running a business, writing a review, marketing a product, or taking a photograph can be just as valuable.

In this chapter, we discuss how you can advance your current culinary career or break into the food industry at any age and with just about any background. Depending on your personal goals — and when you establish them — you may choose to enter the industry straight out of school, or you may want to pursue a career as an investment banker, a newspaper columnist, a graphic artist, or a construction worker before you make your debut in the culinary arts.

Advancing Your Culinary Career

You've probably spent a good amount of time picturing your future self. When you close your eyes and imagine being at work, what do you see? Do you see yourself working the line in a busy restaurant? Or would you rather be discussing the history of wine with your customers in the front of the house? Are you cutting an elegant cake for guests at a wedding reception or are you in a test kitchen, trying out new recipes?

Regardless of which part of the industry you're most interested in, you probably already know that you're going to have to start at the bottom and work your way up. You understand that you may be washing dishes for a few months, holding camera equipment, or even fetching coffee. You need to accept this fact, because very rarely does a fresh face receive immediate responsibilities without a trial run to test his or her dedication to the industry.

Your entry-level position is only a snapshot of the beginning of your career, however. Where do you see yourself 5, 10, or even 20 years down the line? Do you want to own your own restaurant or catering company? Do you want to be an editor at a company that publishes cookbooks? Do you want all other food artisans to grow green with envy at the mere mention of your name? You can work your way toward achieving these dreams and more by making connections, choosing areas to direct your focus, and even gaining more experience through on-the-job training and education.

Finding a mentor

When you enter the culinary industry, try to meet other people who currently do what you want to do in the future. These connections can form during a simple conversation over a rare ingredient in a grocery store aisle, an interview for an open position, or even a chance introduction at a social gathering. Any culinary professional can teach you a thing or two about working in the industry, but you really want to meet someone who can be your mentor, because that's the type of person who will really help you find your place.

Unfortunately, you can't just pluck someone from a crowd and dub him your mentor. Instead, this relationship develops as you slowly form a professional connection with someone who is (or has been) where you want to go and who is willing to instruct you and support you as you progress in your career. Eventually, in addition to being a tutor, a coach, and a friend, he becomes your mentor.

Sometimes, one or both parties may not even realize that they're in a mentoring relationship. You may not think of someone as your mentor at first, but once you realize that you're turning to them for guidance, the relationship will become clear. On the other hand, the people you consider your mentors may never even realize that they play these roles in your life. Sometimes, the relationship isn't defined or labeled — it just happens.

You can find a mentor anywhere; many times, you'll know if someone is capable of providing you with a bit of guidance after your initial meeting. If their career interests you and they seem to have a hold on what it takes to be successful in the industry, you may want to get their contact information so you can stay in touch. You may find a mentor anywhere, but some popular places include schools, local restaurants, trade shows and food fairs, and even online social networking sites. If you admire someone's work, but you don't have the means to meet them in person, you can always go to their personal websites and write them e-mails.

A working relationship: Thomas Keller and Grant Achatz

In 1996, restaurateur Thomas Keller was named California's Best American Chef by the James Beard Foundation. The French Laundry (TFL), located in Napa Valley, was cited as one of the most exciting places to eat in the country. Keller was at the top of his game, and 22-year-old Grant Achatz wanted to be right there with him. Every week for nearly a year, Achatz sent his resume to Keller at TFL. Although Achatz had very little experience other than training at the Culinary Institute of America (CIA), Keller was impressed by the young chef's determination and took him under his wing as a *commis,* or apprentice.

Keller had always been Achatz's inspiration in the field and, as the two worked together in the kitchen, he soon became Achatz's mentor. Keller taught Achatz everything he needed to know and more, and he even arranged for the young chef to travel to El Bulli, one of the best restaurants in the world at the time, to sample the award-winning and inventive menu. Confident in his ability to prepare and reinvent food, Keller promoted Achatz to sous chef within four years of working at TFL.

In 2001, Achatz expressed an interest in moving to Chicago to run his own kitchen at the already established restaurant Trio. Keller was his biggest supporter. He helped prepare Achatz for the interview and even kept him on the TFL staff when Achatz was initially denied the position. Soon, however, Trio's owners realized their mistake and handed over control of their kitchen to Achatz. Keller enthusiastically supported his mentee's choice, and the two remained in contact despite Achatz's departure.

In 2005, Achatz left Trio to open his own restaurant in Chicago, Alinea. By 2006 and 2007, both *Gourmet* and *Restaurant* magazines had named Alinea one of the top restaurants in the world, and, in late 2007, Achatz claimed victory in a battle against mouth cancer. The next year, the James Beard Foundation named Achatz the Best Chef in the United States. In 2011, Alinea was awarded three Michelin stars. Every year, very few restaurants in the United States are given this honor. Keller's TFL and Per Se (located in New York) are among the very few that also have three Michelin stars.

If asked, Achatz attributes most of his success to Keller's decision to take a chance on him. His training at the CIA may have taught him many techniques and methods, but it was Keller who really showed him what being a chef is all about. Keller's influence is evident in nearly all of Achatz's work and his personal life — Achatz even named his youngest son Keller in honor of his world-renowned mentor.

Learning the ropes

If you're starting out fresh and young (possibly as a graduate of a culinary school), you need to work your way up the ladder if you wish to achieve success in any arena in the culinary industry. The first rung on this ladder is to thoroughly understand the basics.

No matter how menial a task may seem at the time, always produce your best work. Make sure your dishes and floors are the cleanest your employers have ever seen and your white tablecloths show absolutely no trace of food or drink. If you show your employers that you're dedicated to working with them and that you respect them and their work, they'll begin to trust you and give you more challenging tasks.

As you work, pay attention to the jobs being done by your coworkers in the kitchen, in the dining room, on the set, or in the office. If you already have some understanding of how they perform their job responsibilities, you'll be better prepared for any tasks that are handed down to you in the future. Watch how they work and imagine how you would respond to the same challenges. Understanding the demands for other positions in your company or restaurant will help you put a finger on which direction you'd like to take within the company as time passes.

Choosing a specialty

After you learn the basics, the next step is to decide whether you want to choose a specialty. Taking a particular and specific approach to food is optional but highly recommended. In fact, the culinary-arts field hosts so many options that *not* placing your focus on a certain style or technique is almost impossible.

If you want to work in restaurants, your first task is to decide which type of food you want to prepare. French or Spanish? Mexican? Japanese? Maybe Italian? Or how about American? You can even find restaurants that combine a few. By making this simple decision, you're already taking a step toward choosing a specialization.

Next, think about what you want to do with your food. Do you want to alter its textures and tastes using chemical compounds? Do you want to churn out savory vegetarian or vegan dishes? Would you rather work with sugary pastries or fresh vegetables?

Knowing what cuisine you'd like to prepare helps you narrow the list of skills you need to perfect. When you have skills in particular areas, you're more marketable to companies or chefs looking for people who have this experience.

Choosing a specialization is also important for people who don't work in restaurants. If you're a food writer, you have to decide whether you want to write biographies about famous chefs, nonfiction about the history of particular ingredients and cultures, or reviews about products and restaurants. You also have to decide whether your critiques will be about local places or if you'll travel the world for your job. If you're a food scientist, you have to decide which part of the process you'd like to participate in; for example, would you rather try to find the best way to store an item, or would you like to test products for foodborne illnesses? As with cooking jobs, choosing a specialty for writing, research, or whatever field you want to enter will guide what kind of training and experience you need to seek.

Bringing balance to decisions

Choosing a specialty doesn't have to mean putting yourself in a box and smacking a permanent label on it — it doesn't have to be the only thing you do. After you've decided on a specialty and really excelled at it, you can definitely add different interests to your repertoire. For example, opening a cupcakery doesn't mean that you can't also eventually sell meat and potato–filled pasties on the side. Rising to the position of executive chef of a Spanish-influenced restaurant doesn't restrict you from ultimately transferring to a quiet, Italian café.

A rule stating that the choices you make when you're 23 years old are the only decisions you'll make for the rest of your life just doesn't exist. If you grow tired of your specialization, switch it up.

Think about it: How many chefs do you know who are also confident in creating desserts?

(Many, many restaurants and catering companies actually buy their desserts from pastry shops and bakeries.) How many fry cooks go home and blog about their experiences in the food industry? If you want to eventually market yourself to more than one area of the culinary industry, you can. Focus on your main specialization and when you're confident in that area, move on to another.

To go beyond your specialization, find one or two things that you're good at — even if they're seemingly unrelated — and build on those skills. Just because you're a baker doesn't mean you can't make a mean tomatillo gazpacho if, down the road, you'd like to move on to working at a Mexican restaurant (you'll even be able to incorporate your baking background and add churros to the menu!).

Seeking additional training and education

The best way to advance your culinary career is to gain more experience. The better you know how to do something (and the more often you do it), the better your chances are of being hired or getting promoted. You can more effectively market yourself for your dream job if you seek additional training or even education.

At any point in your life, you can consider going back to school to earn certificates or higher-level degrees. If you have your associate's degree, why not complete another year or two and attain your bachelor's? If you already have a bachelor's degree and you have the time and money, you may consider pursuing a master's degree. Many culinary institutions, such as Johnson & Wales University and the Culinary Institute of America, have continuing education classes geared toward students who wish to change their profession and enter the culinary industry. If you don't want to get a degree but still want to learn new skills, talk to college representatives about auditing classes (sitting in on them but not receiving college credits). You can even attend specialty workshops hosted at hotels, restaurants, casinos, or crafts stores on the weekends. The more you know about food, the more impressed your potential employers will be.

Any course you complete or degree you attain should immediately be placed on your résumé. In fact, don't even wait until you've finished a course to include it. If you're in the middle of pursuing your degree (meaning you're actually enrolled and attending courses, not just thinking about doing so), place the name of the program, degree, or certificate in the Education section of your résumé along with the date you anticipate completing it. This information shows employers that you're serious about what you do and are willing to work hard to attain your goals. For more help writing your résumé, check out Chapter 16.

If you're a chef, another way you can move up the proverbial ladder is to earn certifications from the American Culinary Federation (ACF). For each certification, you must complete a certain number of hours in the classroom or the kitchen, and then you must pass practical and written exams. Following are some (but not all) of the ACF's certifications:

- Certified Culinarian (CC)
- Certified Sous Chef (CSC)
- Certified Chef de Cuisine (CCC)
- Certified Executive Chef (CEC)
- Certified Master Chef (CMC)
- Certified Pastry Culinarian (CPC)
- Certified Working Pastry Chef (CWPC)
- Certified Executive Pastry Chef (CEPC)
- Certified Master Pastry Chef (CMPC)

These titles not only will appear on your resume but also can be printed on your chef's jacket. In some arenas, they're as impressive as a PhD or MBA and should be taken seriously. For more information about the ACF's certification programs, see Chapter 3 or visit the ACF's website at www.ACFchefs.org.

Another way to gain experience — regardless of whether you want to film a cooking show, market products, bake cakes, or invent new flavors — is to find internships, externships, and apprenticeships. These positions are often temporary and unpaid but can ultimately lead to paid, full-time, permanent positions with companies or kitchens if you impress your bosses. If you don't have the means to quit your current job and take an unpaid apprenticeship or internship, you may be able to speak with your current employer about flexing your hours so you can remain employed and complete one of these opportunities simultaneously. Your day-to-day schedule will be rough, but it'll be worth it in the end. For more information about discovering these opportunities, see Chapter 3.

Switching Gears: Getting Involved in the Food Industry

It's never too late to get involved in just about any area of the food industry. Deciding at the age of 73 that you want to become a restaurant chef would probably be challenging, but even that goal isn't impossible. But even if you're considerably younger than that, your decision to enter the culinary field may still have come after spending many years in the career you originally pursued.

Perhaps you're tired of doing the same old thing every day, or maybe your hobby of baking cakes has become a successful side business that you want to pursue full time. How you get here doesn't matter — the fact is that you're here, reading our book and ready to switch gears.

You can take two main paths when changing your profession. You can either devote yourself to learning the ins and outs of the industry through formal education or training or, if you have the funds, you can invest or start a new business. And if neither of those options work for you, you can try to incorporate the job skills you already have into a culinary job.

Starting from square one

Say you've been working for 20 years as a construction worker. You always make dinner for your family on the weekends, and everyone for whom you've cooked has complimented your skills in the kitchen. You' determine that you want to change professions, and because you've always enjoyed cooking, you decide you want to be a cook. Maybe you don't want to own a restaurant or even rise to a managerial position in a kitchen, but you'd still like to learn the proper techniques and then find a job in a kitchen.

You're starting with a blank slate, so the best thing for you to do is throw yourself headfirst into the business. You may want to start by enrolling in cooking courses at a local community college or technical school. If you have the time and money, you can even check out a four-year school or a culinary institute. Whether you pursue a degree or certification is up to you, but we definitely recommend taking some introductory courses to the profession so you can approach an employer with knowledge of proper techniques and the understanding of how to work with a variety of ingredients.

In addition to taking cooking classes — or in place of them, if you so choose — you can apply for an entry-level job in a restaurant. The type of restaurant and the position for which you apply depend on what you want to do. If you want to reheat or finish dishes previously prepared in commissary kitchens and shipped to the kitchen, you can easily attain a job as a cook at a fast-food or some family-style restaurants. If you want to work on the dish from preparation to presentation, you may want to apply for a job at a white-tablecloth or fine-dining restaurant where the food is made from scratch.

You may start out washing dishes or dicing onions, but if you show your supervisor that you're dedicated to learning everything there is to know about her kitchen, eventually you'll earn her respect and trust and may find yourself promoted to a station on the line. All newcomers to the business, whether they're 18 or 48, face this issue.

Cooking isn't the only field you many find yourself wanting to get into. Whether you want to be a food stylist, a restaurant reviewer, an artisanal bread maker, or anything in between, the fastest route to success is to immerse yourself in as much education and/or training that you can consume.

Becoming an investor

You can become a member of the culinary world in many other ways, of course. One way in particular doesn't require you to slave away in a hot kitchen, go back to school to learn the basics, or have any additional training. Instead, it requires that you have quite a bit of money — and faith in someone else who happens to have all the previously mentioned credentials.

If you've always wanted to open a restaurant, bakery, pastry shop, or café but don't have any culinary training whatsoever, you can still make it happen. Many restaurant owners around the world have never cooked in their restaurants' kitchens. Instead, they hire executive chefs to run the kitchens, plan the menus, and hire and fire kitchen staff. Meanwhile, the owners invest money, secure loans, and run the business end of things (until they hire consultants or staff to do it for them).

You often hear stories of wealthy businesspeople loaning up-and-coming chefs or bakers the money they need to get their businesses off the ground. Sometimes these culinarians are close friends (or even friends of close friends) of the businesspeople. Occasionally, an investment in a chef's restaurant, diner, bakery, shop, or café is silent, meaning no one knows where the chef got the money. Other times, the partnership is quite public. Every situation is different and highly dependent on the personalities of each partner and the agreement they've made with one another. The sidebar "Floor trader to restaurant owner: Nick Kokonas" tells the story of one such partnership between investor and chef. For more information about starting your own business, see Chapter 18.

From the stage to the kitchen: Mark C. Tafoya

Currently, Mark C. Tafoya is a Certified Personal Chef (CPC) who sits on the board of the National Advisory Council for the U.S. Personal Chef Association (USPCA). He refers to himself as a "self-taught gourmand," which means "one who is interested in good food and drink." This life was not always what he envisioned for himself, however. His path to food stardom came after many years in an entirely unrelated industry.

After graduating with a bachelor of arts in French literature and theater studies from Yale University, Tafoya spent more than ten years as a Broadway actor. During that time, he also worked as a freelance writer for the *Princeton Review*. He received many assignments that gave him the opportunity to write, travel, and learn about international cuisine. Eventually he realized it was time to change professions — working with food had become more than a hobby or side job.

He enrolled in courses at and later graduated from the Culinary Business Academy and then spent time working as a private chef in New York. Today, Tafoya is the executive chef and co-owner of the Culinary Media Network. The business started as an online magazine called *The Gilded Fork* in 2005 and evolved into a multimedia network in 2007 with the world's first all-food podcast channel.

Adding a food-related twist

If don't want to start from scratch but you don't have the money to invest in a fresh-faced professional, you have yet another option for elbowing your way into the culinary industry: Use what you already know.

Examine the work you do on a day-to-day basis. Do you cover local events for a hometown newspaper? Do you teach high school students? Are you a doctor or maybe a graphic designer? Adding knowledge of food to any of these professions (and many more!) can open the door to many possibilities for careers in the food industry.

If you're a journalist or writer, for example, start reviewing restaurants or interviewing up-and-coming chefs. You can write a book about the history of food and culture or you can start a blog centered on your own experiences with making or eating food. If you're a photographer, start taking pictures of food, or if you're a sculptor or a painter, look into food styling. If you're a cameraman, try to get a job on the set of a cooking show.

What if you work with computers? You can probably start a food e-zine or contact food companies and see if they need a new webmaster or a website built from scratch. If you're a graphic designer, you can look for marketing companies that may design food packages or containers.

Floor trader to restaurant owner: Nick Kokonas

For ten years, Nick Kokonas worked in a derivatives trade firm that he developed. He spent long hours on Chicago's trading floor and, according to his wife, was on the verge of developing "trader personality disorder" and becoming the type of person he had always claimed to dislike. So he called it quits and soon found a home in the culinary arts.

In 2001, Kokonas and his wife had lunch at a Chicago restaurant named Trio. At the time, Grant Achatz, a former mentee of The French Laundry chef and owner Thomas Keller, was the executive chef. Kokonas was impressed by the tasting menu and blown away by the meal. He became a regular customer, booking reservations for the first Wednesday of every month. One night, he e-mailed Achatz and asked if the chef could prepare something special for his wife's birthday: a meal of Latvian-, Japanese-, and Thai-influenced food. Achatz did more than just make her a meal she'd never forget — he invited the couple into Trio's kitchen and cooked for them privately. Kokonas and Achatz soon became good friends.

Kokonas understood that Achatz wanted his own restaurant, a blank canvas that he could mold into everything he'd ever wanted. Kokonas saw Achatz's dedication to his profession and had faith that investing his savings into any project the young man was a part of would be a good move. Kokonas and Achatz became business partners, and between 2004 and 2005 they sent more than 1,800 e-mails to each other as they planned for the opening of the restaurant they now co-owned: Alinea.

Within two years, Alinea was named one of the best restaurants in the country and, eventually, the world. Less than four years later, the restaurant received a rating of three Michelin stars — one of the biggest honors in the restaurant world. Kokonas's belief in Achatz's talent and vision had paid off — well.

The duo's business partnership didn't end with Alinea. In 2011, they opened another groundbreaking restaurant named Next and a restaurant and bar named Avery. They also published two books together, a nonfiction cookbook and a joint memoir.

Believe it or not, jobs such as culinary historian, librarian, psychologist, and even anthropologist exist. So if you have training in any of those fields, you can sprinkle in a bit of food knowledge and easily find yourself doing what you love.

So, what if you're a doctor? Or a lawyer? Or an architect? You can design restaurants, represent the Food and Drug Administration, or become a nutritionist or dietician. You can even be a consultant, helping smaller businesses figure out whether their menus are nutritionally sound or whether they're violating a law by substituting glue for milk on the set of an advertising photo shoot. (Hint: They just may be!)

The chances are pretty good that if you're reading this book, you know quite a bit about food already. You're interested in it, you like to work with it, and you especially enjoy eating it. Now, combine those interests with the demands of your current job. Can you make it work? We're willing to bet you can!

Chapter 18

Making Your Own Path: Becoming a Culinary Entrepreneur

At some point during your career, you may decide to start your own culinary business and become a culinary entrepreneur. A *culinary entrepreneur* is someone who owns a culinary business, such as a restaurant, bakery, catering company, or bed-and-breakfast. If you have a passion for some aspect of the culinary world and want to be your own boss, this chapter can help you decide if culinary entrepreneurship is a good route for you.

Owning your own business is rewarding, but it has its drawbacks. New businesses take time to become successful and require hard work, sacrifices, and piles of money. Are you willing to devote every waking hour to your business? How about all your hard-earned cash? Do you have a support system in place willing to help you if you need it? If you didn't scream "No!" in response to any of these questions, you just may have what it takes to become a culinary entrepreneur.

Getting Down to Business: Should You Own Your Own?

Before you determine what type of business you want to own, sit down and consider why you'd like to own your own business. You probably have a bunch of reasons. Get a piece of paper and write them down. While you're at it, write down the pros and cons of being a business owner. When you're finished, read the lists over. These lists will force you to take a hard look at the benefits as well as the drawbacks. If your list is filled with mostly pros, then maybe you should consider going for it. If it's filled with mostly cons, then maybe you should do some more thinking before taking the plunge. These lists can help you decide if owning your own business is right for you.

Knowing the positives

Most people want to own their own business because they want to be their own boss. Becoming your own boss allows you to answer to no one but yourself. You make all the decisions — from the menu to the products offered to the design of your business.

Owning a business makes life exciting, especially if you're at a point in your life where you're bored. Maybe you've worked at the same job for a while now with no room for advancement and you're craving something new. Or maybe you're just entering the workforce and have big dreams. Either way, you won't be bored if you have your own business, but you'll definitely be challenged. In addition to making life exciting, owning something that you can pass on to your children is a feeling like no other. Leaving behind your legacy is priceless.

Considering the negatives

Of course, owning your own business has cons, too. It takes time before your business turns a profit. Do you have the necessary funds to live on if your business doesn't make any money during the first few months or even years? Remember, during this time you still have to pay your staff, pay toward your debts, and pay for supplies. Owning your own business is a huge financial risk and making money — at least at first — won't be easy.

Not having any free time is another downfall. Forget about days off, sick time, vacations, holidays, and weekends, at least in the early days when you're just starting your business. You need to work long hours and be accessible day or night, which can create rifts between you and your family and friends. If you're more comfortable punching in and out at a certain time every day, then a job as a culinary entrepreneur may not be right for you.

The responsibilities that come along with owning your own business can cause a great deal of stress, which can affect you physically and mentally. The list of things to worry about is endless: profits, taxes, staff, customers, regulations, health care, payroll, inspections, and so on. Another cause of stress is the unknown. Not knowing if your business will succeed can rattle even the calmest person.

Choosing What You Want to Do

After you decide that you definitely want to be a culinary entrepreneur, you need to get started on the first of many questions you'll have to answer: What type of business will you own? You have to consider several factors when choosing a business to get into. One of the most important factors is what you like to do. Do you have a knack for decorating beautiful cakes? Perhaps you can open your own bakery. Perhaps you love steak and are an expert griller, in which case a restaurant may be the way to go. Maybe you enjoy canning or pickling. You may be able to sell a product out of your home. Do you enjoy cooking for a crowd and planning parties? Owning a catering company may be right up your alley. Maybe you've already worked in the restaurant business or a bakery and would like to teach workshops or give private cooking lessons. Whatever you choose to do, it should ultimately come down to what you're good at and what you enjoy.

Another consideration is what products or services people are willing to purchase. One way to do this is to walk or drive around the area you wish to open a business. Are there many of the same types of businesses or is the area lacking different types of businesses? Talk to people and ask them about the type of business you'd like to open and see if they're receptive to the idea. Another resource you can use is your local telephone directory. Turn to the yellow pages and look at all the different types of businesses in your area. Ask yourself the same question, "Are there many of the same types of businesses?" How about, "What types of businesses are not located in my area?" Determine if the type of business you want to open would serve a large group of people or be lost in the crowd of other similar businesses.

In addition, you should think about your competition. Canvass the area where you'd like to open your business. If four bakeries are located in the area where you want to open a cake-decorating business, you can choose to find a different location or open another type of business in this location. If there are no coffee shops, you may want to consider opening one. You may also want to think about opening a similar business that offers something that the others don't. For example, if there are four other bakeries, you may want to think about opening a bakery that specialized in only cupcakes or cookies.

Building a Business Plan

After you determine what type of business you want to open, the next step is to write a business plan. A business plan is a blueprint for how you'll run your business. A blueprint should include important information such as the location, or site, of your business; what steps you need to take before opening your business, such as securing permits, licenses, and funds; what you need for the business, such as equipment and staff; and how you'll get the word out about your business. Of course, these aren't the only things that should be contained in your blueprint. You should also include information such as sketches of what your business will look like, your hours, your products and services, as well as any other information pertinent to the business.

The U.S. Small Business Administration offers information and workshops about writing a business plan as well as sample business plans on its website. For more information, visit www.sba.gov.

Choosing a location

Choosing a location is one of the most important decisions you'll make when becoming a culinary entrepreneur and writing a business plan. And by location, we don't mean the city or state your business will be located in, we mean the actual site. (The city or state in which your business will be located is important, but is usually established by where you already live or where you plan to move.) Will you run your business out of your home? Will you rent a space? Or will you purchase a facility? The answers to these questions determine other points on your business plan, such as licenses and permits, equipment, and staff.

Running a business out of your home

One of the easiest ways to own your own business is to run it from your home. This set up is a smart idea for people who would like to try owning a small business before jumping full-fledged into a huge undertaking. With a location already assured, you can get by with less start-up money. You can save money on rent and gas and save time by not having to commute to work. You can also set your own hours and dress as you please. Imagine wearing pajamas to work every day!

But although running a business out of your home may be feasible at first, it may become impractical over time as you build your customer base or expand your product line, because you may run out of space and/or parking. A home-based business may also require special licensing. The requirements for licensing a home kitchen for commercial use vary from state to state. Some states don't allow food to be sold out of home kitchens, while others have very specific guidelines that must be met. So if you want to run a home-based business, find out first if you can legally do so before applying for licenses and permits. Check with your local municipality to obtain this information. For more information see "Securing licenses and permits" later in this chapter.

You may find that some people don't trust home-based businesses because they don't think they're legitimate businesses. If you follow your town's requirements and guidelines and run your business by the book, you shouldn't have to worry about defending the reputation of your home-based business.

Taking on an established business

Another route to owning your own business is to acquire an existing business. The major advantage is that all the hard work has already been done for you. You already have an operational business including staff, equipment, and an existing customer base. However, you must consider the disadvantages that come along with purchasing someone else's business, too. You inherit all the problems the business may have, which can include old and broken equipment and exhausted and unmotivated employees. As the new owner, you're faced with keeping things the way they are or changing them. Pros and cons come along with change. You may increase your business with change or alienate existing customers. The key is to find a balance to make your business successful.

Also ask yourself these questions before deciding to open a home-based business:

✔ Are you the kind of person who can stay focused on work while at home? Having the discipline to work while surrounded by distractions is important — especially when you have orders to fill on a timely basis.

✔ Do you have the space you'll need to run your business? If you don't have much counter space and have a small, cramped kitchen, you may want to reconsider your plan.

✔ Do you have the necessary equipment at home? Without the proper-sized oven, baking a few simple cakes may take you hours, and without a large refrigeration unit, you may not be able to store as many ingredients as you need.

✔ Do you have enough money to cover costs associated with new equipment, licenses and permits, staff, and advertising? Running a business — even a small one — requires a chunk of money, and you most likely won't earn much profit in the beginning.

✔ Will you need to hire a staff to help you? After time, you may find yourself getting more business and may require someone to help you. If you take on more work, do you have the space and funds to hire staff if needed? If not, you may have to cut back on the number of orders you take or consider hiring someone on a part-time basis.

If you decide to hire a staff — even just part time — you need to check your local zoning laws because some municipalities prohibit hiring non-related employees in a home-based business. You should also check with the IRS for specific information on employer tax responsibilities.

Bed-and-breakfasts

Some people choose to open up their homes and run a bed-and-breakfast. A bed-and-breakfast is a home-based business that offers overnight accommodations and typically breakfast to guests. Running this type of business is similar to running a hotel, just on a much smaller scale. Many bed-and-breakfasts have less than 10 bedrooms and guests typically share bathrooms within the establishment.

You should consider many factors before deciding to go this route. Are you comfortable opening your home to strangers? Guests will be staying in your home and using its amenities. Do you enjoy cleaning up after people? Bed-and-breakfast owners are responsible for chores such as cooking, cleaning, shopping, and laundry. They are also responsible for day-to-day operations and management responsibilities, such as bookkeeping, advertising and marketing, organizing check-ins, taking reservations, and so on. Hours are another factor to consider as most bed-and-breakfasts are open seven days a week and require you to be up early to prepare breakfast and clean guests' rooms. The answers to these questions will help you decide if opening a bed-and-breakfast is the right move for you.

✔ How will potential customers learn about your business? Will you pay for advertising or hire someone with sales and marketing skills? Or will you take care of your own marketing needs? Either way, you'll need to come up with a plan to get your name out there and advertise your services. If you don't plan on advertising your business, how will you grow a customer base?

Think about your answers to these questions carefully before deciding to open a home-based culinary business.

Another thing to consider before opening a home-based business is the type of business you want to run. Not all types of businesses are well suited to homes. Space and parking are two common reasons that many businesses aren't located out of homes. Following are a few examples of good home-based business ideas:

✔ Baked goods (breads, cakes, cupcakes, cookies, pastries, pies, and so on)

✔ Homemade candy

✔ Canned and pickled goods (honey, jams, pickles, salsa, sauces, spices, and so on)

✔ Catering services

✔ Food and gift baskets

✔ Prepared meals (focusing on a particular type of food such as soups, sandwiches, hoagies, tacos, wraps, and so on)

✔ Jerky and other dried foods or fruits

✔ Pet food and treats

✔ Workshops, classes, or private cooking lessons

✔ Packaged teas, coffees, or other beverages

Renting or purchasing a facility

Some types of culinary businesses need large equipment, workspaces, areas for clients to shop or dine, inventory storage rooms, and enough space for a whole crew of employees to work. These types of businesses are not meant to be run from a home, so if your dream business fits that bill, you need a facility. You can either rent or purchase a facility for your business. Take a look at your business's needs to determine how much space you need.

You also have to decide whether you want to rent or purchase a facility. This decision may be easy. You need a big down payment to purchase a building, so if you don't have this kind of cash on hand, then renting is the way to go. And in any case, renting is sometimes wise at first until you determine whether your company is going to be successful. This way, if your business doesn't make it, you don't have to worry about selling a building. Also consider what will happen if you needed more room in the future. If you rent a property, you can always move to a larger facility. But if you own, you have to build an addition or sell your property.

Although, if you own your own space, you are free to design it to fit your needs. If you need more seating, for example, you can tear down a wall to create the space you need — something that you can't do when you're renting a facility.

If you're working with contractors to construct your business, you should make sure you have all the necessary building permits and inspections. This will save you time, money, and many headaches during the construction process. For more information about obtaining building permits, contact your local municipality.

If you rent or purchase a space that's already fitted for the type of business you want to open, it may already have all the equipment you need. In that case, working out of a facility instead of your home can actually save you money in the long run.

The food truck

Food trucks are popping up all over the streets of big cities throughout the United States, serving everything from waffles to cupcakes to tacos. These mobile kitchens are gaining in popularity and giving traditional restaurants a run (or a ride) for their money.

Operating a food truck is an alternative for people looking to own their own restaurant or bakery. Food-truck operators usually prep and cook their products either on the truck or at an off-site commercial kitchen and then sell their products out of the truck. Although food-truck owners don't have to worry about a permanent site, they do have to worry about finding a prime place each day to park and set up their business. Food trucks must also adhere to government regulations, licenses, permits, and zoning rules as well as other regulations that vary from state to state.

Food-truck vendors are gaining a following on the Internet and are using it to their advantage. More and more food-truck vendors are marketing their products through social media sites such as Twitter and Facebook that allow followers to track the location of their favorite truck.

If you want to be a culinary entrepreneur and can't afford a space of your own or your home isn't feasible for your business needs, don't give up. Be creative and talk to others who may be able to help you. If you need to use a commercial kitchen to prepare and cook your products, look for a business that may allow you to rent its space. How about the bagel shop around the corner that's closed at night? Maybe the owners would allow you to rent its kitchen while the shop is closed? How about a small restaurant that is only open for the evening? Its owners may allow you to use their kitchen in the mornings. You may even develop close relationships with the owners of these businesses that can help you down the road. Maybe they will sell your products at their business or help you get your name out there. Consider renting space in churches, recreation centers, culinary schools, or commissary kitchens.

Following are a few examples of businesses that require a site outside the home:

- ✔ Large bakeries and pastry shops
- ✔ Butcher shops and delicatessens
- ✔ Large catering companies
- ✔ Food delivery services (delivering prepared meals)
- ✔ Grocery stores
- ✔ Hotels and spas
- ✔ Restaurants
- ✔ Specialty stores (selling cookware or specialty foods)

Securing licenses and permits

Another part of your business plan should include information on needed licenses and permits, which require fees that can eat into a hefty chunk of your savings. Whether you decide to open a business out of your home or chose to rent or purchase a space, you must acquire licenses and permits. First, you must apply for a business license, which is required to run a business and is separate from the license and permits needed to prepare and sell food. Since the regulations for business permits vary from state to state, contact your state government for more information. (Many software packages are available to assist business owners with these operations, such as *Quicken Home & Business* and *QuickBooks*.) After you've secured a business license, you need to obtain a food-handler permit and food-preparation license. Some states require certifications such as ServSafe, which is a food safety certification offered by the National Restaurant Association for those in the food service industry. You also need to have your kitchen inspected by the health department and obtain liability insurance to protect your business and other assets just in case your products sicken someone or someone is injured at your business.

To find out what permits and licenses you'll need in your location for your particular type of business, contact your local small business association, chamber of commerce, health department, and/or cooperative extension.

Procuring funds

Every business plan should include a section on finances. You need money to start and operate a culinary business — or any business, in fact. You need cash for expenses such as permits and licenses, equipment, rent or mortgage, staff, taxes, insurance, advertising, and ingredients. If you need more money than you have, consider making money by obtaining a part-time job, selling personal items, moving to a cheaper apartment, or taking a second mortgage on your house. You can choose to borrow funds from a bank, but remember that you'll have to pay back the loan plus interest.

You can also look for a partner or an investor to help finance the business. Talk to your family members, friends, former colleagues, and other acquaintances to see if they'd be interested in becoming partners or investors in your business. You can even search forums online or take an ad out in a local publication to find a potential backer. But if you choose to go this route, remember, you have to split your profits with your partners or investors and perhaps give them a say in how you run the business. And because money is involved, you'll need to hire a lawyer and get everything in writing before you accept money from another person — even if it's a family member.

Purchasing equipment

Your business plan should include everything that you need to start your business, including equipment. Some of the money you need to start a culinary business will be used to purchase necessary equipment. Equipment is everything other than food that you need to run a business. From canning jars to industrial-strength mixers, knives, and even a computer, you may be surprised at how long the laundry list of items needed to run your business is when you write it out.

If you purchase or rent a facility to open a restaurant that wasn't previously used as a restaurant, for example, you need to purchase tables, chairs, decor, utensils, glassware, plates, ovens, fryers, grills, tools, cooking appliances, refrigeration units, dishwashing machines, computer systems, uniforms, and so on. The good news is that some of this equipment may be tax-exempt. Be sure to check with the Internal Revenue Service (IRS) as this will save you money.

Because many people do not plan properly for entering the restaurant industry, some businesses don't succeed. This is good news for other passionate and daring entrepreneurs who are on the hunt for gently used and affordable restaurant equipment. You can find these deals online on sites such as eBay or craigslist.

If you're lucky enough to rent a space with everything you need in it or if you run a business out of your well-equipped home, you won't need to purchase much equipment. If you're planning to run a business out of your home, you will most likely need to purchase some type of refrigeration unit to store your business ingredients separately from your other food, though. You may even need additional space for this refrigeration unit, in which case you may need to construct a room or convert a closet in your home.

Hiring staff

Because you've written a clear and concise business plan, you should know whether you'll need to hire staff. Depending on the size and nature of your business, you may not be able to go it alone. If you open a large business, such as a restaurant, you need a large staff to prepare and serve food efficiently. If you run a small, home-based business, you probably won't need a large staff to help you make the products. You may be able to get by with hiring help on an as-needed basis. If you're a caterer, you can hire people just for the day of the event. How many people a business may need to operate can fluctuate on a daily or even weekly basis, depending on how much work the business has.

In addition to preparing your products, you need to set aside time to work on day-to-day tasks such as ordering supplies, making a daily, weekly, or monthly schedule, answering phones, taking orders, checking and replying to e-mails, filing, advertising, making financial decisions, cleaning, and other routine tasks. If you're not able to do all this by yourself, you may need to hire someone to help.

When considering hiring a staff, you need to figure out how much you can pay as wages and decide whether you will offer benefits such as health-care coverage, sick time, vacation time, and 401(k) plans. Some states have mandates on benefits, such as healthcare, so check your state laws to determine what regulations you must follow regarding employee benefits. If you own a home-based business, you should check your local zoning laws to determine if you're able to hire employees. All businesses should check with the IRS for specific information on employer tax responsibilities.

Just because you can't do everything yourself doesn't mean you're a bad business owner or you've failed at running your own business. Delegating work is perfectly okay. If you can't afford to hire a staff at the beginning, see if you can get your spouse, family, or friends to help you out for a while.

Marketing your business

Even the most well-structured businesses can fail because the owners didn't include marketing in their business plans. If no one knows about your business, how will customers know you exist? Marketing and advertising are key ways to make customers aware of your business. But because you're starting a new business, you probably don't think you have the funds to advertise, right? Think again. You can advertise your business in many ways, and not all of them cost an arm and a leg.

Word of mouth is a great free way to advertise, but chances are if you're a new business, you don't have that many customers yet. Give your business an online presence by creating a website as well as a blog or social-network page on Twitter, LinkedIn, and Facebook. Your friends, family, and current customers can interact with your business by using social networking sites to help spread the word about your business. You can also create inexpensive fliers and brochures advertising your business and hang them in other local businesses, libraries, churches, or throughout your neighborhood. Business cards are also an effective and inexpensive way to get your name out there. Leave them everywhere you go.

Although pricier, radio and television commercials are great ways to inform a larger audience about your business. If you can afford them, ads in newspapers and local magazines can also reach more potential customers.

Other ways to generate buzz about your company are to host charity events, hold contests or giveaways, or purchase a booth at tradeshows, local bazaars, or festivals.

In time, you may be able to hire someone who has public relations and marketing experience to take care of your advertising needs and help you manage a client base.

Career Profile

Each culinary entrepreneur's role is different, depending on the type of business. People open their own businesses every day. Some succeed, while others fail. Before you dive in and become a culinary entrepreneur, make sure you do your research so you know what you're getting yourself into ahead of time. The following sections give you a good head start on understanding some of the aspects of owning a culinary business.

Personality traits

Culinary entrepreneurs should be detail-oriented, passionate, and confident to handle the challenges of owning a business. They should also be very hard working, but that doesn't mean they have to do all the work themselves. In fact, good culinary entrepreneurs know how to work well with others. They delegate tasks and forge relationships with employees, partners, and other business associates.

Culinary entrepreneurs should also be humble, because they need to realize when they need help, and resilient, because they need to be able to roll with the punches when times are tough and when business is booming. They should be able to remain calm under pressure and be flexible so they can adjust when things don't work out as planned. What happens if you're getting ready to deliver a cake and accidentally drop it on the ground? You can't give up and tell your customers that you don't have their order. You need to be able to adapt and put a plan in place to remedy the situation.

Culinary entrepreneurs should be competitive and driven to do everything they can to ensure their business thrives.

Salaries

The salary for a culinary entrepreneur varies according to many factors, such as the size, type, and location of the business. Some culinary entrepreneurs make a great deal of money while others just squeak by and take second jobs to supplement their income.

Another way to possibly earn money as a culinary entrepreneur is to sell your business. It may be hard to give up your business that you grew from nothing, but it may ensure you're able to retire — possibly even early — and live comfortably. Selling your business not only provides you with cash, it also gives you free time, which you may consider more valuable than money. Selling your business isn't always a guarantee of making money. To make money, you have to price your business high enough so you don't lose money on it, and you also have to find an interested buyer — which may be difficult, especially if you own a small or home-based business, such as selling jams or decorating cakes.

Education and training

Although a culinary background is not required to own your own business, you can increase your chances of success by having at least some culinary experience (or even a culinary degree) and knowing something about the culinary field you want to enter. For example, if you'd like to start your own catering business, you should first work for a caterer to gain the knowledge and experience you need for your business. If you'd like to sell cakes out of your home, first work in a bakery to see how it's done.

You should also have some knowledge about how to run a business. Pursuing a business-related degree, such as management, isn't a bad idea. Business classes can teach you how to perform the many necessary tasks for opening and running a business, including writing a business plan, securing funds, obtaining permits, finding a location, hiring staff, and on and on. A degree in hotel/restaurant management or hospitality management, blending business and culinary studies, may be a good choice depending on what field you want to enter.

Advancement prospects

Culinary entrepreneurs are already at the top of their field, so they really can't advance into any higher roles. If their business is successful, they may think about opening another business, whether it's another outlet of the same business in a different location or a different business entirely.

Culinary entrepreneurs who own a successful business may decide to turn their business into a franchise. When you turn your business into a franchise, you sell the rights to an individual or group to market your business's goods or services. For example, whoever buys the franchise to your restaurant essentially owns a copy of your restaurant, but must operate it according to specific guidelines and may not be able to change anything such as the food or decor. Some examples of franchises are McDonald's, Burger King, and Subway.

Culinary entrepreneurs may also decide to sell their business to pursue a different career.

Unions and associations

Although culinary entrepreneurs usually don't belong to any sort of union, numerous associations exist that they can join. Some examples include national, state, and location associations, general culinary entrepreneur associations, and more specific culinary entrepreneur associations, including the American Home Business Association (AHBA), American Hotel & Lodging Association, American Restaurant Association, Artisan Baker Association, Home Baking Association, Home Business Association, National Association of Home Based Businesses, National Association of Catering Executives (NACE), National Federation of Independent Business (NFIB), National Restaurant Association, National Small Business Association (NSBA), and the United States Association for Small Business and Entrepreneurship (USASBE). These associations provide culinary entrepreneurs with information about owning a business, writing a business plan, permits and licenses, state and local regulations and laws, as well as certification information.

Employees of culinary entrepreneurs may belong to unions such as the United Food and Commercial Workers International Union (UFCW), Service Employees International Union (SEIU), and the Hotel Employees and Restaurant Employees International Union (HEREIU).

Part VI
The Part of Tens

The 5th Wave   By Rich Tennant

"Let me know when you've got enough lettuce on that taco."

In this part . . .

*1*t just wouldn't be *For Dummies* without the Part of Tens. In this part, we include our culinary top-ten lists. The first list gives you ten reasons to consider a career in the culinary industry. The second list covers ten tips to help you thrive in the culinary industry. These chapters are short and may be good references for you, so flip to them as often as needed.

Chapter 19

Ten Reasons to Work in the Culinary Industry

· ·

In This Chapter

▶ Checking out reasons why a culinary career may be right for you

▶ Examining the best perks of the industry

· ·

You may decide that you want a career in the culinary industry for a number of reasons. Many of these reasons may be tied directly to the type of job you want. Maybe you're an early bird and the early-morning hours of a baker are more appealing to you than a 9-to-5 job. Or perhaps you enjoy the challenge of a fast-paced, hot kitchen more than you like the idea of sitting at a desk, crunching numbers and writing business plans.

The possibility also exists that at this point in your life, you're still unsure of whether you'd like to work in the culinary industry. If that's the case, we completely understand — choosing a career (or deciding to change careers entirely) is difficult for many people. Sometimes listing the pros can sway you toward a choice, and this chapter just may list enough good points about the culinary industry to convince you to commit to an exciting, food-related field.

In this chapter, we list the most common reasons people become involved in the culinary industry. Examine this list and see how many of these have already crossed your mind. If these are similar to the reasons you'd list for wanting to work in the industry, then a culinary career is probably right for you!

You Love Food!

If you're going to work with food all day (and oftentimes all night!), you need to love it. You need to admire its smells, its textures, and its tastes. You need to love preparing it and eating it. You should jump at the chance to grill burgers and hot dogs at summer barbeques, and when you get a new spice grinder for your birthday, you shouldn't be ashamed to enthusiastically thank your new favorite gift-giver.

Although not every job in the culinary industry requires you to handle food directly, you still need to enjoy working with it. Whether you want to photograph it, distribute it, or write instructions on how to use equipment that cooks it, you're going to find that your job is much easier if you know quite a bit about different types of food and beverages. As an aspiring culinarian, you should have the utmost respect for food of all kinds, from Italian meats to French pastries.

You Enjoy Staying Active

Even if you're not cooking or baking, your job in the culinary industry may still be physically demanding. Unless you're a food writer (although you will still be using your hands to write!) or a restaurant owner who stays away from the kitchen, you're most likely going to get your hands dirty at work. Even working at a grocery store requires you to cut meats, stack bottles of spaghetti sauces, and arrange produce displays.

If you think you'd enjoy actively working with the items you're marketing, photographing, styling, selling, or preparing, then you'll most likely enjoy just about any career in the industry. Even executive chefs or general managers who may do much of their work on computers or at their desks always have the option of leaving their offices to arrange tableware, dice vegetables, or garnish plates.

Because many of the jobs in the food industry are physically challenging, you may start to feel the industry's effects on your body at a young age. Your back and knees may hurt and your fingers and wrists may ache. Lifting a 50-pound bag of flour and standing for eight to ten hours each night may become harder for you over the years. You may not encounter these issues for a while if you stay active and in shape; however, when your body starts telling you its time to quit, you may want to listen. Making a change doesn't mean you have to stop working with food, though. Just switch things up a bit. See Chapter 17 for more information on changing careers.

You Want to Keep Learning

The culinary industry is always evolving. Although you may find many traditionalists in the business, you'll also encounter an abundance of professionals who enjoy working with the latest and greatest ingredients and equipment. Lucky for them, something new to play with always seems to be emerging in this industry.

Food scientists and engineers work to develop new approaches to preparing food every day. They may add new functions to old kitchenware such as microwaves or stovetops or they may use their knowledge of biology and chemistry to create completely new flavors. Even chefs need to constantly put new twists on old food combinations to keep their menus current.

Because of these advancements in kitchens, factories, and laboratories across the nation, culinary professionals are able to continue to learn about food throughout their entire careers. This field is exciting and dynamic; if you enjoy educating yourself and trying new things, you'll fit in well.

You Know People Have to Eat!

Food is a basic necessity for all humans; we need it to survive. Whether someone is preparing a simple salad at home or sitting down to a porterhouse steak in a popular restaurant, he or she is able to do so because of a multitude of culinary professionals.

The food on your table is available to you because of artisans, farmers, scientists, and test-kitchen cooks. It may have been prepared by a professional chef in a large kitchen, or it may have been frozen by a commissary cook for you to defrost and heat at your convenience. Many of these professionals were originally taught basic skills by culinary instructors throughout the country.

The food service industry is always thriving; you probably won't be surprised to know that it's one of the largest employers in the United States. And in addition to food service, you can sell, market, photograph, and write about food. You can also grow, style, test, and eat it. There are — and always will be — jobs available for you in this industry.

Depending on your location and the state of the economy, you may have to spend a bit of time looking for jobs, even in the food service industry. Although they may be hard to find at times, we can assure you that they're definitely out there. Walk or drive around your town and stop in places of interest to see if they're hiring, check out "help wanted" ads and peruse online job sites until something catches your eye.

You Want a Career That's Easy to Get Into

One of the biggest draws to many professions in the culinary industry is that you don't need a college degree, or sometimes even experience, to enter the field. Many careers allow you to start from the bottom and work your way up, learning as you go. You don't need anything more than a high school diploma (some companies don't even require that!) to wash dishes, wait tables, prep salads, slice deli meats, or make cheese.

If you want to work with food at a capacity that requires a college education and quite a bit of experience, entering the field still isn't all that difficult. Many companies offer internships and apprenticeships that you can complete while taking classes so you'll obtain both experience working in the industry and an education before you even land your first full-time job. The more experience and education you have, the easier it is to find the job you want and move through the ranks.

You Don't Want a Desk Job

Let's face it — not everyone has the attention span necessary to sit at a desk for eight hours a day. Although these jobs may not require you to be on your feet in a hot room, they're still physically challenging and mentally draining. Many successful professionals turned to the culinary industry because they couldn't see themselves with a desk job, and you may very well be in the same boat.

You know that plenty of jobs exist in the industry that require you to sit at a desk and work on a computer for most of your day. These may include restaurant-supply buyers, food writers and marketing professionals, and menu and kitchen designers. But if these jobs and work styles don't appeal to you, don't worry — you can do so many other things.

Restaurant-supply salespeople, artisans, and food-truck owners travel every day, visiting local businesses and popular areas to promote their products. Executive chefs and general managers often have their own offices, but they also have responsibilities in the kitchen and dining room. These professionals may have a bit of paperwork to do at the end of the day and may have to spend an hour or so on the computer ordering items they need, but they're on their feet, working with their hands and hearts for the better part of their day.

You Like Meeting New People

No matter what job you take in the culinary industry, you'll almost always be part of a team and will rarely be in charge of an entire product — not because employers don't think you're capable of seeing the project from beginning to end, but because many times involving multiple people is simply more efficient. This work environment is great news for you if you enjoy meeting new people.

If you work at a restaurant, for example, you'll meet people who work in the kitchen and the dining room. You'll also meet salespeople, delivery men and women, and possibly kitchen and menu designers. If the restaurant is part of a chain, you may also meet district managers and marketing specialists. While talking to these people, you'll most likely find common ground and make connections that may prove valuable when looking for another job or a character reference.

Greet all visitors to your store, restaurant, or office with a smile. Being polite and helpful keeps them coming back for more. If you have the time, make small talk. After so many visits to deliver ingredients or sell equipment, these people will begin to recognize you. Although you may never be good friends, you may be able to contact them if you need help finding a particularly rare product or are looking for a way to make a little extra money in the future.

You Love a Good Challenge

Working with food can be quite difficult at times because it's time-sensitive. It loses its shape, texture, and taste quickly when in the wrong environment. It may spoil or freeze in inappropriate temperatures. Most of the work you do with food has to be quick — unless you have the option of using fake food, in which case it doesn't really matter how long it takes. (See Chapter 14 for more information on food styling.)

Food and beverages are also difficult to work with because developing tasty food pairings and menu items is challenging. If you put two ingredients together, you have to be sure that each flavor is represented (and that the taste is attractive, not repulsive!). Developing a new flavor pairing requires you to take risks and predict what people will buy and eat. You have to define your audience and then figure out what they're hungry for.

The environment you work in also makes some culinary careers more challenging than your average desk job. Kitchens of all types may be hot and cramped, and art studios where food is styled and photographed may be large and rather cold. If you're working on location as a stylist, photographer, cameraman, or television host, you may need to work hard to make food look its best in the mountains, the woods, or on the beach.

You Need a Paycheck

If you've skimmed the salaries sections of any of the chapters in this book, you've probably figured out which careers pull in the big paychecks and which ones may require you to keep clipping coupons and wearing last season's styles. Although the pay may not be that great when you enter the field, if you work your way up the ladder, you'll most likely see an increase in funds.

We won't lie to you — food-service industry wages can be hard-earned. Wait staff rely heavily on tips (and some customers are *horrible* tippers), and if you receive a salary instead of hourly pay, you won't receive additional pay for working overtime. If you're a salesperson who works on commission, you essentially determine your own fate, and you may have to really pound the pavement to earn the amount you want.

Set aside these difficulties for a second, though, and visualize yourself working in the industry as a line cook, an assistant pastry chef, a flavor chemist, or a cookbook editor. If you were to dedicate yourself to your career and show your supervisors that you're willing to go the extra mile, you'll most likely be rewarded at the end of the day. Raises and promotions will come easily, and so will respect from your peers and management staff. As you work your way to a bigger paycheck, you'll start to realize that you're getting paid to do what you love, and that should feel quite satisfying.

The more experience and educational accomplishments you have, the better your pay will be from the start. Show your employers that you're worth the extra money by attaining a technical or college degree or by attending courses to further your education on the weekend. Get certified, choose a specialization, and always be ready to show your employers what you can do.

You Never Have to Leave

As we discuss in Chapter 17, you can find a career in food with just about any background. English students can write food critiques and cookbooks, doctors can become nutritionists and food psychologists, and teachers of all backgrounds can become culinary instructors if they also have experience in kitchens. Because so many careers exist in the industry, you never really have to leave.

As you get older, you may want to get off your feet and give your back a rest. With your knowledge of food, you can start a food blog, write reviews for your local newspaper, or offer private in-home cooking lessons to people in your neighborhood. You can also decide to go into restaurant ownership and hire your own kitchen staff. If you don't want to stop working with food, you don't have to. There will always be a place for you in the culinary industry.

Chapter 20

Ten Tips to Help You Thrive in the Culinary Industry

In This Chapter

▶ Finding out more about the areas you're most interested in

▶ Choosing a specialty and making yourself more marketable

▶ Staying up-to-date on culinary trends through reading and research

The most successful culinary professionals know how to manage their time and work well with others. They understand that to achieve your goals, you need to devote yourself to your craft — even if this means starting at the bottom and climbing the ladder to success one rung at a time.

In this chapter, we offer ten brief tips that will help you thrive in the culinary industry, no matter which career you'd like to pursue. Keep this advice in mind when you start your first job, and (with a little luck and a lot of patience) you'll move through the ranks quickly.

Start at the Bottom

Whether you want to be a chef, food stylist, or flavor chemist, you should be prepared to start at square one — especially if you don't have any prior experience or educational accomplishments listed on your résumé. Even with a college or technical degree under your belt, finding a job that embodies exactly what you want to do will be difficult and frustrating. However, after you find entry-level employment, you can work your way up the ranks by showing your skill and dedication to your craft.

Don't let the idea of being stuck at the bottom for a year or so deter you. Simply landing a job in your field is a step in the right direction. As long as you're in a restaurant, who cares if you're only washing dishes or prepping salads for now? And as long as you can observe the process of setting up and holding a culinary photo shoot, does it really matter that all you've done all day is fetch coffee and carry the camera bag?

You may not realize it at first, but even though you may not be cooking food or personally developing recipes, you can still take something away from your seemingly uneventful days. Entry-level jobs give you the opportunity to see the industry up close and take notes. They let you watch others tackle challenging tasks and then picture yourself doing these same tasks. You can think about whether you would do anything differently or whether another approach would work better. Eventually the time will come when you can put what you've learned to use.

Entry-level jobs not only allow you to learn about the industry, but also help you learn more about yourself. You may discover that you have a talent for fondant rolling or that you despise making Mexican food. Sometimes, the most valuable thing you take from an entry-level job is the discovery of what you definitely *don't* want to do with your life. Obtaining this knowledge early in your career is best so you don't waste thousands of dollars on school and decades doing a job you simply don't enjoy.

Take Courses Related to Your Interests

Many careers in the culinary industry don't require you to have a college or technical degree, so if you don't want to step foot inside a classroom, you never have to. However, if you're interested in pursuing a degree or certification, or if you just like learning, taking college courses or courses offered through weekend workshops is a great way to show future employers that you're serious about your career.

One of the great things about the culinary industry is that you can apply what you learn in nearly any type of course to food-related work. If you want to take English courses, you can use what you learn there to be a food writer. If you're interested in biology or chemistry, you can apply this knowledge to a career as a food scientist. Anthropology courses can help you become a food anthropologist (a person who studies the history of food gathering, distribution, preparation, storage, and more within a culture or cross-cultures), and business and marketing courses are extremely valuable if you become a general manager or restaurant owner.

Today, courses are offered in just about anything. Even if you don't want to complete a whole degree or certification, you can still enroll in classes that interest you the most. From cake decorating or nutrition, soups and sauces to purchasing, you are likely to find some kind of class that looks good on a résumé and may help you land your dream job.

Find a Mentor in Your Field

As we discuss in Chapter 17, one of the best ways to learn and grow in the culinary field is to find a mentor. A mentor is someone who may have your dream job (or at least knows a lot about the field you want to work in) and who teaches you what you need to know to help you reach your goals.

Mentors' jobs are two-fold: They act as both teachers and friends. They can teach you about the latest techniques and ingredients one minute and then give you advice on your relationship with your significant other the next. Mentors often cross the line between coworkers and friends — but that's okay. They need to know what's going on in their mentees' personal lives to send the mentees down the professional path an appropriate way.

You may not always work with the people whom you consider your mentors. (And you may actually have more than one.) They may be employed in other kitchens, bakeries, or labs — they may even live in a different state and converse with you online. No matter where they're located, mentors can still give you advice about the field.

Good mentors always tell you the truth — even if the truth is something you don't want to hear. They talk about their own ups and downs in the business and use those experiences to come up with advice for you. Remember, mentors know what they're talking about. They've been where you want to be and can help you get there, too.

Work Well with Others

As a child, you were taught to share. This lesson is one you should keep in mind when you enter a professional setting. If you want to work in a kitchen, you must learn to share your space and your tools. Although you may have your own knife set, the majority of the equipment and cookware you use belongs to the restaurant and therefore is available for everyone.

And although sharing tools is definitely important, sharing ideas is even more so. In a professional setting, you should always do what you're told. However, if you're aware of a more efficient way to complete a task (and if this approach will save your employer some money!), respectfully and professionally present your ideas to your superiors.

Also keep in mind that even though you may think your way of doing things is always correct, you may occasionally be wrong. When your coworkers or supervisors come to you with criticism or want you to try something different, remain open to their ideas. Consider what they're asking you and try to put your own spin on it so that you're following their lead but continuing to produce work that still feels like yours.

Make Time to Read

To truly be successful in this industry, you *need* to know what's going on in it at all times. You need to be aware of new trends and know whether they're thriving or failing horribly. You should understand how to use and procure the latest ingredients and equipment. If a certain technique is suddenly popular in another part of the world, do your best to find out why people are praising it.

How are you supposed to know learn about trends in your industry? Read! Read newspapers, magazines, journals, blogs, and cookbooks. If you subscribe to newsletters, e-zines, or online catalogs, this information will find its way directly to you.

Don't get us wrong —you don't need to spend hours researching food every weekend. (Although that much reading certainly couldn't hurt.) Instead, we're merely suggesting that when you have a few minutes, check out the food section of your local newspaper, navigate to a credible food blog, or pick up a magazine. The more you read, the more you'll know about the business — and the better (and easier) your decisions will be in the future.

When you're looking for something to read, don't be afraid to grab a culinary book that's been on the shelf for a few years (or longer). Understanding older techniques helps you see how preparing food has (or hasn't!) changed throughout the years. Examining Auguste Escoffier's original recipes and reading books about the history of salt or pickling, for example, makes you more knowledgeable about the industry as a whole.

Choose a Specialization

As we discuss in Chapter 17, in the culinary industry, choosing a specialization is optional but strongly recommended. So many options are available to you in the culinary industry that *not* specializing in something is nearly impossible.

Choosing a specialization can be as easy as figuring out the type of food you want to work with: Italian? Thai? Polish? Another way to specialize is to choose a way to work with this food. Do you like to experiment? Perhaps you'd like to try a hypermodern approach and practice gastronomy, or maybe you prefer to keep it traditional and rustic.

Specializing in a particular area or technique means knowing more about that approach to working with food than the average chef, baker, writer, or scientist. So if you're going to label yourself a specialist, you have to be able to prove it. Take extra courses, read the appropriate literature, and perfect your skills in this area before you tell potential employers you have a specialization.

Don't allow other people to pressure you into a specialization. Just because you're good at decorating cakes doesn't mean you *have* to do it for a living. If your passion lies in simple baking, you should pursue a career that will allow you to bake breads, pastries, and muffins and perhaps dabble in cake decorating in your free time. Make the decision that's right for *you* — not your boss, your spouse, or even your mom.

Manage Time Wisely

The most successful culinary professionals in the world became successful because they knew how to manage their time. Time management is important in every industry, but it's especially important when you work with food.

Because food can lose texture and temperature and spoils easily, it's considered a time-sensitive product. Whether you're packaging, photographing, styling, dissecting, or cooking it, pay attention to its color, smell, and texture. You need to work quickly so you can deliver it to your clients before it has the chance to go bad.

To better manage your time, try making lists of what you need to do. Arrange the tasks in chronological order so you know what needs to be done first. When you have your list in order, write down the amount of time you think each task will take you. Factor in the time you spend preparing for the task (finding the appropriate tools, setting up your work area, and so on) and extra time in case you make a mistake and have to repeat the process. Examine the list and determine if you need help completing it. Is it realistic? Can you really bake and frost 500 cupcakes in five hours by yourself? If not, you may need to call in reinforcements or rethink your plan of attack.

When tackling the items on your list, try to finish each task within the allotted time. Don't think too far ahead of the task at hand, or you may get frustrated and overwhelmed and make the entire project more difficult than it needs to be.

Open Yourself Up to New Ideas

As new techniques, equipment, and ingredients become more popular in the culinary industry, you may want to consider adjusting your approach to working with food to keep up with recent trends. This adjusting doesn't mean you need to incorporate every change or trend that emerges into your work. Simply being open to trying something new earns you more respect than refusing to consider the options at all.

Every now and then, you may need to upgrade your equipment or replace an old dish on your menu. Think carefully about which new products are on the market that may help you and what your competition is doing with new ingredients that may work in your menu. Choose items that are not only right for you and your business but that also help you remain a strong competitor.

Stay Fit

If you want to work in any type of kitchen, you should be prepared to spend 40 to 60 hours a week on your feet. All this standing can influence your physical health significantly — your back, neck, legs, and feet will all feel the effects of a long day in a hot kitchen. Your hands and arms may also ache for a while after your shift ends.

One of the best ways to deal with these drawbacks is to stay in good physical shape. The stronger your muscles are, the more easily you'll be able to lift 50-pound bags of flour, cut through chicken bones, whip sweet liquids into light and airy creams, and push through a day on your feet.

Drink lots of water when you work in a kitchen. Because kitchens are typically warm environments, you may find yourself sweating quite often. Drink water whenever you get the chance so you stay hydrated and alert. At many busy restaurants, employees may not get the chance to take adequate breaks. Even if you don't have time to eat a full meal, be sure to make time to drink a glass of water.

Broaden Your Horizons

You may come across some great opportunities if you choose to specialize in a particular area of the culinary industry. But you may find even better jobs if you keep your eyes and ears open and continue to learn new skills.

The more you can do, the more marketable you are to future employers. In the culinary industry, you can combine nearly any interest with food to make a career. If you're a computer whiz, you can design food-purchasing software or websites. If you're artistic, you can style or photograph food or design menus for restaurants. If you love writing and eating, you can blog about your dining experiences, write recipes and reviews, or team up with an experienced chef to write a bestselling cookbook.

If you can promise more business, you may be a shoo-in for the position.

Index

• *Z* •